BEFORE THERE WAS A BIBLE

BEFORE THERE WAS A BIBLE

AUTHORITIES IN EARLY CHRISTIANITY

Lee Martin McDonald

t&t clark
LONDON • NEW YORK • OXFORD • NEW DELHI • SYDNEY

T&T CLARK
Bloomsbury Publishing Plc
50 Bedford Square, London, WC1B 3DP, UK
1385 Broadway, New York, NY 10018, USA
29 Earlsfort Terrace, Dublin 2, Ireland

BLOOMSBURY, T&T CLARK and the T&T Clark logo are trademarks of
Bloomsbury Publishing Plc

First published in Great Britain 2023

Copyright © Lee Martin McDonald, 2023

Lee Martin McDonald has asserted his right under the Copyright, Designs and
Patents Act, 1988, to be identified as Author of this work.

Cover image (top): 2DA8Y5X © WHPics / Alamy
Cover image (bottom): *Church Fathers*. Artist: Byzantine Master
© Heritage Image Partnership Ltd / Alamy

All rights reserved. No part of this publication may be reproduced or transmitted
in any form or by any means, electronic or mechanical, including photocopying,
recording, or any information storage or retrieval system, without prior
permission in writing from the publishers.

Bloomsbury Publishing Plc does not have any control over, or responsibility for,
any third-party websites referred to or in this book. All internet addresses given
in this book were correct at the time of going to press. The author and publisher
regret any inconvenience caused if addresses have changed or sites have ceased
to exist, but can accept no responsibility for any such changes.

A catalogue record for this book is available from the British Library.

Library of Congress Control Number: 2022020585

ISBN: HB: 978-0-5677-0579-2
PB: 978-0-5677-0578-5
ePDF: 978-0-5677-0580-8
eBook: 978-0-5677-0582-2

Typeset by Newgen KnowledgeWorks Pvt. Ltd., Chennai, India

To find out more about our authors and books visit www.bloomsbury.com
and sign up for our newsletters.

For Richard Payant
Fellow military officer, capable lawyer, careful thinker
about the Christian faith, and my dear friend for over forty years

CONTENTS

Preface ... ix

Introduction ... 1

1 Judaism and Early Christianity: Similarities and Differences ... 7
   1. Early Jewish Christianity and Late Second Temple Judaism ... 7
   2. Important Differences between Late Second Temple Jews and Early Christians ... 9
   3. Early Jewish-Christian Beliefs and Other Jewish-Christian Sects ... 11
   4. The Early Church's First Scriptures ... 15
   5. Issues Leading to the Separation of Christians from Judaism ... 24
      A. When Christians Ceased Being Jews ... 24
      B. The Causes of the Separation and Hostilities ... 29

2 Major Challenges for the Early Christians ... 35
   1. Introduction ... 35
   2. Roman Persecutions and Philosophical Disputes ... 37
   3. Early Christianity and Emerging "Heresies" ... 44
      A. Ebionites ... 47
      B. Marcionites ... 49
      C. Gnostics and Gnosticism ... 56
      D. Montanists ... 61
   4. Influences of Heresy in Early Christianity ... 64

3 Primary Authorities in Early Christianity: Jesus and His Scriptures ... 67
   1. Jesus of Nazareth as Lord of the Church ... 67
   2. The Scriptures of Jesus ... 69
   3. The Scriptures Cited in the NT Authors ... 82
   4. The Church's First Scriptures ... 85
   5. The Words of Jesus and the Beginnings of a *Christian* Scripture ... 85
   6. Conclusion ... 93

4 Other Important Authorities and Guides: The Episcopate, Sacred Traditions, Core Creeds, and Hymns ... 95
   1. Introduction ... 95
   2. From the Apostles to the Episcopate ... 96
   3. Sacred Tradition in Early Christianity ... 98
   4. Early and Later Church Creeds ... 100
      A. NT Creeds ... 100
      B. Creeds Addressing the "Heresies" ... 104
   5. An Expansion of the Early Creeds ... 105

6. The Core of the *Regula Fidei*	109
7. The *Regula Fidei* and Christian Scripture	110
8. Hymns, Songs, and the Early Core Traditions	112

5 The Lectionaries, Manuscripts, and Their Texts — 117
  1. Introduction — 117
  2. The Act of Writing — 118
  3. The Lectionaries — 122
  4. The Manuscripts and Christian Scripture — 124
  5. Majuscule/Uncial Manuscripts from the Second to Fifth Centuries — 127
  6. The Textual Variants and Their Importance — 128
  7. Ancient Acknowledgment of Textual Variants — 140
  8. A Stabilized Greek Text — 142
  9. Final Remarks and Conclusion — 143

6 The Ancient Artifacts: *Nomina Sacra*, Translations, and the Councils — 147
  1. The Literary Artifacts of Antiquity and Their Importance — 147
  2. The Christian Use of *Nomina Sacra* — 148
  3. Early Translations of the Church's Scriptures — 152
  4. Local Council Decisions and the Church's Scriptures — 159
  5. The Emergence of Christian Scriptural Canon Lists — 163
    A. OT and/or NT Canon Lists from the East — 164
    B. OT and NT Canon Lists from the West — 165
  6. Conclusion — 166

7 Pseudepigrapha and Apocrypha in Early Christianity — 169
  1. Introduction — 169
  2. The Origin and Meaning of Pseudepigraphal Writings — 170
  3. Jewish Production and Use of Pseudepigrapha — 175
  4. Christian Production and Use of Pseudepigrapha — 179
  5. Canonical Pseudonymous Literature — 187
  6. The Importance of Pseudonymous Writings — 190
  7. Conclusion — 191

8 Final Thoughts and Conclusions — 193

BIBLIOGRAPHY — 199

INDEX OF BIBLICAL AND OTHER ANCIENT REFERENCES — 223

SUBJECT AND AUTHOR INDEX — 241

PREFACE

The following study has its origin in my attendance and participation in multiple church denominational worship services over many years. Knowing that the early churches did not have a Bible for centuries after the birth of the early church I began to inquire into how those churches survived and even grew despite the lack of a clear collection of its first scriptures and no formed New Testament (NT) until centuries later. How was the essence of their early faith maintained in their challenging years with no set scriptural base, only a few influential leaders, and with few prominent persons among them? How could they maintain and advance their core beliefs that identified the essence of Christian faith and eventually become a widespread movement? Their beginning raised many questions in my mind, and I also reflected on the church services that I attended or participated in from the beginning of my journey of faith that was instructed through the church's preaching, teaching, singing, baptismal and eucharistic affirmations, and by volunteering to participate and help as I was able. My faith was born before I knew any Bible verses or could even find them during church worship services and Sunday school classes. Soon my journey of faith was enabled to grow with the encouragement and teaching of many others in the church, most of whom were simple faithful followers of Christ, and they were happy to share with me what they could.

As I reflected on my early days in church as a teenager (I did not grow up in church but came to faith in my late teens), I remembered that some of the older people could not read or write but still came to church. Some carried Bibles with them that they could not read but brought their Bibles faithfully to church, sang their favorite hymns and spiritual songs that they learned from hearing them from long repetition over years. They were blessed to attend church and participate when and where they could to advance the life and ministry of the church they loved. As I studied the early church and its remarkable growth amid many disappointments and challenges, I asked how the church was able to advance its faith and mission when so few could read or write and when no one had a Bible like we have today, and most of those followers were simple persons who could not articulate the details of their faith or many of the more complex doctrines that were emerging in the churches.

The answer, of course, was not as complicated as it might now seem when most Christians have a Bible and can follow along the reading of scripture in worship in their own Bibles. Many have college and advanced degrees and not a few have influential positions in society and some churches have remarkable resources to advance their mission through multiple media presentations. That was not true in antiquity and yet the church grew despite its many challenges and disappointments. The success and early growth of the churches was not a secret and not as complicated as we might think. The early Christians were regularly reminded of the core elements in the church's teachings and early creeds (e.g., Rom 10:9) and in other ways as we will see below and they were always reminded of what God had done for them in Jesus the Christ and how that should be manifest in their living and church mission.

While the full scope of that faith was still rough around the edges for a while, most followers of Jesus knew that God made forgiveness of sins available to them in Jesus who had a special relationship with God and brought hope to them. It took time to deal with issues of ethnic prejudice, the consequences of their faith in daily living, and how best to accomplish their mission as a community of followers of Jesus the Christ. That early faith was made clear, of course, in the church gatherings, the songs they sang (Phil 2:6–11), the teachings they heard, the simple early creeds they cited (e.g., Acts 2:42; Rom 10:9), and in the affirmations they heard as they broke bread together (e.g., 1 Cor 11:23–26; *Did.* 9:1–5) or in baptismal affirmations (Acts 8; *Did.* 7:1–4). That was sufficient to advance the life and mission of the early churches when most could not read or write, but they learned the essence of their faith in multiple ways that were continual reminders of the core traditions circulating among them.

I am reminded again of my earlier church attendance when I remember some wonderful persons in my first church home who went to church regularly but could not read let alone understand the Bible. Some of them were largely illiterate but still came to church, sang the songs of the faith that were familiar to them, prayed, served the Lord to the best of their ability, and even carried a Bible that they could not read. Some of those people were in my own family. They also certainly affirmed the church's key teachings about Jesus and their faith in him and often they would be involved in various voluntary ministries of the church. How could simple persons who were less literate have an informed faith? The answer, of course, is just like the early Christians who often could not read but could nevertheless learn from others who could both read and teach the core faith that brought life changes to them. That is not unusual even today in mission activity and quite common among some persons of advanced years who can no longer read or study their Bible but love it and love singing their favorite hymns and spiritual songs from memory. The preaching, teaching, creedal affirmations often read congregationally in their worship, as well as baptismal and eucharistic affirmations, and spiritual songs all regularly informed the faith of the early followers of Jesus and reminded them of their core beliefs.

This book took shape as I was questioning how early churches could survive without having a Bible. I have spent years trying to understand the Bible and to teach it in churches as well as in academic institutions and seminaries. I know how valuable the Bible is for the church today, but what about those who did not have access to it throughout much of church history? The benefits of having a Bible and studying those writings closest to the time of Jesus as well as those scriptures that informed the faith and teaching of Jesus himself are a remarkable treasure for persons of faith; for many centuries most followers of Jesus did not have access to all that we have today but their faith continued to grow and they have left behind many treasures for us that have blessed the church through many centuries. I am impressed that the faith of many ancient saints has moved many to carry on the mission of the church just like the early Christians advanced the church's life and mission as they were able and often during challenging circumstances. History is strewn with the blood of martyrs, even to the present day, who refused to deny the faith that they learned in churches many centuries ago that enabled them to grow and advance in their faith. The same is true today especially in some third world countries where that faith can be quite costly as we have witnessed through the modern media. Although Christian faith has often been quite costly throughout history, it nevertheless continues to thrive even when and where its candle is dim.

I have examined the emergence of early Christianity for years now, and as I began to reflect on several parallels between the past and present I hope the following may fill a gap for those raising similar questions about the early churches before they had a Bible. My thinking on such matters and after further investigations led me to ask about the authorities in the early churches before there was a Bible. It was clear early on that the churches existed before the full scope of its Old Testament (OT) was settled and before any of the NT books were written. So, the question of how the faith of those early churches was transmitted and how there could be any stability in the message and faith they proclaimed was an important part of the story I wanted to tell. I am aware that for many centuries and still today there are different perspectives of the Christian faith circulating in our world, and those differences led to considerable debates, but the core teachings of that early faith have not changed much even as churches grew and addressed emerging crises and challenges facing them (see Chadwick 1993, 1990: 21–61). Many perspectives circulating in the churches brought challenges to the followers of Jesus, but soon clearer direction and guidance for their faith emerged that enabled them to continue.

Biblical scholars today acknowledge that the majority of those who became followers of Jesus in antiquity were not literate and they depended on those who were literate and informed to teach them the substance and meaning of their faith and their sacred traditions. The transmission of Christian faith through the centuries took place in multiple ways as we will see later. Much of what took place then is also like many Christian expressions of faith today. The following reflects my examination of those areas in early Christianity and what eventually emerged as the church's core traditions supported by their emerging OT and NT scriptures. May what follows be a help and encouragement to readers that will aid in their understanding of some of the challenges facing churches and multiple expressions of Christian faith today.

I must also express my appreciation here to T&T Clark at Bloomsbury for accepting this volume in their impressive collection of scholarly works. I am deeply appreciative and I owe significant thanks to Dominic Mattos for his welcome of this manuscript, his encouragement, and suggestions on how to improve it. I owe appreciation to the careful work of Saranya Manohar, the project manager for Bloomsbury, who discovered much that needed to be changed or corrected. I also want to thank the helpful work of Jonathan Nash, production editor at Bloomsbury Academic, in getting this manuscript ready for publication. I could not ask for a better team of capable and even expert workers who brought this book to publication. While they were all helpful and encouraging and I owe them much, any remaining mistakes or errors are, of course, my responsibility.

Finally, I want to say how much I have appreciated my dear lawyer friend, Richard Payant, to whom this volume is dedicated. He has long been an active member of his church and takes his beliefs and actions as a Christian seriously. He often offers excellent and thoughtful advice to me. We have known each other now over forty years and we met when we were both in the military and he faithfully attended my chapel services and was most helpful to me then. Our friendship has long been a special blessing to me.

Introduction

I have often spoken and written on the value of knowing the scriptures and I encourage people to read their Bibles regardless of the translation they are using. We learn from the Bible who God is, what God wants from us, how to live and how to serve God who created us, and everything in heaven and earth. The New Testament (NT) gives to us our best picture of who Jesus is, what he has done that benefits those of us who put our faith in him, what he taught, and the remarkable things he has done. It also clarifies to us how we ought to live and why we need to proclaim Jesus and his message. Those who put their faith in him are not disappointed and we learn *most* of what we know about him in the NT writings.

But what about those early Christians who did not have Bibles like we have today? Most early churches appear to have had copies of several of their favorite scriptures or portions of those scriptures but nothing like a complete Old Testament (OT) or NT. In other words, the early churches existed and even functioned as churches without a Bible. By the term "Bible," I am referring to both OT and NT and not limited copies of some of their sacred scriptures. There is little evidence that all of the OT or NT scriptures were present in any or even a few early churches until much later.

The value and benefit of having a copy of the church's sacred scriptures is not in question in what follows and much of what I have to say is affirmed in them, but the earliest followers of Jesus did not have a Bible like we have today. They did know of many sacred texts that give to them their understanding of God's direction for living and today we call those texts our OT scriptures, though the full scope of those scriptures was uncertain for centuries to come and what we have in our current Bibles is different from what most early churches possessed or even were familiar with until much later. What they knew about Jesus and the faith he proclaimed was first preserved and proclaimed orally in church gatherings and that was at the heart of the sacred traditions in the early churches. That story was passed among the early churches first by those (generally apostles) who were closest to Jesus and learned from him, but subsequently also from those they taught and were placed in leadership roles in the churches. Christian faith was a response to what was heard or recited in churches or reflected on in the teachings of the early followers of Jesus as they proclaimed his story and cited multiple Jewish scriptural texts with a Christological focus, as we will observe below.

The focus here is not so much on the formation of the Bible that I have addressed at length elsewhere but more on life in the early churches before the Bible was formed and how their core beliefs and practices were formed and transmitted before there was a Christian scripture. That also includes the time before there was a complete OT collection of scriptures that was generally settled for most churches, namely the middle to late fourth century. We know that the churches functioned and even grew during that time before the Bible came to its current shape. How did churches carry on their teaching, worship or liturgical, and missional activities for centuries before there was anything like a complete Bible? That will be our focus in what follows.

I should also say that throughout this volume I will use the designation "Jewish-Christian" to identify the first followers of Jesus, but I am also aware that the earliest followers of Jesus did not use that designation to identify themselves. They were all Jews then who did not distinguish their Jewish identity from their faith in Jesus who they believed was their anticipated Jewish Messiah. I will use that designation for convenience to distinguish the first followers of Jesus, Jews who followed Jesus, from those who came to faith in him later and apart from an observance of the Law, namely the Gentiles. I should also add that the designations "Christian" and "Christianity" are later used designations, and I acknowledge that the *earliest* followers of Jesus did not initially call themselves by those terms, but eventually they were used to identify those who followed Jesus. Hopefully that will be simpler than employing several designations that are more complicated.

Finally, I am focusing on "authorities" in early Christianity. Not all of them are of creeds that summarize early Christian beliefs for most of the churches, but some are rather models that were followed as in the cases of baptisms, hymns expressing early Christian beliefs, liturgies, and organizational structures. Some of the models early Christians followed functioned like authorities even though they were not always express commands to follow as in the cases of some hymns and art. It has been brought to my attention by an early reader that I need to clarify notions of authority in early Christianity, and I agree. The primary notion of "canon" is rule or guideline and in that sense, there were many early "canons" of faith before there was an official biblical canon. Some texts functioned as canon or rule before they were called scripture or officially commanded by church councils as a guide to follow. These include early texts later attributed to apostles but were not called scripture immediately, but by the second century some of those writings began to be called "scripture" and that was a first step before later forming a "biblical canon" (a closed collection) of the church's scriptures. Again, the primary focus of this volume has to do with what authorities or guides were followed in churches before there was a biblical canon, that is, a Bible.

The primary questions and focus of this volume are on how the early followers of Jesus grew and survived without a Bible like ours and how they preserved the core traditions that are central to the Christian faith. They did not have the privileges that we have today of reading the multiple images of Jesus that we see in our scriptures and how what Jesus taught and proclaimed affects how we should live now (the Gospels and Epistles especially). The scriptures that we have in our Bibles today clarify most of the questions that Christians have about God, Jesus, their own identity as followers of Jesus, and their mission in the world. That is a blessing and privilege for moderns that the earliest followers of Jesus did not have. Many questions arise from that situation, and we may well want to know what the theological or doctrinal discussions in antiquity would have been like if Jesus' followers had a settled OT and NT like we have today. The scope of the scriptures that Jews now call their Hebrew Bible (HB) or Tanak was not complete or finished in the first century, as we will see below, and the scope of books that eventually went into it was fluid for several centuries for both Jews and Christians.

The authorities in early Christianity before there was a Bible is a story that is seldom told and almost always is assumed by well-intentioned church members, namely that times then were much like they are now. What was the life like among the early followers of Jesus and how did their understanding of their faith grow and how was it passed along from the beginning when there was no Bible? Also, how was the sense of the authority of God manifested in the early churches before there was a notion of a Bible or even a complete Bible such as churches today have? As we see in the NT citations of the Jewish scriptures, the authors were often *writing with scripture* and citing Jewish scriptures, not unlike the practice of their contemporary Jewish siblings. They clearly welcomed several of the Jewish sacred scriptures and affirmed the authority of Jesus in multiple ways that identified their communities of faith. There never was a time for the churches without the presence and recognition of the authority of scriptures in early Christianity, but the scope of those scriptures was not clear in the first century CE. Nevertheless, the church's most important authority from its foundation was Jesus, who began to be called the Lord of the church soon after the reports of his resurrection.

The church existed *before* there was a *fixed* collection of the Hebrew scriptures (the OT) and certainly before there were any written NT scriptures. When Christians met together, their *first* scriptures were read to them that they later called their "Old Testament" and they transmitted orally their shared faith about Jesus that they also believed was a fulfillment of their earliest collection of sacred scriptures. The traditions about Jesus were transmitted orally and within decades were put in writings that circulated in the churches and eventually became a part of their *Christian* scriptures (NT).

The more important challenges the early Christians faced were not only the fact that Jesus had not returned as his followers had hoped but also that the churches lost their *religio licita* status as a licensed or legally recognized religion after they and their Jewish siblings separated. That loss eventually led to *local* Roman persecutions and by the mid-third century an empire-wide persecution under the Roman Emperor Decius and subsequently in the fourth century under Emperor Diocletian. Along with the above, the death of the apostles left an important vacuum in the Christian community. This was accompanied by the emergence of various so-called "heresies" that emerged in the churches in the late first century and throughout the second.

In recent discussions of how the churches got their Bible, there is little attention given to the earliest primary authorities circulating among Jesus' followers that eventually gave rise to the formation of the church's Bible. From the church's beginning, authority played a major role in the faith and life of its multiple communities. Without question, that faith was centered on the recognition of Jesus' special relationship with God and the significance he played in God's plan of salvation for humanity. It also focused on the importance of his teachings, activities, death, and resurrection for the communities of faith. The churches' first sacred scriptures (HB or OT) were circulating throughout Palestine in the first century, but it is not certain which ones were recognized by Jesus or his earliest followers since not all the later HB scriptures are cited either by Jesus or the early church fathers. From the scripture texts cited by Jesus in the Gospels and the other NT authors, it appears that Deuteronomy, Isaiah, and the Psalms were among the most cited and recognized scriptures among the early Christians, but that does not mean those were the only recognized scriptures in the early churches. Two-thirds of the Jewish scriptures that later were called the Tanak, and much later, the HB were also cited by the NT authors. This is also like the Essenes at Qumran who produced or made copies of the now famed Dead Sea Scrolls (DSS). It is not possible to say with certainty which specific scriptures the residents at Qumran acknowledged as scripture since they were all placed side by side without obvious distinctions. Similarly, Jesus and his first followers recognized sacred scriptures but did not leave behind a list of all the texts they welcomed as scripture.

Because the scriptural texts cited in the NT and by early church fathers were often intended to address specific circumstances facing the churches, it is quite likely that they welcomed more than what is cited in the NT and in early church fathers' writings. No one in the first century listed or identified all the scriptural texts that comprised their recognized sacred scriptural books. There was no discernible interest in identifying a complete list of all recognized scriptures at that time. It appears from the NT and the DSS that several religious texts that were not later included in the later HB or Christian OT were also cited and welcomed among the sacred religious texts of that time. That is certainly true also for the early churches. In what follows, I will show that the *notion* of a "Bible," that is, a *fixed* collection of sacred scriptures, was a later development in early Christianity and that discussion of a biblical canon was not a significant factor in the early church's development until largely the fourth and fifth centuries following the Council of Nicea when the identity of Jesus was more settled and clearer for most churches. It is difficult to imagine a NT canon of scriptures before most churches were in broad agreement on the identity of Jesus and when that came, multiple lists of the church's scriptures began to emerge.

Also, in what follows I will focus on how several other authorities or guides for the early churches were circulating in early Christianity from its beginning and how they offered clarity to churches in their transmission of the sacred story that gave rise to their faith and enabled them to deal with the many challenges facing them. The churches addressed those challenges noted above first by adopting a stronger episcopate (essentially enhancing the role of the bishop) along with regular citing of creeds that identified who Jesus was and the core elements of their faith. In the second century, apostolic authority was attributed beyond first-century apostolic leadership in churches but later was attached to writings believed to be written by them. As the authority of those writings emerged, the notion of *Christian* scripture was also beginning to emerge in the second century. It was then that texts written in apostolic names or by their assistants in church ministries (Luke, Mark) began to be read alongside the church's first (OT) scriptures and many of those writings began to *function* like scripture before the end of the second century when several were beginning to be called scripture. Eventually, that collection began to be firmed up and by the middle to the end of the fourth century biblical canons, or lists of books recognized as the church's scriptures that could be read in churches, emerged that gave guidance to churches for which scriptures could be read in their liturgies or rejected altogether, although these "biblical canons" are now what most call a "Bible." Of course, "Bible" was not a common or popular designation among the Christians for their scriptures until many centuries later. The first known use of the term was when Jerome referred to the church's sacred scriptures as "the holy books" in the early fifth century. "Books," of course, in Greek is *biblia* the plural of *biblos* and "Holy Books" (= "Holy Bible") became a common designation for the church's scriptures among the Christians by the ninth century, though even at that time the books in the collections of scriptures were not always the same. For centuries, however, and despite considerable overlap in the books welcomed in the Christian scriptures, still other now-called "nonbiblical" books were often welcomed and read in some churches like scripture, including some that later were dubbed apocryphal or pseudepigraphal books. Regarding those "additional" books, the production and use of pseudonymous texts was common in the Greco-Roman world and in late Second Temple Judaism among their Jewish siblings, but it was also eventually common in early Christianity. It is not surprising to find that some of those texts also circulated in the Christian communities and some of them likely remained in the church's scriptures, for example, 2 Peter, Jude, the Pastorals, and possibly others. Several NT writings were written anonymously (Gospels, Acts, Hebrews, 1, 2, 3 John), and apostolic names were later attached to them (e.g., Matthew, Mark, Luke, John, Paul).

As we will see, the core traditions and beliefs of the early Christians circulating in the churches from their beginning were regularly repeated in their emerging summarizing creeds and liturgies. The surviving biblical manuscripts and the ancient canon lists not only show the considerable overlap in the sacred writings circulating in the churches but also reflect some of the variations in those collections in the early churches. While the initial churches did not have a collection of Christian scriptures, the core beliefs of the early churches were regularly cited in early creedal formulations in the NT and by the early church fathers.

Some Jewish and Christian writings that were not eventually included in the church's OT or NT, often called "Apocrypha" and "Pseudepigrapha," also influenced some early Christian authors and the churches they served. Multiple church traditions and art are sometimes reflected in those disputed writings that were eventually widely rejected or excluded from the church's scriptures, but, as we will see, some of them were recognized as scripture in some early churches, at least for a time and some of them continue to this day. The church's first scriptures later called their OT were regularly but not exclusively interpreted Christologically or eschatologically to advance the Christian proclamation.

I will also focus on the most common authorities in early Christianity *before there was a Bible*, namely Jesus, the apostles, the church's core traditions circulating in the early churches, the first summarizing creeds of those traditions, along with hymns and spiritual songs that were not as authoritative as the church's scriptures but nevertheless they taught the people the core beliefs circulating in the early churches. I will also focus on the importance of what we can discern in the surviving ancient church manuscripts of their sacred texts, and the later lectionaries that were read in the churches.

I also acknowledge in advance, as David deSilva has rightly noted in a jacket endorsement of the volume by John J. Collins, Craig A. Evans, and myself, that there has been "something of an obsession with the boundaries of canon" among biblical scholars. I agree and add that this obsession has often excluded any focus on what took place in the early churches *before* there was a Bible. Much of the biblical canon inquiry has focused on ancient church father citations and ancient lists or catalogues of various writings or books recognized as scripture. While those are important for understanding the formation of the church's Bible and cannot be ignored, I want to say that they are not the whole story of the early church before it got its Bible. The "operative" scriptures of early Christianity were those that were read in the churches and those are seen primarily in the surviving manuscripts and the lectionaries from antiquity. In other words, the scriptures read in the early churches are seen largely in the surviving "biblical" manuscripts and in the lectionaries read in church liturgical settings. Hurtado has observed that perhaps only 1 percent or so of the approximately 500,000 books produced in early Christianity have survived (Hurtado 2006: 24–5). As a result, some caution must be taken in my assessments of the surviving manuscripts from that time. He also correctly reminds us that our conclusions about antiquity must be open for correction given that so much from antiquity has been lost. Also, because most of the manuscripts that we now have were found in Egypt, where the warm dry weather allowed for greater preservation than in places with more moist weather, caution is needed before assuming that they represent more churches than those in ancient Egypt. Do those manuscripts tell us what churches in the east or west were thinking at the same time? To what extent were perspectives unique in the locations where manuscripts were found reflective of a greater number of churches whose manuscripts are now lost because the weather conditions did not allow long-time preservation? Also, there were lectionaries read in synagogues and churches from their beginning (e.g., Luke 4:16–19), but the ones that have survived are largely from the fourth century and later, so what has survived is not likely reflective of all churches in all locations. These and several other related issues will be addressed in the following chapters and in them we will see more clearly how they functioned before there was a Bible. The primary focus of this volume is not on the formation of the Bible since I have written on that subject at considerable length elsewhere but rather on early Christianity before there was a Bible. Occasionally some issues related to canon formation will be summarized in some of the chapters to let readers unfamiliar with this matter know the larger picture of emerging authorities in early Christianity.

The next chapter will address the implications of the Jewish context in which early Christianity was born and how that context helped frame some of the key teachings and practices in early Christianity. I will also summarize the distinctions and divisions between adherents of the common beliefs and practices of the various Judaisms of late Second Temple Judaism and early Christianity. I will conclude with a focus on some of the causes that led to the separation of the early followers of Jesus that had a considerable impact on early Christianity and its subsequent developments.

CHAPTER 1

Judaism and Early Christianity: Similarities and Differences

1. EARLY JEWISH CHRISTIANITY AND LATE SECOND TEMPLE JUDAISM

As is well known, Christianity began as a Jewish sect in first-century Judaism and it follows that there would be many similarities between the current first-century Jewish beliefs and practices and the early followers of Jesus, and Jesus himself doubtless reflects many parallels with his Jewish siblings. The book of Acts, without any qualifications or disputes, specifically identifies the early followers of Jesus as a Jewish "sect" (Acts 24:5, 14; 28:22). This is readily seen in the early Christians' recognition of the authority of the Hebrew scriptures circulating in Palestine *at that time* including their observance of the Law of Moses (Pentateuch), other Hebrew religious texts (the Prophets), as well as Temple sacrifices, the practice of circumcision, times of prayer, observance of the Sabbath, and the multiple holy days such as Passover, Pentecost and Feast of Dedication. Like their fellow Jews, they participated in the multiple religious traditions current in the first century CE, including synagogue participation. Jesus, his disciples, and his earliest followers regularly observed and endorsed the commonly held Jewish religious teachings and practices of their day.

Many first-century Diaspora Jews and their early Jewish-Christian siblings appealed to a *similar* collection of Hebrew scriptures translated in Greek in the Septuagint (LXX) that eventually formed later Christian Old Testament (OT) scriptures circulating in the early churches. Some scholars contend that the books not later included in the HB, but were included in the *Christian* copies of the LXX, were not viewed as scripture by the Jewish population in the first or second centuries. Of course, there was no discernible OT canon of scriptures in the first century, but the texts functioned like scriptures circulating among the Jews both in Palestine and Alexandria and throughout the Mediterranean world in the first century BCE and CE and included several of the books later included in the Christian LXX collection of Jewish scriptures, but not in the HB or Tanak. Some of those writings as we will see below were among the Dead Sea Scrolls without any obvious distinction from the later canonical Hebrew Bible (HB)/Tanak scriptures.

Similarly, some of them were found among the collection of sacred texts in the famed Cairo Geniza and there are multiple verbal parallels with them in some New Testament (NT) texts cited like scripture. Even though they do not have the usual scriptural introductions, such as "as the scripture says," "the scripture says," or "as it is written," those designations are not uniformly used through the NT writings as we will see in Matthew and Hebrews and elsewhere. All NT references to the Jewish scriptures are *not* introduced with any of those usual introductions, but they are clearly introducing scripture, for example the scriptural citations in Hebrews and the example of Jesus citing Daniel as a prophet (Matt 24:15) without using those introductions. Even among the scriptures cited in rabbinic Judaism there are over eighty references to Sirach as scripture, but it was eventually dropped. The scriptures of the early Christians are those that were circulating among the Jews (mostly Pharisaic and Essene) of the first century CE *before* their separation from them. Why would some early Christians welcome the deuterocanonical writings as scripture without an antecedent in their Jewish siblings? The Christian copies of the LXX that we have in the fourth and fifth centuries reflect current Jewish sentiments about scripture before their separation and later the rabbinic Jews established a more restrictive collection by the end of the second century CE.

Despite the many different interpretations of those sacred texts, all the Christian bodies, whether Orthodox, Catholic, or Protestant Christians, agree on the books in the Hebrew scriptures later formed as the Tanak and even later as the HB. Catholics and Orthodox welcome other books often called deuterocanonical books by Catholics and inspired noncanonical OT scriptures by the Orthodox, and apocrypha by the Protestants, but all welcome all the HB books in their OT.

It is also the case that neither Jesus nor his earliest followers intended to start a new movement outside of the Jewish people having several common beliefs and practices of popular views of Palestinian Judaism in the first century, nor was there initially a plan to start a new community called the church as opposed to the synagogue or "Christian beliefs" currently common among many Palestinian Jews in the first century. Likewise, there was no initial intention to write new scriptures that would eventually become their NT. However, the above similarities with their Jewish siblings do not mask several important differences among the early followers of Jesus, especially in welcoming Gentiles into their community without circumcision or the observance of the Sabbath and the Laws of Moses.

It is fundamental to our understanding of early Christianity that Jesus and his earliest followers were Jews and that they began a religious movement or sect *within* first-century Judaism and believed that they were those who best followed the Jewish scriptures, traditions, and their hopes, and were the successors of blessings promised to the Jews, including their ability to interpret their sacred scriptures more faithfully. Although they eventually welcomed Gentiles as a part of their community of faith, there was significant opposition within the early Jewish-Christian community to that decision (Acts 11:1–18; 15:1–11; Gal 2:11–14). The earliest Christians claimed that their salvation came through their faith in Jesus their Messiah/Christ (Acts 4:12). Eventually, his Jewish and Gentile followers saw themselves as the "true Israel" of God (Gal 3:6–16; Rom 2:25–29). For Paul, the welcoming of the Gentiles was in the plan of God (Gal 3:6–14) and even *for a time* had been given priority over the Jews (Rom 11:13–24).

The earliest Jewish-Christians continued to gather for worship and prayers in the Jewish Temple and in the various Jewish synagogues mostly until as late as 100–125 CE, but some continued meeting in synagogues well into the late second century at Sepphoris (Zippori), the capital of Galilee, with regular contact with fellow Jews (*Abod. Zar.* 16b). The initial separation of Jews and Jewish-Christians began largely when the Jewish-Christians fled to Pella southeast of the Sea of Galilee on the east side of the Jordan river following the death of James the brother of Jesus (*c.* 62–64). The final separation of Jewish Christians from fellow Jews, though not their religious practices, followed the Jewish Bar Kochba rebellion against Rome, a messianic movement in the Land of Israel (132–35 CE). Jewish Christians were widely excluded from participation in synagogues in Palestine because they did not support the messianic movement that was led by a self-proclaimed messianic figure, Simon Bar Kozibah (Kochbah), since by doing so implied a rejection of Jesus as their Messiah.

Biblical scholars have long recognized that Jesus and the early Jewish-Christians are closer in their perspectives and beliefs to the Jewish sect of Pharisees mentioned in the NT than to any of the other first-century sects of Judaism. This can be seen in their commitment to keeping of the Law (Matt 5:17–20; Acts 21:17–26), table fellowship (Acts 10:9–29; 11:2–12; Gal 2:11–14), acceptance of the same sacred scriptures (Luke 24:44; John 5:39), their affirmation of the resurrection of the dead (Rom 8:11, 18–23; 10:9; 1 Cor 15:3–11), and their eschatological beliefs. As we see in the Gospels, Jesus and his followers often disagreed with the Pharisees over the Jewish *oral* traditions, including how to observe the Sabbath (e.g., Mark 2:13–3:6; 7:1–13; Luke 11:37–52). The Pharisees are mentioned ninety-nine times in the NT, and eighty-six of those are in the Gospels. Some of the Pharisaic views and practices are listed in Josephus's detailed description of them (*c*. 75–79 CE; *Ant*. 13.12–15; 18.171–72; *Life* 10–12). The Pharisees held strict observance of the Law, the tradition of the elders, divine providence with human accountability, a future resurrection, and, for some, the coming of a messianic figure (Schnabel 2009: 491–6).

Rabbinic Jews of the second through the sixth centuries have views that are similar to those of the first-century Pharisees, especially in terms of their teachings about agricultural law, Sabbath keeping, festival observance, and purity regulations. After the destruction of the Temple in 70 CE, the Pharisees took the lead in establishing a center of Jewish religious life in matters of Law and purity at Jamnia (Yavneh), following the destruction of the Temple. Rome recognized the Pharisaic teachers as the governing body for the internal life of the Jewish people in the Land of Israel (Ferguson 2003: 514–15). The *primary* expressions of the sects of Judaism that survived the first century in the Land of Israel and in Babylon are reflected in rabbinic Judaism whose roots largely go back to first-century Pharisaic rabbis, especially Hillel, Gamaliel, and Simon. Some scholars debate whether Pharisaic Judaism is the only surviving voice of first-century expressions of Judaism, but there are several traits among them that appear to establish a close relationship with rabbinic Judaism (Neusner 1984: 45–61).

2. IMPORTANT DIFFERENCES BETWEEN LATE SECOND TEMPLE JEWS AND EARLY CHRISTIANS

Despite the many common perspectives and practices in early Christianity that have their roots in late Second Temple Judaism, there are also several important distinctions. Jewish religious opposition to the teachings of Jesus and his followers, especially from the Sadducees and Pharisees, was present from the beginning of Jesus' ministry (Mark 2:23–3:6; 14:1–2, 53–65; Acts 4:1–6; 5:17–42, *passim*) and that opposition became more intense over the emerging Christian views regarding the Law, observance of purity rituals, Sabbath keeping, and especially for their inclusion of Gentile converts without having them observe the Law, including their welcome of uncircumcised Gentiles into their fellowship (see Gal 2:11–14 and Acts 15).

Jewish opposition to Christians grew as they claimed that they were the heirs of the divine hopes and promises to Israel through faith in Jesus the Christ, and especially when they abandoned the requirement for Gentiles to observe the Law (Gal 3:6–9; 6:15–16; Rom 4:1–15). Another distinction had to do with Christian claims that the promised outpouring of the Holy Spirit at the end of the ages (Acts 2:16–33) promised to Israel (Dan 12:2, Joel 2:28–32; Ezek 36:26–27) was now manifest in the emergence of the church and its ministries. For several centuries there were many attempts to convert Jews to the Christians' way of thinking with some initial success, but such attempts eventually gave way to hostility. Some early Christians, especially Paul, believed that all Jews and others eventually would accept Jesus as their Messiah (Rom 1:16–17; 11:25–36; Phil 2:6–11). Although that did not happen, the early church's mission to Jews continued for centuries and is especially seen in various reported dialogue engagements and debates with Jews in the second century and following. The best known of these dialogues was Justin's *Dialogue with Trypho* (c. 150 CE), but in most of these supposed dialogues, the Jews involved regularly lost the debate with Christian debaters and often became followers of Jesus. Despite Jewish rejection of Jesus as the Messiah and often opposition to Christians, many of them continued to remain attracted to Judaism. Chrysostom (c. 347–407), for instance, gave several warnings to Christians to stay away from the Jewish synagogues (*Against the Jews*, Homily 8, and *Discourse* 1.3.3 and 1.4.2).

With their common roots in first-century expressions of Judaism and sharing most of the same sacred scriptures in their OT, mutual comparisons and even contacts between rabbinic Judaism and early Christianity could be anticipated. The NT writers themselves show considerable familiarity with the first-century Jewish matrix. Indeed, along with Philo, Josephus, and the Dead Sea Scrolls, the NT Gospels are widely acknowledged by Jewish and Christian scholars alike as one of the primary resources for understanding the Jewish context of late Second Temple Judaism (Levine 2017: 118–19, 249–50, 759–63). This can be seen in several NT criticisms of the Pharisees that generally focused on accusations of legalism, self-righteousness, and hypocrisy, but that was not in reference to the God they served or the scriptures they read. The biggest difference between Christians and Pharisees, of course, had to do with how to obtain divine salvation, namely, whether through faith in Jesus the Christ or through the keeping of the Law and its traditions. Josephus offers a description of the Pharisees' commitment to the Law and Jewish tradition (*Ant.* 13.171–173, 288–298; 17.41–44; 18.11–15; see also *War* 1.107–114; 2.162–166). He sheds little light on their emphasis on ritual purity, agricultural taboos, festivals, and the like (Neusner 1984: 54).

The important differences in the surviving Jewish and Christian traditions, of course, have to do with their understanding of Jesus, eventually the role of the Law and its traditions, and the Christian notion of supersession that claimed that Christians had replaced the Jews as the people of God, even if according to Paul only temporarily (Rom 10:11–14; 11:1–23; Gal 6:15–16). Some of these differences cannot only be seen in the early church fathers but also in some rabbinic traditions though they are fewer in number there. Early Christian literature is generally negative in its assessment of the Jewish beliefs, but it was not initially anti-Semitic as much as anti-Judaistic, namely, they did not have a *racial* conflict with the Jews so much as a *religious* one, though often and later it was every bit as vitriolic (McDonald 1993: 215–36).

Many first-century Jewish beliefs and perspectives are reflected in later rabbinic Judaism in its *Mishnah* and in its subsequent interpretations.[1] Rabbinic writings have

---

[1] The Mishnah is largely a codified collection of Jewish oral traditions circulating in the first two centuries CE that were subsequently interpreted in the two Talmuds, namely the *Palestinian* Talmud regularly identified as

only a few direct references to Jesus, the Christians, and their literature, and this may be because the Mishnah and the two Talmuds are largely focused on *halakah* or law, rather than *haggadah* or history. History as such is not of primary interest in rabbinic literature, and the few references to history in the time of Jesus are generally considered unreliable (Cohen 1979: 253; Van Voorst 2000: 75–134; Neusner 1984b: 54–7). Some initial negative references to Jesus and the Christians were later modified in manuscripts after the Christians gained political influence and power in the Roman Empire following the conversion of Constantine to the Christian faith (Brown: 158–9; Van Voorst 2000: 100–32). I will later focus on the causes and consequences of the separation of the Christians from their Jewish siblings, but first I will observe the many overlapping traditions and parallels among Jews of Late Second Temple Judaism and early Christianity

3. EARLY JEWISH-CHRISTIAN BELIEFS AND OTHER JEWISH-CHRISTIAN SECTS

The Jewish-Christian history of early Christianity is reflected in NT among the first followers of Jesus and its primary advocates were Peter and James, the brother of Jesus. The earliest followers of Jesus have multiple parallels with the common Palestinian Jewish practices of that time whether regarding the scriptures they cited or in their observance of the Sabbath, the practice of circumcision, diet regulations, and distancing themselves from Gentiles.

The various emerging Jewish-Christian sects that followed Jesus will be discussed in more detail in Chapter 2, but here we need to note that not all the Jewish sects were the same as the emerging proto-orthodox followers of Jesus characterized especially by the Apostle Paul. There are references to Jewish Christians in the early church fathers who refer to them as sects. Jerome speaks of the early Jewish Christians as the "Nazarenes" (*Esaiam* 8.11–15; 9.1; 11.1–3; 29.17–21; 31.6–9). Irenaeus speaks of them as the Ebionites (*Haer.* 1.26.2; 3.21.1; 3.33.4), Tertullian (*Praescr.* 32.3–5) calls them Cerinthians (*Haer.* 1.26.1–2; 3.3.4), Epiphanius (*Pan.* 28.1.3; 2.3; 4.1–2) and Origen call them Symmachians (*Matt.* 16.16, see also Eusebius in *Hist. eccl.* 6.17), Ambrosiaster (*ad Gal. Prol.*) and Hippolytus speaks of them as Elkesaites (*Ref.* 9.13.2–3; 9.15.2; 9.17.2; cf. also *Ref.* 7.7–9; 7:33.1–2; 7.34.12; 7.35.1–2).

Along with the Jewish-Christian sects, there were several other Christian sects including the proto-orthodox Christians who were largely followers of Paul. The proto-orthodox were the "winners" among the multiple early sects of followers of Jesus and they were the ones who wrote the early history of the early church, something that "winners" do throughout history. Dunn correctly acknowledges that early Christianity was at first a Jewish sect and that sect grew and soon became multiple sects that followed Jesus whether among the Jews or the Gentiles (Dunn 2013: 197–203). What they all had in common was the centrality of Jesus in their expressions of faith and mission. As we will see in Chapter 2, other well-known expressions of Christian faith included the Ebionites, Docetics, Marcionites, Gnostics, and Montanists that were eventually called "heretical."

---

the *Yerushalmi* or the siglum *y*. and the *Babylonian* Talmud regularly identified as the *Bavli* with the siglum *b*, both third to sixth centuries CE, as well as the *Tosefta* or siglum *t*, *c*. third century CE, along with the various Jewish interpretations of scripture (*Midrash*, *Rabbah*, *Melkita*, and *Targums*, *c*. first century BCE to roughly sixth century CE).

The parallels in first-century CE Jewish sects with the early Jewish Christians can be seen not only in the earliest Christian writings, mostly the NT, but also in several contemporary Jewish texts at Qumran, Philo, Josephus, and in the Mishnah and in the two Talmuds, the later interpretations of the Mishnah. These are seen first with Jesus and his earliest followers with their multiple Jewish religious parallels. When Jesus said that the whole Law depends (Greek, *krematai* "hangs"; Heb., *Tala*) on two commandments, that is, to love God with all oneself and one's neighbor as oneself (Matt 22:37–40), he was reflecting a long-standing Jewish and later rabbinic understanding that many commandments depend or "hang" on one or a few of them. This can be seen in *Siph.* of Lev 19:2 where the command to be holy underlies the rest of the commands. According to Bar Kappara (*b. Ber.* 63a, 18), "what short text is there upon which all the essential principles of the Torah depend? In all thy ways acknowledge Him and He will direct thy paths" (a reference to Prov 3:6; see *b. Ber.* 63a, 18, Soncino trans.). Here, as in the case of the Matthew text, the whole Law depends on a single command.

This is also found elsewhere in rabbinic writings, namely in *m. Hag.* 1.8, *t. Hag.* 1.9, and *t. Er.* 8.23 where other laws, even large ones, are considered like mountains hanging by a hair (a smaller command with an important principle). It is reported that Hillel once received a pagan man based on the principle "what is hateful to you, do not [do] to your neighbor: that is the commentary thereof; go and learn it: that is the whole Torah, while the rest is the commentary" (*b. Shab.* 31a, 12–13, Soncino). Matthew's description of all the Law "hanging" on loving God and one's neighbor is the same principle of a single or smaller command containing the essence of all the commandments. This does not mean that according to Jesus the other parts could be ignored as we see in Matt 5:18 where he says: "not one letter, not one stroke of a letter will pass from the law until all is accomplished" (Daube ([1956] 1998: 250–3).

The above shows that the early Christians owed many of their practices to their roots in late Second Temple Judaism. These Jewish precursors can be seen in Christian baptisms and the Eucharist or communion, though Christian baptism and the Eucharist have different meanings than what we find in those precursors. It is generally acknowledged that early Christian baptism has its roots in the Jewish ritualistic cleansings in the *mikva'ot* that it has several similarities in ancient and even modern Jewish practices, beginning in the baptismal practice of John the Baptist. The baptism of Jesus by John was subsequently practiced by Jesus' disciples including Paul in both in the NT (e.g., John 3:22–24, Acts 2:37–38; 8:12, 36–38; 9:18; 10:44–48; Rom 6:3–4; 1 Cor 1:14–16, passim) and in subsequent church practice. Ferguson has written a massive and standard work on Christian baptism in the first five centuries and has clarified its origin, mode, and theological understanding including the practice of ritualistic baptisms in ancient Judaism and in the baptismal practice of John the Baptist, and his influence on Jesus and his disciples. He has also made clear the differences in the early Christian baptisms from John's practice of baptism. The influence of John's baptism practices on early Christian baptism that was preceded by faith and repentance is clear, but the Christian theological affirmations at baptisms were distinct and regularly affirmed in its practice (*Didache* 7) with later added expansions regarding babies, amounts of water available, and the condition of the baptizands. Although there are multiple examples of ritualistic cleansings in pagan religions, they do not appear to have had any impact on the Jewish practices or the notions behind their *mikva'ot* cleansings (Ferguson 2009: 25–59 and 60–96). Ferguson also shows the parallels and differences between the baptisms in the OT and Judaism of late antiquity and the baptismal practice of John the Baptist and both the parallels and differences in early Christian baptisms. He focuses both on the origin and mode of early Christian baptism in the NT (2009: 99–199) and early Christianity (2009: 201–321) along with a study of the baptismal affirmations (theological) in the first five centuries (113–23, 315–24, and 522–63). A useful summary of many of the more extensive arguments is found in Ferguson (2006: 1:390–5).

Similar claims can be made about early Christian observance of the Last Supper or the Eucharist with its obvious multiple parallels not only in the Jewish Passover but also in Pentecost observances. Stubbs has shown convincingly that the early Christian observance of the Lord's Supper, or Eucharist, has important parallels with late Second Temple Judaism and several OT texts (Stubbs 2020: 238–81). He emphasizes five parallels to the ancient Jewish Passover and the Pentecost observances that are often overlooked in current Jewish and Christian parallels. These include (1) the real presence of God and God's kingdom among God's people; (2) thanksgiving for creation and providence; (3) remembrance of past deliverance; (4) covenant renewal in the present; and (5) celebration of the feast to come (Stubbs 2020: 44–5). The Pentecost parallels are rooted in the interpretation of the reference to the "blood of the covenant" (Exod 24:6–11; cf. Jer 31:31–34) that Stubbs says is prefigured in Jesus' reference to the "blood of the covenant" where that expression is understood to prefigure Jesus' saying, "This is my blood of the covenant" (Mark 14:23–24; Matt 26:28; Luke 22:20).

The Exod 24:6–11 passage is not about the Passover but rather the ratification of the covenant of the giving of the Law that was celebrated at Pentecost. There we see that following their sacrifices the people "beheld God and ate and drank" (24:11). These parallels with early Christian practices of the Last Supper or Eucharist are obvious given the threefold reference to "the blood of the covenant" in the Synoptics. Christianity's debt to both the Jewish Passover and Pentecost observances is important for understanding its Jewish significance for the earliest Christians. Stubbs makes many arguments for expanding the church's focus in the Eucharist to a broader emphasis than the traditional Passover tradition circulating in the first century of the common era. He largely sees the Eucharist as a covenant renewal ceremony that has implications for its celebrations in churches today (Stubbs 2020: 44–5 and 238–81). He adds that in the Gospels God dwells where Jesus is. He is the meeting place between heaven and earth and where the kingdom of God is transmitted. He also examines evidence of temple imagery in Pauline literature and other early Christian writings, where the church is often portrayed as the new Temple, also noting the temple imagery in some early Christian writings (e.g., the *Didache*), and in early Christian art and architecture (Stubbs 2020: 87–94, 99–108). For Stubbs, the Eucharist is "a Christian Sabbath/Passover/Pentecost/Booths feast" (2020: 238).

Other parallels between late Second Temple Judaism and early Christianity include the format of early Christian practice of worship liturgies, organizational structure, the leadership they welcomed (prophets, teachers, bishops, and elders), notions of angels, apocalyptic eschatology (cf. Daniel and Revelation), and their reception of the same religious texts that were circulating in first-century Palestinian Jewish communities. Many of those similarities continue to this day in many churches and that is largely what we might expect from these ancient Jewish siblings. The early followers of Jesus never claimed that the Jews honored the wrong God or read the wrong scriptural texts or organized wrongly. Indeed, Jews and Christians worshipped the same God and appealed initially to most of the same scriptures including the books that later were included in the HB and the Christian OT along with some that were not later included in the HB.

Unlike the later Marcionite and Gnostic Christians, the early Jewish Christians and their late Second Temple Jewish siblings both affirmed a common belief in divine creation of heaven and earth (1 Cor 8:6; Col 1:15; John 1:2–4; Acts 17:24). Also, like their Jewish siblings, they refused to recognize the divinity of the Roman emperors or offer sacrifices to them. After they lost their legal religious status (*religio licita*) when they were no longer viewed as a Jewish sect, they experienced considerable local persecution. Jewish and Christian communities of faith also believed that God had spoken to the Israelite nation through inspired prophetic individuals, some of whom wrote sacred texts that eventually came to be called Jewish, and later among Christians, sacred scripture. Along with their shared beliefs and practices, Jews and the early Jewish Christians shared the common regular readings and interpretations of their sacred scriptures in their religious gatherings, along with the practice of circumcision (even by Paul as in Acts 16:3). Along with this, we can obviously add the ritualistic cleansings (*mikveh*, pl., *mikva'ot*) that are reflected similarly in early Christian baptism, along with their similar worship patterns that included reading of scriptures, singing spiritual songs and hymns, prayers, observance of the Sabbath and Jewish holy days (noted above), and participation in ritualistic Jewish vows (e.g., Acts 18:18b; 20:6, 16; 21:26). Jesus regularly attended the synagogue and read the scriptures in his hometown (Luke 4:16–20). We also saw that the "last supper" observed by Jesus and his disciples was a celebration of the Jewish Passover and Pentecost meals (Mark 14:12–25; //Matt 26:17–30; //Luke 22:7–23). Paul began his preaching and teaching in Jewish synagogues and Jewish places of prayer *first* as we see in the Acts accounts of his ministry (13:14; 14:1; 16:13; 17:1, 10, 17; 18:4; 19:8; 21:26; 28:17–28; cf. also Rom 1:16).

Jesus welcomed and defended the integrity of the Temple as a house of prayer by chasing out the money changers in the Temple courtyard (Mark 11:15–19; Matt 21:12–17; Luke 19:45–48; John 2:13–25) and he made visits to the Temple, not only as a child (Luke 2:41–52) but also after his death, his earliest followers Peter and John (Acts 3:1–11) and James (Acts 21:17–27) and even Paul continued to attend to religious practices in the Temple. Paul's practice of Jewish rituals such as his circumcision of Timothy (Acts 16:3), cutting his hair at Cenchreae (Acts 18:18), and participation in a Temple ritual (Acts 21:26–27) all reflect his Jewish activity among Jesus' earliest followers (1 Cor 9:19–20). Along with this, after Peter met with the household of Cornelius in Caesarea (Acts 10:34–48), he was rebuked in Jerusalem by fellow Jewish Christians for eating with Gentiles (Acts 11:1–18). This reflects, of course, both Jewish sensitivities and *early* Jewish-Christian prejudice against Gentiles (see also Gal 2:11–14), something common in late Second Temple Judaism. There was no initial intentional ministry to the Gentiles let alone a plan to welcome them into their gatherings, but that came after Gentiles began to be attracted to the Christian proclamation both in Caesarea (Acts 10:34–48) and, according to Luke, also at Antioch (Acts 11:19–26). That both surprised, puzzled, and even disappointed some Jewish Christians initially and the matter of whether to welcome Gentiles without the obligation to observe the Law came to a major discussion and was finally decided, but not without objection (Acts 15:1–35).

Paul never rejected his Jewish heritage (Phil 3:1–5) nor did he teach that Jews had to abandon keeping the Law or reject their current activities in Judaism to be a follower of Jesus. In other words, one did not have to be a bad Jew to be a follower of Jesus. He saw his Jewish heritage as an important contribution to his own understanding of the Gospel that was rooted in the promise given to Abraham to all persons of faith (Gal 3:6–14; Gen 12:1–3), and his only exception to it was that Gentile believers could become followers of Jesus by faith alone (Rom 4:1–5; 5:1–11, 18–21; 7:6). While Paul did not abandon the Law (Rom 7:7–12; 1 Cor 9:20–21; Gal 3:19–21), he no longer believed that one was made right with God by the Law (Gal 3:6–10, 21–29). Early Jewish-Christian opposition to welcoming Gentiles in the church is clear in the NT, especially in Acts and the letters of Paul noted above, but because Gentile Christianity eventually won the day in churches, it is easy to forget how Jewish the earliest followers of Jesus were. The earliest Christians were Jews who also observed Jewish Sabbaths, various holy days, Jewish vows, acceptance of circumcision, and the initial Jewish-Christian objection to Peter having contact with the Gentiles at Caesarea and his welcoming them into the faith of the early church. We see this also in Peter's initial objection to having contact with Gentiles at Caesarea but eventually was eating with them (Acts 10:9–48; 11:1–18). He also abandoned his eating with Gentiles when fellow Jews came to Antioch and was condemned by Paul for his inconsistency (Gal 2:11–14). According to Acts, the Gentile reception of the Jewish proclamation about Jesus was taking place also in Antioch on the Orontes and many were coming to Christian faith (Acts 11:19–30). That initiated the church's sponsoring the Gentile missionary activity of Barnabas and Paul when many Gentiles came to faith in Christ (Acts 11:21–26; 13:1–3). This result, of course, came within a few years after the death of Jesus when *some* of his first followers began to welcome Gentiles into their community by faith in Christ alone and without the necessity of circumcision (Acts 15:1–21; see also Levine's discussion of this (2017: 118–19, 232–38, 267–67)).

The above shows the Jewish-Christian parallels with their Jewish siblings' beliefs and practices and shows why none of the earliest followers of Jesus thought of abandoning their Jewish practices common in the Jewish communities in which they had been raised. They, like other contemporary Jews, looked forward to a messianic figure who would free them and all Jews from the tyranny of Rome (Acts 1:6–7). Evans offers a helpful list with backgrounds of those who claimed to be Jewish messiahs before, during, and even as late as the fourth century CE (Evans 2005: 431–43). Such hopes in the Jewish communities ceased for almost three centuries following the defeat of the Simon Bar Kochba rebellion in 132–135 CE and the devastating consequences that followed.

As noted above, the earliest followers of Jesus had no intention of attracting Gentiles into their churches or constructing a body of Christian scriptures, but eventually, they did both. That appears to have happened not because of initial intentions but rather because of the attraction of the Christian proclamation to Gentiles who soon became a part of the early Christian community and largely in the Hellenistic Jewish-Christian communities.

4. THE EARLY CHURCH'S FIRST SCRIPTURES

By far, the most striking parallels between Judaism and early Christianity was the church's adoption of the Hebrew scriptures circulating in Palestine among many Jews before Jews and Jewish Christians separated. The Jewish Christians, like their Jewish siblings, welcomed initially the same sacred scriptures. While the scope of that collection of sacred texts is unclear in the first century CE, we often see in the subsequent Christian manuscripts and later canon lists not only the same books that were included in the HB but also several additional Jewish (Hebrew and Aramaic) texts that were not later included in the HB. The evidence for the reception of these additional Jewish books can be seen in Christian manuscripts of the LXX, multiple canonical lists, and in church father citations. While some scholars claim that the NT authors were familiar with some of the so-called "apocryphal" texts, they never cited them as scripture or made use of the common scriptural introductions, such as "as the scripture says" or "it is written." That argument, of course, shows a lack of awareness of the many times the Hebrew scripture was cited in the NT without use of those designations (e.g., Jesus citing Dan 9:27 in Matt 24:15; see also Matt 10:35–36 citing Mic 7:6 without using the usual scriptural introductions and likewise the author of Heb 1:3 cites Wis 7:25 and multiple other recognized Jewish scriptures without using those designations. Of all of the multiple OT references in Hebrews, only one is with the usual term found in the quote, not produced by the author of Hebrews who only mentions "it is written" once (Heb 10:5–7) and that is in the citation in Ps 40:6–8 itself. This argument also often misses the fact that several HB texts are cited without being introduced by those designations as noted above. Several of those additional texts in the surviving LXX manuscripts copied and transmitted by Christians include several other writings alongside the HB writings and this practice can also be seen in the Dead Sea Scrolls, the NT, and the early church fathers, and in the major fourth- and fifth-century codex manuscripts (Sinaiticus, Vaticanus, Alexandrinus, and others).

The argument that there was no larger collection of writings in the LXX than in the Hebrew scriptures, the Tanak, depends on later and isolated texts from Josephus and the *baraita* in the Babylonian Talmud (*b. Baba Bathra* 14b). It also ignores that some of those writings cited as scripture by the Catholic churches who now call them "deuterocanonical" scriptures and the "readable" or "non-canonical scripture" texts by Orthodox churches, were also present in the Dead Sea Scrolls that includes twelve copies of 1 Enoch, fourteen copies of Jubilees, five copies of Tobit, and two copies of Sirach. The contents of the Cairo Geniza dating largely from the fifth to the ninth centuries include multiple copies of Tobit, Sirach, and the *Damascus Document*. The presence of these noncanonical Hebrew and Aramaic texts among Jewish collections of sacred writings that late underscores the fluidity of the formation of the Hebrew scriptures for centuries and the circulation of some of the deuterocanonical (apocryphal) texts in Jewish collections both in the Dead Sea Scrolls, Egypt, and early Christianity. According to Edrei and Mendels these additional writings were circulating in the LXX and were also well known in Diaspora Judaism (2007: 91–137).

Their presence in early Christian LXX manuscripts can hardly be a Christian innovation but rather a collection of sacred texts that were not included in the late HB/Tanak. The early churches welcomed them from their Jewish siblings and included many of them in their own OT manuscripts, and listed some of them in the later canonical lists (see these lists in Gallagher and Meade and further arguments in McDonald 2017: 1:232–67, 396–418). These additional texts that are not in the later HB/Tanak were welcomed by some Jews and many early Christians and were included in the LXX Greek translation of the Hebrew scriptures. While it is true that the Christians preserved and transmitted the only surviving texts of the LXX, there is no evidence that the Christians themselves uniquely included the additional Jewish texts in their OT. The Diaspora Jews were likely unaware of the Babylonian decisions about the scope of their scriptures that we see in the *baraita* (*b. Baba Bathra* 14b, *c.* 180–200 CE) until well into the ninth century (see also McDonald 2019: 397–413 and Edrei and Mendels 2007: 91–137).

The early Christians *generally* adopted the Greek translation (the LXX) of the Hebrew scriptures and it included other books not eventually included in the HB/Tanak. Most of the early Christians also adopted the quadripartite or fourfold divisions of the Greek scriptures along with the larger number of books included in them. It may be that the Christian "takeover" and adoption of the LXX, as C. F. D. Moule once remarked, was "one of the most remarkable takeover bids in history" (cited in Rajak 2009: 279, fn3).

Martin Hengel wrote similarly that the Christians "snatched it away from the Jews" (Hengel 2002: 41, 43, and 50).

The additional so-called apocryphal and pseudepigraphal texts in the LXX were circulating in first-century Jewish communities some of which were acknowledged as sacred texts by some Jews and later by some Jewish and Gentile Christians. This LXX includes not only the books that Jews and many Christians held in common (the HB/Tanak), though with a different order and with the books not included in the HB. In about 90 percent of the NT citations of the OT writings, the NT authors are citing the Septuagint (LXX). Jerome (late fourth to early fifth century) was the first church father who translated his Latin Vulgate OT from the Hebrew scriptures and although he included several of the additional LXX books in it, because he was under pressure to do so, his preference was to accept into the OT only the books in the HB.

The early Christians appealed more and more to the LXX and adopted it as their OT scriptures and appealed to the legendary *Letter of Aristeas* (c. 130 BCE) to support their decision and affirmed its divine inspiration. Interestingly, they also debated with the Jews claiming that the Jews changed the meaning of the Hebrew text when it was different from the LXX, even claiming that the scriptural texts were clearer and more accurate in the Greek LXX than in the Hebrew. For example, in his *Dialogue with Trypho the Jew* (71.1–2), Justin made references to the Hebrew text that he argued were clearer in the Greek. Interestingly, Tov makes a similar argument regarding several LXX texts that he claims are based on earlier and more reliable Hebrew antecedents than those that the later Masoretic scribes employed in producing their Hebrew text of the HB. Those antecedents (proto-Masoretic) he found among the Dead Sea Scrolls, the LXX, and Samaritan Pentateuch (Tov 2002: 234–51).

On the other hand, later rabbinic Jews accused Christians of changing the Greek text to support their own Christian perspectives and consequently they commissioned a new Greek translation of the Hebrew scriptures and selected Aquila, a Gentile who had earlier converted to Christianity but subsequently to Judaism (Rajak 2009: 294–313). A return to the Hebrew text of the Jewish scriptures for the Christian OT scriptures was controversially made by Jerome in preparing his Latin Vulgate translation of the OT that initially was without widespread support among the church fathers of that period. Jerome's appeal to the Hebrew text instead of the LXX caused no small controversy with Augustine and others after him. It appears that the compromise for Jerome was to include in his OT translation the additional books in the LXX (1556) that were later called "deuterocanonical" scriptures and that he himself did not make the translation of most of them.

Interestingly, Evans has argued that the versional changes and widespread openness to new translations (e.g., Greek, Latin, Syriac, and others) likely come from Jesus himself who quoted and paraphrased the books of Moses and most of the Prophets and did not seem devoted to one text, whether Hebrew, Aramaic, or Greek (2017: 95–107; and his 2020: 1–31, 427–49). Jerome's Latin translation of the Hebrew scriptures was eventually adopted in the Western churches. The Eastern churches continued to affirm the LXX Greek text for their OT and kept the additional LXX books in it. The eventual acceptance of Jerome's translation in the West came to fruition in the reformation period when it became obvious to many Christians that the translation of their OT should be from the "original Hebrew," but the question was what to do with the additional books not included by the rabbis in their HB. The churches in the West affirmed not only in the HB books but also the books affirmed in local councils (Laodicea in 360, Rome in 382, Hippo

393, Carthage 397 and 419) long before the Council of Trent in 1546. The churches of the West adopted not only the books of the LXX but also the Latin translation of their HB books. This was done, of course, at the expense of the Greek translation of the Hebrew text that formed the scriptures of most of the early Christian churches.

As noted above, Jewish communities in the first centuries BCE and CE welcomed some books that were not later included in the HB and those texts are *now* generally called apocryphal or deuterocanonical and pseudepigraphal books. Some first-century Jews and later some Jewish and Gentile Christians accepted some of those books, including 1 Enoch and the LXX apocryphal or deuterocanonical books. Although the early Christians held to most of the same scriptures as their Jewish siblings before their separation, they often interpreted them in different ways, that is, Christologically and eschatologically. An example of this can be seen in Justin's *Dialogue with Trypho* regarding the continuing function of the Law and its use or lack thereof by Christians.

Protestants later adopted the same OT scriptures as those in the HB, but their arrangement of those scriptures generally follows what is often called the LXX "quadripartite" divisions of Law (or Pentateuch), history, poetry and wisdom, and prophets (Major and Minor). The Hebrew order that is affirmed in the rabbinic "tripartite" divisions of Law, Prophets (Former and Latter), and Writings is possibly a later order not clearly introduced until the late second century CE (*b. Baba Bathra* 14b). Is this difference simply a reflection of how books were received and circulated in the Hebrew scriptures (HB) and the Greek scriptures (LXX)? Did the Christians intentionally reject the Jewish tripartite divisions of the Christians' OT scriptures because the Jews had adopted it or because it is the way that the LXX translation had arranged them? Although there are no arguments from the early church fathers on the order or sequence of their scriptures except in the broad categories of Law and Prophets, Christians may simply have followed the LXX order that they had *inherited* and not *invented*. Because no one in antiquity makes an argument for the four-part order of the LXX as opposed to the three-part order in the HB, it is likely that the Christians inherited their order from copies of the LXX they called their OT. The early Christians were not unanimous in their adoption of a quadripartite order for their OT canon, as we saw in Jerome and in the codices Sinaiticus and Alexandrinus that followed roughly the HB tripartite order, but none of the Christian translations or texts follow the HB order exactly. Daniel, for instance, is regularly included after the three major prophets, Isaiah, Jeremiah, Ezekiel, in the Christian OT, and most often before the Twelve Minor Prophets, but not always. Sometimes in the canonical lists the Twelve (Minor Prophets) appear *before* the three major prophets in some of the surviving manuscripts.

Since early Christianity initially began as a Jewish sect, we obviously must ask what the surviving Jewish sources from roughly the time of Jesus tell us about the *operative* scriptures of that era. That discussion involves a study of Philo, the Dead Sea Scrolls, Josephus, early rabbinic texts, as well as the religious literature written in the first centuries BCE and CE that is sometimes called pseudepigraphal writings or, as James Sanders calls them, "non-Masoretic" texts (Sanders 1997). Those collections regularly cite more from the books later included in the HB and that suggests their popularity in the time of Jesus and throughout the first century. However, we do find other religious (scriptural?) texts at Qumran among the Dead Sea Scrolls as we observed earlier and some of them have parallels in the LXX.

While the primary authorities in the early churches began with Jesus and his deeds and words, what were the scriptures welcomed in the first churches that eventually made up their OT? Without question the most frequently cited LXX texts in early Christianity were from the books in the later HB/Tanak, but occasionally some of the deuterocanonical writings as well. Most often those Hebrew scriptures were read in churches outside of Palestine in the Greek Septuagint (LXX). These authorities were accompanied by the sacred traditions about him (initially oral) that were often summarized in early creedal formulations about Jesus in the NT (e.g., Rom 10:9; Phil 2:6–11). After the deaths of Jesus and the apostles, the leadership in the churches was guided by the empowered bishops and their interpretations of the church's first scriptures.

Plato famously argued that written texts were unworthy instruments of communication because they discouraged the use of memory and the texts could be changed by later copiers (Plato, *Phaedrus* 275AC). Some Pharisees similarly argued that the "oral Torah" (the Jewish religious traditions that were codified in the Mishnah) should *not* be put into writing (*b. Gittin* 60b; *b. Temura* 14b). The sacredness of the Jewish scriptures was always maintained as distinct from Jewish oral traditions, but the oral traditions that some rabbis called the "Oral Torah" were gathered and organized by Rabbi Judah the Prince (c. 200–220). Those traditions were called the *Mishnah* (Heb. = oral instruction or study as opposed to *miqra'* for the study of scripture). It is comprised of sixty-three tractates that had authoritative religious status, and soon after their formation, an interpretation (*gemara*) of them emerged that culminated in the two *Talmudim* (*Yerushalmi* and *Bavli*). These oral traditions and their interpretation were viewed as sacred religious literature but were *never* called "scripture" or described as "defiling the hands," that is, the Jewish notion of inspired sacred literature (Lim 2010). Together the written scriptures and the "Oral Torah" (Mishnah) including its interpretation (primarily the two *Talmudim*) formed Jewish sacred literature. The parallels with the church's written traditions (OT and NT) and various regulations for organization, behavior, and church practice are apparent but without clear dependence on Judaism's model.

As noted above, the early church, as a Jewish sect and without any initial intention to separate from their Jewish siblings or their common Jewish practices in first-century Judaism and initially, had no plans to welcome Gentiles into their community. The earliest followers of Jesus, like him, continued their observance of various Jewish laws regarding Sabbath keeping, circumcision, and other Jewish rituals including the observance of other Jewish holy days and practices (e.g., Acts 13:14–45; 16:3, 13; 17:1–2; 18:14, 18). According to Acts, the Gentile mission appears to have begun within a decade of the church's beginning and was launched both in Caesarea Maritima (10:1–11:18) and in Antioch on the Orontes (Acts 11:19–26).

Before that, and after the welcome of the Gentiles, Chadwick concludes that the unity in early Christianity depended on two things: "a common faith and a common way of ordering their life and worship." He goes on to say that despite their differences in race, class, or education, what brought Christians together was "their loyalty to the person and teaching of Jesus" (Chadwick 1993: 32). While I disagree with Chadwick on when the NT canon of Christian scriptures appeared, he is right that eventually the emergence of a NT canon of scriptures aided considerably in the unity found in most churches and in their doctrinal affirmations. What held them together after the deaths of the apostles, he contends, was the emergence of the strong authoritative role of the bishop along with the "rule of faith" that summarized the core elements of their Christian beliefs, and eventually also a NT canon of Christian scriptures (Chadwick 1993: 41–5).

Along with the recognition of Jesus' authority, the not yet fully formed Hebrew scripture collection functioned as a primary authority both by Jesus' Jewish followers in Palestine and throughout the Diaspora. Those scriptures were not always the same books that eventually comprised the later HB, as we will show below, but the authority of the Jewish scriptures was paramount to Jesus and for his earliest followers. None of their scriptures could be ignored or violated (see Matt 5:17–19). Although their collection of scriptural texts was not yet complete or fixed in the time of Jesus, or even for churches for several centuries later, the earliest churches nevertheless welcomed most of the same OT scriptures. The authority of these sacred texts can be seen in the NT writings, whose authors regularly wrote *with scripture* as they made their case for Jesus' identity, teachings, and mission, and for their core beliefs, guidance for Christian behavior, and mission. I am following here Jacob Neusner and W. S. Green's term, "writing with scripture" (1989). Their illustrations are especially helpful for seeing how the NT authors not only cited but also included their sacred scriptures among their own comments often without the usual scriptural citation introductions ("as it is written" or "as the scripture says") to advance their message. Writing *with* scripture was a form of writing often without formal citation of scriptural texts.

From the church's beginning some NT writers and early church fathers made regular use of many books not later included in the Jewish Tanak/HB collection of scriptures. However, the scope of those scriptures was not clear for most Christians until much later despite considerable overlap in the texts they cited. For some Jews, apparent clarity on the scope of their scriptures took place around the end of the first century CE (Josephus, *AgAp*. 1.37–43), but for most others in the rabbinic tradition the specific books in their scriptures were seldom clear until much later, including the tripartite order of the HB canon. There continued to be questions among the rabbis about the scope and contents of some of the books among the Prophets and Writings for several centuries.

The most commonly disputed HB books among the rabbis included: (1) Ecclesiastes (*m. Yadayim* 3:5; *b. Berakhot* 48a; *b. Shabbat* 100a; *Ecclesiastes Rabbah* 1:3; 11:9; *Leviticus Rabbah* 23; *Avot of Rabbi Nathan* 1; cf. Jerome on Eccl 12:14); (2) Esther (*m. Megillah* 4:1; *b. Megillah* 7a; *b. Sanhedrin* 100a; cf. *t. Megillah* 2:1a; 2 Macc 15:36; Josephus, *Ant*. 11.184–296); (3) Ezekiel (*b. Shabbat* 13b; *b. Hagigah* 13a; *b. Menahot* 45a; cf. Jerome, *Epistle* 53.8, and Sirach 49:8); (4) Proverbs (*b. Shabbat* 30b); (5) Ruth (*b. Megillah* 7a); and (6) Song of Songs (*m. Yadayim* 3:5; *m. Eduyyot* 5:3; *t. Sanhedrin* 12:10; *t. Yadayim* 2:14; *b. Sanhedrin* 101a; *b. Megillah* 7a). These are also among the least cited OT books in early Christianity. For further discussion of this, see Lewis (2002: 154–7) and Dunne (2014: 155).

Although some Jews set forth the scope of the Hebrew scriptures by the end of the second century in the *baraita*[2] *b. Bathra* 14b that listed the books in the Prophets and Writings (including the Torah or Law of Moses in *b. Baba Bathra* 14a), that catalogue was not accepted by all rabbinic Jews until later in the Talmudic period (roughly 200–500 CE). It is seldom clear why the rabbinic sages and some church fathers rejected several popular religious texts such as Wisdom, Sirach, 1–2 Maccabees, and other so-called deuterocanonical books, and also why they included Song of Songs, Ecclesiastes, and Esther. By the end of the second century CE, Esther was regularly read in synagogues annually during the feast of Purim (to celebrate the deliverance of the Jews from Persian persecution) on the fourteenth—fifteenth of Adar (usually in March). This is noted earlier

---

[2] A *baraita* is a written tradition dating generally sometime in the tannaitic period (first and second century CE and most after 70 CE) but not included in the Mishnah and later appears in the two Talmudim, including the *amora 'im* Tosefta and Midrash, and other texts. It reflects texts that were not widely approved in the tannaitic period but became so eventually among rabbinic sages in the later period of the Talmudic period.

by Josephus (*Ant.* 292–295) and subsequently in the Mishnah (*m. Megilla*), but debate about Esther continued among some rabbinic Jews later. Earlier Esther was not included in the scrolls of Qumran or in several Christian canon lists later. For further examination of this topic see McDonald (2017: 1:467–75 and 2:320–47).

The early church fathers generally accepted most of the Hebrew scriptures doubtless because they welcomed as scripture their Jewish siblings, but the scope of those scriptures is seldom clear and that is reflected in the multiple OT canons that continue in the various Christian bodies today. Many of the HB/Tanak books are regularly cited as scripture in the church fathers and, like the NT authors, most often in the LXX, for example, Clement of Rome (*1 Clem.* 45.2–3). Clement of Alexandria, citing fragment 10 of *Kerygma Petruo* (*Strom.* 6.128.3), says, "we say nothing apart from the scripture." He is speaking here primarily of the churches' first scriptures, their OT. Some early church fathers even claimed that they came to Christian faith by reading their OT scriptures (Justin, *Dial.* 8.1; Tatian, *Oratio ad Graecos* 29; and Theophilus, *Ad Autolycum* 1.14). As we saw above, most early Christians read their scriptures not from the Hebrew HB or OT but rather in the Greek Septuagint (LXX) OT and they generally agreed with the *Letter of Aristeas* regarding the inspiration and authority of those scriptures in Greek (e.g., Justin, *1 Apol.* 31.1–5; *Dial.* 71.1; 84.3, later Irenaeus, *Haer.* 3.21.2).

As the later Jewish sages debated the acceptance of several books that are now in the HB, especially Song of Songs, Ecclesiastes, and Esther, the Ante-Nicene and Nicene church fathers also debated the same books. There was considerable debate among Jews over Esther, and it is missing among the Dead Sea Scrolls, likely because of its disputed calendar. Dunne has produced a useful summary of Esther's reception both by Jews and Christians in antiquity (2014: 95–130). Some of the early Christians also questioned the authority of Esther, especially Melito of Sardis and Athanasius who omitted it in his *Thirty-Ninth Festal Letter* that listed his biblical canon in 367. Some church fathers would not read it in their worship services. It was likely rejected by Amphilocius of Iconium (*c.* 380), but some others may have accepted the book only with the multiple additions to it in the LXX that included references to God. As late as 367 CE, Athanasius did not include Esther in his OT biblical canon list. The lack of a stable sequence or order in the HB canon, especially regarding the Prophets and the Writings, can also be seen in the fluid order in the LXX books. The historical books of the Writings (Ketuvim) are placed after the Kings as we see in the place of the Chronicles, Ezra-Nehemiah, and Esther, but the location of Chronicles varies in the surviving HB texts. It most often follows Kings in the LXX but differently in the HB.

Does this distinction in the order of the books in the HB and LXX make any difference? Not if we follow the early Christians and Jews who did not possess a single codex with all their scriptures in one volume until the fourth century for the Christians (Codices Vaticanus and Sinaiticus) and even later for the Jewish adoption of the codex. Until then the Jews circulated their scriptures in rolls or scrolls and no scroll was large enough to include all the Hebrew scriptures and consequently the order in the collections varied for centuries. Similarly, the order of the Christian OT scriptures varied considerably until the codex was technologically advanced enough to be able to include all the Christian scriptures in one volume, but even then (fourth century CE), variations in their order continued in both the OT and NT scripture collections. It is difficult to find any discussion of or argument for the order of the books in the individual collections that comprised either the HB or the LXX.

All Christians did not eventually agree on the scope of their OT scriptures even though all of them eventually accepted the books in the HB canon. Since all books that were included in the HB are also in the Christian canons, it is strange that the Christians would have adopted those books but not their order or divisions in the HB (Tanak) unless they were not yet in place when the Jews and Christians parted ways mostly from the last half of the first century and first half of the second century. It is more likely that *the order* in the LXX preceded that in the HB Tanak and that would account for the broad Christian acceptance of a different order (for arguments see McDonald 2019: 408–10).

It appears that some Christians from the fourth century onward acknowledged not only all the HB books but also some of the apocryphal-deuterocanonical books, especially Wisdom of Solomon, Wisdom of Jesus ben Sira, Tobit, Judith, but sometimes Psalms of Solomon and occasionally 1 Enoch. Some early church fathers did not accept Esther or Ecclesiastes as some of the canonical lists show, but eventually they were included in the church's OT. Some of the apocryphal/deuterocanonical books have close verbal parallels in several NT texts and several of those books were cited as scripture by several church fathers and were included in several Christian biblical manuscripts.

Interestingly, at roughly the same time, both Jews and Christians added additional books to their earlier HB and OT scriptures, namely the Jews added the Mishnah, Tosefta, and two Talmudim that are not called scripture but are regularly treated authoritatively in similar ways. Likewise, the Christians added a "New Testament" to their scripture collection and began to call their first scriptures their "Old Testament" by the last third of the second century, though the precise parameters of that collection were not firmly decided by that time in the second-century churches even though the process of canonization had already begun. By then, several Christian books were recognized as scripture and interest in the full scope of the Christian OT was only beginning for some Christians as we see in Melito of Sardis *c.* 170–180 CE (Eusebius, *Hist. eccl.* 4.26.13–14).

As it became clear to the church fathers and their communities that another collection of sacred texts was important to their development and continuing ministry by the end of the second century, they *began* to identify their inherited First scriptures as their "Old Testament." They also began recognizing their new collection of *Christian* scriptures that was beginning to form their "New Testament." Those designations were not in the common lingua franca until well into the fourth century, but by that time there were two clearly identified collections of scriptures for most Christians. Similarly, the Jews supplemented their Torah (the Tanak) with the "Oral Torah" (essentially the Mishnah), two Talmudim, the Tosefta, and various *midrashim*.

The Christians and the Jews saw the need for something more for the continuing life of their respective communities. Although the rabbinic sages did not identify the Mishnah and the various supplemental texts as scripture, those writings nevertheless functioned like that in their communities. It is not likely that the HB books, and those alone, were acknowledged as their sacred scriptures before the second century *for some Jews*, but not for all of them. In rabbinic Judaism there were subsequent debates after the end of the second century over the sacredness of some of the books noted above that were later included in the HB (Esther, Song of Songs, Ecclesiastes, Ezekiel, and Sirach). Sirach was not eventually included, but for a time it was treated as, and even called, scripture by some rabbis for centuries. It appears that there was also considerable debate about the value of Esther in the Christian OT for centuries.

Although the full collection of Jewish apocalyptic texts is uncertain in Second Temple Judaism, it appears that following the Bar Kochba rebellion (132–135 CE) such texts diminished in significance and influence in ancient Judaism but not in early Christianity. Again, initially Jewish apocalyptic texts were welcomed as scripture by some Jews, especially those at Qumran and by many early Christians. Early Christianity emphasized Jewish apocalyptic well into the late second century through the Montanists, but *generally* with much less focus or influence after that.

One of the more interesting discussions about the distinctions between Christian scriptures and later rabbinic texts has to do with whether the popularity of the Christian Gospels in Palestine led rabbinic sages of the second and third centuries CE to be more specific about the books that they welcomed in their HB/Tanak. Long ago, George Foote Moore suggested that during the second and third centuries CE rabbinic sages forbid fellow Jews from reading the Christian Gospels and during this time discussions of canon formation took place among the Jews. He concluded that the popularity of the Christian Gospels in Palestine likely influenced rabbinic decisions about the scope of the Jewish scripture canon. He more precisely concludes, "the attempt authoritatively to define the Jewish canon of the Hagiographa begins with the exclusion by name of Christian Scriptures," which was formed in part due to the rise of "Christian heresy and the circulation of Christian writings" in the Jewish community in Palestine (Moore 1974: 101–2, 125). Moore cites as evidence for his conclusions the following two Tosefta texts:

> The books of the Evangelists [Heb. = *haglionim*] and the books of the *minim* they do not save from a fire. But they are allowed to burn where they are, they and the references to the Divine Names which are in them. R. Yosé the Galilean says, "On ordinary days, one cuts out the references to the Divine Name which are in them and stores them away, and the rest burns." Said R. Tarfon, "May I bury my sons, if such things come into my hands and I do not burn them, and even the references to the Divine Name which are in them. And if someone was running after me, I should go into a temple of idolatry, but I should not go into their houses [of worship]. For idolaters do not recognize the Divinity in denying him, but these [Christians] recognize the Divinity and deny him." (*t. Shabbat* 13:5 A–F, Neusner, *Tosefta*, 405)

See also:

> The Gospels [Heb. = *haglionim*] and heretical books do not defile the hands. The books of Ben Sira and all other books written *from then on*, do not defile the hands. (*t. Yadayim* 2:13; trans. Leiman 1976: 93, 109)

That text also contends that from the time of Sirach and thereafter all subsequent texts are uninspired and reflects the second-century BCE belief that the Spirit had departed from Israel (1 Macc 4:46; 9:27; 14:41). Leiman also offers several other instances of books that "defile the hands," a reference to sacred texts, and other rabbinic texts that reflect the sacredness or lack thereof of various ancient texts, whether Sirach, Eldad and Medad, Esther, Ezekiel, and others (Leiman 1976: 104–20).

Although few scholars have followed Moore's suggestion, and neither of these texts say how popular the Christian Gospels were, nevertheless that the rabbinic sages in the early third century condemned the reading of them is suggestive. Of course, there would have been no need for the rabbinic sages to condemn reading the Gospels if there were no Jews reading them.

5. ISSUES LEADING TO THE SEPARATION OF CHRISTIANS FROM JUDAISM

Undoubtedly, one of the most important issues that ultimately led to the separation of the majority of Jews from the Jewish followers of Jesus was the latter's acknowledgment of Jesus *as Lord* and *as their anticipated Messiah*. Over time, the hostilities between Jews and Christians became intense, especially when the early Jewish Christians welcomed Gentiles into their fellowship without the requirements of keeping the Law and the practice of circumcision. As the Romans eventually recognized the separation of the Christians from the Jews, Christians lost their Roman recognition as a legitimate or acknowledged religion (*religio licita*) along with the privileges and safety that recognition afforded them. When that happened, it was not uncommon for *some* zealous Jews to turn Christians into Roman authorities as we saw in the *Martyrdom of Polycarp* 12–13, 17–18 (*c.* 155–156 but the later verses 19–22 are likely *c.* 170–180; other examples of this are in McDonald 1993: 215–52). Such hostilities characterized Jewish and Christian relationships for centuries and when the Christians eventually became the dominant religion in the empire, the vituperative language turned into acts of violence that betrayed their faith.

From the church's beginning, the early followers of Jesus, like Jesus himself, were often at odds with the religious leaders of the Jewish nation. Jewish-Christians were but one of several Jewish religious sects in the first century CE along with the Pharisees, one of the two major Jewish sects that survived the turmoil of that century. The Pharisees are not well portrayed in the NT often because of their strict religious observances that reportedly took priority over human need and that brought them into conflict with Jesus who gave human need higher priority than religious observances of cleanliness and Sabbath observance (see Mark 2:1–3:6).

A. When Christians Ceased Being Jews

As a first-century Jewish sect, along with the Pharisees, Sadducees, Essenes, and Zealots, what distinguished them from their fellow Jews was their acceptance of Jesus of Nazareth as their Messiah and calling him their Lord coupled with their welcome of Gentiles without observance of Jewish laws including circumcision. This made it difficult for the Jewish Christians to continue within the broader community of Judaism despite some of them continuing to practice various elements of Judaism for several centuries. They were marginalized by the emerging majority of Gentile Christians (e.g., Justin, Irenaeus, and Tertullian). The Jews were known among the Romans as a people who would not associate with Gentiles and who also refused to eat pork, or any meat sacrificed to idols. Most abhorrent to Gentiles was that Jews also circumcised their male children (Chadwick 1993: 9–23). The earliest Christian Jews believed that if something new happened (e.g., a crisis or blessing), it would be consistent with their faith in the God of the Jews who was also creator of heaven and earth and the Lord of human history who inspired their scriptures. They, like their Jewish siblings, were also a people of "the book," or Jewish scriptures, from their beginning. They were in solidarity with Israel in multiple ways as indicated above, but unlike them they were also mindful that there was continuity between the actions of God in the past with his present activity in Jesus of Nazareth (Chadwick 1993: 9–13).

Christianity largely ceased being a sect of Judaism by the end of the first century and no later than the end of the second century (Dunn 1991 and his 1994: 101–19; with correctives in Lieu 1994: 355–68). Boccaccini argued that Christianity is one of the two *main* voices of ancient Judaism, the other being the rabbinic sages who survived the first century (1991: 16–18). The separation was complete when the majority of churches ceased observing the Law, the practice of circumcision, and the celebration of special holy days, and also when Jesus was venerated to the position of divinity. The Jewish churches did not seek for that break, nor did they advocate such a position. From their beginning they continued their worship in the Temple in Jerusalem until persecution broke out (c. 62) and James, the leader of the church in Jerusalem, was executed.

A conference of Jewish religious leaders, mostly Pharisees, met at Jamnia (Javneh) (c. 90 CE) to deal with the issues facing the survivors of the Jewish rebellion against Rome in 66–70 CE that led to the destruction of the Temple along with its sacrificial system that was so prominent among the various Jewish sects. At that time there was a rapidly growing intolerance of Jewish Christians within mainstream Judaism by those who were not supportive of the Jewish rebellion against Rome. That increased following the subsequent second rebellion against Rome led by Shimon Kosiba, a messianic claimant, and called the Bar Kochba rebellion (132–135 CE). The intolerance was most pronounced in the formal anathema against the Christians who did not support the rebellion because doing so would conflict with their belief that Jesus was their Messiah. The *Birkath ha-Minim* (initially c. 100 CE) that later became a part of the synagogue liturgies included, "May the Nazarenes [Jewish Christians] and the heretics be suddenly destroyed and removed from the Book of Life." I have more about this below.

More and more, the Gentile congregations saw themselves as having taken the place of the Jews in the plan of God and this sense of supersessionism, which was in effect a formal separation from Judaism, was set in motion in a direction from which the church would never return. Often this process was justified by citing Rom 11:17–24, but Paul himself shuddered at the thought of the church replacing the Jews in the plan of God. To him the setting aside of the Jews from receiving God's salvation in Jesus Christ was only a temporary measure and he believed and hoped that all Jews would eventually convert to faith in Jesus Christ (Rom 11:25–32; cf. Phil 2:10–11).

The early church fathers' vituperative language against the Jews from the second to the fifth centuries, and even later, reflects the pain of the fateful separation of Christianity from Judaism. The process was often filled with hate, anger, and even violence from both the Jews and the Christians. The Christians, who saw themselves as the legitimate heirs of the Jewish religious traditions, including the Prophets, who were called believers in Christ and were appropriated into the Christian tradition, were at pains to demonstrate that they had superseded the Jews and denied to them the ability to interpret their own scriptures, challenging their method of interpretation, and even their future as the people of God (Origen, *In Lib. Jud. Hom.* 8.2, GCS, 7.510.14). Ignatius of Antioch, for example, claims that the "Prophets also do we love, because they have announced the Gospel, and are hoping in him [Christ] and waiting for him, by faith in whom they also obtain salvation, being united with Jesus Christ, for they are worthy of love and saints worthy of admiration, approved by Jesus Christ, and numbered together in the Gospel of the common hope" (*Philad.* 5.2).

Some Christians began to teach that the Hebrew scriptures became the sole possession of the Christians, because only they could properly understand and interpret them, and their fulfillment was only found in Christ (Clement of Alexandria, *Strom.* 6.28.1). According to Justin, the Christians had become the "true spiritual Israel," because the Jews had despised and forsaken the law of God and his holy covenant, and had hardened their hearts, refusing to see and perceive the will of God given to them through the Prophets (Justin, *Trypho* 11, 12). Justin argued from the example of Abraham for the inclusion of the Gentiles and for the exclusion of the Jews (cf. *Trypho* 110). In Rom 11:25–27 Paul speaks of a temporary situation that allowed for the inclusion of the Gentiles while maintaining the Jews as the elect people of God. He uses the example of Abraham in Gal 3:6–9, 13–14 and Rom 4:1–18 not to exclude the Jews but to include the Gentiles. In time, however, the inclusion of the Gentiles was viewed as also excluding the Jews. Siker has noted similarly that Deut 7:1–6 was used by the Jews as a way of including the Jews and excluding the Gentiles (Siker 1991: 254 n.13). Justin Martyr, however, may be the first Christian writer to argue specifically that it is the Christians who are the "true spiritual Israel," who have replaced the Jews (*Dial.* 1, 123, 135). We should note that it is not clear that this was Paul's intention in Gal 6:18, especially considering his strong affirmation of the Jews as God's elect in Rom 11:28–29, but clearly Justin could have taken that text in Gal 3:5–18 to justify his claim. Matthew comes close to this position in Matt 21:42–43 and perhaps paves the way for it in Justin's interpretation. Such arguments by Christians would obviously be met with strong opposition by the Jews. In this context, a battle ensued for the Jewish traditions and heritage that the church laid claim to, that was contested between Christians and the survivors of first-century Judaism, rabbinic Judaism.

Justin distinguished between the laws in the Hebrew scriptures, noting that the laws relating to the keeping of the Sabbath, observance of holy days, and circumcision came later after Abraham and were given because of the obstinance of the Jews who violated the whole law of God given to Abraham and those later laws were not part of God's original law given to Abraham, noting that neither circumcision nor the keeping of the later ritualistic laws were present at that time but came later with Moses, but Abraham believed God and was counted as righteous without the later legalistic requirements of the Mosaic Law (*Dialogue with Trypho* 10:3; cf. 19:3–4). Justin writes,

> For if circumcision was not required before the time of Abraham and if there was no need of Sabbaths, festivals and sacrifices before Moses, they are not now needed (23:3; see also *Dial.* 19:5–6; 22:11), but God gave them because of Israel's sins in their sacrifice to the golden calf and to ensure that Israel kept God before their eyes and abstained from unjust and impious acts. (*Dial.* 46:5)

Barber shows how Justin's arguments have their roots in the NT arguments from Jesus and Paul concerning the keeping of the Law of God (Barber 2011: 67–90). Justin's arguments against Christians keeping all the ritualistic aspects of the Law are repeated and argued even more strongly by Irenaeus (*Haer.* 1.110.1–3; 3.33.1; 4.9.1) and he affirms the Ten Commandments but not the other Mosaic laws. He contends that those laws were not needed from their beginning (4.15.1; 4.17.3) and Abraham was imputed righteousness without circumcision and the observance of the Sabbaths (*Haer.* 4.16.2). Tertullian likewise presents similar arguments saying that the primordial law was essentially to love God and one another and to keep the Ten Commandments (*Against the Jews* 2; see also his *Against Marcion* 2.18). Since for Tertullian, the secondary laws were written later, they were therefore temporary and need not be continued or kept since the Gospel has replaced that part of the Law (*Against the Jews* 2 and 4 and *Against Marcion* 4.11). These same arguments are in the *Didascalia Apostolorum* (1.6.7–11; *c.* 220–240 CE) and also affirm the Ten Commandments (6.15.2). The "Secondary Legislation" (Laws of Moses) is also similarly argued by Augustine (*Contra Faustus* 19:13), Athanasius

(*Festal Letter* 19.3–4), and Chrysostom (*Adversus Judaeos* 4.6.4–5). The church fathers following Justin generally made a distinction between the decalogue and the rest of the laws, Israel's worshipping the golden calf triggered the secondary laws or legislation, and the Patriarchal age of Abraham was the precedent for the church not to follow the Laws of Moses after the decalogue (Barber 2011: 89–90).

Under such titles as *Adversus Judaeos* and *Altercatio cum Judaeo*, the early church fathers produced many harsh polemical writings against the Jewish people. The frequency and intensity of this phenomenon is also accompanied by the strange contradiction of its presence in *Christian* literature! Most of these criticisms are religious in nature, that is, they are anti-Judaistic, but they also oppose those (Jews) who followed its precepts. The criticisms are not racial in their orientation, although many of the writings containing them are unusually intense even to the point of condemning the Jewish people as a whole and, in some cases, even suggesting or encouraging hostilities toward the Jews. Anti-Jewish sentiment was nothing new when the church was born, but the Christian anti-Judaic rhetoric was different from that of the Greco-Roman world, even though it may have been influenced by it. What at times may appear in the church fathers to be a reference to race, that is, Jews being condemned as a people or nation, is most often a reference to their *religious* identity rather than to their ethnic origins. However, a "religious" anti-Judaism, however, was often just as hostile and even dangerous to Jews. Marcel Simon argues, "a Jew was characterized by his religion. If he was converted, he ceased to be a Jew, and the ultimate aim [of the Church] was just that, the conversion of Israel" (Simon 1986: 398). In the *Dialogue of Timothy and Aquila*, for example, after Aquila (the Jew) converted to the Christian faith and was renamed Theognostos he was described as one who "became the receptacle of the Holy Spirit—*he who was once a Jew*, but now a Christian by [the grace of] God; he who was once a wolf, but now has become Christ's sheep" (trans. Williams 1935: 78).

In the NT there are negative comments about *some* Jews, especially those who opposed the early Jewish Christians and were in favor of crucifying Jesus and those who subsequently persecuted Jewish Christians, but there was no invective toward all Jews nor were all Jews vindictive against the Jewish Christians. Paul argued the temporary rejection of followers of Judaism, but he longed for their conversion (Rom 11:11, 15, 23–24). There is little doubt that "theological anti-Judaism" (see this term in Poliakov 1962: 23) had its origins in the NT writings, especially Johannine writings where "the Jews" were seen as those who oppose Jesus (John 5:10–18; 6:41–59; 7:1, 10–13; 8:48–59). This is like Paul (Rom 11:17–30; Gal 3–4; 1 Thess 2:14–16), but the anti-Jewish comments in Paul, who was himself a Jew, are more focused on religious matters such as the Law, its ritual, and the failure of the Jews to convert to the Christian faith than it was on Jews as a race. The charges against the Jews of obduracy, blindness, crimes committed against the Prophets, and finally the crucifixion of Jesus are all part of the Christian tradition from its beginning. The charge of blindness is found in the Jesus tradition (Matt 23:16; cf. Mark 12:37–40), which included judgment from God for killing the prophets (Matt 23:29–36). The charge of Jewish obduracy is like Paul's charge against the Jews in Acts 28:25–29 citing to them Isa 6:9–10. The charge of deicide against the Jews by Melito in Sardis (c. AD 180) is not far removed from the words of Paul in 1 Cor 2:8. Ruether contends that anti-Judaism is essential to Christian theology claiming that John gives the "ultimate theological form to that diabolizing of 'the Jews' which is the root of anti-Semitism in the Christian tradition," and concludes that there is no way to eliminate anti-Judaism from Christianity without overhauling its Christological hermeneutic (Reuther 1974: 116).

The charges against the Jews in the writings of the church fathers began to expand to include God's ultimate and final rejection of the Jews. By the fourth and fifth centuries it appears that the early anti-Judaism stance began to be more anti-Jewish than before and a rejection of the Jewish people themselves. Several scholars have shown that it is unlikely that anti-Semitism was present at all in the ancient world and that the racial overtones in the negative language against the Jews are more commonly connected with modern post-Holocaust times. The anti-Semitism (racism) is almost totally absent in ancient rhetoric, but rather it was the Jewish religion and Jewish manners and practices that were called into question by the ancient pagan world (see Cohen 1987: 76; Klassen 1985: 1:5–12; Simon 1986: 395–400). Some of the most intense Christian writings against the Jews (Aphraat, Ephraem, Chrysostom, Cyril of Alexandria, and even Augustine of Hippo) are from the fourth and fifth centuries. By this time the anti-Judaism positions in elements of the earlier churches led to open hostilities against the Jews as in the case of Cyril of Alexandria (*c.* AD 414) who tried to get the Christians to throw the Jews out of the city (Wilken 1971: 9–38). His success in this endeavor is not known, but his language against the Jews is. He calls them "the most deranged of all men," "senseless," "blind," "uncomprehending," and "demented" (*In Lucam, Homily* 101). John Chrysostom accused the Jews of being "bandits," "killers of the Lord," "licentious," "possessed by demons," and the like (see his *Homily* 8, *Against the Jews*, PG 48.927–42). Tertullian earlier argued that God's grace had ceased working among the Jews because they had despised and rejected Jesus as their Messiah with impiety, which was foretold about them in the scriptures (*An Answer to the Jews* 13).

The separation of the church from Judaism by all accounts was not a peaceful one and left many bitter feelings in its wake. By the end of the fifth century, the vast collection of Christian literature that mentioned the Jews at all did so, with a few exceptions, in a negative manner. Eusebius claimed Philo in Alexandria had not only met some Christians but also "welcomed, reverenced, and recognized the divine mission of the apostolic men of his day" (*Hist. eccl.* 2.17.2 [LCL]). This could be Eusebius's fantasy or based on some tradition handed to him, but it does show that not all Jews were considered diabolical by the early Christians. It should also be noted that the "apostolic men" were, in the words of Eusebius, "of the Hebrew origin, and thus still preserved most of the ancient customs in a strictly Jewish manner" (Wilde 1949: 80–2, 173–7, 192–8, 212–16).

In time, partly because of both the Jewish opposition to the church and partly because of their failure to convert to Christianity, some church fathers encouraged Christians to take hostile actions against them. For example, when Christians in Callinicum in Asia, led by their bishop, burned down a Jewish synagogue, the local governor required them to rebuild the synagogue at the bishop's own expense. Ambrose, bishop of Milan (*c.* 339–97), upon hearing of that decision, appealed the sentence to the emperor, Theodosius the Great, and publicly refused him communion until he reversed the governor's sentence (Ambrose, *Ep.* 40 and 41). The obvious implication drawn from Ambrose's actions was that it was okay to do such things to the Jews. Similar harsh comments can also be found in Ignatius (*Magn.* 8–10; Phld. 5–6), *Epistle of Barnabas* (2–3, 4.6–8, 6.6–8; *Diogn.* 3–4), Melito (*On the Passover* 259–279, 732–747), Tertullian (*Ag. Marc.* 2.19, 3.23 and 5.4), and others. Some of these writers evidently had frequent contacts with the Jews and maintained dialogue with them well into the fourth and fifth centuries even after the church had won a prominent role in the Roman Empire.

B. The Causes of the Separation and Hostilities

The factors that led to the complete separation of Christianity from Judaism are largely obvious. The most important reason for their separation was, of course, not only a difference in the Jewish Christians' understanding of Jesus as the hoped-for Messiah but also their understanding of the nature and role of the Torah. From the very beginnings of the Christian movement, many Jews stumbled over the notion of a crucified Messiah (1 Cor 1:23). In Justin, *Dial.* 10.3, Trypho objects to the Christians' hope of the blessing of God because they are "resting their hopes on a man that was crucified." Justin addresses this objection with an argument on the resurrection and the second advent of Jesus (cf. 32.1–3).

The Christological formulations about Jesus, namely that he was "Lord" and "Christ," were also considered incompatible with the Jewish understanding of the person and role of the Messiah (see arguments on this in Segal (1986: 154–60) and Lazare 2010: 31). Flusser contends that a high or divine Christology regarding Jesus posed problems for Jews, but he stresses that even those Jews who were prepared to accept Jesus as their Messiah were less prepared to accept him as the divine Son of God (Flusser 1988: 620–5). It was also difficult for most Jews to square the Gentile–Christian attitude toward the Law with their own understanding of Torah and the necessity of living within God's covenant (Segal 1986: 143, 156, 161). This, of course, made the eventual separation of Christianity from Judaism inevitable, even though a significant number of Jewish Christians (Ebionites, Elkasaites, Cerinthians, and Nazoreans) did not see that as necessary.

The earliest ancient resources for understanding the theology of early Jewish Christianity are the books of Matthew, James, Hebrews, and the *Didache* 1–6. The fourth-century *Clementine Homilies and Recognitions* (*Pseudo-Clementines* likely from Syria) depends on the late-second-century *Preaching of Peter* and provides a post-second-century understanding of conservative Jewish Christianity. These Jewish Christians survived the first century, but their theological stance is much debated. Most agree that their Christological formulations were incompatible with Gentile Orthodox positions on the divinity of Jesus (see also Callan 1986: 27–52, 65–6 for a summary of the Jewish-Christian theological positions). The Jewish Christians eventually survived the first century, but their theological stance on the identity of Jesus was strongly debated (see the discussion of the Ebionites in Chapter 2). But this still does not account for the level of vindictive rhetoric and eventual hostilities that existed between Jews and Christians, or for their negative preoccupation with each other for hundreds of years. According to a third-century document (*Did. apost.* 5.14.23), the chief reason for celebrating Easter was not only to observe the passion of Jesus but also "to obtain forgiveness for the guilty and unfaithful Jews." But what moved the relations from debate and separation to open hostilities? Several answers are possible and to some extent it is likely that all the following played some role in the increase of hostilities.

First, of course, was the failure of the Jews to convert to Christianity. As is well known, many early Christians had three major expectations that did not materialize in the way they had hoped: (a) that Jesus would soon return to the earth and establish his kingdom, (b) that the city of Jerusalem would become the religious capital for the Christian faith, and (c) the Jewish nation would soon come to accept Jesus as the promised Messiah. Stephen Neill discusses these hopes in early Christianity (1976: 32–7), concluding that the last of these hopes proved most frustrating for the early church that was preoccupied for centuries with Jewish failure to become followers of Jesus. So powerful was the influence of the Jews in the empire that the Christians could not be certain even in the fourth and fifth centuries that the gains they had acquired under Constantine would not be overturned. To understand the Christians' fears, one need only recall the actions of the emperor Julian, who tried to return the empire to its former pagan ways. After rejecting his Christian upbringing, he attempted to reverse the gains of the Christians, partly by promoting the welfare of the Jews over the Christians but also by trying to rebuild the Temple in Jerusalem. Twice earlier during the reigns of Hadrian and Constantine the Jews attempted to rebuild their Temple but were unsuccessful. Had Julian's attempt been successful, one of the Christians' most enduring arguments against Judaism would have been blunted. They had long claimed that the destruction of the Temple and the expulsion of the Jews from Jerusalem under Hadrian were evidence of God's rejection of the Jews, and proof of the consequent election of the Christians to take their place. So common was this claim that one can scarcely believe that Julian, who was raised in the Christian religion, was unaware of it. Socrates, the church historian (c. AD 380–450), tells of Julian's promotion of and financial support for the Jews to rebuild the Temple in Jerusalem, and describes in detail the supernatural intervention of God by an earthquake and fire to prevent it from happening. He also emphasizes that Cyril, bishop of Jerusalem, had predicted the demise of the structure, thereby denoting divine intervention in the matter. Because of this belief in divine activity, he says, many Jews "confessed that Christ is God: yet they did not [do] his will" even after a cross miraculously appeared on their garments afterward (see Socrates Scholasticus, *Ecclesiastical History* 3.20) (c. AD 380–450). Other examples of Christian arguments against Jews include Justin (*1 Apol.* 47, 53; *Dial.* 117), Irenaeus (*Haer.* 4.4.1–2; 4.13.4), and Origen (*Cels.* 7.20 and *Hom. Jerem.* 14.13). The Jews themselves even gave this as evidence of God's judgment of them but not, of course, as evidence that God had replaced them in favor of the Gentiles or Christians (cf. Justin, *Dial.* 16, 40, 92). Eusebius indicates that one of the purposes of his work was to "add the fate which has beset the whole nation of the Jews from the moment of their plot against our Saviour" (*Hist. eccl.* 1.1.2 [LCL]). He describes in detail the destruction of Jerusalem and the temple (2.6.3–7; 3.5–6), concluding that "such was the reward of the iniquity of the Jews and of their impiety against the Christ of God" (3.7.1 [LCL]). Ruether gives several other examples of similar conclusions (Ruether 1974: 144–5).

Whatever it was that happened in Jerusalem to terminate Julian's plan, his early death from wounds received in battle in the east brought a cessation to any further plans for rebuilding the Temple. Christians saw all this as proof of God's rejection of the Jews and validation of the Christian claims. Sozomen (c. 425–430), emphasizing the divine role in this event, claims that after the destruction of Julian's temple in Jerusalem, "many [Jews] were hence led to confess that Christ is God, and that the rebuilding of the temple was not pleasing to Him" (*H.E.* 5.22). Whether or not there is any truth to this part of the story, the tendency in ancient histories is often to be self-serving. In this case one can at least see the importance of the failure to rebuild the Temple for the Christian apologetic.

Given the level of Christian anti-Judaic rhetoric, it is inconceivable that Jews did not respond in some way to the Christian polemic against them. Or conversely, that the Christian polemic happened in a vacuum instead of as a response to hatred toward them, but therein is an important problem. There are very few Jewish sources from the earliest days of the church to document such a response from the Jews. If the Jews produced polemical writings against the church, how is it that so few of them currently exist? Moore suggests that the answer probably lies in the fact that such literature was expunged from the Jewish community after the Christian triumph over the empire (Moore 1921: 200;

cf. Segal 1986: 147). Meagher, however, argues that the infrequency of a vilification of Jesus in Jewish writings shows that the real issue against the Christians for the Jews had to do with Christians' abdication of the Law and not with Jesus. He argues that Christians, like Stephen in Acts, were persecuted because they abused the Law, not for their views about Jesus' messiahship (Meagher 1979: 19–20). He adds that when the Christians retaliated against Jewish persecution, they eventually gained the upper hand (20–1). Whatever the reason(s) for the scarcity of the Jewish rhetoric against the Christians, the Christian writings themselves offer abundant evidence for the circulation of Jewish polemic against the church in the Roman Empire. In Origen's *Contra Celsum*, an unknown but thoroughly conservative Jew shows considerable awareness of the Christian faith and feeds Celsus with many substantial objections to the Christian faith (*C. Cel.* 2.4.1–2; 2.9.1; 2.13; 2.18, 26, 28, 34, 39, 41, and elsewhere). Porphyry was also aware of similar Jewish criticisms against the Christians and made wide use of them in his arguments against the Christian religion.

Part of Ambrose's primary argument to the emperor Theodosius that Christians should not be forced to rebuild the Jewish synagogue destroyed by the Christians in Callinicum was that the Jews themselves had destroyed several Christian churches. In complaining about the Roman laws that required Christian responsibility for the rebuilding of the synagogue, Ambrose asks, "Where were those laws when they [the Jews] set fire to the domes of the sacred basilicas [Christian churches]?" (Letter 40 to *Theodosius*). Hence, nothing was done about reparations. Similar comments come from Cyril of Alexandria who tried to have the Jews expelled from that city because of their hostilities against Christians that resulted in the deaths of several Christians. Evidence for this story can be found in Socrates Scholasticus (*Hist. eccl.* 7.13, and elsewhere in 3.20 and 5.22). He does not hesitate to criticize Cyril for his behavior and the Jews there received severe prejudicial treatment.

It has been quite popular since Adolf von Harnack to question whether the Christian treatises against the Jews reflect a genuine attempt to deal with real objections by the Jews against the Christians, but some scholars have since concluded that there were many contacts between the Jewish and Christian communities throughout the first five centuries and that Christian writings often reflect many of the actual issues raised by the Jews (Cohen 1967 35–53, 229, 327–8; Simon 1986: 143–5).

Jewish evidence for their polemic against the Christians is slim but worth noting. The first is found in the *Birkath ha-Minim*, namely, the benediction (or malediction) against heretics, found in the twelfth of the *Eighteen Benedictions*, or the *Shemonah Esrey*, which forms the basic prayer of the Jewish liturgy. It reads,

> And for the separatists [Nazoreans or Christians] and for the heretics [*minim*] let there be no hope; and let all wickedness perish as in an instant; and let all thy enemies be cut off quickly; and mayst thou uproot and break to pieces and cast down and humble the arrogant kingdom quickly and in our days. Blessed art thou, O Lord, who breakest enemies and humblest the arrogant. (*PB* 50 [48]; Maccoby 1988: 208)

I will say more on the designation "Nazorean" and "Nazarean" in Chapter 2, but for now, this is suggestive of a Jewish polemic against early Jewish Christians and eventually against all Christians.

Some have doubted that the *Birkath ha-Minim* contains a direct reference to the Christians in its earliest formulation, but when did *minim* become a common Jewish designation for Christians? Marius Heemstra, in his discussion of the factors that led to the divide between Christianity and Judaism, includes the loss of the *religio licita* status for Christians but focuses especially on Christian claims to have superseded the Jews as the people of God (Heemstra 2010). There are some versions of the twelfth benediction dating from the fourth century that contain the word *noserim* that came to refer to the "Nazoreans," or Christians. It is possible that this was strictly a reference to Jewish Christians, but Tertullian, for example, indicates that Nazoreans was used by the Jews as a reference to all Christians. Explaining the meaning of the word, he states, "the Christ of the Creator had to be called a *Nazarene* according to prophecy; whence the Jews also designate us, on that very account, *Nazarenes* after Him" (*Adv. Jud.* 4.8.1 ANF). Flusser offers a detailed history of the origin and use of the *Birkath ha-Minim* and rejects the notion that it was ever used *only* of Christians, claiming that instead it was directed first against the Essenes and then only later against "Nazoreans," whom he believes were *Jewish* Christians (Flusser 1988: 637–43). Segal is probably correct when he says that the term *minim* was a reference in the benedictions that included, but was not limited to, all Christians (Segal 1986: 150).

Justin also appears to substantiate this when he refers to a curse directed against all Christians. Explaining to Trypho some of the reasons for the calamities that had befallen the Jews (probably referring to the events surrounding AD 66–70 and 132–35), he writes, "Accordingly, these things have happened to you in fairness and justice, for you have slain the Just one, and His prophets before him; and now you reject those who hope in Him, and in Him who sent Him—God the Almighty and Maker of all things—*cursing in your synagogues those that believe on Christ.*" In references to actual persecutions of the Christians, he continues, "For you have not the power to lay hands on us, on account of those who now have the mastery, *but as often as you could, you did so*" (*Dialogue* 16.4 ANF [emphasis added]; see also 16, 47, 96, 137). Justin (*1 Apol.* 131) also accuses the Jews of cruel punishments and even of killing the Christians. Along with Justin, we also see that from Origen (*Hom. Jerem.* 10.8.2), Epiphanius (*Pan.* 29.9.1), Jerome (*Ep.* 112.13) to Augustine, all saw the *Birkath ha-Minim* as a curse against the Christians.

Along with the *Birkath ha-Minim*, there are several references in the Palestinian Talmud and the subsequent *Toldoth Yeshu*, which offer an anthology of Talmudic references put together for use against the Christians. Evans has collected a sample of those texts in the Talmudic literature that reflect the tensions between Jews and Christians. He has shown that the Babylonian Talmud casts aspersions against Mary, the mother of Jesus, who is sometimes also confused with Mary Magdalene. He also notes that Mary is described as "one who was the descendent of princes and governors, played the harlot with carpenters [Joseph]" (*b. Sanh.* 106a). On the matter of Jesus' death, he was excommunicated and condemned for worshipping an idol (*b. Sanh.* 107b; *Sota* 47a). Regarding Jesus' ministry, Evans shows that his practice of healing was described in some Jewish texts as sorcery: "Jesus the Nazarene practiced magic and led Israel astray" (*b. Sanh.* 107b; see the interesting parallel in Mark 3:22) (Evans' trans. in his 2005: 342–409 and 418–30). He observes that Jesus' crucifixion is described in similar negative terms in both the Babylonian (*Bavli*) and Jerusalem (*Yerushalmi*) Talmuds:

> On the eve of Passover they hanged Jesus the Nazarene. And a herald went out before him for forty days, saying: "He is going to be stoned, because he practiced sorcery and enticed and led Israel astray. Anyone who knows anything in his favor, let him come and plead in his behalf." But, not having found anything in his favor, they hanged him

on the eve of Passover (*b. Sanh.* 43a; cf. *t. Sanh.* 10.11; *y. Sanh.* 67a; *y. Sanh.* 7.16). (Evans' trans. in his 2005: 342–409 and 418–30)

Even the reports of Jesus' resurrection are spoken of disparagingly in terms of him being a magician: "He then went and raised Jesus by incantation" (*b. Gitt.* 57a, MS. M). "Woe to him who makes himself alive by the name of God" (*b. Sanh. 106a*). Rokeah's conclusion that "the Jews clearly had no hand in the persecutions of Christians by the imperial authorities: Jews neither informed on Christians nor turned Christians over to the Roman authorities" (Rokeah 1989: 2–3) cannot be substantiated by any fair treatment of the primary sources, both Jewish and Christian. Another example of this can be seen in the author(s) of Polycarp's martyrdom that refers to Jewish participation in exciting the anger of the crowds to kill Polycarp and even desecrate his body by not allowing a proper burial (*Mart. Pol.* 12.2; 13.1; 17.2; 18.1). Again, there is no reason to reject the essential reliability of this report that the Jews incited the crowds against the Christian community.

Equally unfounded is Rokeah's contention that the Christian polemic and persecutions directed against the Jews were caused *only* by Christian frustration over the failure of the Jews to convert to Christianity (Rokeah 1989: 4). He does not give sufficient weight to the long list of references in the patristic writers who refer not only to Jewish rhetoric against the Christians but also to their persecutions of them. See, for example, Justin (*Trypho* 16, 17, 32, 34, 117, 131, 133, 136, 137), Irenaeus (*Adv. Haer.* 4.21.3), Hippolytus (*In Gen.* 49.86), who also says that Jews joined with pagans against the Christians (*In Dan.* 1.29.21), and Origen (*Genes. Hom.* 13.3).

If Jewish participation in Christian suffering did not occur, as Rokeah argues, we are without an adequate cause for the hateful intensity of the Christian polemic against the Jews. Johnson has shown that Jewish polemic against pagans was quite common in ancient times, and that some of the very language later used by Christians against the Jews was also used earlier by the Jews in reference to their pagan enemies (see Johnson 1989: 19–41). He observes the rather crude language in Philo's *On the Embassy to Gaius*, where he describes his Alexandrian neighbors as "promiscuous and unstable rabble" (18.120) and, again, states that the Egyptians were a "seed bed of evil in whose souls both the venom and temper of the native crocodiles and wasps are reproduced" (26.166). Other similar examples are found in Philo's *On the Contemplative Life* and in the earlier author of the *Wisdom of Solomon* (*c.* first century BC in Alexandria). Johnson lists numerous references in Josephus to Jewish violence and hostilities, including Josephus's own use of malicious terms to describe his opponents and the enemies of the Jews, which are plentiful in his *Against Apion* (Johnson 1989: 422, 434–5).

Further, perhaps to overcompensate for past injustices, Johnson is also right when he says that in today's world theologians treat first-century Jews as if they were pacific in their relations either to Jesus or to the early church, and they treat "uncritically" the Pharisaic traditions' own self-portrayal and "dismiss any possibility of frailty." As proof of Jewish culpabilities, he lists twenty-one references from Josephus that show that the Jews were often fanatical and violent (1989: 421–2 and 439). Numerous parties from the ancient world made use of such language. Understanding this can rob the polemic of much of its disproportionate force (1989: 441). All of this is not to relieve Christians from any responsibility for their own actions but rather to balance the picture and remind readers that some Jews like some Christians were sometimes irresponsible and did unkind acts in ancient times not unlike they occasionally are today.

The church went to great lengths in its earliest years to maintain the unity of the God of the Hebrew scriptures with the God of Jesus and the apostles, and to stress that their roots were firmly rooted in the Jewish religious tradition. Jewish Christians, as we observed earlier, did not seek to leave Judaism or its synagogues, but this separation was eventually imposed upon them by the leading voices of Judaism that emerged from the first century. Unfortunately, the recognition of Christian indebtedness to their Jewish heritage did not prevent Christians and Jews from sometimes extreme and hostile competition over who was the rightful heir to that heritage. A large body of angry, anti-Judaistic rhetoric exists in the writings of the early church fathers that became especially pronounced in the fourth and fifth centuries. Whether this was in response to Jewish persecution and their polemic against the church, or whether the Christian polemic against the Jews itself led to Jewish polemic against the Christians, may be debated but not the fact of Jewish opposition to Christianity, which is seen first in the NT and then in the church fathers. Gager rejects this and points to Christian opposition to Jewish leadership and their opponents arguing that much of the NT focus against the Jews and Judaism in fact refers to Gentile Judaizers (Gager 1983: 117–20), but given that, even if true, it still does not account for all the anti-Jewish statements in the NT, for example, 1 Thess 2:14–16; Acts 28:17–31.

I have argued that Jewish opposition to early Christianity resulted both from the early followers of Jesus' Christological perspective and their teachings on the role of the Law and its ritual for Gentile Christians. Flusser makes an important case for this (1988: 619–25) and Segal adds a focus on the Christological issues that divided Christianity and Judaism (Segal 1986: 154–60). When Christianity was a small Jewish sect, it could easily be ignored by its Jewish siblings, though there is little evidence that they did, but with the church's significant growth in the second and subsequent centuries, Christian faith was perceived as a greater threat to Judaism and drew serious Jewish reactions to it. On the other hand, the survival of Judaism posed a threat to Christianity's argument that the church had replaced Judaism and had become heir to its antiquity and sacred scriptures. It is hard to imagine how the two groups could have stayed together for long given their many differences, but the hostilities between them unfortunately damaged all hope for reconciliation or for a separation that led to centuries of pain and bad behavior. In both communities the faith transmitted in both of their respective scriptures was too often ignored and a terrible price for both communities was paid because of it. Christianity, before there was a Bible, had much going for it but their essential core traditions were sometimes ignored. As we have seen, both communities of faith occasionally bear witness to their mutual failures. The arguments and evidence in this section largely come from McDonald (1993: 215–52).

We will now focus on the primary authorities in early Christianity beginning with Jesus, of course, including the scriptures he cited, and the origin of the *Christian* scriptures and how they were cited in early church fathers before there was a Bible.

CHAPTER 2

Major Challenges for the Early Christians

1. INTRODUCTION

Before the end of the first century, *Christians* were facing several significant challenges. Jesus had not returned as his early followers had hoped and his closest disciples had died. The presence of a "living voice" of eyewitnesses to the story of Jesus and his fate was gone. Jesus and his earliest followers were all Jews who had no intention of separating from their Jewish siblings and their multiple first-century Jewish practices continued among the Jewish Christians. We saw that those practices of Jesus' first followers included participating in Temple sacrifices, synagogue attendance, recognition of Sabbath and other holy days, circumcision, and recognition of the sacredness of the Law of Moses and other prophetic literature. They had no intention of beginning a new community of faith or to depart from their involvement in those multiple expressions and practices of Judaism. Nothing in the Gospels or Acts suggests that the first followers of Jesus broke with or separated from participation in the major expressions of Judaism.

A not often noticed challenge for the early followers of Jesus was to find a useful designation that identified them, whether it was "The Way" or "the community/assembly (*ecclesia*) of the Lord" (= "church") or "Christian" or such like. It is difficult to find in the New Testament (NT) a common and consistently used expression to describe those who followed Jesus. James D. G. Dunn correctly observes that there was more than one expression of Christian faith within the Jewish people and that the earliest followers of Jesus were simply another Jewish sect with no intention of abandoning the broader expressions of late Second Temple Judaism practiced in the time of Jesus. He acknowledges that the designations "Christian" and "Christianity" were not used initially and only gradually took root among *some* early followers of Jesus, and, as a result of his inquiry, speaks of those early followers of Jesus as "embryonic Christianity," but with considerable reservations (Dunn 2013: 183). While I agree with Dunn's reservations and acknowledge that most authors regularly use "Christian" anachronistically for the earliest followers of Jesus, I will use "Christian" and "Christianity" regularly here to distinguish between those who followed Jesus and acknowledged his role in God's salvation for humanity from those who did not. I am aware that the designation "Christian," although present in the NT (Acts 11:26; 26:28; 1 Pet 4:16), was not a common designation for the earliest followers of Jesus or the name for their churches until much later. Dunn was also aware that the earliest followers were known as a Jewish "sect" (Acts 24:14; 28:22) that had no intention of leaving the broader Jewish community or abandoning their common contemporary expressions of Judaism. The multiple Christian sects in the first century were even more numerous in the second century as the Gentile Christians began to outnumber the Jewish-Christian followers. As the Jewish Christians welcomed uncircumcised Gentiles into their communities, it became more difficult for their Jewish siblings to continue welcoming the Jewish Christians in their synagogues or at their other Jewish observances (Dunn 2013: 183–205).

By the end of the first century and throughout the Roman Empire, the Christian community had grown to somewhere around a hundred thousand followers (Johnson 1989: 423). That number was nonetheless quite small when compared to the almost seven million Jews who were living in the Roman Empire at that time with perhaps one to two million of them residing in Palestine. The size of the Jewish community in the first century CE varies in scholarly writings, but the above numbers are considered reasonable (Perelmuter 1989: 18). Meeks (1983: 34) estimates that there were easily five to six million Jews in the first century in the Greco-Roman Empire out of an estimate sixty to seventy million persons in the population. Poliakov (1962: 5) puts the figure at three to four million Jews living in the Diaspora and one million in Palestine. Others put the total Jewish population at around six to seven million. The obvious point here is that scholars of this period agree that the Jews were a sufficiently large community and significantly outnumbered the Christians in the first three centuries and possibly even well into the fifth or sixth century.

Both the growth and wide dissemination of the Christian message throughout the Roman Empire made communication among the churches more difficult and something was needed to bring a level of harmony and communication among them. Because of the distance between churches and the lack of a national postal service, the writing of letters or epistles and their circulation by couriers, though often difficult for regular communication, eventually became a common means of communication that enabled Christians to find out what was going on elsewhere in their mission. The letters were also used to teach and instruct new converts in the faith and to help maintain some sense of unity among the churches. During the first and second centuries, along with Paul's letters, the Catholic Epistles (James, 1 Peter, 1 John, and subsequently 2 Peter, 2–3 John, and Jude) were circulating in some churches. In the late first and early second centuries, other letters were circulated by Clement of Rome, Ignatius, and Polycarp to specific churches or individuals. By the third and fourth centuries other Christian leaders were regularly circulating their own letters (e.g., Origen, Cyprian, and Athanasius) to address relevant issues to churches and individuals.

In the following I will address several of the most significant challenges for early *Christianity*. These noted in the previous chapter included the delay of Jesus' return, the deaths of the apostles, Jewish and Roman opposition, and the various perceived heretical issues in the second to fourth centuries. By the end of the first century and in the early part of the second century, the delay of Christ's return to establish his kingdom upon the earth had begun to cause a change in outlook among Christians. The apocalyptic message of the earlier disciples, which had focused upon the imminent return of Christ and the overthrow of all existing kingdoms on the earth, was no longer as appealing to Christians as it had been. Jesus had not returned as the early Christians had hoped and some were losing patience. Some authors from that period and later reflect this concern and they continued the apocalyptic message urging Christians to steadfastness, patience, and preparation for the coming day of Christ's return (2 Tim 3:16–18; Rev 1:3; 3:10–11; 22:20; 2 Pet 3:3–7; Rev 22:12).

By the middle of the second century much of the earlier apocalyptic message and the prophetic movement in early Christianity declined in influence in churches often because of abuse (*Did*. 11–13; cf. reference to Lucian's *Passing of Peregrinus* below). The focus on the return of Christ coupled with the coming of the Kingdom of God declined and it appears that most Christians were no longer anticipating a return of the risen Christ soon.

John's Gospel, for example, has almost no references to the coming apocalyptic kingdom of God frequently mentioned in the Synoptic Gospels (see John's exceptions in 3:3 and 5:25–29 for references to that coming kingdom). The primary message in John is about the eternal life that is already present in Jesus (John 10:10; 1 John 5:11–13) and on becoming the children of God at the present time (John 1:11–12). This emphasis on the present and eternal and the move from the focus on the apocalyptic coming of the Son of Man has some parallels with the rise of the gnostic Christian message in the early second century. The delay of the coming (*parousia* or coming return) of the Christ was difficult for many Christians. How was the church supposed to address its believing community when Jesus had not yet returned after some sixty years since his death? Some late-first- or early-second-century Christians had begun emphasizing a "realized" eschatology or already present (cf. John 1:12; 20:31; 1 John 5:12; cf. 2 Thess 2:2; Luke 17:20–21), and differences arose over the matter of the time of the return when the promises that the Christians had eagerly awaited would be fulfilled. But that had subsided and, in that context, a new movement in the church emerged. The Montanists emerged near the end of the second century reemphasizing the role of the Spirit and the prophetic movement, and they were quite influential for a time as we will see below and attracted some notable followers.

The delay in the return of Jesus, the death of the apostles, and the decline of the prophetic (apocalyptic) voices in the churches eventually led to a gradual collection of Christian writings that began to function like scripture in the churches. While there was a living testimony of eyewitnesses who had witnessed the activity of God in Jesus the Christ, some preferred that over written documents. As noted earlier, in the first third of the second century, Papias preferred the living voice of eyewitnesses over the written texts as in the cases of Mark and Matthew (Eusebius, *H.E.* 3.39.4) (see Gamble 1995: 30–2).

The vacuum of authority, if we may speak of one after the deaths of Jesus and his followers, began to be filled by strengthening the office of the bishop (*1 Clement*, *Didache*, and especially *Ignatius*) and that continued to grow in the second century and was helpful for the church to address its many challenges at that time and thereafter. The strong organizational structure under the leadership of the bishop along with creedal formulations that summarized the core religious proclamation addressed the problems facing the proto-orthodox Christians in the second and later centuries. We will see this more fully in the discussions of heresy below.

2. ROMAN PERSECUTIONS AND PHILOSOPHICAL DISPUTES

After the separation of Jews and Christians, beginning in 62 CE and largely but not fully completed after the Bar Kochba rebellion against Rome in 132–135, Christians became more vulnerable to local persecutions. That is because they had lost their privileged licensed religion status (*religio licita*) as a Jewish sect that earlier afforded them some freedom to practice their religion under the protection of Rome, but after that was lost Roman hostility began to break out against them in multiple locations. Increased local persecution continued until the middle of the third century when it became empire-wide under Decius (250–251), and finally under Emperor Diocletian (303–305). Until that time all persecutions were local and not empire-wide. They ceased after Constantine abolished them in 313 (see Eusebius, *Hist. eccl.* 8.2.1 and 8.5–6).

The local persecutions were often quite intense but, again, they were local. For example, Claudius Nero (*c.* 37–68), the first Roman emperor to institute a local and specific persecution of Christians in Rome (Pliny, *Ep.* 10.96–97; Tacitus, *Ann.* 15.44; Tertullian, *Ad Nat.* 1.7.8–9; *Apol.* 5.3–4; Eusebius, *Hist. eccl.* 4.26.9), was later followed by Domitian (*c.* 51–96) who was known for his cruelty against Christians (Suetonius, *Dom.* 12.2; more clearly in Pliny, *Ep.* 10.96.1 and Eusebius, *Hist. eccl.* 3.18.4). His murder brought considerable jubilation among Roman senators (Suetonius, *Domitian*, 23.1–2). Because of increased *local* persecutions throughout the empire, the early Christians faced several local hardships (Rev 2:9–10; 3:9–10; Heb 10:32; Acts 16:16–40, passim). As a small religious minority at the turn of the first century, Christians faced additional challenges that often came to religious minorities. The Christians' gracious regard for sinners, the lowly, and the despised was considered distasteful by some. Many false rumors circulating about the Christians were misunderstandings of what the Christians were practicing. For example, they were accused of cannibalism when they partook of the body and blood of Christ in the communion meal. They were even accused of eating children, namely confused with the Son of God (Benko 1984: 54–78). Because they expressed love toward all, and because everyone was a brother or a sister and used such terms as the "love feast," the Christians were often accused of incest and immorality (called "Oedipodean intercourse," based upon the classical story of Oedipus of Thebes marrying his own mother). Their denial of the validity and reality of the state divinities, as well as their refusal to worship the emperor, led to their being accused of atheism. (See, especially, Athenagoras, *Plea* 3; Minusius Felix, *Octavius* 9.) Opposition to Christians was considerable, leading to many local persecutions with greater intensity in the church's first three centuries (see also Wilken 1984). The following quotations offer a sense of how the Christians were perceived and received by state officials, prominent philosophers, and competing propagandists.

1. Suetonius (Gaius Suetonius Tranquillas, *c.* 69–140). Suetonius was a friend of Pliny the Younger and a government official under Emperor Hadrian. He wrote *Lives of Illustrious Men*, some of which have survived, and also *Lives of the Caesars*, which portray the Caesars from Julius to Domitian. Suetonius describes Nero's punishment of Christians as follows: "Punishment was inflicted on the Christians, a class of men given to a new and wicked superstition" (*Nero* 16.2). Again, speaking of the expulsion of the Jews from Rome in AD 49, he writes, "Claudius expelled the Jews from Rome who, instigated by Chrestus [Christ?], never ceased to cause unrest" (*Claudius* 25.4 [LCL]). While many scholars believe that Suetonius' reference to "Chrestus" is a reference to Jesus the Christ, not all are convinced.
2. Tacitus (Cornelius Tacitus, *c.* AD 55–120). Tacitus was a major Roman historian. Among his best known writings are the *Histories* and the *Annals*, as well as *Agricola* and *Germania*. He describes the great fire at Rome in AD 64 and Nero's blaming of the event on the Christians. Although he agrees that the Christians perpetuate a "hideous and shameful" religion and constitute a "deadly superstition," he does not believe that the Christians were guilty of the fire. He writes,

> But all human efforts, all the lavish gifts of the emperor, and the propitiations of the gods, did not banish the sinister belief that the conflagration [the burning

of Rome] was the result of an order. Consequently, to get rid of the report, Nero fastened the guilt and inflicted the most exquisite tortures on a class hated for their abominations [*flagitia*], called Christians by the populace. Christus, from whom the name had its origin, suffered the extreme penalty during the reign of Tiberius at the hands of one of our procurators, Pontius Pilate, and a deadly superstition, thus checked for the moment, again broke out not only in Judea, the source of the evil, but also in Rome, where all things hideous and shameful from every part of the world meet and become popular. Accordingly, an arrest was first made of all who confessed; then, upon their information, an immense multitude was convicted, not so much of the crime of arson, as of hatred of the human race. Mockery of every sort was added to their deaths. Covered with the skins of beasts, they were torn by dogs and perished, or were nailed to crosses, or were doomed to the flames. These served to illuminate the night when daylight failed. Nero had thrown open his gardens for the spectacle, and was exhibiting a show in the circus, while he mingled with the people in the dress of a charioteer or drove about in a chariot. Hence, even for criminals who deserved extreme and exemplary punishment, there arose a feeling of compassion; for it was not, as it seemed, for the public good, but to glut one man's cruelty, that they were being destroyed. (*Ann.* 15.44.2–8; Stevenson trans. 1957: 2–3)

3. Pliny the Younger (*c.* 61–114), an educated member of the Roman aristocracy and governor of Bithynia. Pliny wrote some ten books of letters for publication, which are valuable historical documents covering the period of Trajan's reign as Roman emperor (*c.* 98–117), including an early reflection of attitudes toward the Christians by the emperor. Evidently, being a new governor, he had not yet experienced any trials of the Christians, and he wrote to Emperor Trajan for help in knowing how to deal with them. He also wanted to tell the emperor what his practice had been in regard to the Christians. Some persons had reported to him that certain individuals were Christians and, upon investigating the matter, he found out that there were three kinds of persons coming before him: (1) those who freely confessed that they were Christians and refused to deny their faith, who were consequently executed; (2) those who denied that they ever were Christians and were given the opportunity to perform a pagan religious act (probably pouring out a libation to the gods and/ or the emperor) and to curse Christ upon which act they were released with no recriminations; and (3) those who had actually been Christians but turned away from the Christian faith and returned to pagan practices, who confirmed it by worshipping the pagan images of the gods and cursing Christ. These persons were also released. The following is Pliny's letter to Trajan with his three questions of the emperor:

> It is my custom, lord emperor, to refer to you all questions whereof I am in doubt. Who can better guide me when I am at a stand, or enlighten me if I am in ignorance? In investigations of Christians, I have never taken part; hence I do not know how the crime is usually punished or investigated or what allowances are made. So, I have had no little uncertainty whether there is any distinction of age, or whether the very weakest offenders are treated exactly like the stronger; whether pardon is given to those who repent, or whether a man who has once been a Christian gain nothing by having ceased to be such; whether punishment attaches to the mere

name apart from secret crimes [*flagitia*], or to the secret crimes connected with the name. Meanwhile this is the course I have taken with those who were accused before me as Christians. I asked them whether they were Christians, and if they confessed, I asked them a second and third time with threats of punishment. If they kept to it, I ordered them for execution; for I held no question that whatever it was that they admitted, in any case obstinacy and unbending perversity deserve to be punished. There were others of the like insanity; but as these were Roman citizens, I noted them down to be sent to Rome.

Before long, as is often the case, the mere fact that the charge was taken notice of made it commoner, and several distinct cases arose. An unsigned paper was presented, which gave the names of many. As for those who said that they neither were nor ever had been Christians, I thought it right to let them go, since they recited a prayer to the gods at my dictation, made supplication with incense and wine to your statue, which I had ordered to be brought into court for the purpose together with the images of the gods, and moreover cursed Christ—things which (so it is said) those who are really Christians cannot be made to do. Others who were named by the informer said that they were Christians and then denied it, explaining that they had been, but had ceased to be such, some three years ago, some a good many years, and a few even twenty. All these too both worshipped your statue and the images of the gods, and cursed Christ.

They maintained, however, that the amount of their fault or error had been this, that it was their habit on a fixed day to assemble before daylight and recite by turns a form of words to Christ as a god; and that they bound themselves with an oath, not for any crime, but not to commit theft or robbery or adultery, not to break their word, and not to deny a deposit when demanded. After this was done, their custom was to depart, and to meet again to take food, but ordinary and harmless food; and even this (they said) they had given up doing after the issue of my edict, by which in accordance with your commands I had forbidden the existence of clubs. On this I considered it the more necessary to find out from two maidservants who were called deaconesses, and that by torments, how far this was true; but I discovered nothing else than a perverse and extravagant superstition. I therefore adjourned the case and hastened to consult you. The matter seemed to me worth deliberation, especially on account of the number of those in danger; for many of all ages and every rank, and also of both sexes are brought into present or future danger. The contagion of that superstition has penetrated not the cities only, but the villages and country; yet it seems possible to stop it and set it right. At any rate it is certain enough that the almost deserted temples begin to be restored, and that fodder for victims finds a market, whereas buyers till now were very few. From this it may easily be supposed, what a multitude of men can be reclaimed, if there be a place for repentance. (*Ep.* 10.96, LCL) (Stevenson 1957: 13–14)

4. Trajan (Roman emperor, *c.* 98–117) replied to Pliny the Younger in Bithynia and in so doing gave a timely report on the legal status of Christians in the empire:

You have adopted the proper course, my dear Secunde, in your examination of the cases of those who were accused to you as Christians, for indeed nothing can be laid down as a general ruling involving something like a set form of procedure. They are not to be sought out; but if they are accused and convicted, they must be punished—yet on this condition, that whoso denies being a Christian, and makes the fact plain by his action, that is by worshipping our gods, shall obtain pardon on his repentance, however suspicious his past conduct may be. Papers, however, which are presented unsigned ought not to be admitted in any charge, for they are a very bad example and unworthy of our time. (Pliny, *Ep.* 10.97, LCL; Stevenson 1957: 16)

In the third century, Decius (249–251) forced all empire residents to offer sacrifices to him and obtain certificates of their obedience. Those who refused were tortured and/or executed leading to the numerous Christian deaths. His persecutions ended when Decius was murdered in June of 251. In 303, Diocletian, seeking unity in the empire, sought to destroy the churches and gave orders to destroy their buildings and sacred books. His reign initiated what was later called the "Era of the Martyrs." He abdicated his reign in 305, but the persecutions continued until Constantine's defeat of his successors in 313. During this persecution, Christians had to decide which books to turn over to the authorities. Likely some criteria developed then to distinguish the churches' most cherished books from other religious texts. They often turned over less important writings, but regularly tried to protect the most sacred books, sometimes with their lives. Decisions on which books were *most* valued likely were determined for many churches at this time. An example of this is in McDonald (2017: 2:87–90).

In terms of the arguments of philosophers the following reflects the challenges the Christians faced in the second century and later. Lucian of Samosata (*c.* AD 120–80) was a man who wrote satires about religious and philosophical thought and did not hesitate to make biting comments about individuals with whom he had differences. Among his many writings is the story *On the Passing of Peregrinus*, a satirical depiction of the life and death of a charlatan Christian, Proteus Peregrinus, passing himself off as a prophet. He lived in the early to middle second century and deceived Christians and took them for their money. Some scholars have said that Lucian was writing about the life of Polycarp, who was martyred about the same time when Peregrinus died. They have pointed to some of the parallels in the Christian story of *The Martyrdom of Polycarp*. Besides the interesting but not exact parallels, there is little support for that conclusion. Of special interest, however, is Lucian's detailed description of a wandering charismatic taking advantage of the early Christians and finally their response. Lucian had no respect for the Christians and spoke of them as simple and gullible people. Lucian wrote at length about Proteus Peregrinus, saying,

> It was then that [Proteus] learned the wondrous lore of the Christians, by associating with their priests and scribes in Palestine.[1] And—how else could it be?—in a trice he made them all look like children; for he was prophet, cult-leader, head of the synagogue, and everything, all by himself. He interpreted and explained some of their books and even composed many, and they revered him as a god, made use of him as a lawgiver, and set him down as a protector, next after that other, to be sure, whom they still worship, the man who was crucified in Palestine because he introduced this new cult into the world.

---

[1]Since Christians did not have officeholders called priests or scribes in their churches at this time, this may be Lucian's confusion of Judaism with Christianity. The term "priest" was not adopted by the church until much later, well after the time of Lucian.

Then at length Proteus was apprehended for this and thrown into prison, which itself gave him no little reputation as an asset for his future career and the charlatanism and notoriety-seeking that he was enamored of. Well, when he had been imprisoned, the Christians, regarding the incident as a calamity, left nothing undone in the effort to rescue him. Then, as this was impossible, every other form of attention was shown him, not in any casual way but with assiduity; and from the very break of day aged widows and orphan children could be seen waiting near the prison, while their officials even slept inside with him after bribing the guards. Then elaborate meals were brought in, and sacred books of theirs were read aloud, and excellent Peregrinus—for he still went by that name—was called by them "the new Socrates."

Indeed, people came even from the cities in Asia, sent by the Christians at their common expense, to succour and defend and encourage the hero. They show incredible speed whenever any such public action is taken; for in no time they lavish their all. So it was then in the case of Peregrinus; much money came to him from them by reason of his imprisonment, and he procured not a little revenue from it. The poor wretches have convinced themselves, first and foremost, that they are going to be immortal and live for all time, in consequence of which they despise death and even willingly give themselves into custody, most of them. Furthermore, their first lawgiver [Jesus] persuaded them that they are all brothers of one another after they have transgressed once for all by denying the Greek gods and by worshipping that crucified sophist himself and living under his laws. Therefore, they despise all things indiscriminately and consider them common property, receiving such doctrines traditionally without any definite evidence. So, if any charlatan and trickster, able to profit by occasions, comes among them, he quickly acquires sudden wealth by imposing upon simple folk.

However, Peregrinus was freed by the then governor of Syria, a man who was fond of philosophy. Aware of his recklessness and that he would gladly die in order that he might leave behind him a reputation for it, he freed him, not considering him worthy even of the usual chastisement. (*On the Death of Peregrinus* 11–14 LCL)

This passage reflects, among other things, that the early Christians were often persecuted for their faith and that by and large they did not have many among them from the wealthy and learned classes. The early Christians were known for worshipping Jesus as a divine being and for caring for those of their number who were imprisoned by reason of their witness. Further, there was a perception on the part of the non-Christian world that many of the Christians were not afraid to face the consequences (imprisonment or death) for being Christians, and that their eschatological hope was a primary source of encouragement to them. This supports the NT witness in these matters. The above source also notes that the interpretation of their scriptures by a prophet inspired by the Spirit was commonplace, and that they were generous in their giving.

Among the most important critics of early Christianity, Celsus (fl. *c.* 178–180) was more familiar with early Christian writings and also with the core beliefs and practices of the Christians than his contemporaries. He apparently read several Christian writings besides merely listening to the rumors being spread about them. His arguments against the Christians, which were the most serious of the second century and even later, were examined in detail and answered some fifty years later by Origen in his *Contra Celsum*. Celsus, like Lucian, objected to the simplicity of the Christians, and criticized their choice of faith over reason. He also objected to their doctrine of the incarnation of Christ, that is, God becoming a human being. According to Origen, from whom we know of Celsus, he claims,

> Celsus urges us to "follow reason and a rational guide in accepting doctrines" on the ground that "anyone who believes people without so doing is certain to be deceived." And he compares those who believe without rational thought to the "begging priests of Cybele and soothsayers, and to worshippers of Mithras and Sabazius and whatever else one might meet, apparitions of Hecate or of some other demon or demons. For just as among them scoundrels frequently take advantage of the lack of education of gullible people and lead them wherever they wish, so also," he says, "this happens among the Christians." He says that "some do not even want to give or to receive a reason for what they believe and use such expressions as "Do not ask questions; just believe," and "Thy faith will save thee." (Origen, *Contra Celsum* 1.9 LCL)

Celsus charges that Christians are unprofitable members of society and are weak, women, and slaves:

> Their injunctions are like this. "Let no one educated, no one wise, no one sensible draw near. For those abilities are thought by us to be evils. But as for anyone ignorant, anyone stupid, anyone uneducated, anyone who is a child, let him come boldly." By the fact that they themselves admit that these people are worthy of their God, they show that they want and are able to convince only the foolish, dishonorable and stupid, and only slaves, women, and little children. Those who summon people to the other mysteries make this preliminary proclamation: "Whoever has pure hands and a wise tongue." And again, others say: "Whoever is pure from all defilement, and whose soul knows nothing of evil, and who has lived well and righteously." Such are the preliminary exhortations of those who promise purification from sins. But let us hear what folk these Christians call. "Whosoever is a sinner," they say, "whosoever is unwise, whosoever is a child, and in a word, whosoever is a wretch, the kingdom of God will receive him." He asks, "Why on earth this preference for sinners?" (Origen, *Contra Celsum* 3.44, 59, 64 LCL)

Celsus also had a negative attitude toward Jesus about whom, according to Origen, Celsus wrote, "He was brought up in secret and hired himself out as a workman in Egypt, and after having tried his hand at certain magical powers he returned from there, and on account of those powers gave himself the title of God" (Origen, *Contra Celsum* 1.38 LCL). He even accused Jesus of practicing sorcery (*Contra Celsum* 1.6, 68). At this point, he showed a lack of knowledge about Jesus, but generally he had a good understanding of the low economic and educational status of the Christians and the simple outline of their faith. He shows the kinds of philosophical criticisms the early Christians faced as they took their message into the Roman world.

Finally, some slanderous ancient graffiti on a stone in a guard room on Palatine Hill in Rome reflects a popular rejection of the second- and third-century Christians. Its precise date is difficult to establish, but it is probably from the middle to late second century. The etching depicts the figure of a man with the head of an ass hanging on a cross. Next to the figure is a man, of whom nothing is known, standing by the cross with his head raised in a gesture of adoration (Ferguson 2003: 561). The inscription reads, "Alexamenos worships his god." These and many other negative perspectives of the early Christians reflect the many challenges facing them well into the fourth century.

3. EARLY CHRISTIANITY AND EMERGING "HERESIES"

By the late first century and throughout the second, Christians faced many challenges, including the delay of the anticipated return of Jesus the Christ that led to mockery (e.g., 2 Pet 3:3–7 responds to that), and the deaths of the apostolic figures with the subsequent vacuum of authority, accompanied by several severe *local* persecutions of some Christians. These were accompanied by the emerging "heresies" in churches that some church fathers believed were outside the mainstream of Christian teachings/tradition, especially Docetism, Marcionism, Gnosticism, the Montanists, and Ebionite views of Jesus (see discussion of their teachings below). The identity of Jesus was a major issue confronting second-century Christianity and later. There were multiple positions circulating in the churches on the identity of Jesus, for example, whether he was a spirit and not fully human (Docetism) or was fully human but divinely inspired (Ebionite) or was both divine and human (proto-orthodox), and so on.

Who was Jesus and what was the church's core beliefs about him? We know who the "winner" eventually was, namely the proto-orthodox church fathers, but their answers to those questions were not always clear. What were the implications of this for understanding the church's mission and guidance for church life? These and other questions occupied considerable time in second- and third-century church fathers. To safeguard the essence of Christian faith, several second-century church fathers gradually welcomed not only the first-century primary early Christian authorities (Jesus as Lord of the church, their Old Testament [OT] scriptures, and apostolic authority) and subsequently recognized an enhanced episcopal authority along with the sacred traditions of and about Jesus summarized in first- and second-century creeds. Some early-second-century authors began citing a few of the NT writings in a scriptural manner, especially some of the canonical Gospels (mostly Matthew) and some writings by the Apostle Paul to churches. Christian beliefs transmitted in the summary creeds and supported by the NT authors were the new additional witnesses that formed additional authorities for the churches. Those texts that initially functioned authoritatively and later were called "scripture" in a growing number of churches formed the core of the NT writings.

These authorities (Lord, OT, apostles, creeds, episcopate, NT writings) were often cited to address several of the so-called "heretical" teachings circulating in some churches. The death of the apostles was addressed by an emerging and significantly more powerful episcopate led by the church's bishops who some church fathers argued were in the line of succession from the apostles who passed on to them not only legitimate leadership but also the sacred traditions that were entrusted to the apostles (Irenaeus, *Haer.* 3.3.3). While there were some theological controversies present in the first century (e.g., Gal 1:6–8; Col 2:20–23; 1 Tim 4:1–5; 6:20; 2 Tim 3:1–9; 1 John 4:2–3; Jude 5–8; Rev 2:6, 14, 20, 24), they became more widespread and *likely* more influential in the second and third centuries. Several second- and third-century church fathers, especially Irenaeus, Hegesippus, Tertullian, Hippolytus, and Origen, dealt with the divergent late first- and second-century heretical movements described earlier. Their responses to the multiple challenges facing the churches generally focused on tradition, creeds, leadership, and an emerging Christian scripture defending the core elements of the church's earliest proclamation and beliefs about Jesus. In what follows here I will focus largely on those authorities and how they addressed the needs of the developing and ever-expanding churches in the second to the fourth century.

The failure of Jesus to return, as the earliest followers of Jesus had hoped would happen in their lifetimes (1 Thess 4:14–18; Acts 1:9–11; John 14:28), brought growing skepticism in the late first and second centuries (see a response in 2 Pet 3:1–4). Along with the deaths of the apostles and the decline of the prophetic voices in churches multiple expressions of Christian faith and multiple so-called "heresies" emerged that focused on the identity of Jesus and other issues related to the church's Jewish heritage.

Several necessary and important responses from the ancient churches to the crises they were facing had a major impact on emerging Christianity, including an expanded role for bishops and church order, clarification of the rule of faith (or *regula fidei*, and church tradition), and the *recognition* of *Christian scriptures* that likely, following the Hellenistic model and Jewish Tanak, later emerged as a fixed Christian biblical canon. I will begin with the sacred tradition (*regula fidei* or "rule of faith"), summarized in early NT creeds, and supported later by the church's Christian scriptures.

As we turn to focus on the role or function of heresy in early Christianity and how it led to a strengthened episcopate and a more precisely argued proto-orthodoxy, we should note in advance that the designations "heresy" and "heretic" are later designations for those who earlier held beliefs contrary to those of the "proto-orthodox" followers of Jesus. Those designations that are now common were not so clear earlier and they became designations by the "winners" of the early controversies who began to label those with different perspectives than their own as "heretics" and their teachings as "heresy." There were multiple understandings of Jesus in antiquity when such designations began to appear. As we will see below, they recognized that Jesus had a special relationship to God and in God's plan of salvation for his people. As we saw earlier in the Jewish benedictions against the Christians, the Jewish religious leaders believed that the followers of Jesus were heretical.

When the Christian message began to appeal to Gentiles, many of the earliest followers of Jesus questioned the legitimacy of welcoming them into the church without circumcision, keeping the Law of Moses, the Sabbath, and other Jewish rituals. Paul, of course, made it clear that Gentiles did not have to become Jews to become followers of Jesus and conversely that Jews did not have to abandon Judaism to follow Jesus. Christianity was a Jewish sect first and many objected to opening their churches to Gentiles without their keeping the Jewish practices. What is more important to observe here is that all the earliest followers of Jesus did not adopt the proto-orthodoxy of Paul. As we will see below in our discussion of the Ebionites, the earliest Jewish followers of Jesus no doubt considered the proto-orthodox teaching of Paul on Gentile freedom from the Law as heretical and wrong.

From its beginning, there were multiple voices among the followers of Jesus. The most significant issues for them to deal with was the identity of Jesus and how to deal with Gentiles coming to faith in Jesus as the Christ. The now common designations (heresy and heretic) were not regularly used in the first century, but the emergence of views contrary to those held from the beginning were often called into question and even condemned as we will see. Today "heretics" usually refers to those who make a conscious or willful rejection of beliefs that are now considered normative for the church or for a group of churches. Roman Catholics, for instance, define a heretic as a member of the church who denies the truth of any revealed teaching of the church. Protestants usually define a heretic as one who rejects any truth taught in the Bible. The term is not generally used of non-Christian groups, such as Buddhists or Hindus, but only of those who claim to be Christian and reject *major* teachings in the Christian scriptures. Of course, *"major"* is always a debatable issue and not always agreed upon by all followers of Jesus!

Normally those terms refer to theological positions or individuals and groups *within* the Christian tradition who have strayed from orthodoxy, especially in reference to the nature of God or Jesus. The difficulty in defining heresy in antiquity is that normative Christianity (orthodoxy) had not yet been fully defined or *universally* acknowledged in early Christianity until there was a major move in that direction such as the early or "proto-orthodoxy" promoted in the second- and third-century church fathers, especially by Irenaeus, Hippolytus, Athenagoras, Tertullian, Origen, and Cyprian. Helmut Koester acknowledges that there was a free oral tradition paralleling the synoptics until around 150 CE and orthodoxy and heresy were "not distinct categories before the time of Irenaeus" (Koester 1957). While such categories were not clear until the later second century, the notion of something circulating that was not in compliance with the earliest traditions of the church was well known, as in the case of the Docetic controversy (1 John 4:2–3; cf. also Col 2:8–16, 20–23). Church leaders did not make their decisions about heresy based on an already formed Christian Bible but rather on what they believed were the earliest traditions and creeds passed on in the churches and safeguarded by their apostolic transmission to the bishops of the churches. There were departures from that almost from the beginning, but lengthy arguments against heresies were more common in the latter half of the second century. For added support for their teachings, the church fathers regularly appealed to first-century Christian writings that were not initially identified as scripture but later were included the church's NT canon. From the middle to the end of the first century, it appears that many divergent theological issues were circulating in the early churches (1 Cor 15:12–19; Col 2:8, 20–23; 2 Thess 2:1–3; 1 John 4:1–3; Rev 2:14–15, 20–24). It is clear that several of the early Christian traditions and teachings circulating in many churches also found in several first-century Christian writings were not infrequently challenged in the first- and second-century churches.

In the second century the so-called heretical groups were by no means insignificant in number, and indeed, if combined, it has been argued that they may well have outnumbered those in the proto-orthodox churches (Bauer 1971). In response, the second- and third-century orthodox church fathers sought to anchor their beliefs and practices in what they believed were the *earliest* traditions and creeds of the church supported by the *earliest* known Christian writings (hence, both an apostolic criterion and an appeal to antiquity). They believed that these sources supported their proto-orthodox traditions and provided the best foundations for Christian belief over those of the other sects of Christianity that the orthodox considered outside of the boundaries of the earliest church teachings. They believed that those core beliefs had been handed on in the earliest churches by the apostles.

By the mid-second century, church leaders had already recognized the value and usefulness of early Christian writings in their worship, instruction, and apologetic and dealing with perceived heresies in the church. By the mid- to late second century, the words "Gospel" and "apostle" (sometimes "Lord" and "apostle") represented the words of and traditions about Jesus and the writings attributed to the apostles (Gospels, Acts, Epistles, Revelation). They began to be read alongside the "prophets" and sometimes instead of the "prophets" (their OT scriptures), and these writings all served as primary authorities in the second-century church fathers. Some were calling these texts "scripture" in the first half of the second century and some of them were already functioning like "scripture" before being so called.

The focus in what follows is whether the second-century heretics and those who espoused their views had a significant influence on the emerging churches of that time. Several scholars (Harnack, von Campenhausen, Metzger, and others following their lead) contend that the proto-orthodox church leaders responded to four major second-century heretical groups (Ebionites, Marcionites, Gnostics, and Montanists) by establishing a biblical canon or selection of books that could be read in the churches. However, there is little convincing evidence that the second-century proto-orthodox church fathers' responses to their opponents led them to establish the select writings that later formed the church's Bible. Rather than focusing on a select collection of Christian scriptures in dealing with their opponents, they responded to what they believed were divergences from the acknowledged apostolic traditions and core beliefs with a *canon of faith* (*regula fidei*). That canon of faith was the sacred traditions and proclamations of the church that were transmitted to the churches from the beginning, whether orally or in Christian writings. Those teachings and beliefs were the rule to follow in dealing with their opponents. No second-century evidence supports that any church fathers had an interest in producing a fixed collection of sacred writings in response to any heresy circulating in the early churches.

I will now summarize the basic views of each of the best known four "heretical" Christian groups in the second and later centuries and how the proto-orthodox church fathers responded to them. I should say in advance that the following "heresies" emerged before many churches had a developed theological framework that defined the parameters of their faith. What we know of the four groups comes mostly from the "winners" of the theological debates in the second and later centuries, namely the proto-orthodox followers of Jesus. The point of identifying these groups is to show the divergent views in multiple followers of Jesus *before there was a Bible* later identified as the church's OT and NT.

A. Ebionites

From the church's beginning the first followers of Jesus were Jews who practiced the Law and kept the Jewish traditions current in late Second Temple Judaism or the first century CE before the destruction of the Temple in 70 CE. The NT reflects similarities and differences that emerged between the Jewish Christians and the Hellenistic Jews who followed Jesus, especially Paul who did not impose the traditional Jewish regulations of the Law, including circumcision, on Gentile Christians (e.g., Acts 11:2–3; 15:1–5; Gal 2:11–14; 3:8–14, 21–29; 4:5:2–15; 5:11–12; 6:12–15). The early Jewish Christians, like Jesus and his family, observed the Law, circumcision, Sabbath keeping, Jewish holy days, and the recognition of the importance of the Temple and its sacrificial system. The Ebionites likely descended from the first-century Jewish Christians who affirmed Jesus as their Messiah, and also the importance of observing the Law of Moses and other Jewish scriptures and traditions, but not necessarily his divinity, virgin birth, or preexistence. They are likely the same as the "Nazareans" who were among the Jewish Christians who generally not only acknowledged Jesus as the Son of God and their Messiah but also observed the Law. Eusebius acknowledged two groups of Jewish Christians that went by the name Ebionites. One of them denied the virgin birth and the other accepted it. Both rejected the letters of Paul and only used the *Gospel according to the Hebrews* but also observed the Jewish ceremonials and met on Sundays in commemoration of the Savior's resurrection (*Hist. eccl.* 3.37.1–6). Both Ebionite groups were condemned because they denied the divinity of Jesus, affirming only his humanity and that he kept the law perfectly and he was the Christ. Apparently, the Nazareans were also assumed to be the "heretical" Ebionites (Klugkist and Reinink 1999: 1–31).

The designation "Ebionites" derives from the Hebrew term *ebyon*, meaning "poor." The early church fathers disagreed over its meaning but sometimes used it in mockery as we see in Origen who accused them of being "poor in understanding" (*On First Principles* 4.3.8). He said there were two kinds of Ebionites with one affirming Jesus' divinity and the other denying it (*Contra Celsum* 5.61; *Matt. Comm. Ser* 79). He also observed that the Ebionites rejected the virgin birth of Jesus (*Epist ad Titum* 3.11; *Hom in Luk* 17) but observed the Law (*Epist. ad Rom.* 3.11; *Contra Celsum* 2.1) and circumcision (*Hom in Gen.* 3.5) and rejected Paul (*Hom in Jer* 19.12; *Contra Celsum* 5.65). Origen claimed that all Ebionites observed the Law and wanted to be imitators of Christ.

Eusebius likewise speaks with mockery about the name saying,

> The first Christians gave these the suitable name of Ebionites because they had poor and mean opinions concerning Christ. They held him to be a plain and ordinary man who had achieved righteousness merely by the progress of his character and had been born naturally from Mary and her husband. They insisted on the complete observance of the Law and did not think that they would be saved by faith in Christ alone and by a life in accordance with it. (*Hist. eccl.* 3.27.1–2)

He also goes on to say that there was another group with the same name who did not deny that the Lord was born of a virgin and the Holy Spirit, and nevertheless agreed in not confessing his preexistence or being the Logos and Wisdom, but like the other Ebionites they "were zealous on the literal observance of the Law." It appears that both groups rejected Paul and his letters, read only the *Gospel according to the Hebrews*, and like the other Jewish or Judaizing sects observed "the sabbath and the rest of the Jewish ceremonial, but on Sundays celebrated rites like ours in commemoration of the Savior's resurrection." Eusebius sarcastically concludes that the Ebionites obtained their (deserved?) name because of "the poverty of their intelligence, for the name means 'poor' in Hebrew" (*Hist. eccl.* 3.27.3–6, LCL trans.).

Ehrman suggests that the Ebionites took their name because they chose to follow the early church example of selling their property and giving it to the poor (e.g., Acts 2:44–25; 4:32–37), making the givers of their property "voluntary poor" individuals (Ehrman 2003: 99–100). He refers to a sect of early Jewish followers of Jesus who did not agree with the emerging proto-orthodoxy of Paul and Hellenistic Christianity but who mostly lived in the east side of the Jordan River (after the death of James) and identified Jesus not as divine but rather as the human son of Joseph and Mary. They believed that the Holy Spirit descended on him at his baptism, and he perfectly kept the Law. They rejected the letters of Paul because of his rejection of circumcision for Gentiles and their keeping of the Law. They perhaps appealed to an earlier form of the Gospel of Matthew (Aramaic?) that may be an apocryphal Gospel by another name (Irenaeus, *Haer.* 1.26.2 and 3.11.7). The so-called *Gospel according to the Ebionites* that they read may be an earlier form of the Gospel of Matthew instead of an apocryphal Gospel like the Gospel of Matthew without its first two chapters that focus on Jesus' virgin birth. It appears that the Ebionites did not accept the virgin birth of Jesus or his divinity but did accept his messiahship as well as the belief that he died for the sins of humanity and was raised from the dead (Ehrman 2003: 99–103). Eusebius says the Ebionites made use of the *Gospel of the Hebrews* (Eusebius, *Hist. eccl.* 3.27.4).

Little is known of the Ebionites until the fourth or early fifth centuries and what we know then comes mostly from their opponents. The primary sources about them are from Eusebius (just cited) and Epiphanius of Cyprus in the late fourth and early fifth century (*Haer.* 30). Since their story was told by the "winners" of the ancient debates and not by the Ebionites themselves, it is unfortunate that we do not have their own representatives telling their story. Epiphanius, like Eusebius, indicates that they used the *Gospel of the Hebrews*. As noted above, it is likely that they emerged from the earlier group of Jewish Christians sometimes called the "Nazarenes." The identity of Jesus was certainly a major issue that divided them from some other early Jewish-Christian followers of Jesus, like Paul, who followed the proto-orthodoxy emerging in the first century. In the first and second centuries there were several positions on the identity of Jesus circulating in the churches, for example, whether he was a spirit and not fully human (Docetism), or that he was fully human but divinely inspired (Ebionite), or that he was both divine and human (proto-orthodox), and so on. They may have anticipated the doctrine of the so-called "adoptionists" who claimed that God adopted Jesus as his son at his baptism (Mark 1:11; Luke 3:21–22; Matt 3:16–17) and at his transfiguration (Mark 9:7; Luke 9:35; Matt 17:5). For a more detailed summary of their story and the multiple sects of Christianity, see David Antony (2016: 14–19).

The Jewish followers of Jesus were not all the same, and we see references to them in several early church fathers often by different names that suggest that there were several Jewish-Christian sects, for example, the "Nazarenes" (Jerome, *Esaiam* 8.11–15; 9.1; 11.1–3; 29.17–21; 31.6–9), "Ebionites" (Irenaeus, *Haer.* 1.26.2; 3.21.1; 3.33.4; Tertullian, *De Praesc.* 32.3–5; Hippolytus, *Ref.* 7.34.12; 7.35.1–2), "Cerinthians" (Irenaeus, *Haer.* 1.26.1–2; 3.3.4; Hippolytus, *Ref. Prol.* 7.7–9; 7.33.1–2; Epiphanius, *Pan.* 28.1.3; 2.3; 4.1–2), "Symmachians" (Origen, *in Matt.* 16.16; Eusebius, *Hist. eccl.* 6.17; Ambrosiaster, *ad Gal. Prol.*), and "Elkesaites" (Hippolytus, *Ref.* 9.13.2–3; 9.15.2; 9.17.2). Of these only the first two are considered primarily Jewish-Christian sects with some teachings in common with the later proto-orthodox Christian positions advocated by Paul, but not accepting Paul's letters because of his advocacy of Gentile freedom from the Law.

B. Marcionites

Marcion (active *c.* 140–160), a wealthy shipowner and native of Sinope in Pontus, was like many of his contemporaries who recognized the importance of several authoritative Christian writings to be read in his churches (Barton 2002: 341–54; Lieu: 2015: 17–25). His primary concern was to eliminate Jewish influences in the churches, including their first scriptures and references to the God of the Jews whom he thought was evil. He selected a limited collection of Christian writings that he edited to define more clearly his Gospel and eliminate Jewish influences. It is not clear that Marcion called these writings (Luke and ten letters of Paul) "scripture," though the writings he selected most likely functioned that way for him and his followers. The church at large did not respond to Marcion with a longer biblical canon but rather with its rule of faith (*regula fidei* noted earlier) that had its roots in the traditions passed on in the churches by those closest to Jesus. Marcion imitated the familiar Gospel-apostle tradition that was circulating in the churches. Von Campenhausen (1972: 153) suggests that Marcion created the Gospel-apostle form that was later adopted by the broader church, but this conclusion is neither required nor even likely. The Gospel-apostle order more likely grew out of the church's recognition of its threefold canon of authority—Law, Gospel (= Jesus), and apostle that was well attested before the time of Marcion.

Marcion, however, is best known for three important positions related to the scriptures and God: (1) he rejected the Jewish scriptures concluding that they could only be made relevant to the church by allegorizing them, an interpretive methodology that he rejected; (2) he denied that the God of the Jews was the same as the loving and unknown God of Jesus; and (3) he limited his collection of readable Christian writings to an edited version of the Gospel of Luke and ten letters of Paul. His followers did not follow Marcion's collection only but occasionally cited the Gospel of Matthew and other Christian writings besides. Raymond Collins suggests that Marcion was one of the first persons to call one of the canonical Gospels a "Gospel." Marcion apparently assumed that when Paul spoke of "his Gospel" he was referring to the Gospel of Luke. Collins argues that Marcion evidently presumed that Paul had in mind a written source, so he set out to restore it by cutting out the Jewish elements in it that were offensive to him (1983: 22). However, "Gospel" is found earlier in the *Didache* ("as the Lord commanded *in his gospel*"— ὡς ἐκέλευσεν ὁ κύριος ἐν τῷ εὐαγγελίῳ αὐτοῦ, *Did.* 8.2), an obvious reference to Matt 6:5.

Marcion's primary aim was the separation of Christian tradition from its Jewish heritage and its origin in Judaism. We have no indication *from Marcion* that he called the writings of Paul and Luke sacred "scripture," but they appear to have functioned that way in the communities he founded. He freely deleted from his truncated collection all references to the Jewish scriptures. Bishop Epiphanius of Salamis (315–403) identifies the specific books in Marcion's collection as follows:

> Such is Marcion's spurious composition, which contains the text and wording of Luke's gospel and the incomplete writings of the apostle Paul, meaning not all of his letters, but only Romans, Colossians, Laodiceans,[2] Galatians, First and Second Corinthians, First and Second Thessalonians, Philemon, and Philippians. But he includes none of First and Second Timothy, Titus, and Hebrews [and even?] those he includes [are mutilated?], so that they are not complete, but are as though corrupted. (*Pan.* 11.9–11; trans. by Hultgren and Haggmark 1996: 115)

Epiphanius, like Tertullian before him (see *Marc.* 3.473–475), criticized Marcion for something that was not unique to Marcion, namely cutting out texts from Christian writings and inserting something else. That was common in ancient Judaism as well as in early Christianity. There are multiple examples of that practice in the surviving NT manuscripts such as in Matthew's and Luke's corrections and changes of the Markan text, but also the insertions in the NT manuscripts as in John 3:13b, the *Johannine Comma* in 1 John 5:7–8, John 7:53–8:1–11; and the multiple additions or insertions after Phil 3:1b, Mark 16:9–20, and insertions of two more sections in 2 Corinthians (8:1–9:13). The point here is not that Marcion did something new or unheard of but only that he added or deleted those things that Tertullian and Epiphanius did not like.

Many consider it strange that Marcion did not include the Pastoral Epistles or Hebrews, but perhaps he simply did not know about them or that he, like others, was unconvinced

---

[2] Some scholars are convinced that "Laodiceans" is a reference to what we now know as Paul's letter to the Ephesians. The designation in Ephesus (Greek = *en epheso*) in Eph 1:1 is missing from the earliest manuscripts of that letter, and it is unlikely that it was sent to Ephesus alone since Paul had been there and knew some of the people in that church, but the letter does not reflect Paul's knowledge of the Ephesians.

of their Pauline authorship. As many scholars know, the Pastoral letters are also missing from P[46], the earliest manuscript collection of Paul's letters, and are also missing in *Codex Vaticanus* (c. 350–375),[3] and since they are not frequently cited by church fathers before the late second and third centuries, not much can presently be made of their omission in Marcion. Their absence in Marcion's collection may be because they did not exist in their current form when he wrote, or that their contents did not meet his criteria for inclusion. Tertullian claims that Marcion specifically rejected them because he rejected writings *to a person* rather than to the whole church and therefore excluded 1 and 2 Timothy and Titus, but this does not account for his inclusion of Philemon. He concludes this was because "all treat of ecclesiastical discipline. His aim, I suppose, was to carry out his interpolating process even to the number of (St. Paul's) letters" (*Marc.* 3.473–475). It is also possible Marcion was unfamiliar with many books that later became the church's NT canon though that is uncertain. Again, his later followers sometimes cited other NT texts, including the Gospel of Matthew.

There was no canonical list of books circulating in churches during Marcion's lifetime. Also, because Hebrews included so many citations of the Jewish scriptures, he simply dismissed it. This is guesswork, of course, since we have no surviving source from Marcion himself to determine what might be true here, but we know that the Gospel of Luke in Marcion's collection is shorter than other versions of it and is missing the birth of Jesus story, the only known version of Luke without a birth story, and that it begins at Luke 4:1. Whether he was aware of any other letters attributed to Paul or the other NT writings is debatable, though, given the popularity of the Gospel of Matthew in the second century, he was likely familiar with it and his later followers certainly knew this Gospel and often cited it, as we will see below.

Marcion knew that the Jewish scriptures and several NT texts told of God's creation of the world, but he rejected that and taught that the "god" who created the world was also a *Demiurge*[4] who was both vengeful and evil. He encouraged his followers to read the Jewish scriptures so they would know their incompatibility with Christian teaching, and unlike widespread Christian practice in the second century, he rejected the spiritualizing or allegorizing of the Jewish scriptures to make them relevant and compatible to the Christian community. In the ancient world, allegorizing ancient texts was a recognition of their sacredness. Barton observes that allegorizing a text was "the characteristic mark of a holy text in the ancient world" (1997: 61). He adds that Origen's defense against Marcion is enhanced by the comments of Celsus, the foremost critic of early Christianity, who despised the unsophisticated Christians; nevertheless, Celsus acknowledged positively that among them there were "intelligent people who readily interpret allegorically" (*Contra Celsus* 1.23; see Barton 1997: 53–5 and Barton 2002: 349). Celsus saw the use of allegory as a sign of sophistication.

---

[3]Because *Codex Vaticanus* ends in the middle of Heb 9:24 and is a fragmented text, the absence of the Pastorals, Philemon, and Revelation may have been included originally, but that is unclear. *Codex Sinaiticus* and *Codex Alexandrinus* do include the Pastorals following Hebrews, so it is possible they were originally included in *Vaticanus*.

[4]"*Demiurge*" or "craftsman" (Gk. *dēmiourgos*) is Plato's term for the inferior creator of the universe. In the second and third centuries CE, the creator-god was also referred to by some gnostics as "Ialdabaoth," a nonspiritual being (Layton 1987: 12–16). Ptolemy, head of the Valentinian gnostic school in the second century, claimed that the Demiurge was an angel, the parent of all animate things, who was the God of Israel and *ordinary* Christians (Layton 1987:: 279).

Marcion's rejection of the Hebrew writings as scripture supported his belief that Christianity was something completely new. He stressed that the God of the Law was a *Demiurge*, a creator-god like the creator-god discussed in Gnosticism (King 2003a; Perkins 1980; Wink 1993). Because he believed that the God of the OT was not the same as the unknown God of Jesus, he argued for a separation of Christianity from its Jewish roots and influences. He appears to have rejected all Jewish influences on the early Christian proclamation, but acknowledged that Jesus and Paul were Jews. Marcion's rejection of Jewish teachings may have stemmed from the current anti-Jewish sentiment that was widespread in the Roman Empire following the Jewish Bar Kochba rebellion against Rome in Palestine (132–135 CE).

According to Harnack and others after him, Marcion established "the first biblical canon" and church leaders subsequently responded to his challenge first by excommunicating Marcion and then by establishing a larger collection of Christian scriptures that they now called their NT and reemphasized their acceptance of the Jewish scriptures (Harnack 1908). This view was popular in academic circles throughout most of the last century and it still has some adherents, but some now acknowledge that Marcion's purpose was not so much an insight into the value of a limited number of NT writings or even to establish a biblical canon (Barton 1997: 34–62). Rather, Marcion believed that the Christian Gospel was absolute love that was contrary to what he believed was the legalistic and oppressive law of the Jewish scriptures that was taught by the early church's leaders in Jerusalem, especially Peter and James.

Marcion wrote the mostly lost *Antitheses* that is partially reconstructed by Tertullian and through ancient citations of it that supported his rejection of the OT and his limited NT Prologues to Luke and ten letters of Paul (e.g., see Theron 1980: 79–83; Lieu 2015: 172–89). The *Antitheses* was essentially Marcion's doctrinal handbook arguing for the incompatibility of the Jews' Law and the church's Gospel and for an understanding of Marcion's Gospel. He believed that Judaism heavily influenced Peter and James and that only Paul adequately separated himself from it. BeDuhn offers valuable information about Marcion's collection of Christian writings and some of the implications from that collection (2013: 203–59).

Earlier scholars accused Marcion of being a gnostic Christian, or at least that he was heavily influenced by them, and it appears that he borrowed the name of the evil god of creation from the gnostic community, but he may not have been a gnostic Christian. Irenaeus identifies Marcion as a gnostic claiming that the gnostic Cerdo took his system of philosophy from the followers of Simon Magus (Acts 8:9–24) and that "Marcion of Pontus succeeded him [Cerdo] and developed his doctrine" (*Haer.* 1.27.1), but unlike several of the Gnostics, Marcion rejected *all* the Jewish scriptures and all allegorical interpretations of them. He avoided any focus on secret knowledge and had little sympathy for the mythological speculations that were characteristic of the Christian gnostic movement. He apparently was also something of an ascetic and taught sexual abstinence. According to Eusebius, "The so-called Encratites proceeding from Saturninus and Marcion preached against marriage, annulling the original creation of God, and tacitly condemning him who made male and female" (Eusebius, *Hist. eccl.* 4.29.1–2, LCL).

It has been speculated that Marcion's churches outnumbered, or at least equaled, those of the orthodox Christians in the mid-second century, but whether true or not, his influence can be seen in the large number of important orthodox church teachers who attacked his views at the end of the second century and well into the fifth century (Justin, Irenaeus, Hippolytus of Rome, Clement of Alexandria, Tertullian, Origen, Eusebius, Epiphanius, and Cyril of Jerusalem). Since all of Marcion's works have been lost or more likely destroyed, we are dependent on his opponents to reconstruct his views and activities. Fortunately, they appear to be consistent with each other in much of how they describe him and his followers, but, as in all anti-heretical literature of ancient times, his orthodox opponents also make *ad hominem* attacks against him. The "winners" in history always write the books about the "losers."

Tertullian's criticisms of Marcion are included in his *The Five Books against Marcion* (c. 190–200). Those books show not only the difficulty that the church fathers had in answering Marcion's teachings but also his significant influence in many churches for a considerable period. Marcion's excommunication from the churches in Rome and elsewhere resulted in many strong criticisms of him by multiple church fathers even long after his death. Commenting on Marcion's two best known teachings, Tertullian states,

> Marcion's special and principal work is the separation of the law and the gospel; and his disciples will not deny that in this point they have their very best pretext for initiating and confirming themselves in his heresy. These are Marcion's *Antitheses*, or contradictory propositions, which aim at distinguishing the gospel from the law in order that from the diversity of the two documents[5] that contains them, they may contend for a diversity of gods also. (*Marc.* 1.19, adapted from ANF)

He later adds that "Marcion expressly and openly used the knife, not the pen, since he made such an excision of the Scriptures as suited his own subject matter" (*Praescr.* 38.7, ANF). More specifically, Tertullian mentions Marcion's process of excising the Jewish elements from Luke: "Now, of the authors whom we possess, Marcion seems to have singled out Luke for his mutilating process" (*Marc.* 4.2, ANF). He also comments on Marcion's editorial work on Paul's Epistles: "As our heretic is so fond of his pruning knife, I do not wonder when syllables are expunged by his hand, seeing that entire pages are usually the matter on which he practices his effacing process" (*Marc.* 5.18.1, ANF). Tertullian offers multiple examples of this "effacing process" in Ephesians (= "Laodiceans"), that he (and evidently Marcion) believed was written by Paul (*Marc.* 5.16–18). Later notions of inviolable scripture were obviously not present when Marcion was active. His cutting what he did not like from Luke's and Paul's writings is incompatible with later notions of scripture. According to Tertullian, Marcion added nothing new to these documents except perhaps his prologues. For a useful collection of the Marcionite *Prologues*, see Theron (1980: 78–83). Had Marcion accepted Luke and Paul's letters as scripture in the sense that it was later understood, it is hard to reconcile his mutilation of that literature with such notions of the inviolability of scripture. For more discussion of this, see Dahl (1978: 233–77). Whether Marcion himself produced all of the prologues attributed to him is debated, but they were friendly to his positions and most likely came from the later second or third century. It may be that the church fathers responded to these prologues by producing their own (see Grant 1941: 231–45), such as Jerome who produced his own Gospel prologues (Theron 1980: 51–5).

As late as the fifth century, Cyril of Jerusalem warned his parishioners to avoid Marcionite churches (see Clabeaux 1992: 4:520–1) and attacked Marcion as "that mouthpiece of ungodliness" and the "second inventor of more mischief" (Simon Magus of Acts 8 being the first). He writes,

---

[5] He does not specifically identify the "two documents," but they are likely a reference to the Gospel tradition that Marcion espoused and the Jewish scriptures or even Judaism itself.

> Being confuted by the testimonies from the Old Testament which are quoted in the New, he [Marcion] was the first who dared to cut those testimonies out and leave the preaching of the word of faith without witness, thus effacing the true God: and sought to undermine the Church's faith, as if there were no heralds of it. (*Catechetical Lectures* 6.16, NPNF)

Perhaps more clearly than others of his day, Marcion recognized the difficulty of a literal interpretation of the Hebrew scriptures for the early church. Paul himself spoke of the inability of the legal aspects of the law to bring persons into a right relationship with God and denied works of righteousness (or keeping the law) as a means of attaining salvation (Gal 3–4; Rom 4:5). Marcion believed that this supported his rejection of the law. He also argued that the God of the Jewish scriptures was harsh, even cruel, and especially vengeful and changeable. The moral standard of an "eye for an eye" was hard for him to reconcile with Jesus' call to "turn the other cheek" and to love one's enemies (e.g., Matt 5:38–48). Marcion said the Jewish scriptures were no longer binding on Christians. This was especially true of the legal and moral codes and traditions associated with keeping the law. Taking his cue from Paul, he argued that Christians are free from the law and, therefore, have no reason to give allegiance to that which has been rendered obsolete by faith in Jesus Christ.

Barton concludes that Marcion was important for two reasons: he rejected the OT, viewing it as the document of an alien religion, and he saw the role of Jesus as one who would deliver those in bondage from the evil creator-god of the OT (Barton 2002: 354). Marcion concluded that only by the *arbitrary* means of interpreting by allegory or typology, that is sometimes known as *pesher* exegesis, could Jewish scriptures have the slightest camouflaged meaning at all (Campenhausen 1972: 148–74). Marcion's rejection of the OT writings, together with his use of a literal hermeneutical approach for interpreting it, stripped the church not only of its first scriptures but also of its prized claim to the heritage of Israel's antiquity and to being the religion of historical fulfillment (Campenhausen 1972: 151).

Because others made use of a limited collection of Christian writings (Luke or Matthew using Mark), Marcion thought that he was doing nothing unlike what other Christians before him had done, namely, adopting a particular Gospel, the Gospel of Luke, and welcoming besides several letters from Paul. It is unlikely that any first-century churches possessed all of the canonical Gospels, and most probably only had one of them and a few of the Pauline letters at best and perhaps one or more of the Catholic Epistles (perhaps 1 Peter and 1 John) and possibly Acts; but there is no evidence that any first- or second-century church possessed all of the NT writings. Marcion evidently acknowledged the value of the Gospel-apostle traditions in the church, but that is not why he was criticized.

Barton rightly concludes that Marcion was not responsible for other Christians adopting the NT in response to him, but rather was responsible "for their retaining the Old Testament." He argues that "Marcion was not a major influence on the formation of the New Testament; he was simply a Marcionite" (Barton 2002: 350, 354). Marcion's apparent rejection of some of the NT writings and all the Jewish scriptures suggests that some of those NT writings were already functioning authoritatively in some churches though not all of them, or that they were not yet viewed as Christian scripture. Harnack's argument was that objections to Marcion led the church to establish a NT canon, but remarkably none of his many second-century critics accused him of seeking to establish a fixed scripture collection or a Christian NT scripture. Although Marcion advanced the use of some Christian writings in his churches, that is not the same as inventing a biblical canon. Had he intended that, it is amazing that not even his followers followed his example since they cited and interpreted Christian literature from more than Luke and Paul. Hahneman has shown that later Marcionites welcomed verses from the other Gospels observing that Ephraem Syrus claimed that Marcionites had not rejected Matt 23:8 and that Adamantius (early fourth century) in his five-volume dialogue, *De recta in Deum fide*, claimed that the Marcionites quoted John 13:34 and 15:19 and corrupted Matt 5:17. Origen even quotes a Marcionite interpretation of Matt 19:12 (Hahneman 1992: 91). Hahneman adds further that the Armenian Marcionites appear also to have received Tatian's *Diatessaron* (Hahneman 1992: 92–3; see also Cassey 1938).

We cannot be certain that Marcion had access to all four canonical Gospels since even his contemporary, Papias, refers only to Matthew and Mark. It is probable that Marcion was at least aware of the Gospel of Matthew since his followers made use of it. Matthew was the most cited Gospel along with the Gospel of John in the second century when Marcion lived. It is also doubtful that Marcion's collection of letters of Paul was the first collection of Pauline Epistles, as some have suggested. In fact, it makes more sense to assume that his collection was possible only because churches before him had made use of a collection of Paul's writings that had circulated in churches before him (Col 4:16 should not be considered an isolated case). Dahl contends that a ten-letter Pauline corpus was available before the time of Marcion and that he simply made use of it and edited it (Dahl 1978). That makes more sense.

Marcion's rejection of Judaism can be seen in his (or his followers') prologues to the Epistles of Paul, which survive only in Medieval Latin Vulgate manuscripts. It is not clear how they managed to be included among the prologues to the scriptures of the orthodox community, but they are indicative of what is known of Marcion's or his followers' feelings toward those with Judaizing tendencies in the church. The following prologues to Paul's letters to Romans, 1 Corinthians, and Titus are not all of the prologues but are representative of this line of thought.

> The Romans "live" in the regions of Italy. False apostles had reached them beforehand, and under the name of our Lord Jesus Christ they were misled into the Law and the Prophets. The apostle [Paul], writing to them from Corinth, calls them back to the true evangelical faith.

> The Corinthians are Achaeans. And they similarly heard the word of truth from the Apostles, but they were subverted in many ways by false apostles—some were misled by verbose eloquence of philosophy, others by a sect of the Jewish law. [Paul], writing to them from Ephesus by Timothy, calls them back to the truth and evangelical wisdom.

> He [Paul] reminds and instructs Titus concerning the constitution of a presbytery and concerning spiritual walk and heretics who believe in Jewish books [Hebrew scriptures], and who must be avoided. (Cited in Theron 1980: 79–83)

Marcion undoubtedly was an important catalyst that led multiple second-century church fathers to respond strongly to his rejection of their first scriptures. He may have also led the church to affirm more NT writings than he was willing to accept, but this does not mean that he or anyone else in the second century had a fixed collection of scriptures in view. All evidence for that position is inferential and considerably later. In the surviving second- and third-century documents, there was never a time when the Gospel of Luke was cited more than the Gospel of Matthew. Marcion may have been responsible for spurring the church to make clearer that it prized its inherited Jewish scriptures as well as its Christian writings, but that was not his intention. The church fathers responded to Marcion with a more precise canon of faith (its *regula fidei*), namely the reiteration of the traditions of faith that had been passed on to the churches by the apostles and the succeeding bishops from the church's beginning. The multiple reactions to Marcion were intended to make clear a prior commitment to the Jewish scriptures, that the God of the Jews was also the God of Jesus. Marcion appears to be an interesting counterpart to the Ebionites, who, according to Irenaeus, "use the Gospel according to Matthew only, and repudiate the Apostle Paul, maintaining that he was an apostate from the Law" (*Haer.* 1.26.2, ANF).

It is often argued that Marcion constructed the first *known* list of Christian scriptures with the aim of separating Christianity from its Jewish/Judaism roots (Frend 1984: 212–17), but the proto-orthodox churches continued to affirm their acceptance of the Jewish scriptures. Interestingly, Marcion's followers both felt free to edit his work and to recognize a different collection of sacred texts that included Matthew. It is important to note that for Marcion's followers his collection of Luke and ten Pauline letters did not mean a fixed catalogue (canon) of scriptures to which nothing could be added or taken away (Hahneman 1992: 92).

C. Gnostics and Gnosticism

One of the most influential heresies of the second century is commonly known as Gnostic Christianity. What the adherents of this group (or groups) of Christians taught or espoused is usually identified as "Gnosticism." The term *gnostic* derives from the Greek *gnōstikos* (γνωστικός = "cognitive" or "capable of discerning") that has ancient roots stemming from the word *gnōsis* (Greek = γνῶσις, "knowing" or "knowledge"), suggesting something like "capable of attaining knowledge," but this notion of *gnōstikos* was rare among the Greeks. The designation came to refer to disciplines of study that suggested something along the lines of that which "leads to knowledge" as in the famous dictum "know yourself." The Greeks themselves did not speak of gnostics as those who pursued a particular form of knowledge for religious purposes. The term *gnostic* appears to have become a later designation attached to gnostic adherents by their opponents and appears interchangeable with the word heresy.

Although the term "gnostic" eventually became associated with the ancient and highly diverse systems of thought in second-century Christianity, we do not know the precise origin or date of such views, or even with certainty the circumstances that gave rise to it. In antiquity it was common to conclude that Simon Magus (Acts 8:9–24) was the founder of this community and all heresy in the churches, but this is more ancient lore than factually based information. In the fifth century, for example, Cyril of Jerusalem states that "the inventor of all heresy was Simon Magus: that Simon, who in the Acts of the Apostles, thought to purchase with money the unsalable grace of the Spirit" (*Catechetical Lectures* 6.14, NPNF). Those drawn to this group were generally better educated than most, had little hope for the world improving (much like the Jewish apocalyptic writers), and produced a considerable amount of esoteric literature that generally denigrated the created world and focused on self-awareness (Leyton 1987: 5–9).

Although there is much that is not known about the communities that were identified as gnostic Christians, there are some things about them that are known both from their opponents and from their own writings. We can say for certain that in the second century, a significant community of gnostic Christians emerged with a system (or several systems) of thought that challenged the basic underlying beliefs of traditional Christianity. Adherents of this new philosophy were labeled "gnostics" in subsequent generations (and especially in the modern era), and what they taught or believed is now called "Gnosticism." They apparently flourished throughout the second and third centuries and continued to have adherents much longer than that in some areas (e.g., the Mandeans in the East) (see Lupieri 2002). They produced a vast amount of literature, and apparently were not interested in any fixed collection of Christian scriptures. Much of their literature is allegorical or spiritual interpretations of the OT and NT scriptures, including pseudonymous writings attributed to biblical figures. *It may be* that they drew selectively from various Jewish and Christian writings, and their own writings were viewed as supplements to these for the sake of dialogue and clarification of the meaning of the former texts.

With the discovery of nearly fifty gnostic documents at Nag Hammadi, Egypt, in 1945, scholars were able for the first time to see direct information about the gnostic community in their own writings and expressing their own perspectives (for helpful translations of these works, see Layton 1987; Robinson 1990; Meyer 2007). Before that discovery, scholarship was solely dependent upon the opponents of Gnosticism—namely, proto-orthodox and later orthodox Christians. The orthodox Christians defined gnostics in polemical contexts as heretics, especially Irenaeus, who leveled severe attacks against them in book 1 of his *Against Heresies*. Remarkably, Irenaeus's collection of charges against the Gnostics are consistent with what is found in gnostic literature itself. With the discovery of the Nag Hammadi gnostic documents, which originally came from outside of Egypt and were later translated into Coptic, it is now possible to view gnostic Christianity from a gnostic perspective from around the mid-fourth century and even before.

It is difficult to date the origins of gnostic belief and even more difficult to define or identify its adherents with a scheme of beliefs and practices. It is also a challenge to identify all of the characteristics attributed to them from an examination of their writings. There were apparently a variety of views and practices among gnostic sects. Irenaeus, for example, criticizes the heretical teachings of Marcion, Tatian, Saturninus, and Valentinus because, he claims, they formed "one set of doctrines out of totally different systems of opinions, and then again others from others, they insist upon teaching something new, declaring themselves the inventors of any sort of opinion which they may have been able to call into existence" (*Haer.* 1.28.1, ANF). After criticizing these individuals, he goes on to say, "besides those, however, among these heretics who are Simonians [supposed followers of Simon Magus], and of whom we have already spoken, *a multitude of Gnostics have sprung up, and have been manifested like mushrooms growing out of the ground*" (*Haer.* 1.29.1, ANF, emphasis added).

Gnostic Christians apparently included in their systems of thought an amalgamation of several theological and philosophical perspectives circulating in antiquity, including those of Iranian Zoroastrian theology, Jewish apocalypticism, Platonism, Hellenistic philosophy, and various elements of early Christianity, especially the notion of Jesus as redeemer. They saw themselves as Christians, that is, members of the greater church, but tended to have an elitist perspective of themselves believing that while other

Christians had a place in the family of God, they themselves had a higher standing because of their greater knowledge. They rejected all political and religious institutions and the values, authorities, and most of the moral codes connected to those religious institutions. Some gnostic Christians became ascetics, and others were antinomian. Some rejected marriage and the pursuit of physical pleasure, while others entertained numerous spouses and sexual partners and embraced physical pleasures. Their adherents stretched from western Persia (now Iraq) in the east, to Lyon, France, in the west, and from Egypt in the south to Ancyra (now Ankara, Turkey) and Satala (in Asia Minor) in the north. Although we now have a valuable collection of their literature, it is not a complete collection, and we are not yet certain about its date or the provenance. Where their literature was found does not indicate where it was written. Scholars have suggested dates for the gnostics ranging from roughly 10 BCE to the death of Plotinus the Neoplatonist in 270 CE.

Wink suggests that the key to understanding the diversity within this large gnostic community is their understanding of the "powers," that is, "the social structures of reality, political systems, [and] human institutions such as the family or religion" (Wink 1993: vii, 17). Gnostics demonized all of these powers or institutions, believing that none of them will be saved from final destruction. Wink also observes that in gnostic thought salvation is not deliverance from personal sin, since that is based on imposed moral codes that the gnostics rejected, but rather on deliverance from the powers of the social and religious institutions that enslave. He claims that they emphasized that a "waking up" (special *gnosis*) is needed (cf. 1 Thess 5:5–7) to find deliverance from such evils. The author of the gnostic *Gospel of Philip*, for instance, appeals to readers to recognize the root of evil (i.e., the powers), so they can be destroyed and have no power over them:

> Let each of us dig down after the root of evil that is within us and let us pluck it out of our hearts from the root. It will be plucked out if we recognize it. But if we are ignorant of it, it takes root in us and produces its fruit in our heart. It masters us. We are its slaves. It takes us captive, to make us do what we do not want; and what we do want we do not do. It is powerful because we have not recognized it. While it exists, it is active. (*Gospel of Philip* 83.18–30; adapted from Wink 1993: 37)

Wink claims that the gnostic enterprise is both similar and contrary to what the NT teaches noting,

> gnosticism taught escape from a world imprisoned under tyranny of evil powers. The New Testament teaches liberation from the tyranny of evil powers in order to recover a lost unity with the created world. This world is not only the sphere of alienated existence, but also the object of God's redemptive love. Therefore we are not to flee the world, but to recall it to its Source. (Wink 1993: 52)

Gnostic Christians generally believed that there was a divine spark (Spirit) from God in humanity and that it was their goal through special knowledge to be restored to God through the work of a redeemer, Jesus, who removed ignorance and restored self-knowledge to those who were spiritual (Grant 1961: 16). Despite this common understanding, scholars of this ancient phenomenon generally agree that they have yet to find a satisfactory definition that fits all traces of Gnosticism in antiquity, or even find a convenient term for its literature. Karen King provides an informed evaluation of this religious movement (King 2003a: 5–19 and 2003b; see also Jonas 1963; Rudolph 1983; and Perkins 2002: 355–71: 355; Layton 1987; Logan 1996). Although there is little agreement on a meaningful and accurate definition of Gnosticism, scholars continue to use "Gnostic" since there is little else to put in its place.

By way of summary, *generally speaking*, (1) gnostic Christians denied that the Christian God, the God of Jesus, was also the creator of the world. For them, matter was evil and was created by a Demiurge, an evil and distant emanation from the *plērōma* ("fullness") of the divine. In this they were similar to the Marcionites. (2) They often rejected the Jewish (Hebrew Bible [HB]/LXX) scriptures but not uniformly. Unlike Marcion, they often allegorized them to find meaning for Christian faith, for example, as in Ptolemy's *Letter to Flora* that cites favorably several OT texts but rejects others and instructs Flora on how to interpret them. (3) They distinguished the heavenly Savior/Redeemer from the human Jesus of Nazareth, a teaching not unlike various earlier Docetic teachings that claimed that Jesus only "seemed" or "appeared" to be human, but he was not human. This teaching, as noted above, is what stands behind the condemnation in 1 John 4:2 and it is condemned especially more frequently in the *Letters* of Ignatius (e.g., Ign. *Eph.* 7.1–2; *Trall.* 10.1; *Smyrn.* 2.1). (4) The gnostic Christians also believed that *full* salvation was only for the pneumatics or spiritually elite (themselves), but that a lesser degree of salvation could be obtained by those who only have faith without special *gnōsis*. Those completely involved in the world, however, had no hope of salvation. (5) They also claimed that they had received secret Gospels from the apostles themselves.

The esoteric writings of the gnostics, along with their claims to secret revelations from the apostles, were rejected by the proto-orthodox church fathers and especially Irenaeus, who argued instead for the legitimacy of the Christian truth and its tradition, or rule of faith (*regula fidei*). He contends that this tradition was passed on in the church by apostolic succession through its bishops. He explains, "For if the apostles had known hidden mysteries, which they were in the habit of imparting to 'the perfect' apart and privately from the rest, they would have delivered them especially to those to whom they were also committing the leadership of the churches themselves" (*Haer.* 3.3.1, adapted from ANF). One can scarcely challenge Irenaeus's logic here.

In his highly influential volume, *The Mission and Expansion of Christianity in the First Three Centuries* (1914), Adolf von Harnack cited the following passage from Tertullian (*c.* 200) criticizing the gnostics:

> What shall I say about the ministry of the word? Their [the heretics'] concern is not to convert the heathen, but to subvert our folk [orthodox Christians]. The glory they seek comes from bringing the upright down, not raising the fallen up. Since their work results from no constructive operations of their own, but from the destruction of the truth, they undermine our constructions to build their own. Take their complaints against the Law of Moses and the prophets and God the Creator away from them, and they have nothing to say. So it comes about that they find it easier to pull down standing buildings than to build up the fallen ruins. (*Praescr. Haer.* 42)

King contends that while Tertullian's claim and assertion carried the day against the Gnostic Christians, and despite Harnack citing him with approval, she rejects that assessment of the gnostics and has selected three important gnostic texts, namely, *The Epistle of Peter to Philip*, *The Apocryphon of James*, and *The Gospel of Mary*, to show how each of them demonstrates a commitment to mission and preaching the Gospel even knowing that they will suffer as Christ did in pursuing that same mission. She also shows how the history of the winners (orthodoxy) is always the last written word about the losers (Gnosticism), but that such histories are not always an accurate portrayal of the losers. As support for this she cites multiple reflections of early non-orthodox Christian texts well into the fourth and fifth centuries (King 2003a and 2013: 441–55).

It is appropriate to ask, as many have, whether such writings prompted the proto-orthodox Christians to distinguish the church's earliest Christian writings from the Gnostic writings and call the former a NT canon and the latter a heresy. In their confrontation with the gnostic Christians, did the proto-orthodox decide that the best way to deal with gnostics was to decide which Christian writings were sacred and which were not? There is nothing in the second and third centuries that suggests that was the case. Did the gnostics consider what they wrote as sacred scripture and binding upon their readers? Again, we have no evidence that allows us to draw that conclusion. Perkins concludes that the gnostics "never set up individuals as heroes of the divine" and did not observe the ecclesiastical structures that began to develop in the second and third centuries of the church (Perkins 1980 and 2002: 355–71). According to her, Irenaeus accused the gnostic Christians of saying that the scriptures were incorrect, that they were not authoritative, that they were ambiguous, and that the truth cannot be discovered by someone who is ignorant of their truth (*Haer.* 3.2.1). Perkins challenges a common notion that gnostic Christians and orthodox Christians had dueling scripture canons. She surveys the major texts that reflect the primary notions of Gnosticism that promulgate gnostic views and how they interpret several familiar OT texts and provides three helpful tables showing references in the Nag Hammadi library to various OT texts, Pauline Epistles, and the canonical Gospels. Genesis appears to be the most frequently cited OT book by the Gnostic Christians, but also Second Isaiah. Most references to the NT literature come from Matthew and John (Perkins 2002: 368–9). Generally, however, Perkins acknowledges that although these works were cited, there was "little engagement" with them (Perkins 1980: 199–200).

Perkins further challenges the tendency among scholars to assume that the gnostic Christians simply "followed the orthodox canon with one of their own." She concludes, "It should be apparent by now that nothing could be farther from the truth. These Gnostic writings reflect the liturgy, teaching, preaching and polemic of their respective communities. But they never claim to do more than to embody true tradition." Perkins concludes that the gnostics did not have a normative text that gave them the limits of their theological reflection (Perkins 1980: 201–2), or that "gnostic exegetes were only interested in elaborating their mythic and theological speculations concerning the origins of the universe, not in appropriating a received canonical tradition," and finally she concludes that "hermeneutics, not canon formation, is the central point at issue between Irenaeus and his Valentinian opponents" (Perkins 2002: 371).

Did the Gnostics' production of esoteric literature force the Christians to come to grips with the scope of their own scriptures? Since gnostics did not claim that they had produced sacred inspired scriptures that were binding on all, arguments against them cannot be based on establishing binding Christian scriptures for all. They may well have also been among some of the first to acknowledge some NT writings as scripture or at least they likely used them as authoritative sacred texts without specifically identifying them by the familiar scriptural designations. The gnostic Basilides of Alexandria may well have been among the first to recognize some NT writings as Christian scripture (John, Luke, and Matthew and Romans, 1–2 Corinthians, and Ephesians; cited by Hippolytus, *Refutations of All Heresies* 7.22–26; *c.* 220–230 CE). Irenaeus and others argued against the gnostics in the second and third centuries though not with a canon of scripture but rather with a proto-orthodox canon of faith (*regula fidei*) that they believed had been passed on by the apostles to their successors in the churches, the bishops. Some scholars have a way of assuming that the Bible was already established or settled before the gnostic versus orthodox debates began and assume realities that were not present at that time, namely fully formed notions of heresy or Christian scripture. Both assumptions can lead to inappropriate conclusions.

D. Montanists

Montanus, possibly a priest of Cybele, and two women named Priscilla and Maximilla, came to Phrygia in Asia Minor around 170 CE claiming to be inspired by the Paraclete (Holy Spirit) and having an announcement of the Parousia (the second coming of the Lord). The three of them had a major impact on the people of Phrygia and were received with enthusiasm by many Christians throughout the Greco-Roman world. The Montanists were by far the most popular charismatic Christian sect in the second and third centuries. Their message had an apocalyptic focus and, according to Frend, they strongly advocated their interpretation of the book of Revelation and emphasized prophecy, rigid asceticism, martyrdom, and the presence and power of the Holy Spirit (1984: 253). He points to the long history of prophetic movements in this region and observes that orthodox Christians were simply unprepared to deal with them (1984: 254–5). Unlike in many other religious groups at this time, both men and women could become prophets in Montanism. In his discussion of Montanism, that he calls the "Cataphrygian heresy," Eusebius mentions several times that women were a significant part of that movement (*Hist. eccl.* 5.14–19). The Montanists began to be called "Cataphrygians" in the fourth century (Frend 1984: 256). By 200 they had expanded their influence on Rome and North Africa and their primary influence was among rural communities.

What is most surprising about the Montanists is that Tertullian was their most famous and most influential convert who was also a teacher and apologist for their views. His conversion to the Montanist sect was perhaps because of the Montanists' emphasis on a rigorous ascetic lifestyle. He was already a highly disciplined man with little toleration for weak and undisciplined Christians. His hesitation to baptize converts or children too early, for example, is well known and illustrates his call for careful and consistent behavior:

> According to circumstance and disposition and even age of the individual person, it may be better to delay baptism; and especially so in the case of little children. Why, indeed, is it necessary—if it be not a case of necessity—that the sponsors too be thrust into danger, when they themselves may fail to fulfill their promises by reason of death, or when they may be disappointed by growth of an evil disposition? ...
> For no less cause should the unmarried also be deferred, in whom there is an aptness to temptation—in virgins on account of their ripeness as also in the widowed on account of their freedom—until either they are married or are better strengthened for

continence. Anyone who understands the seriousness of Baptism will fear its reception more than its deferral. Sound faith is secure of salvation! (Tertullian, *Baptism* 18.4; cited in Jurgens 128–9)

Tertullian also may have been impressed with the charismatic focus of the Montanists, which was acknowledged in the greater church as a legitimate and authentic expression of Christian faith but which had declined significantly in the second-century churches perhaps because of its abuse by some wandering charismatics who claimed prophetic gifts as we see in Lucian's *Passing of Peregrinus* and in the abuses addressed in the *Didache* (11.1–10).

The most vigorous opponents of the Montanists in Asia Minor were the so-called *Alogi* who looked askance at both the Gospel of John and the book of Revelation because of their supposed gnostic origins. The Alogi even called the book of Hebrews into question because of its view of the hopeless condition of the apostate Christian, which also coincided with the Montanists' harsh penitential practice (R. Collins 1983: 26; von Campenhausen 1972: 232). The response of the church at large to the Montanists was a rejection of their movement and a reserve toward the Gospel of John because of its focus on the Paraclete (Spirit) and a similar reserve toward the book of Revelation (especially in the Eastern churches) because of its apocalyptic and esoteric emphasis.

Von Campenhausen concludes that the emergence of Montanism was a significant factor in prompting orthodox Christians to determine the scope of their NT scriptures. His view is based on an observation from Hippolytus of Rome who claimed that the Montanists produced "innumerable books" (*Elenchus* 8.19.1). Von Campenhausen concludes from this that the church was forced to make a decision about the scope of its canon because of the ever-growing number of Montanist books. He explains,

> It is obvious that such an attitude can no longer be content with recognizing a rough list of sacred writings and with rejecting others as heretical forgeries; it now has to be clearly decided which books are to belong to the "New Testament" and which are not. At this point the final stage of the formation of the Canon has begun. It did not at once reach its goal; but the necessity of a "closed" canon had been grasped in principle. (Campenhausen 1972: 231–2)

In other words, according to von Campenhausen, the Montanists generated numerous books that they believed were divinely inspired, and the greater church therefore saw the need to identify more precisely what literature was inspired by God and therefore could be read in the churches (Campenhausen 1972: 227–32). Hippolytus's well-known criticism of the Montanists and their books has a bearing on that debate. He writes,

> But there are others who themselves are even more heretical in nature [than the foregoing] and are Phrygians by birth. These have been rendered victims of error from being previously captivated by [two] wretched women, called a certain Priscilla and Maximilla, whom they supposed [to be] prophetesses. And they assert that into these the Paraclete Spirit had departed; and antecedently to them, they in like manner consider Montanus as a prophet. And *being in possession of an infinite number of their books*, [the Phrygians] are overrun with delusion; and they do not judge whatever statements are made by them, according to [the criterion of] reason; nor do they give heed unto those who are competent to decide; but they are heedlessly swept onward,

by the reliance which they place on these [imposters]. And they allege that they have learned something more through these, than from law, and prophets, and the Gospels. (*Refutation of All Heresies* 8.12. Adapted ANF and emphasis added)

Schneemelcher challenges this assessment and questions whether the Montanists produced any literature (1991–2: 685 n.2). Tertullian, however, acknowledges that the Montanists wrote newly inspired books and defends the appropriateness of recent revelation. Von Campenhausen, citing Tertullian's edits of the *Passio Perpetuae* that included its introduction and conclusion, says Tertullian defended the production of new books that the Montanists believed were inspired by God and that it was mere prejudice "to heed and value only past demonstrations of power and grace." Further, he argued, "those people who condemn the one power of the one Holy Spirit in accordance with chronological eras should beware." Von Campenhausen cites Tertullian's justification of the new literature as follows: "It is the recent instances to which far higher respect ought to be paid; for they already belong to the time of the End and are to be prized as a superabundant increase of grace." Von Campenhausen adds a final quote from Tertullian who argues that prophecies coming from "End Times" are from "God, *in accordance with the testimony of scripture*, has destined for precisely this period of time."

Von Campenhausen citing the "Introduction" to *Passio Perpetuae* states that mainstream churches rejected the Montanist prophecies essentially on the grounds that their prophecies were contrary to the NT scriptures (Campenhausen 1972: 229–31). Eusebius relates the testimony of a certain Apolinarius who challenged the practice of the Montanists adding what he called "false prophecy" to the Christian writings circulating in the churches. Apolinarius evidently did not reject the writings that were in accord with what had already been received and circulated in the churches but rather rejected the new so-called prophecies that were added.

> For a long and protracted time, my dear Abercius Marcellus, I have been urged by you to compose a treatise against the sect of those called after Miltiades, but until now I was somewhat reluctant, not from any lack of ability to refute the lie and testify to the truth, but from timidity and scruples lest I might seem to some to be *adding to the writings or injunctions of the word of the new covenant of the gospel, to which no one who has chosen to live according to the gospel itself can add and from which he cannot take away*. But when I had just come to Ancyra in Galatia and perceived that the church in that place was torn in two by this new movement [the Montanists] which is not, as they call it, prophecy but much rather, as will be shown, false prophecy, I disputed concerning these people themselves and their propositions so far as I could, with the Lord's help, for many days continuously in the church. Thus, the church rejoiced and was strengthened in the truth, but our opponents were crushed for the moment and our adversaries were distressed. (*Hist. eccl.* 5.16.3–4, LCL. Emphasis added)

Von Campenhausen attempts an explanation of this passage, concluding that what was intended was that "the composition of new authoritative writings was now thought of as outrageous presumption" (Campenhausen 1072: 230). This passage is difficult to understand since it appears from Eusebius's quote that Apolinarius was fearful that he himself would, by addressing the Montanist concern, be adding new books to a closed collection to which nothing else could be added. It is difficult to know precisely what

Apolinarius had in mind. Surely, he would not have feared to respond to what he thought was heresy since that already had precedence in the churches and would not have added new texts to the scriptures.

From this and the other criticisms of the Montanists, von Campenhausen argues that the church could no longer have a roughly defined canon of scriptures and could no longer be content with rejecting heretical forgeries as they appeared. He concludes that the Montanists with their production of new so-called inspired books was the primary factor that led the churches to define more precisely which books belonged in their NT and which books did not. Against this is the fact that the proto-orthodox church fathers argued against the Montanists by employing the church's *regula fidei* that summarized the church's traditions and the apostolic writings.

Schneemelcher acknowledges that the sayings of Montanus and his prophetesses were collected and passed on in their churches as authoritative inspired teachings, and even used and defended as prophetic texts by Tertullian, but it is not clear that the Montanist writings were viewed as Christian scriptures to be added to other Christian scriptures. The Montanists believed that the Spirit could still speak in new divinely inspired writings, and this was supported by Tertullian (Schneemelcher 1991–2: 686–9). It is difficult to argue against Tertullian here since the greater church *up to that time* had never concluded that the Spirit had ceased speaking in or to the churches or even that newly written inspired writings could no longer emerge. That came much later in the churches (fourth and fifth centuries). It appears rather that what the church did not like *at that time* was *what* the Montanists wrote, but not to affirm that the Spirit had ceased speaking in the churches. Schneemelcher rightly questions von Campenhausen's view that the Montanists influenced the church to establish its own biblical canon (1991: 24). I have addressed this issue elsewhere (McDonald 2017: 2:158–64).

4. INFLUENCES OF HERESY IN EARLY CHRISTIANITY

We must be reminded again that the heretical challenges of the second and third centuries were not responded to by the creation of an established list of scriptures that could be read in the churches but rather by emphasizing the earlier transmitted traditions and beliefs of the churches, their *regula fidei*. This was the case in churches before there was a notion of a fixed collection of the church's scriptures. The response of the second-century churches to these divergences was to argue from their core teachings that had been passed on to the churches from the beginning. Other factors later contributed to the forming of a canon of OT and NT scriptures that will not be dealt with here but are discussed in detail in McDonald (2017: vol. 2). There is no record that the second-century churches were interested in producing a fixed or even fluid biblical canon of Christian writings. How did the churches keep their sacred traditions and beliefs of the churches before there was a Bible? That will be the focus in the next three chapters.

By the end of the second century only some of the NT writings had received scriptural designations and cited as "the Scripture says" or "as it is written." Goppelt correctly observes that although some of the NT Epistles were likely read instead of a sermon in the early churches, the term "scripture" was reserved initially only for the church's OT scriptures until well into the second century (Goppelt 1970: 164). While the NT writers regularly cite and anchor their teachings in their first scriptures that they later called their "Old Testament" scriptures, but soon in the second century they also were anchoring their teachings in their emerging NT writings. As we will see next, there were several important authorities and models that the early churches affirmed and employed to respond to the multiple challenges they faced and to advance their mission in their formative years *before there was a Bible.*

CHAPTER 3

Primary Authorities in Early Christianity: Jesus and His Scriptures

1. JESUS OF NAZARETH AS LORD OF THE CHURCH

From the church's beginning, the first and foremost authority for the early Christian movement was Jesus of Nazareth who was acknowledged to be their anticipated Messiah with a special relationship with God and who would bring freedom from Roman domination of their land. After his resurrection, he was confessed as the Lord of the church (Acts 1:36; Rom 1:3–4; 10:9; Phil 2:9–11). He was widely known for his remarkable teachings, his affirmation of the Hebrew scriptures, and his proclamation of the coming soon Kingdom of God and how to prepare for it. His proclamation was oral and there is no indication that he wrote any books or letters. The writings that he cited in his teachings were also the first scriptures of his followers and they eventually became the church's Old Testament (OT) scriptures. Jesus taught that the way to prepare for the coming Kingdom of God was to repent of sins, be baptized, and obey his commands. His message was like that of John the Baptist who also called for repentance, baptism, and doing deeds of kindness to others and to those especially in need (Mark 1:4–8, 14–15; Matt 3:1–6; 25:34–46; Luke 3:3–14; 13:1–3; Matt 28:19–20, passim). After his death, Jesus' immediate followers (later called the apostles) were the leaders of the early churches. Their authority was paramount in the earliest churches and after their deaths that authority went to their successors, the bishops of the churches. Those three authorities were the primary authorities in the earliest churches, but as we will see in the next chapter, the scope of the church's leadership and its scriptures were affected by the sacred traditions already welcomed by most of the followers of Jesus. For now, we will focus on the *primary* authorities in early Christianity.

Although the early followers of Jesus of Nazareth were deeply indebted and loyal to their understanding of the Hebrew scriptures that they later called their "Old Testament," they began largely as an oral religion with no writings by Jesus or any direction from him to his followers to produce written traditions or scriptures about him or his message. His activities, teachings, and fate were the primary authorities of his earliest followers, and they interpreted their Hebrew scriptures mostly Christologically to understand him (e.g., Isa 53:4–9, cf. Acts 8:28–35; Hos 11:1, cf. Matt 2:15; Ps 2:7 and 2 Sam 7:14 and Deut 32:43, cf. Heb 1:5–6, passim). Only later after his death and resurrection did his followers produce the writings that now make up the church's New Testament (NT) and others as well.

Again, and without question, Jesus was the most important authority in early Christianity. He was the Lord of the church. Those who recognized his special relationship with God, accepted his teachings, and understood his death and resurrection on their behalf believed that they had received in him forgiveness of their sins, and hope for the future. For them, Jesus was the "Lord" of his followers. His teaching and healing activity led his early followers to conclude that he was that anticipated messianic figure who would liberate the Jewish nation from Roman rule. After his death and reports of his resurrection he became the core authority and central figure in all early Christian confessions of faith and creeds. After his death and resurrection, Paul and others with him proclaimed Jesus' death for humanity's sins and his resurrection from the dead that affirmed to them that he was the Son of God, Christ, and Lord of the church (Rom 1:3–4; cf. 10:9 and 1 Cor 15:3–11; cf. Heb 13:20–21; Jas 1:1; 5:7–11; 1 Pet 1:1–3, passim). Much of the unity in the early churches was based on the affirmation of these beliefs.

Because of Jesus' popularity, his reported remarkable deeds (healing miracles), and his teachings, it is likely that some stories about him were written *while he was still living* and decades later they were included in the Gospels, especially as the memory of him began to fade and his first disciples were dying. It is possible that some of the teachings of Jesus and even the stories of his miracles, especially the so-called Q material in Matthew and Luke, were written before Jesus' death and later included in the Gospels. Given Jesus' popularity in the Galilee region as well as in and around Jerusalem, it should not be surprising that some of his literate followers put stories about him in writing. Dunn has argued that stories of Jesus' teachings and activities were circulating among his followers before his death and, since the "Q" material in Luke and Matthew does not include the death and resurrection of Jesus, it is likely that they were written before his death. He concludes that "Jesus made an impact on those who became his first disciples, *well before* his death and resurrection. That impact was expressed in the first formulations of the Jesus tradition, formulations already stable before the influence of his death and resurrection was experienced" (Dunn 2005: 77; but more extensively in his 2003: 173–254). This "living tradition," as Dunn put it, was passed on orally by Jesus' disciples from the beginning and was recalled in the earliest days of the beginning of the church. It is unclear when some of that tradition was written down after his resurrection and included in the canonical Gospels, but many other stories about him were also remembered after his death and resurrection and it is possible, if not probable, that some of the memories about him *before* his death were remembered and written before the canonical Gospels were produced in their present form. What was remembered about him before his death no doubt formed at least the core of the oral traditions circulating about him after his death and was likely at the heart of much of the early church's teaching about him later (Acts 2:42).

The Gospel of Luke begins by referring to the "*many* who have undertaken to set down an orderly account of the events that have been fulfilled among us" (1:1), that is, earlier *written* stories about Jesus produced before he wrote his Gospel. The term "many" (πολλοί) suggests more than Luke's widely acknowledged use of Mark and "Q" (those writings found in Matthew and Luke, but not in Mark). Those writings that are peculiar to Luke, including multiple parables, that are sometimes identified as "L" (writings peculiar to Luke) suggest that the author of Luke was familiar with several written texts about Jesus including his activities, teachings, and healings. Whatever the reasons for producing his Gospel, he certainly perceived a need for the traditions about Jesus to be preserved in writing and he was following others in doing so but wanted to put those activities in

Jesus' life in a more "orderly account" (1:3). Despite the written sources about Jesus circulating, his followers transmitted *orally* his story and regularly cited multiple Hebrew scriptures as evidence of his messiahship and his message about the coming Kingdom of God. The Christological and eschatological interpretations of those Hebrew scriptures that were common among Jesus' earliest followers along with their interpretation of the Hebrew scriptures was often similar to those at Qumran who produced/copied the Dead Sea Scrolls. What is in view here is the use of *pesher* or *midrashic* exegesis to interpret the Hebrew scriptures in light of their own circumstances and finding their fulfillment in Jesus and in their own circumstances.

The earliest proclamations and teachings about Jesus were largely those committed to memory and proclaimed orally. The likelihood of an expansion of the primary story about Jesus is well known in antiquity and not unlike what we find in Jewish traditions in late Second Temple Judaism and in early Christianity. An important question, of course, is how much expansion of the traditions about Jesus took place in the early churches and whether or how the faith of his later followers were influenced by those expansions. Scholars are aware of multiple other gospels written mostly in the second and third centuries that expanded the story of Jesus often in ways that conflicted with the canonical Gospels. It is common among some biblical and historical scholars to focus on the perceived expansions of that story about Jesus in early Christianity, but in the Gospels that were eventually acknowledged as scripture in the churches there is still considerable overlap in the proclamation about him. This overlap continues despite multiple differences in how that story was told or in their telling of some of the same stories, for example, in the genealogies in Matthew and Luke, the baptism of Jesus, his arrest, execution, and resurrection. Although there were multiple differences in the stories about Jesus in their written traditions, the ancient churches nevertheless continued a proclamation about Jesus that is summarized in their core creeds or confessions in the NT and in the early church fathers' confessions that are also at the heart of the early traditions about him.

Although some scholars claim that some of the sayings attributed to Jesus are inauthentic *in their current form*, for example, Mark 8:34–35 and Matt 28:19–20, most agree that the canonical Gospels are the primary sources for our knowledge of the teaching and preaching of Jesus (Bauckham 2006). Several Jesus sayings found outside of the canonical Gospels and frequently identified as the *Agrapha* are acknowledged as genuine (of the more than two hundred, no more than eight to twelve are possible), but most of them do not have credibility among scholars and those that do make little or no advance in our understanding of Jesus and simply and generally support the Jesus we find in the canonical Gospels. For a discussion of these texts, see J. Jeremias (1964: SPCK), Stroker (1989), Hofius (1992: 88–91; 1991: 336–60), Charlesworth and Evans (1994: 479–533), and Evans (2002: 185–92). It is unlikely that we will ever know with certainty the writings that Jesus acknowledged as sacred scripture, but we are able to draw some preliminary conclusions about the matter. In our pursuit of this goal, we begin by describing an appropriate methodological approach and then examine the resulting evidence that permits some qualified questions raised earlier.

2. THE SCRIPTURES OF JESUS

As the primary authority for the followers of Jesus, the authoritative scriptural texts that he cited are, of course, likely to have been similar to those that his followers also appealed to in their mission to advance the story and mission of Jesus. The primary sources for knowing what scriptures influenced Jesus and the ones he cited the most are, of course, in the canonical Gospels. In them we can see which sacred texts influenced Jesus' teachings the most and which ones he cited as scripture. In some instances, scholars disagree whether it was Jesus speaking or his later interpreters, but they generally agree that the canonical Gospels are the most fruitful starting place for any investigation into this matter. Establishing a universally acknowledged database of Jesus' citations of biblical texts and his allusions to or familiarity with other sacred texts is problematic as we noted earlier, but below some of the database that is recoverable from the canonical Gospels aids in our awareness of the scriptures he cited more frequently.

According to the Synoptic Gospel writers, Jesus appealed to most of the texts now in the Hebrew Bible (HB), but he cited Isaiah, Psalms, Deuteronomy, and Exodus more frequently than the other HB books. He also showed familiarity with other Jewish religious texts that we now call noncanonical (or apocryphal and pseudepigraphal) texts. The Synoptic Gospels indicate that Jesus frequently cited or alluded to four of the books of the Law, but only one time did he refer to Numbers (Num 28:9–10, cf. Matt 12:5). In John, like in the Synoptics, Jesus cited the Psalms, Isaiah, Deuteronomy, and Exodus more frequently, but other HB books to a lesser extent as well (e.g., Daniel). Below is a collection of these and other texts that have some parallels in verbal and subject matter with the teachings of Jesus, but for here and in summary, according to John, Jesus cited all five Torah books and especially Deuteronomy. According to the Evangelists, Jesus was also quite familiar with several of the Prophets, especially Isaiah. Likewise in all four Gospels, Jesus cited frequently the book of Psalms as we see in his reference to Ps 22:1, and probably all of that psalm (see Mark 15:34), as well as the reference to Ps 69:4–9 cited in reference to Jesus cleansing the temple court in John 2:17. No one seriously doubts that Jesus made use of Ps 22:1 at his crucifixion since it is not the kind of text that the early church would have placed in the mouth of Jesus without some justifiable basis, since it appears to report Jesus' loss of faith. Martin Dibelius offers an earlier interpretation of the meaning of this passage claiming that the reference to Ps 22:1 was in fact a reference to the whole of psalm (1982: 193–4).

While Jesus referred to Daniel and Zechariah on several occasions, he did not cite all the Prophets or all the Writings in the HB. More specifically, Jesus makes no reference to or citation of Joshua, Judges, Ruth, 2 Samuel, 1 Chronicles, Ezra, Nehemiah, Esther, Job, Ecclesiastes, Song of Songs, Lamentations, Obadiah, Nahum, Habakkuk, or Haggai. Nothing in the Gospels suggests that Jesus was either aware of them or that he rejected them. They are simply not mentioned, alluded to, or cited in the canonical Gospels. On the other hand, there is nothing in the canonical Gospels or in early Christianity that suggests that Jesus restricted his understanding of scripture to any well-defined collection that eventually became fixed in early Judaism and subsequently in early Christianity. For more specific scriptural citations by Jesus, see below.

From the church's beginning, the words of Jesus were not only the primary authority for the early Christians but also the sacred texts that Jesus himself acknowledged as scripture. Some scholars contend that a fixed biblical canon of the Hebrew scriptures, the church's first scriptures, was current among the Jews *long before* the time of Jesus, and a few are bold enough to argue that Jesus passed on this fixed collection of Hebrew scripture to his disciples, a biblical canon if you will, that was essentially the same as that recognized by the Pharisees and that collection was the first scriptures of the earliest Christians that they later called their OT canon. Roger Beckwith, for instance, argues that "the New Testament shows Jesus and his apostles endorsing a canon wider than that of the Samaritans and indistinguishable from that of the Pharisees, which now seems to have been the standard (if not, indeed, the only) Jewish canon" (Beckwith 1993: 100–2). It is strange and even anachronistic to argue that Jesus or his apostles endorsed any biblical canon. In what follows, I will use the terms "canonical" and "noncanonical" to identify literature that did and did not eventually find a place in the current HB or Protestant OT, but I am fully aware that these are anachronistic designations later imposed on the ancient religious texts that informed early Christianity. Such designations admittedly are imposed *back* on the religious writings that had no such designations in the time of Jesus. I use them in what follows for the sake of identifying the literature that now comprises the church's Bible and the literature that was not later accepted as canonical literature in the churches.

Jesus was well informed by many of the religious texts circulating in Palestine, most of which were later included in the HB and some that were not, but there is no indication in the writings that tell his story (the Gospels) that he produced any writings or called on his followers to produce sacred texts about him or his mission. The writings that focused on his life and ministry, the Gospels, do not suggest that he or his immediate followers had any direction or plans to produce any writings about him or his movement, let alone a new collection of scriptural texts. Presently, there is no clear evidence to substantiate the claim that Jesus had a fixed biblical canon, that is, a fixed collection of sacred scriptures that informed his teachings and beliefs. At least, no one has been able to say *for sure* what was in it even though many guesses have been posited over the years. Scholars are generally certain that most if not all of the writings that are now in the HB were among the scriptures that Jesus and his contemporary Jewish siblings acknowledged, but for some there were other books not later included in the HB that also influenced both Jesus and his early followers. James VanderKam acknowledges that the word *canon* is not used in its later technical sense of a closed or fixed collection of sacred texts by the biblical authors or by those contemporary with them. He rightly concludes, "Since the specialized use of the term [canon] originated among patristic writers, it cannot serve as a useful point of entry into the problem with which we are concerned. There appears to be no single word in Jewish texts of the second-temple age that expresses this specific sense of *canon*" (VanderKam 2000: 2; cf. also 2002: 91–2). It is also unlikely that Jesus ever recognized a fixed collection of the scriptures and *none* of his disciples or the early church fathers ever suggested that he did.

Ultimately, it appears that the writings that were believed to have best conveyed the earliest Christian proclamation and that also best met the growing needs of local churches in the third and fourth centuries were the writings that the later churches selected for their sacred scriptures. Conversely, it appears that the literature they deemed no longer relevant to the church's needs, even though it may have been considered relevant at an earlier time, was simply eliminated from further consideration (*1 Enoch, Shepherd of Hermas, 1 Clement, Epistle of Barnabas, Didache,* and others). Widespread use in churches and especially in the larger churches of the third through the fifth centuries is probably the primary key to understanding the preservation and canonization of the books that make up both the OT writings and the current NT (McDonald 1996: 127–8).

Besides the lists supplied below, the following examples of Jesus' familiarity with either the noncanonical texts or the oral traditions circulating about them in the first century are also worth noting. It appears, for instance, that Matthew made use of the language of *Wisdom of Solomon* in his telling the story of Jesus. For example, in *Wisdom* 2:13 we read, "He professes to have knowledge of God and calls himself a child of the Lord." There is some coincidence of language in Matt 27:43 where we read, "He trusts in God; let God deliver him now, if he wants to; for he said, 'I am God's Son'" (see also parallels in thought in *Wisdom* 2:18–20). Likewise, in *Wisdom* 3:7, the words *"In the time of their visitation* they will shine forth and will run like sparks through the stubble" have some parallel with the words in Luke 19:44 where Jesus says, "because you did not recognize *the time of your visitation from God*." In both Wisdom 5:22 ("The water of the sea will rage against them, and rivers will relentlessly overwhelm them") and Luke 21:25 ("distress among nations confused by the roaring of the sea and waves"), the judgment of God comes upon the disobedient through raging waters. The following examples show other parallels in word and thought:

1. Compare 2 Macc 3:26: *"Two young men also appeared to him, remarkably strong, gloriously beautiful and splendidly dressed, who stood on either side of him* and flogged him continuously, inflicting many blows on him" with Luke 24:4: "While they were perplexed about this, suddenly *two men in dazzling clothes stood beside them*."
2. Compare Tob 12:15: "I am Raphael, one of the seven *angels who stand ready and enter before the glory of the Lord*" with Matt 18:10: "Take care that you do not despise one of these little ones; for, I tell you, *in heaven their angels continually see the face of my Father in heaven*" and Luke 1:19: "The angel replied, '*I am Gabriel. I stand in the presence of God*, and I have been sent to speak to you and to bring you this good news.'"
3. Compare Tob 14:5: "But God will again have mercy on them, and God will bring them back into the Land of Israel; and they will rebuild the temple of God, but not like the first one *until the period when the times of fulfillment shall come*. After this they all will return from their exile and will rebuild Jerusalem in splendor; and in it the temple of God will be rebuilt, just as the prophets of Israel have said concerning it" with Mark 1:15: and saying, *"The time is fulfilled, and the kingdom of God has come near*; repent, and believe in the good news" and Luke 21:24: "They will fall by the edge of the sword and be taken away as captives among all nations; and Jerusalem will be trampled on by the Gentiles, until the times of the Gentiles are fulfilled."
4. Compare Sir 9:8: "Turn away your eyes from a shapely woman, and *do not gaze at beauty belonging to another; many have been seduced by a woman's beauty*, and by its passion is kindled like a fire" with Matt 5:28: *"But I say to you that everyone who looks at a woman with lust has already committed adultery with her* in his heart."
5. Compare Sir 10:14: *"The Lord overthrows the thrones of rulers and enthrones the lowly in their place"* with Luke 1:52: "He has brought down the powerful from their thrones and lifted up the lowly."
6. Compare Sir 11:19: "when he says, '*I have found rest, and now I shall feast on my goods!' He does not know how long it will be until he leaves them to others and dies*" with Luke 12:19–20: "And I will say to my soul, 'Soul, you have ample goods laid up for many years; relax, eat, drink, be merry.' But God said to him, 'You fool! This very night your life is being demanded of you. And the things you have prepared, whose will they be?'"

7. Compare Jdt 29:10–11: "Lose your silver for the sake of a brother or a friend, and *do not let it rust under a stone and be lost. Lay up your treasure according to the commandments of the Most High, and it will profit you more than gold*" with Matt 6:20: "but *store up for yourselves treasures in heaven, where neither moth nor rust consumes and where thieves do not break in and steal.*"
8. Compare Sir 51:23: "*Draw near to me, you who are uneducated, and lodge in the house of instruction*" with Matt 11:28: "*Come to me, all you that are weary and are carrying heavy burdens, and I will give you rest.*"
9. Compare Sir 51:26–27: "*Put your neck under her yoke, and let your souls receive instruction*; it is to be found close by. See with your own eyes that I have labored but little and found for myself much serenity" with Matt 11:29: "*Take my yoke upon you and learn from me*; for I am gentle and humble in heart, and you will find rest for your souls."
10. Compare Wis 6:18: "and *love of her is the keeping of her laws* and giving heed to her laws is assurance of immortality" with John 14:15: "*If you love me, you will keep my commandments.*"
11. Compare Wis 16:26: "so that your children, whom you loved, O Lord, might learn that it is not the production of crops that feeds humankind but that *your word sustains those who trust in you*" with Matt 4:4: "But he answered, 'It is written, "*One does not live by bread alone, but by every word that comes from the mouth of God.*"'"
12. Compare *Jub.* 5.3: "*For no one takes plunder away from a strong man*, so who is going to take (anything) from all that you have done, unless you give (it)?" with Mark 3:27: "But *no one can enter a strong man's house and plunder his property* without first tying up the strong man; then indeed the house can be plundered."
13. Compare Jub. 5.9–11: "*You feed the birds and the fish*, as you send rain to the wilderness that the grass may sprout, to provide pasture in the wilderness for every living thing, and if they are hungry, they will lift up their face to you. *You feed kings and rulers and peoples, O God, and who is the hope of the poor and the needy*, if not you, Lord?" with Matt 6:26: "*Look at the birds of the air; they neither sow nor reap nor gather into barns, and yet your heavenly Father feeds them. Are you not of more value than they?*"
14. Compare *1 En.* 15.6–7: "Indeed, you, formerly you were spiritual, having eternal life, and immortal in all the generations of the world. That is why formerly I did not make wives for you, for the dwelling of the spiritual beings of heaven is heaven" with Mark 12:25: "For when they rise from the dead, they neither marry nor are given in marriage, but are like angels in heaven." (Note: The similarity here is in thought rather than verbal parallels, namely angels do not marry and neither do those who go from this life to the next.)
15. Compare *1 En.* 16.1: "*they will corrupt until the day of the great conclusion*, until the great age is consummated, *until everything is concluded upon the Watchers and the wicked ones*" with Matt 13:39: "and *the enemy who sowed them [evil children = weeds] is the devil; the harvest is the end of the age, and the reapers are angels. Just as the weeks are collected and burned up with fire, so will it be at the end of the age.*"
16. Compare *1 En.* 22.9–10: "the spirits of the dead might be separated. And in the manner in which the souls of the righteous are separated [by] this spring of water with light upon it, in like manner, *the sinners are set apart when they die and are*

buried" with Luke 16:26: "Besides all this, *between you and us a great chasm has been fixed, so that those who might want to pass from here to you cannot do so, and no one can cross from there to us.*" The similarity is more in the notion of separation in the afterlife.

17. Compare *1 En.* 38.2: "and when the Righteous One shall appear before the face of the righteous, those elect ones, their deeds are hung upon the Lord of the Spirits, he shall reveal light to their righteous and the elect who dwell upon the earth, *where will the dwelling of the sinners be, and where the resting place of those who denied the name of the Lord of the Spirits? It would have been far better for them not to have been born*" with Matt 26:24: "The Son of Man goes as it is written of him, but *woe to that one by whom the Son of Man is betrayed! It would have been better for that one not to have been born.*"

18. Compare *1 En.* 51.2: "And he shall choose the righteous and the holy ones from among [the risen dead], *for the day when they shall be selected and saved has arrived*" with Luke 21:28: "Now when these things begin to take place, stand up and raise your heads, because *your redemption is drawing near.*"

19. Compare *1 En.* 62.2–3: "*The Lord of the Spirits has sat down on the throne of his glory, and the spirit of righteousness has been poured out upon him. The word of his mouth will do the sinners in*; and all the oppressors shall be eliminated from before his face. On the day of judgment, all the kings, the governors, the high officials, and the landlords shall see and recognize him—*how he sits on the throne of his glory, and righteousness is judged before him, and that no nonsensical talk shall be uttered in his presence*" with Matt 25:31 and 19:28: "*When the Son of Man comes in his glory, and all the angels with him, then he will sit on the throne of his glory.*"

20. Compare *1 En.* 69.27: "Then there came to them a great joy. *And they blessed, glorified, and exalted the Lord on account of the fact that the name of that Son of Man was revealed to them.* He shall never pass away or perish from before the face of the earth" with Matt 26:64: "*Jesus said to him, 'You have said so. But I tell you, from now on you will see the Son of Man seated at the right hand of Power and coming on the clouds of heaven.'*" (Note: The parallel is the exaltation of the Son of Man.)

21. Compare *1 En.* 94.8: "*Woe unto you, O rich people!* For you have put your trust in your wealth. You shall ooze out of your riches, for you do not remember the Most High" with Luke 6:24: "*But woe to you who are rich*, for you have received your consolation."

22. Compare *1 En.* 97.8–10: "Woe unto you who gain silver and gold by unjust means; *you will then say, 'We have grown rich and accumulated goods, we have acquired everything that we have desired. So now let us do whatever we like; for we have gathered silver, we have dilled our treasuries with money like water.'* And many are the laborers in our houses. Your lies flow like water. For your wealth shall not endure but it shall take off from you quickly, for you have acquired it all unjustly, and you shall be given over to a great curse" with Luke 12:19: "*And I will say to my soul, 'Soul, you have ample goods laid up for many years; relax, eat, drink, be merry.'*" The parallel is in the notion of putting confidence in worldly good and losing all of one's wealth.

23. Compare Sir 24:19–22: "*Come to me, you who desire me, and eat your fill of my fruits.* For the memory of me is sweeter than honey, and the possession of me

sweeter than the honeycomb. Those who eat of me will hunger for more, and those who drink of me will thirst for more. *Whoever obeys me will not be put to shame*, and those who work with me will not sin." See also Sir 51:23, 26: *"Draw near to me, you who are uneducated, and lodge in the house of instruction ... Put your neck under her yoke, and let your souls receive instruction;* it is to be found close by" with Matt 11:28–30: *"Come to me, all you that are weary and are carrying heavy burdens, and I will give you rest. Take my yoke upon you, and learn from me;* for I am gentle and humble in heart, and you will find rest for your souls. *For my yoke is easy, and my burden is light."* (This is like the examples in items 8 and 9 above.)

There are other parallels mentioned in Peter Stuhlmacher (1991: 8–10) including the close parallels in Matt 11:25–28 and the apocryphal psalm 154 (11QPs^a XVIII, 18.3–6).

There are other parallels between "the Book of Parables" in *1 Enoch* (chs. 37–71, *c.* first century BCE) and the teaching of Jesus in the canonical Gospels, especially regarding references to the apocalyptic Son of Man. These are listed below. What makes it unlikely that the *Book of Parables* is a Christian document, as some have argued, is that it concludes by identifying Enoch and not Jesus as the Son of Man (71:5–17). Given the fact that the title "Son of Man" was Jesus' most frequent self-designation, it is unlikely that any Christian group would have created *1 Enoch* and given that title to another hero (Charlesworth 2005: 436–54). It is worth noting that those who deposited the scrolls at Qumran also had a high regard for the Enoch tradition. The recent interest in the books that make up the Enochic collection, written between 300 and 40 BCE, has resulted in several critical works now examining the influence of these texts in early Christianity (Charlesworth 2005: 436–54; Gabriele Boccaccini 2005: 1–14, 417–25; VanderKam 1996: 33–101; 2000: 19–27). These scholars offer multiple examples of the influence of the Enoch tradition both at Qumran and in early Christianity. There are also several significant word parallels between *Joseph and Aseneth* and the canonical Gospels.[1] It is difficult to date *1 Enoch* before the beginning of the Christian era, but is unlikely that Christians wrote it, as some have supposed, since Christian theological issues are not obvious in the document, even though the NT and early church writers drew freely from it (see Kramer 1998). For a careful examination of this document, see also Gideon Bohak (1996).

Some have argued that since Jesus cited books from each of the threefold collections of the Hebrew scriptures, namely the Law (*Torah*), Prophets (*Nebiim*), and Writings (*Ketubim*)—that is, the *Tanak*, he must have acknowledged all three parts of the HB and that they were complete and fixed in the time of Jesus (e.g., Ellis 1991: 37–46, 125–30; and Beckwith 1985: 111–15, 221–2). However, that argument assumes unconvincingly that the tripartite Hebrew scriptures, the Tanak, was present in the time of Jesus. It also ignores that the earliest and only NT reference to three collections of Jewish scriptures

---

[1] These include Matthew (e.g., Matt 1:18–21 cf. *Jos. Asen.* 21.1; 5.13; cf. *Jos. Asen.* 11.4; 5.43–48; cf. *Jos. Asen.* 29.5; 6.19–21, cf. *Jos. Asen.* 12.15; 6.23; cf. *Jos. Asen.* 6.6); 23 in Mark (e.g., 1:10; cf. *Jos. Asen.* 14.2; 1.17; cf. *Jos. Asen.* 21.21; 6.3; cf. *Jos. Asen.* 4.10; 10.21; cf. *Jos. Asen.* 10.11), 54 in Luke (e.g., 1:5; cf. *Jos. Asen.* 1.1; 1.48; cf. *Jos. Asen.* 11.12; 2.52; cf. *Jos. Asen.* 4.7; 7.44; cf. *Jos. Asen.* 7.1; 11.7; cf. *Jos. Asen.* 10.2; 15.18; cf. *Jos. Asen.* 7.4), and 28 in John (e.g., 1:4 *Jos. Asen.* 12.2; 1.10; cf. *Jos. Asen.* 12.2; 1.27; cf. *Jos. Asen.* 12.5; 3.5; cf. *Jos. Asen.* 8.9; 13.23; cf. *Jos. Asen.* 10.4; 20.22; cf. *Jos. Asen.* 19.11; 20.28; cf. *Jos. Asen.* 22.3) (see Delamarter 2002: 90–3).

in the NT is in Luke 24:44 when Jesus speaks of the "law of Moses, the prophets, and psalms." Although Beckwith contends that "psalms" refers to all the later "Writings" and that this text refers to the later defined Law, Prophets, and Writings making his arguments from the "fifths" (Beckwith 1985: 111–15, 438–47), there is nothing in Luke to suggest that the reference to "psalms" is anything more than psalms that were in circulation in the time of Jesus. Which psalms Jesus refers to is not always clear, but there is nothing in the NT or first-century Jewish literature that clearly identifies the books that make up the Prophets and the Writings. Further, attempts to make "psalms" in Luke 24:44 a reference to all the books that are later called the Writings (*Ketubim* or *Hagiographa* that form the last third of the HB canon) in later rabbinic traditions are unconvincing speculation. As noted above, those who make that claim seldom refer to Luke 24:27 that tells of Jesus explaining to his disciples: "beginning with Moses and all the prophets he interpreted to them the things about himself *in all the scriptures*" (ἐν πάσαις ταις γράφαις). Why would he omit the Psalms here when Jesus clearly cited it as scripture in other Gospel texts? It is not uncommon in the NT and early church literature to find books called "prophets" that were later placed in the Writings in the Jewish HB scriptures. The notion that "psalms" in Luke 24:44 is a clear reference to the third division of the HB is, however, both anachronistic and flawed (Evans 2002: 190–1; McDonald 2017: 1:277–85).

There are no *clear* references in the NT or elsewhere at that time to the three-part HB that now exists until the last third of the second century CE, and even those designations for the Jewish scriptures were not popular designations among the Jews. The limited twenty-four sacred books of the HB are identified *for the first time* only in a Babylonian *baraita*, *b. Baba Bathra* 14b (*c.* 180–200), where they are grouped into the three distinct sections identified as *Torah*, *Nebiim*, and *Ketubim* (or *Hagiographa*). There is no such listing in Palestine (the Dead Sea Scrolls) or Philo (Egypt) in the first century or any Jewish designations referring to a fixed canon of their scriptures. While the *Prologue* to Sirach, Philo's *De Vita Contemplativa* 3.25–26, 28, 4QMMT, and Josephus, *Ag. Ap.* 1.37–43 all suggest multiple categories or genres of the Jewish scriptures, those *categories* and the books that comprise them are not identified. Although there were some Jews who identified all the scriptures of the Jews in *b. Baba Bathra* 14b (*c.* 180 CE) cited earlier, that text was clearly not representative of all Jews until much later; otherwise it would have been included in the Mishnah. Indeed, centuries after that text was produced, many of the rabbinic sages still only spoke of their scriptures as Law and the Prophets. A tripartite biblical canon was probably in its early stages of development in the late second century, but there is no tradition that is clear on this matter before the late second century and in the rabbinic text noted above (McDonald 2019: 397–413). There is no evidence that the Jewish rabbis fully agreed on the scope of all their scriptures until centuries later (McDonald 2017: 1:372–96).

More importantly, when the rabbis of the eastern diaspora and in the Land of Israel finally agreed on the scope of its sacred literature (likely by the fourth and fifth centuries), there is no evidence that their views had much influence on the Diaspora Jews in the western Jewish diaspora until the eighth or ninth centuries CE. They had little contact with the rabbis in the east (from Jerusalem to Babylon) and for centuries continued to make use of the apocryphal and pseudepigraphal writings that were rejected in the east along with most of the books that comprise the HB. Arye Edrei and Doron Mendels argue convincingly that the limits on the scope of the Jewish sacred literature in the rabbinic tradition did not reach western Jews for centuries afterward and they continued to make use of the apocryphal and pseudepigraphal writings as well as the books of the HB well into the ninth century CE. They also bring to our attention that there are only a handful of references in the Talmud to the Jews in the Western diaspora and since those in the West only spoke Greek, they would not have known the rabbinic traditions including the Mishnah and two Talmudim that were written in Hebrew (Edrei and Mendels 2007: 2:91–137).

Further, there is little evidence that *b. Baba Bathra* 14b was even known among the Jews even in Palestine in the second century CE, even though Josephus who was influenced by Hillel from Babylon does speak of a collection of twenty-two sacred books among the Jews (*Ag. Ap.* 1.37–43). If this tradition was widely known and broadly accepted in the Jewish community in Palestine, it is strange that it was not included in the *Mishnah* that codified the Jewish oral religious traditions of the first two centuries CE or even later in the *Tosefta* that followed. There is no evidence that the Jewish community in Palestine accepted this Babylonian tradition in the first or second centuries CE.

Again, the assumption that since Jesus cited writings from all three collections of books that now make up the HB and that he must have affirmed all the books that now comprise the whole of the HB is, of course, anachronistic thinking and assumes without sufficient evidence a firmly fixed tripartite biblical canon well before the time of Jesus. It assumes also that if Jesus cited the psalms, which he did, he also recognized Chronicles, Esther, and the other books now in the Writings (*Ketuvim*) that he does not mention in the Gospels. The argument is, of course, one of silence and without clear ancient textual support. If a threefold HB existed in the time of Jesus, it is quite remarkable that the early church fathers did not know of it or divide their OT scriptures into the same three divisions that later became the Tanak (= T̲orah, N̲ebi'im, and K̲etuvim) until later by just two fifth-century church fathers (Cyril and Jerome). Interestingly, no church fathers made a case for the tripartite structure of their OT scriptures over their own much more common quadripartite divisions in their OT canon that they most likely obtained from copies of their LXX. For more discussion of this, see McDonald (2019: 397–413, especially 402–10). It appears that both the threefold division of the HB canon and the books that comprised it were established for the Jews long after the time of Jesus and after the separation of the Christians from the Jews. It appears also that Jews in the west and those in the north or south apparently were unaware of any tripartite order of the HB canon until centuries later and they largely only had access to their scriptures in the LXX that does not follow the Law–Prophets–Writings order in the HB and included other books not in the HB.

There is ample evidence in the NT that the Law, most of the Prophets, and some of the books that are later referred to as the Writings formed the core of the scriptural collections of the earliest Christian churches, even though several HB/OT books apparently played little or no role in the life and ministry of Jesus or the early church. In the NT, the Jewish scriptures are most often referred to as the "Law and the Prophets," or "Moses and the Prophets," for example, Matt 5:17; 7:12 and Rom 3:21. John 10:34 cites Ps 82:6 as the "law." Paul likewise speaks of the designation "law" when he cites a series of references from the Psalms in Rom 3:10–19. In 1 Cor 14:21 he also introduces Isa 28:11–12 with "in the law it is written." The designation "Law and the Prophets" frequently refers to all the church's First scriptures as we see in Luke 4:17, John 1:45, Acts 13:27 and 28:23. According to Acts 13:15, both the Law and the Prophets were apparently read regularly in synagogues: "After reading the law and the prophets, the rulers of the synagogue sent to them [Paul and Barnabas], saying, 'Brethren, if you have any word of exhortation for the people, say it'" (NRSV) (Leiman 1976: 40). What comprises the categories of "Law" and "Prophets" does not appear to have been fixed in their current shape in the time of Jesus, or for more than a century later until *some* Jews in the east made those distinctions, and even later for most church fathers.

The numerous other NT references to a two-part collection of sacred writings, namely Law and Prophets, with only one NT text that refers to a third category of psalms (Luke 24:44), suggests that when the first-century Christian writings emerged there was no widespread recognition of a three-part biblical canon. Rather, all sacred literature for the Jews was widely acknowledged as "the Law [or "Moses"] and the Prophets." The "Prophets" could also have included what is now called noncanonical writings as well as those writings that comprise the Writings, or third part of the HB. This does not deny that a three-part biblical canon may have been *emerging* during the late first century CE, nor that there are signs that more than two divisions of scriptures were emerging in several Jewish traditions, namely, *Prologue to Sirach* (c. 116–110 BCE), 2 Macc 2:13–15 (c. 105–95 BCE), 4QMMT (or 4Q394–99, C, 6ab–12b; c. 150 BCE), Philo, *On the Contemplative Life* 3.25–26, 28 (c. 20–40 CE), Luke 24:44 (c. 60–70 CE), and Josephus, *Ag. Ap.* 1.37–43 (c. 90–94 CE). The contents of the emerging categories, however, were not yet settled or known by most Jews at that time. They and the NT authors knew only the Law and Prophets as their sacred scriptures, even though "prophets" later became a "catch-all" designation for all Hebrew scriptures (Justin, *1 Apology* 67). A third part of the HB was likely emerging by the end of the first century CE, but its contents were unclear and unidentified in either the Jewish or Christian communities *at that time* with the possible sole exception of "psalms" in Luke 24:44. There is also no evidence for a fixed tripartite Hebrew biblical canon *in the Mishnah*.

The fact that the Christians never organized their OT in the same way that rabbinic Jews did, namely Law, Prophets, and Writings, is significant. Had the three-part HB been widely known in the time of Jesus and before, it is strange that most of the early church fathers did not know or follow that model although they clearly had already accepted the Jewish scriptures that were widely known and used among first-century Jews. Nothing in the NT suggests that Christians were out of step with their fellow Jews regarding the writings they recognized as scripture.

Melito (c. 170–180 CE), the earliest Christian writer to identify a collection of books that comprised the OT for the church, lists the whole collection of HB scriptures, except for Esther, including the rest of the *Hagiographa* (Writings or Ketuvim), but still referred to them only as the "Law and the Prophets" and he most likely also includes the Wisdom of Solomon (Eusebius, *Hist. eccl.* 4.26.13–14) that we see in subsequent OT canonical lists from the church fathers and in the major pandect manuscripts (Codices Vaticanus, Sinaiticus, and Alexandrinus). While Melito listed books that were placed in the Writings by the Jews, he was apparently unaware of this third category and simply listed books from that category (e.g., Daniel, Ezekiel, Ezra) as among the "Law and the Prophets." For him there was no third category among the Jewish scriptures. Differentiating between the Prophets, that for long was all the writings besides the Law or Pentateuch, was much later and the Christians did not adopt the same categories for their HB or OT scriptures as noted earlier.

The following lists of Jesus' citations of the Jewish scriptures are not complete but do reflect most citations of, allusions to, and parallels in subject and verbal matter with the OT/HB and *some* of the so-called apocryphal writings. The following examples are adapted from the latest Nestle/Aland's *Novum Testamentum Graece*.[2]

---

[2] N/A[28], pp. 770–806, especially pp. 869–78. A more detailed collection of references can be found in Steve Delamarter, *A Scripture Index to Charlesworth's The Old Testament Pseudepigrapha* (Sheffield/New York: Sheffield

1. Jesus' Citations of HB Books in the Synoptic Gospels.
   Gen 1:27 (Mark 10:6/Matt 19:4); 2:24 (Mark 10:7–8/Matt 19:5); 4:1–8; cf. 2 Chron 24:20–22. (Matt 23:35/Luke 11:51); 4:24 (Matt 18:22); 6–7 (Matt 24:37–39/Luke 17:26–27); 19 (Matt 10:15/11:23–24/Luke 10:12); **Exod** 3:6 (Mark 12:26/Matt 22:32/Luke 20:37); 20:7 (Matt 5:33); 20:12 (Mark 7:10/Matt 15:4); 20:7 (Matt 5:33); 20:12–16 (Mark 10:19/Matt 19:18–19/Luke 18:20); 20:13 (Matt 5:21); 20:14 (Matt 5:27); 21:12 (Matt 5:21); 21:17 (Mark 7:10/Matt 15:4); 21:24 (Matt 5:38); 23:20 (Mark 1:2/Matt 11:10/Luke 7:27); 24:8 (Mark 14:24; Matt 26:28); 29:37 (Matt 23:17, 19); 30:29 (Matt 23:17, 19); **Lev** 13–14 (Luke 17:14); 14:2–32 (Mark 1:44/Matt 8:4/Luke 5:14); 19:2 (Matt 5:48/Luke 6:36); 19:12 (Matt 5:33); 19:18 (Mark 12:31/Matt 5:43; 19:18; 22:39/Luke 10:27); 24:9 (Mark 2:25–26/Matt 12:3–4/Luke 6:3–4); 24:17 (Matt 5:21); 24:20 (Matt 5:38); **Num** 28:9–10 (Matt 12:5); **Deut** 5:16–20 (Mark 10:19/Matt 19:18–19/Luke 18:20); 5:17 (Matt 5:21); 5:18 (Matt 5:21); 6:4–5 (Mark 12:29–30/Matt 22:37/Luke 10:27); 6:13 (Matt 4:10/Luke 4:8); 6:16 (Matt 4:7/Luke 4:12); 8:3 (Matt 4:4/Luke 4:4); 13:2 (Matt 24:24); 19:15 (Matt 18:16); 23:22 (Matt 5:33); 24:1 (Mark 10:5/Matt 5:31/19:8); 30:4 (Matt 24:31); **1 Sam** 21:2–7 (Mark 2:25–26/Matt 12:4/Luke 6:3–4); **1 Kgs** 10:4–5. (Matt 6:29/Luke 12:27); 10:13 (Matt 12:42/Luke 11:31); 17:1, 8–16 (Luke 4:25–26); **2 Kgs** 5 (Luke 4:27); **2 Chron** 24:20–22 (Matt 23:35/Luke 11:51); **Ps** 6:9 (Matt 7:23/Luke 13:27); 8:3 (Matt 21:16); 22:2 (Mark 15:34/Matt 27:46); 22:2 (Mark 15:34/Matt 27:46); 24:4 (Matt 5:8); 31:6 (Luke 23:46); 37:11 (Matt 5:5); 48:3 (Matt 5:35); 50:14 (Matt 5:33); 110:1 (Mark 12:36; 14:62/Matt 22:44; 26:64/Luke 20:42–43; 22:69); 118:22–23 (Mark 12:10–11/Matt 21:42/Luke 20:17); 118:26 (Matt 23:39/Luke 13:35); **Isa** 5:1–2 (Mark 12:1/Matt 21:33/Luke 20:9); 6:9–10 (Mark 4:12/Matt 12:4; 13:14–15/Luke 6:4); 8:14–15 (Matt 21:44/Luke 20:18); 13:10 (Mark 13:24–25/Matt 24:39/Luke 21:25–26); 14:13, 15 (Matt 11:23/Luke 10:15); 23 (Matt 11:21–22/Luke 10:13–14); 29:13 (Mark 7:6–7/Matt 15:8–9); 32:15 (Luke 24:49); 34:4 (Mark 13:24–25/Matt 24:29/Luke 21:25–26); 35:5–6 (Matt 11:5/Luke 7:27); 53:10–12 (Mark 10:45/Matt 20:28); 53:12 (Luke 22:37); 56:7 (Mark 11:17/Matt 21:13/Luke 19:46); 58:6 (Luke 4:18); 66:1 (Matt 5:34–35; 11:5/Luke 7:22); 61:1–2 (Luke 4:18–19); **Jer** 6:16 (Matt 11:29); 7:11 (Mark 11:17); **Ezek** 26–28 (Matt 11:21–22; Luke 10:13–14); **Dan** 7:13 (Mark 13:26; 14:62/Matt 24:30; 26:64/Luke 21:27; 22:69); 11:31 (Mark 13:14/Matt 24:15); 12:11, cf. 9:27 (Mark 13:14/Matt 24:15); **Joel** 4:13 (Mark 4:29); **Hos** 6:6 (Matt 9:13); 10:8 (Matt 23:30); **Mic** 7:6 (Matt 10:35–36/Luke 12:53); **Jonah** (Matt 16:4; cf. 12:39); 2:1 (Mark 8:31); 3:5–9 (Matt 12:41/Luke 11:32); **Zech** 9:9 (Mark 11:1–10/Matt 21:1–11/Luke 19:29–40); 13:7 (Mark 14:27/Matt 26:31); **Mal** 3:1 (Matt 11:10/Luke 7:27); 3:23–24 (Mark 9:12–13; 11:14/Matt 11:10/Luke 7:27; 17:11–12; 12:12 (Matt 24:30).

   What we see from this survey is that the Evangelists attribute to Jesus the use of the Pentateuch, especially Deuteronomy, the Psalms, and Isaiah, but others as well.

2. Jesus' Citations of HB Books in the Gospel of John.

It is commonly recognized today that the Gospel of John, known by that name from the time of Irenaeus (*Adv. Haer.* 3.11.1–9), has more archaeological, topographical, and chronological data in it than all three Synoptic Gospels combined (Anderson 2006: 596; Wahlde 2006: 583–86). While there is considerable debate about the amount of theology that prevails in this Gospel, scholars are beginning to reassess its value for constructing the life of Jesus. For more than a century its historical value as a reliable witness to the historical Jesus has been minimized, but recent attention to its historical accuracy has been corroborated through archaeological activity and has led to a new appreciation of its attention to historical detail. Several studies of John's Gospel highlight this emerging change in reassessing its historical features including Charlesworth (1988: 118–27), Charlesworth (1995), Wahlde (2006: 523–86), and Anderson (2001). This does not mean that John's Christological affirmations are any more acceptable to critical scholarship now than before, but only that John's Gospel needs to be given more consideration for its historical value in reconstructing the story of Jesus. In terms of the scriptural citations of Jesus, John is largely like the Synoptic Gospels in that he also shows that Jesus cited the Psalms, Deuteronomy, and Isaiah more frequently than several other Hebrew/LXX scriptures, but he was also acquainted with many other HB/OT books. These include:

Gen 1:1 (John 1:1); 4:7 (John 8:34); 17:10–12 (John 7:22); 21:17 (John 12:29); 21:19 (John 4:11); 26:19 (John 4:10); 28:12 (John 1:51); 40:55 (John 2:5); 48:22 (John 4:5); **Exod** 7:1 (John 10:34); 12:10, 46 (John 19:36); 14:21 (John 14:1); 16:4, 15 (John 6:32); 22:27 (John 10:34; 18:22); 28:30 (John 11:51); 33:11 (John 15:15); 34:6 (John 1:17); **Lev** 17:10–14 (John 6:53); 20:10 (John 8:5); 23:34 (John 7:2); 23:36 (John 7:37); 23:40 (John 12:13); 24:16 (John 10:33); **Num** 5:12 (John 8:3); 9:12 (John 19:36); 12:2 (John 9:29); 12:8 (John 9:29); 14:23 (John 6:49); 16:28 (John 5:30; 7:17); 21:8 (John 3:14); 27:21 (John 11:51); **Deut** 1:16 (John 7:51); 1:35 (John 6:49); 2:14 (John 5:5); 4:12 (John 5:37); 11:29 (John 4:20); 12:5 (John 4:20); 17:7 (John 8:7); 18:15 (John 1:21; 5:46); 19:18 (John 7:51); 21:23 (John 19:31); 22:22–24 (John 8:5); 24:16 (John 8:21); 27:12 (John 4:20); 27:26 (John 7:49); 30:6 (John 3:13); **Josh** 7:19 (John 9:24); **2 Sam** 7:12 (John 7:42); 13:25? (John 11:54); **2 Kgs** 5:7 (John 5:21); 10:16 (John 1:46); 14:25 (John 7:52); 19:15 (John 5:44); 19:19 (John 5:44); **Neh** 12:39 (John 5:2); **Job** 24:13–17 (John 3:20); 31:8 (John 4:37); 37:5 (John 12:29); **Pss** 2:2 (John 1:41); 2:7 (John 1:49); 15:2 (John 8:40); 22:19 (John 19:24); 22:23 (John 20:17); 25:5 (John 16:13); 31:10 (John 12:27); 32:2 (John 1:47); 33:6 (John 1:3); 35:19 (John 15:25); 35:23 (John 20:28); 40:11 (John 1:17); 41:10 (John 13:18); 51:7 (John 9:34); 63:2 (John 19:28); 66:18 (John 9:31); 69:5 (John 15:25); 69:10 (John 2:17); 78:24 (John 6:31); 78:71 (John 21:16); 80:2 (John 10:4); 82:6 (John 10:34); 85:11 (John 1:17); 89:4 (John 7:42); 89:27 (John 12:34); 92:16 (John 7:18); 95:7 (John 10:3); 107:30 (John 6:21); 118:20 (John 10:9); 119:142, 160 (John 17:17); 122:1ff. (John 4:20); 132:16 (John 5:35); 145:19 (John 9:31); **Prov** 1:28 (John 7:34); 8:22 (John 1:2); 15:8 (John 9:31); 15:29 (John 9:31); 18:4 (John 7:38); John 24:22 (John 17:12); 30:4 (John 3:13); **Eccl** 11:5 (John 7:38); **Isa** 2:3 (John 4:22); 6:1 (John 12:41); 6:10 (John 12:40); 8:6 (John 9:7); 8:23 [9:1] (John 2:11); 9:2 (John 4:36); 11:2 (John 1:32); 12:3 (John 7:37); 26:17 (John 16:21); 35:4 (John 12:15); 37:20 (John 5:44); 40:3 (John 1:23); 40:9 (John

12:15); 42:8 (John 8:12); 43:10 (John 8:28, 58); 43:13 (John 8:58); 43:19 (John 7:38); 45:19 (John 18:20); 46:10 (John 13:19); 52:13 (John 12:38); 53:7 (John 8:32); 54:13 (John 6:45); 55:1 (John 7:37); 57:4 (John 17:12); 58:11 (John 4:14); 60:1, 3 (John 8:12); 66:14 (John 16:22); **Jer** 1:5 (John 10:36); 2:13 (John 4:10); 11:19 (John 1:29); 13:16 (John 9:4); 17:21 (John 5:10); **Ezek** 15:1–8 (John 15:6); 34:11–16 (John 10:11); 34:23 (John 10:11, 16); 36:25–27 (John 3:5); 37:24 (John 10:11, 16); 37:25 (John 12:34); 37:27 (John 1:14); 47:1–12 (John 7:38); **Dan** 1:2 (John 3:35); **Hos** 6:2 (John 5:21); 4:18 (John 7:38); **Obad** 1:12–14 (John 11:50); **Mic** 5:1 (John 7:42); 6:15 (John 4:37); **Zeph** 3:13 (John 1:47); 3:14 (John 12:15); 3:15 (John 1:49); **Hag** 2:9 (John 14:27); **Zech** 1:5 (John 8:52); 9:9 (John 12:15); 12:10 (John 19:37); 13:7 (John 16:32); 14:8 (John 4:10, 7:38); **Mal** 1:6 (John 8:49); 3:23 (John 1:21).

3. Allusions to or Verbal and Subject Parallels with Apocryphal and Pseudepigraphal Texts Attributed to Jesus in the Synoptic Gospels.

  3 Ezra 1:3 (Matt 6:29); **4 Ezra** 4:8 (John 3:13); 6:25 (Matt 10:22); 7:14 (Matt 5:1); 7:36 (Luke 16:26); 7:77 (Matt 6:20); 7:113 (Matt 13:39); 8:3 (Matt 22:14); 8:41 (Matt 13:3; 22:14); **1 Macc** 1:54 (Matt 24:15); 2:21 (Matt 16:22); 2:28 (Matt 24:16); 3:6 (Luke 13:27); 3:60 (Matt 6:10); 4:59 (John 10:22); 5:15 (Matt 4:15); 9:39 (John 3:29); 10:29 (Luke 15:12); 12:17 (Matt 9:38); **2 Macc** 3:26 (Luke 24:4); 8:17 (Matt 24:15); 10:3 (Matt 12:4); **4 Macc** 3:13–19 (Luke 6:12); 7:19 (Matt 22:32/Luke 20:37); 13:14 (Matt 10:28); 13:15 (Luke 16:23); 13:17 (Matt 8:11); 16:25 (Matt 22:32/Luke 20:37); **Tob** 2:2 (Luke 14:13); 3:17 (Luke 15:12); 4:3 (Matt 8:21); 4:6 (John 3:21); 4:15 (Matt 7:12); 4:17 (Matt 25:35); 5:15 (Matt 20:2); 7:10 (Luke 12:19); 7:17 (Matt 11:25/Luke 10:17); 11:9 (Luke 2:29); 12:15 (Matt 18:10/Luke 1:19); 14:4 (Matt 23:38/Luke 21:24); **Jud** 11:19 (Matt 9:36); 13:18 (Luke 1:42); 16:17 (Matt 11:22); **Sus** 46 (Matt 27:24); **Bar** 4:1 (Matt 5:18); 4:37 (Matt 8:11/Luke 13:29); **Ep Jer** 6:24, 28 (Matt 11:29); 7:14 (Matt 6:7); 7:32–35 (Matt 25:36); 9:8 (Matt 5:28); 10:14 (Luke 1:52); 11:19 (Luke 10:19); 13:17 (Matt 10:16); 14:10 (Matt 6:23); 20:30 (Matt 13:44); 23:1.4 (Matt 6:9); 24:19 (Matt 11:28); 24:21 (John 6:35); 24:40.43 (John 7:38); 25:7–12 (Matt 5:2); 27:6 (Matt 6:12); 28:18 (Luke 21:24); 29:10 (Matt 6:20); 31:15 (Matt 7:12); 33:1 (Matt 6:13); 35:22 (Matt 16:27/Luke 18:7); 37:2 (Matt 26:38); 40:15 (Matt 13:5); 44:19 (John 8:53); 48:5 (Luke 7:22); 48:10 (Matt 11:14; 17:11/Luke 1:17; 9:8); 48:24 (Matt 5:4); 50:20 (Luke 24:50); 50:22 (Luke 24:53); 50:25 (John 4:9); 51:1 (Matt 11:25/Luke 10:21); 51:23 (Matt 11:28); 51:26 (Matt 11:29); **Wis** 2:13 (Matt 27:43); 2:16 (John 5:18); 2:18–20 (Matt 27:43); 2:24 (John 8:44); 3:7 (Luke 19:44); 3:9 (John 15:19); 5:22 (Luke 21:25); 6:18 (John 14:15); 7:11 (Matt 6:33); 8:8 (John 4:48); 9:1 (John 1:3); 15:1 (Luke 6:35); 15:3 (John 17:3); 15:8 (Luke 12:20); 15:11 (John 20:22); 16:13 (Matt 16:18); 16:26 (Matt 4:4); 17:2 (Matt 22:13); 18:15 (John 3:12); *Pss. Sol.* 1:5 (Matt 11:23); 5:3 (John 3:27); 5:9 (Matt 6:26); 7:1 (John 15:25); 7:6 (John 1:14); 16:5 (Luke 22:37); 17:21 (John 7:42); 17:25 (Luke 21:24); 17:26, 29 (Matt 19:28); 17:30 (Matt 21:12); 17:32 (Luke 2:11); 18:6 (Matt 13:6); 18:10 (Luke 2:14); *En.* 5:7 (Matt 5:5); 16:1 (Matt 13:39); 22:9 (Luke 16:26); 38:2 (Matt 26:24); 39:4 (Luke 16:9); 51:2 (Luke 21:28); 61:8 (Matt 25:31); 62:2 (Matt 19:28; 25:31); 63:10 (Luke 16:9); 69:27 (Matt 25:31; 26:64/John 5:22); 94:8 (Luke 6:24); 97:8–10 (Luke 12:19); 103:4 (Matt 26:13).

4. Allusions to or Verbal and Subject Parallels with Apocryphal and Pseudepigraphal Texts Attributed to Jesus in the Gospel of John.

   4 Ezra 1:37 (John 20:29); 4:8 (John 3:13); **1 Macc** 4:59 (John 10:22); 9:39 (John 3:29); 10:7 (John 12:13); **4 Macc** 17:20 (John 12:26); **Tob** 4:6 (John 3:21); **Bar** 3:29 (John 3:13); **2 Bar** 18:9 (John 1:9; 3:19; 5:35); 39:7 (John 15:1); **Sir** 16:21 (John 3:8); 24:21 (John 6:35); 24:40, 43 (John 7:38); 44:19 (John 8:53); 50:25–26 (John 4:9); **Wis** 2:16 (John 5:18); 2:24 (John 8:44); 3:9 (John 15:9–10); 5:4 (John 10:20); 6:18 (John 14:15); 8:8 (John 4:48); 9:1 (John 1:3); 9:16 (John 3:12); 15:3 (John 17:3); 15:11 (John 20:22); 18:14–16 (John 3:12); *Pss. Sol.* 5:3 (John 3:27); 7:1 (John 15:25); 7:6 (John 1:14); 17:21 (John 7:42); *1 En.* 69.27 (John 5:22).

3. THE SCRIPTURES CITED IN THE NT AUTHORS

Since Jesus was acknowledged as the Lord of the early Christian community, it is understandable that the early Christians also accepted and made use of most of the same sacred texts that he favored in his teaching. What books did the early Christians use as sacred texts? Did the rest of the NT writers and the early church also acknowledge as scripture some of the books that we now call noncanonical writings? Peter Stuhlmacher lists several parallels and allusions to noncanonical literature in the NT writings. Daniel J. Harrington challenges the view that there was considerable dependency on the deuterocanonical writings in early Christianity but acknowledges the use of *Tobit*, *2 Maccabees*, and *Sirach* (2002: 196–210). He claims that there were two clear tendencies at the end of the first century CE in Judaism, namely a tendency toward a three-part scripture canon and a growing acceptance of a wider and more inclusive OT canon among the Christians. The following examples reflect some use of these writings:

1. Mark 10:19 appears to make use of Sir 4:1 along with Exod 20:12–16 and Deut 5:16–20.
2. 2 Tim 2:19 appears to cite Sir 17:26 along with Numb 16:5.
3. It is likely that Paul, in Rom 1:24–32, makes use of Wis 14:22–31.
4. In Rom 5:12–21, Paul apparently makes use of the ideas present in Wis 2:23–24. *Wisdom's* canonicity does not appear to concern Paul but only the theological arguments in it [Barton makes this point (1988: 25–34)].
5. In 1 Cor 2:9, Paul appears to cite as "scripture" either the *Ascen. Isa.* 11:34 or a lost *Elijah Apocalypse* derived from Isa 64:3.
6. Jude 14 expressly mentions Enoch who "prophesied" and refers to *1 En.* 1.9.
7. The author of 2 Pet 2:4 and 3:6 shows knowledge or awareness of the traditions in *1 En.* 10.4 and 83.3–5 respectively.
8. The author of Heb 1:3 makes clear reference to and citation of Wis Sol 7:25–26.
9. Jas 4:5 appears to cite an unknown scripture.

The pseudepigraphal *Life of Adam and Eve* (= *Vita*) and the *Apocalypse of Moses* (= *Apoc. Mos.*) also have several parallels in the writings of the NT. For example, see the following:

1. Compare Heb 1:6 with *Vita* 13–14, which focuses on angels worshipping the one who is in the image of God.

2. Compare Jas 1:17 with *Vita* 29:2 and *Apoc. Mos.* 36:3 where the focus is on "the Father of lights;" Rev 22:2 speaks of a tree of life and Paul has parallels with this text regarding Eve as the source of sin.
3. Rom 5:12–21, 2 Cor 11:3, and 1 Tim 2:4, like *Apoc. Mos.*, speak of death that follows the sin of Adam and Eve (*Vita* 44:1–5; *Apoc. Mos.* 24:1–26:4).
4. The understanding of death as the separation of soul and body in 2 Cor 5:1–5; and the appearance of Satan in the brightness of an angel in 2 Cor 11:14, cf. *Vita* 9:1; *Apoc. Mos.* 17:1.
5. The location of paradise is in the third heaven in 2 Cor 12:2, cf. *Apoc. Mos.* 37:5.
6. Paul's reference to *epithumia* ("covetousness") as the root of all sin in Rom 7:7 is like *Apoc. Mos.* 19:3.

By themselves these parallels do not necessarily reflect either the NT writers' acknowledgment of these noncanonical writings as scripture, or necessarily reflect a conscious dependence upon them. No ancient author was specific about a limited or selected collection of the church's scriptures in the first or second century. In the second century some were opposed to some writings, for example, *Gospel of Judas* and Gnostic writings, but that did not lead them to specify the books in their OT or NT. The second-century sources simply reflect a shared knowledge or perspective, *regula fidei*, that was common among the Jewish Christians of the first century and Jewish and Gentile Christians in the second century. The cumulative effect of these and other parallels, however, suggests the tenuous boundaries of sacred scripture collections in the first century. Stuhlmacher argues convincingly that several themes of the NT also have their roots in the apocryphal and pseudepigraphal literature and cites the above examples as evidence (1991: 1–12). Those examples, however, do not necessarily show that the NT writers thought that this literature was sacred, but they reflect common themes and in some cases words or phrases that suggest dependence. It is highly unlikely that such verbal or idea parallels would be present if that literature had been officially condemned or rejected by anyone at that time.

The Law or Torah formed the essential core of sacred scripture for Jesus, as it was for most other first-century Jews and early Christians. Although Jesus regularly cited the Psalms as scriptural support for his teachings, the Torah still formed the backbone of his scriptural collection. There is little question that most of the books of the HB, and several others that were not eventually included in this collection, informed both Jesus and the NT writers and the early church. Most of the references and quotations in Clement of Rome's letter to the Corinthian Christians (*1 Clement*), for example, are from the HB/OT writings with a few references to some NT writings. The apocryphal and pseudepigraphal literature was in many cases marginal in the sense that those writings were not widely cited in early Christianity, even if some do appear to have impacted both Jesus' teachings and those of his early followers.

The early Christians had in common with fellow Jews a commitment to a collection of Hebrew scriptures circulating in Palestine in the first century, though in many instances they had significantly different interpretations of those scriptures. Their interpretations of those sacred texts gave them their identity and affirmed their Christological beliefs about Jesus. Later Jewish and Christian interpretations of the same scriptures were often at odds and especially when rabbinic sages narrowed their shared sacred books to those that now comprise the HB canon. The early Christians continued to cite as scripture several other sacred texts that were circulating in Palestine as scriptures before the separation, especially the Wisdom of Solomon, the Wisdom of Jesus ben Sira, 1 Enoch, Tobit, Judith, and others that now comprise the so-called apocryphal or deuterocanonical texts including some pseudepigraphal texts.

Jesus *most often* referred to or cited scriptural texts that later comprised the HB, but as we saw he also appears familiar with other religious texts that were not later included in the HB. While Jesus did not specifically identify those texts, his second century and later followers did. It is unlikely that Jesus cited all the literature that he and his followers acknowledged as scripture since most of his teaching was *ad hoc* in nature and addressed specific concerns that he faced in his ministry. For example, in the temptation stories in Luke 4:1–12 and Matt 4:1–11, Jesus cited specific texts to address the challenges of his temptations. In his *Against Heresies*, Irenaeus cited several books that were later included in the OT and NT of the church, but he did not cite all the books in the current biblical canon. That, of course, does not mean that he rejected any of them but only that he cited texts that advanced his arguments.

Like other church fathers of that time, Irenaeus did not list all the books that he considered sacred except in the case of the specific Gospels that he recognized as sacred Christian scripture. He left behind no biblical canon despite using and citing many of the books that later formed the NT. He accepted only the four canonical Gospels and specifically excluded *The Gospel of Judas* (*Haer.* 1.31.1). Simply listing the books that Irenaeus cited does not equal a fixed collection of books that he acknowledged as scripture except in the case of the Gospels, since he was writing about specific heresies circulating in some churches and cited only those texts that were most relevant and supportive of his arguments.

If we possessed everything that Jesus said, and no one makes this claim (John 20:30–31), what other texts might he have cited as scripture? It is quite possible that he and his disciples accepted as scripture several other Jewish writings circulating in the Land of Israel or Palestine in the first century, but this is largely an argument from silence. No one at that time produced a list of all of the OT or NT texts welcomed as scripture in the churches. It is unlikely that we will be able to discern all the writings that Jesus considered sacred scripture since he himself never identified them, but as we saw above it is possible to show from his teachings which sacred texts were most influential in his ministry.

Jesus and his earliest followers welcomed as their *first* scriptures a commonly cited collection of Hebrew scriptures circulating among the Jews in the first century. Although the parameters of that first-century collection are unknown, it doubtless included much of the collection that later comprised the HB scriptures. As we saw in the Dead Sea Scrolls, the NT writings, and in the early church fathers, the scope of that collection was still fluid for centuries but the majority of those writings were widely accepted and most of them formed the HB and Christian OT (McDonald 2021: 73–96). Some of those Hebrew sacred texts were not later included in the HB or in the church's OT canon (e.g., 1 Enoch cited in Jude 14, and others).

From the church's beginning, and before there was a Bible, Christians recognized the value of their not yet fully defined Hebrew scriptures. Further, most of the OT citations in the NT writings were generally from the Greek translation (LXX) of the HB scriptures. Those texts most cited were those that initially aided the Christians in defining for them the identity of Jesus, the essence of their faith, and guidance for their mission and conduct. Although the designations "Law" or "Law of Moses and Prophets" were present in NT times, what was in them is not clear.

4. THE CHURCH'S FIRST SCRIPTURES

I noted in the previous chapter that the early followers of Jesus welcomed the Hebrew scriptures that were recognized as divinely inspired sacred texts despite the ambiguity of the scope of that collection in the first century CE. The collections of the church's First scriptures, later called their OT, were fluid for centuries and the early church fathers did not make a case for the precise parameters of that collection despite considerable agreement on the majority of texts that eventually made their OT as we see in their citations and the surviving biblical manuscripts. As we saw in Chapter 2, the early Christians frequently interpreted Christologically and eschatologically many of their OT scriptures. They did not see themselves as a distinct community separate from their Jewish compatriots but rather as the true Israel (Gal 6:15–16) that understood their scriptures and traditions more appropriately than their fellow Jews. Their hope was, with Paul, that "all Israel would be saved" (Rom 11:25–32). They shared many of the views and priorities common in all sects of Judaism of the first century such as circumcision, Temple worship, synagogue attendance, sacrifices, celebrations of Jewish holy days, strict observance of the Law of Moses, and adherence to the Jewish traditions about how to observe those common laws. For example, Acts, the Letters of Paul, Hebrews, and James all reflect a common acceptance of the Jewish traditions and practices by the early Christians. In short, early Christianity was well within the boundaries of Judaism in the first century CE, even with different interpretations of the same scriptures they had in common with their first-century fellow Jews.

But the question here is about the emergence of Christian scriptures. The place to begin is, of course, with the authority of Jesus that was present in churches from their beginning. Since he was recognized as the church's Messiah and for many also the Lord of the church, what he did and said were of pivotal importance to his early followers and whatever scriptures he cited had immediate relevance and significance for his followers and certainly for the authors of the NT. However, as Stuhlmacher correctly concludes, "Nowhere in the New Testament writings can any special interest in the canonical delimitation and fixing of the Holy Scriptures be detected" (Stuhlmacher 1991: 2). But what about the origin of Christian scriptures? When were the early Christian writings recognized as *Christian* scripture? What initiated that recognition? That will be our next focus.

5. THE WORDS OF JESUS AND THE BEGINNINGS OF A *CHRISTIAN* SCRIPTURE

The story of Jesus' and the proclamation about him was first transmitted orally and subsequently in written form that eventuated in the production of the canonical Gospels decades after Jesus' death. Nothing in the Gospels or elsewhere in the NT suggests that Jesus or his followers advocated the production of a new collection of sacred scriptures, but they freely cited those scriptures they had in common with many fellow Jews. It appears that the earliest followers of Jesus were sure that the risen Christ would soon return to establish his kingdom and so it was unlikely that producing new writings or a new scripture was of much interest to them. Nevertheless, from the church's beginning the followers of Jesus transmitted his story and significance orally. Soon thereafter, as we see in the NT, core elements of that story were summarized and transmitted in multiple creeds whether in the affirmations at baptisms or in the Eucharist or communion affirmations (McDonald 2013: 74–121).

There is no evidence from Jesus, the NT, or the Apostolic Fathers that Jesus gave any command to his disciples *to write anything, let alone produce a Christian scripture* and that may explain why some early Christians preferred oral traditions over those that were written. Papias, bishop of Hierapolis in Asia Minor (fl. *c.* 120–130), famously preferred oral traditions over the written texts saying, "I did not suppose that information from books would help me so much as the word of a living and surviving voice" (*Hist. eccl.* 3.39.4). He said this despite knowing about the Gospels of Mark and Matthew (3.39.14–6). As the early witnesses died and as memory of the sacred traditions began to fail, as is normal over time, it is understandable that greater focus was given to *written* traditions and the NT books in the churches, namely those writings closest to the time of Jesus and to those who first followed him.

From the church's beginning, the words, actions, and fate of Jesus were authoritative for his followers and the most familiar of those words and traditions were regularly repeated in liturgical settings and in the churches' teachings and proclamation. Whatever Jesus, the Lord, said was authoritative and *functioned* like scripture among his followers even before his words were written down and later *called* scripture. While there is no indication that the early followers of Jesus intended to produce new scriptures, by the late second century the notion of a body of *Christian* scriptures became an essential feature of early Christianity even though no list or scope of Christian scriptures is mentioned until much later when local church councils made such decisions (Grant 1972: 297; Barr 1983: 12).

Doubtless, the Gospels were quite valuable in churches from their beginning because they told the story of Jesus, the Lord of the church (e.g., Rom 10:9; Matt 28:19–20), but they were not initially called scripture until we begin to see references to them in second-century church father citations. They *functioned* like scripture before they were *called* scripture and the writings that told the story of and about Jesus would obviously be viewed as highly valued and authoritative from the beginning of their circulation in churches. The Gospels themselves were not initially cited *as scripture* but rather the focus in the citations was on words of Jesus and his actions in them. Matthew was the most popular Gospel in early Christianity, but the Gospel itself was not generally called scripture. The Gospels themselves did not receive that designation until the middle to end of the second century, but because they contained the words of Jesus, the central authority for the churches, they *functioned* like scripture before they were called scripture. For example, in 1 Tim 5:18 (likely a second-century text) the words of Jesus are clearly cited as authoritative scripture along with Deuteronomy, but the Gospels in which those words are found are not mentioned. There the author cites both a Deuteronomy text and sayings of Jesus in Matt 10:10 and Luke 10:7 as "scripture." Jesus' words were a final authority for the author's readers. Through much of the second century, the words of Jesus in the Gospels were cited like scripture, but the texts in which they were found were not generally called scripture or introduced with the usual scriptural designations such as "the scripture says" (*hē graphē legei*), "it is written" (*gegraptai*), "that which is written" (*to gegrammenon*), or any comparable formulas regularly used in citing the OT or NT writings in the Apostolic Fathers. For a list of these designations and use and their meaning in early Christianity and late Second Temple Judaism, see Metzger (1968: 52–63) and Penner (2010: 62–84). As we saw earlier, the absence of these citation formulae alone does not determine the scriptural status of the books cited. However, those designations where used do indicate the acceptance of some writings as sacred scripture. Before those designations were used of NT writings, those writings functioned like scripture in many early churches but not all were so cited at the same time and place.

Scholars of the second-century CE Christianity do not agree on *when* such scriptural designations were applied to NT writings, but most agree that the words of Jesus had a scripture-like status from the church's beginning (e.g., 1 Cor 7:10, 12, 17, 25; 14:37; 1 Thess 4:15; Matt 28:18). He was, after all, the Lord of the church and from the church's beginning his words had significant authority attached to them. For example, Clement of Rome acknowledges the authority of the teaching of Jesus for the church as follows:

> And so, we should be humble-minded, brothers, laying aside all arrogance, conceit, foolishness, and forms of anger; and we should act *in accordance with what is written. For the Holy Spirit says*, "The one who is wise should not boast about his wisdom, nor the one who is strong about his strength, nor the one who is wealthy about his wealth; instead, the one who boasts should boast about the Lord, seeking after him and doing what is just and right." *We should especially remember the words the Lord Jesus spoke* when teaching about gentleness and patience. For he said: "Show mercy, that you may be shown mercy; forgive, that it may be forgiven you. As you do, so it will be done to you; as you give, so it will be given to you; as you judge, so you will be judged; as you show kindness, so will kindness be shown to you; the amount you dispense will be the amount you receive." Let us strengthen one another in this commandment and these demands, so that we may forge ahead, obedient to his words (which are well-suited for holiness) and humble-minded. For the holy word says, "Upon whom will I look, but upon the one who is meek and mild and who trembles at my sayings." (*1 Clem.* 13.1–4, LCL, emphasis added)

And again,

> Why do we divide and tear asunder the members of Christ, and raise up strife against our own body, and reach such a pitch of madness as to forget that we are members one of another? *Remember the words of the Lord Jesus*; for he said, "Woe unto that man: it were [would have been] good for him if he had not been born, than that he should offend one of my elect." (*1 Clem.* 46.7–8, LCL, emphasis added)

Clement's appeal for order is based on the admonition of Jesus that he introduces with "remember the words of the Lord Jesus." Metzger notes, however, that these are the only two direct references to the "words of Jesus" in 1 Clement, compared with over one hundred references to the OT scriptures (Metzger 1987: 41–2). Clement was also aware of Paul's Epistles and Hebrews and refers to them throughout his letter but does not call *them* scripture (Metzger 1987: 41–2). Had Paul's letters been viewed as scripture in the first century it is remarkable that those who cite Paul in the late first and early second centuries do *not* call his writings "scripture."

But, in reference to Jesus' words, they had a scriptural value from the beginning. In his *Letter to Flora*, gnostic teacher Ptolemy (*c.* 160) frequently referred to the "words of the Savior" (e.g., 3.5, 8; 4.1, 4; cf. 7.5, 10) as the authority for his instruction. Ptolemy's devotion to the teaching of Jesus may be seen in his explanation of the proper way to understand the Law of Moses and see his reference to those who have misunderstood it:

> That is what happens to people who do not see what follows from the *words of the Saviour*. For a house or city divided against itself cannot stand, *our Saviour declared*. Furthermore, the apostle says that the creation of the world was peculiar to Him and

that all things were made through him, and apart from him nothing was made, refuting the flimsy wisdom of these liars; not the creation of a god who corrupts, but of a just God who hates evil. That is the opinion of heedless men who do not understand the cause of the providence of the Demiurge, who are blind not only in the eye of the soul but also in that of the body.

How they have strayed from the truth is clear to you from what has been said. Two groups have gone astray each in their peculiar fashion, the one through ignorance of the God of justice, the other through ignorance of the Father of All, whom only he who alone knew him revealed at his coming. Now it remains for us who have been granted the knowledge of both of these, to explain the Law to you with accuracy, what its nature is and the one by whom it has been given, the Lawgiver, proving *our demonstrations from the words of our Saviour,* through which alone it is possible without error to travel toward the comprehension of reality.

First one must learn that the whole Law which is contained in the Pentateuch of Moses has not been decreed by some one person, I mean by God alone; but there are also some commandments in it given by men; and that it is tripartite *the words of the Saviour teach us.* For one part is ascribed to God himself and his legislation; another is ascribed to Moses, not meaning that God gave the law through him, but that Moses legislated starting from his own understanding; and the third is ascribed to the elders of the people, who are themselves found from the beginning introducing ordinances of their own. How this came about *you may learn from the words of the Saviour.* When the Saviour was talking somewhere to those arguing with him about divorce, which was allowed by the Law, he said to them, Moses because of the hardness of your hearts permitted a man to put away his wife; from the beginning it was not so. For God joined them together, and what God has joined, let not a man, he said, put asunder. Here he shows that the law of God is one thing—it forbids a woman to be divorced by her husband—and the law of Moses is another—it permits this bond to be sundered because of hardness of heart. So, in this way Moses ordains a law contrary to God, for divorce is contrary to no divorce. (Stevenson 1957: 92–3, emphasis added)

For Clement of Rome and Ptolemy, the *words of Jesus* in the passages above undoubtedly functioned like sacred scripture even without the usual specific scriptural formulae to introduce them. The origin of Christian scripture doubtless must first be connected to the words of Jesus circulating in the early churches, many of which were later included in the Gospels. Our knowledge of the growth and development of that collection of Christian scriptures has some limitations because it depends on scattered witnesses from the earliest church and through the second and third century. Those witnesses are few in number and there are several gaps in our knowledge of those times. Hurtado reminds us that only about 1 percent of an estimated five hundred thousand manuscripts from the early church period have survived and conclusions drawn from such limited resources must be cautiously interpreted. He nonetheless concludes that early Christianity was largely driven by a commitment to religious texts (Hurtado 2006: 24–5). Obviously, some of the early church traditions about Jesus began to be written early (e.g., Luke 1:1–3) and perhaps even before Paul's letters (*c.* 49–58) or perhaps even before Jesus' death, as Dunn suggests (2003: 881–4) noted above.

Many earlier traditions about Jesus were later "codified" into creeds in the NT and the early church fathers. They mostly focus on Jesus with occasional references to God, and later some ecclesiastical regulations on behavior and church governance also emerged. It is most likely that the writings about Jesus, or most of them, were initially welcomed and functioned as Spirit-inspired traditions (Nelson 1991: 1.374). The eventual triumph of Christian proto-orthodoxy and later orthodoxy in the Roman Empire no doubt had its roots in what was believed to reflect the early core traditions about Jesus, including his relationship with God and his role in God's salvation for the people. Later they also had a significant effect on which books to include in the church's NT scriptures along with the disappearance of many noncanonical books. Books not supportive of the orthodox tradition about Jesus with its claim of being rooted in the church's creeds and early church traditions generally ceased being copied and read in churches, and in time most of them disappeared.

Citations of or allusions to the words of Jesus in the Gospels (mostly Matthew) and to a lesser extent the few examples in the NT Epistles (e.g., 1 Cor 7:10–11:23–25) were common in the first and the second centuries, but the books in which these citations of the words and activity of Jesus are found were not yet recognized as sacred scripture or even cited until the end of the second century for the most part. In other words, initially the words and deeds of Jesus in the Gospels functioned as scripture in the churches. The process of establishing a *Christian* scripture begins with the esteem and authority of the words and activities of Jesus that were circulating in the early churches before they were put in the writings now known as the canonical Gospels. Although the Gospels themselves were not immediately called "scripture" or given a scriptural status in the earliest churches, those texts doubtless *functioned* like scriptures from their beginning because they focused on Jesus, the Lord of the church.

It is interesting that about the same time both Jews and Christians began to be open to an additional collection of sacred writings. For the Jews it was the "oral law" comprising the sixty-seven tractates that eventually comprised the Mishnah and while not technically called scripture they began to function that way shortly after they were collected in their final form by Judah the Prince (Ha Nasi) *c*. early third century CE; and very soon thereafter the *gemara* or interpretations of these additional writings were beginning to be interpreted in the two Talmudim in Palestine (the *Yerushalmi*, *y*.) and in Babylon (the *Bavli*, *b*).

At about the same time several Christian writings were functioning like scripture in a growing number of churches, especially the Gospels that had been read in churches from their beginning, but also some writings of Paul began to function like scripture and were cited in an authoritative manner. By the end of the second century some of Paul's writings were also called scripture. Variations in what was recognized as Christian scripture and formed part of the emerging NT continued to vary for centuries. That was especially true about Revelation, Hebrews, James, 2 Peter, 2–3 John, and Jude. Commentaries (interpretations) of several of those texts began to appear in the third century, especially those of Origen. When that took place the scriptural status of those books was already recognized by those who wrote the commentaries and those who read them. Both Jews and Christians saw the need for another collection of sacred texts. While the Mishnah tractates were and are not called scripture, they were and are welcomed and treated like scripture.

Von Campenhausen also adds an important qualification to the emergence of Christian scripture by drawing a distinction between the authoritative words or commands of Jesus and the Gospels that contain them. This was certainly true in their early circulation in churches. He concludes that the words of Jesus were given prominence and recognition in the written and oral tradition and had a scripture-like status in the church from the beginning, but this, he claims, did not extend to the whole Gospel texts themselves (Campenhausen 1972: 118–21). As noted earlier, Papias's mention of Mark and Matthew is not an exception to Campenhausen's argument since Papias preferred the oral traditions circulating in the churches over the written texts. Would that have been likely if he had already recognized their scriptural status? While the Gospels were widely used to convey the Christian proclamation in the second century, they were not initially cited by their authors or specific writings until the middle to late second century except for Papias referring to the Gospel of Mark and *logia* in Matthew cited by Eusebius (*Hist. eccl.* 3.39.14–16). That may also account for the inclusion of many of the variants in the Gospel manuscripts that Koester argues were more prevalent in the second century when their scriptural status was not yet established (Koester 1989: 19–37).

By the mid-second century at the latest, the Gospels were regularly being read in church services and identified by Justin as the "memoirs of the apostles" along with or even instead of "the prophets" in Christian worship services (Justin, *1 Apology* 67), but the Gospels were not yet identified by their specific names at that time. Until the middle second century, churches gave no prominence either to specific authors of the Gospels or to the Gospels themselves *as written documents*, but rather as documents with the words and activities of Jesus in them. The specific names now associated with the initially anonymous Gospels became more commonly used by the time of Irenaeus (*c.* 170–180), though that does not suggest that those names were invented by him or others at that time. Rather, the names later attached to the Gospels were most likely well known in advance of Irenaeus. Papias's reference to the Gospels of Mark and Matthew (in that order) is not a typical exception since he preferred the oral traditions circulating in the churches over Mark and Matthew, but according to Eusebius, as shown above, he did name at least those two Gospels. From their beginning and circulation in churches, the Gospels were likely intended to be read in the churches alongside the OT scriptures, but their early readers did not *yet* call the Gospels scripture (Campenhausen 1972: 123).

The early copiers of the Gospels likely made multiple changes in their texts such as we see in the Gospels of Matthew and Luke who made considerable use of Mark but also felt free to change his text and even soften some of his words. For example, Matthew and Luke corrected Mark's attributing a scripture to Isaiah but which came from Mal 3:1 (Matt 3:3 and Luke 3:4), and both softened or omitted Mark's reference to the weakness of Jesus' disciples (Mark 4:38; cf. Matt 8:24 and Mark 8:17–21; cf. Matt 16:9–12; and omitted in Luke) or the stability of Jesus' family (Mark 3:21 but is absent in Matthew and Luke). Such obvious changes are unlikely if Mark had been considered sacred scripture by the authors of Matthew and Luke. Luke's reference to earlier attempts to tell the story of Jesus (noted in Luke 1:1–2) might well have included Mark's Gospel and other unknown such stories, but he was wanting to offer a more accurate telling of that story. He clearly did not think the earlier attempts to tell the story of Jesus were inviolate; however, those attempts to tell the story of Jesus were the beginning stages of what later formed the core of Christian scripture and regularly, like the Torah or Pentateuch, was given priority of place in the church's NT canon.

The early followers of Jesus met in his name and affirmed him as their promised Messiah and most early Christians also affirmed him as the Lord of the church, and they also welcomed the reading of those writings (mostly Gospels and soon also some letters of Paul) that affirmed their beliefs about him, and they drew the implications of that belief for Christian faith, mission, and guidance for living. By the middle to late second century, some of those Christian writings were beginning to be called scripture and read alongside their first (Hebrew or Greek LXX) scriptures. Near the end of the second century Irenaeus affirmed the four canonical Gospels as a fixed collection and by the end of that century the four Gospels began to be circulated together as we see in the papyrus text P[45] that includes all four canonical Gospels and Acts. No later canonical list includes other Gospels and the four are regularly cited together by that time even though the *Gospel of Peter* was welcomed by some Christians at the end of the second century. By the fourth century Eusebius called the four Gospels the "holy tetrad of the Gospels" (*Hist. eccl.* 3.25.1). However, aside from P[45] noted above all four canonical Gospels were not regularly included in manuscripts together until later. Often only one or two Gospels are in most of the surviving manuscripts before the larger pandects in the later fourth century, but as the manuscripts of the church's Gospels began to circulate together, they were regularly in first place in those manuscripts and regularly took priority of place in the church's NT scriptures.

While there was seldom complete agreement on the sacredness of all NT scriptures, the church fathers often cited one or more of the canonical Gospels, some Pauline letters (mostly to churches), and by the late second century sometimes Acts, 1 Peter, and 1 John were also cited as Christian scripture. While not many churches had a complete collection of their NT scriptures most possessed one or more of the Gospels, the primary staple of the Christian scriptures, and often one or more epistles (generally of Paul). While differences on which books to include in the NT continued for centuries, there was little question about the Gospels. (For a more complete discussion of this, see McDonald 2017: 2:41–59 and 320–47.)

The core of early Christian teaching and preaching included broad but never complete agreement on the identity of Jesus, his significance, and his mission. The essence of Christian faith including the identity of Jesus, the significance of his death and resurrection, and his ethical and wisdom teachings was *generally* at the heart of what was believed by the early followers of Jesus. This core was also at the heart of most of the early and later church creeds, hymns, along with the baptismal and Eucharistic affirmations all noted in Chapter 4. These early core traditions were present in multiple forms from the church's beginning and provided some stability during other difficulties and divisions in the early churches. I will show in Chapter 4 that the acceptance and transmission of those core traditions enabled Christians to survive the multiple challenges facing them *before there was a Bible*.

A collection of stories about Jesus, especially his teachings, healings, and fate (both death and resurrection), circulated orally in churches from their beginning and, as Dunn noted above, it is possible that some of those stories about him were in writing even during Jesus' lifetime and later included in the Gospels. Those stories and others as well (so John 20:30) were told and retold in churches because their primary focus was on Jesus their Lord and Christ. That was especially true when first-century eyewitnesses were no longer available. Strangely, some items in the Gospels are either missing or seldom mentioned in the second century, for example, references to Satan and demons, Jesus' virgin birth, and divine creation, but all become important by the end of the second century and thereafter. These and other issues will be examined in Chapter 4.

We will see later that the surviving manuscripts, lections, and scripture translations show that most early churches seldom possessed large collections of scriptural texts that would even come close to the sizes of the current Bibles. Also, while all Christian doctrine today is rooted in the church's canonical scriptures, that was not a possibility for the earliest churches because they did not have complete Bibles available to them. That suggests that most of the core agreements were on the major issues such as the identity and mission of Jesus. Most churches had only some Hebrew scriptures translated into Greek, Syriac, and Latin (mostly) that were read largely as texts supporting their core proclamation about Jesus. Some of the early churches also followed the typical *pesher* or *midrashic*[3] exegesis common in late Second Temple Judaism and that method of interpretation made it possible for Christians to interpret their first scriptures (OT) in support of their understanding of the Christian faith.

In the multiple ways the early proclamation and early core beliefs about Jesus and his message circulated in the churches, there were important features that remained that were remarkably stable well before there was a Bible and we will see these in the next chapter. The authorities and models that were followed from the first century in early Christianity overlapped considerably and generally functioned well in the developing churches along with their newly formed Christian scriptures. That overlap was certainly in the consistency of what was affirmed about Jesus. While there was obviously some fluidity in the memory of those transmissions, scholars generally agree that the oral stage of transmission in early Christianity was not as fluid as had earlier been thought by other scholars.

Although Christian dependence on Jewish memory techniques has not yet been fully examined, still it is quite likely that the early followers of Jesus employed the use of rabbinic techniques for the transmission of the oral tradition about Jesus and that has been ably argued (Gerhardson 1998: 71–8, 194–223; and his 2001; Riesner 1988). Besides the most memorable parables of Jesus, Paul clearly knew of the oral tradition circulating about Jesus and on occasion cited it to argue his points to his readers (e.g., 1 Cor 7:10; 11:23; 14:37; 15:3–8; Phil 2:6–11; cf. 1 Thess 4:15). Luke also calls on readers to remember "the words of the Lord Jesus, how he said, 'It is more blessed to give than to receive'" (Acts 20:25). Similar examples of that memory can be seen in Polycarp of Smyrna (*c.* 130–140) who quotes Jesus' words beginning with "remembering what the Lord said" (Phil 2:3). Earlier we saw that the "words of Jesus" circulating in the early churches were the memories of Jesus that later formed the Gospels and other Christian texts. It is not yet possible to identify all the oral traditions circulating in the early churches, but most of them can be seen in the core preaching, teaching of the church fathers, and the multiple summaries of early and later Christian creeds. What we have in the Gospels is most likely derived from the best memory their authors possessed along with what was shared with them in earlier writings that included much of what remained in the canonical Gospels (Luke 1:1–2; John 20:30).

Many of the most important oral traditions about Jesus circulating in the early churches are now in the Gospels, but some are in other NT writings (e.g., 1 Cor 7:10; 11:23–25; 14:37). Those oral traditions undoubtedly influenced early Christian preaching and teaching and likely also the decisions about which Christian books were subsequently included in the church's NT. It is clear from the Gospels and other NT writings that those

---

[3]*Pesher* (Heb. = "interpretation" or "realization," pl. *pesharim*) is a form of biblical interpretation like *midrash* (Heb. "interpret" or "inquire") or that sees fulfillment of a passage in the present context by current interpreters. It was a popular form of scriptural interpretation at Qumran, Late Second Temple Judaism (= before 70 CE) and Judaism of Late Antiquity (after 70 CE), and early Christianity.

early oral traditions all contained Jesus' teachings, miracles, his death, resurrection, and the early confessions of faith in and about him.

The canonical Gospels were written at least three decades and longer after the death of Jesus. They reflect the earlier oral traditions about Jesus circulating in the early churches and likely also earlier written traditions about him that also incorporated the Q material and likely an earlier form of Mark, and likely other earlier written traditions referred to in Luke 1:1–2. The canonical evangelists wrote their stories about Jesus *in Greek* and not in Hebrew or Aramaic but, as Papias later indicated, there was evidently an earlier collection of sayings (*ta logia* = "sayings") of Jesus written by Matthew in Hebrew (or Aramaic) and later translated into Greek (Eusebius, *Hist. eccl.* 3.39.4, 14–16). It is quite possible that there were some earlier editions of some of the canonical Gospels, such as *UrMarkus*, a frequently suggested earlier form of Mark's Gospel.

As noted in Chapter 2, from the church's beginning, authority was not only present and vested primarily in Jesus of Nazareth but also in the church's *first* scriptures, the scriptures of their Jewish siblings, and they were believed to have foretold or prophesied about Jesus. Those scriptures were regularly though not exclusively interpreted Christologically, that is, in reference to Jesus as Messiah, and eschatologically, that is, in regard to the church's future and the fulfilled prophetic texts. At the heart of the sacred tradition about Jesus was an acknowledged belief that he was the Messiah that many contemporary Jews anticipated and who believed that he would bring God's salvation to the people. Early on, many followers also recognized Jesus as the Lord of the church in whom final authority rested in all matters related to faith, mission, and guidance for living (Matt 28:19–20; Rom 10:9; Phil 2:6–11). That authority was accompanied by a large unspecific collection of Jewish scriptures most of which later became the church's OT scriptures and an emerging collection of texts that eventually comprised the church's NT. After the death of Jesus and his apostles, the primary leadership of the churches was transferred to the bishops and to others with such titles as presbyter, or elder, and deacon.

6. CONCLUSION

Jesus, the Hebrew scriptures, and the apostles and their successors were the first and the most important authorities in early Christianity. That was followed by the emergence of Christian scriptures that were not present at the beginning of the church. They soon became a factor in the late first and second centuries and their importance continued to grow for centuries. The works cited above have much more detail than can be shared here. I have summarized the conclusions of many standard works above as they apply to our present focus to show the most important authorities in early Christianity before the formation of a Christian Bible. There were several other authorities that we will see in further chapters and the most important among them are the focus of the next two chapters especially for the formation of subsequent creeds, identifying the sacred scriptures that would eventually form the church's Bible, but other models that gave guidance to the early churches.

We will now turn our focus to the three other critically important authorities that allowed the churches to make the necessary responses to the multiple challenges facing them and advance what came to be known as the proto-orthodox understanding of the Christian faith. Eventually these also have an important impact on the formation of the church's Bible and the establishment of their biblical canon. These, of course, include the emerging and more powerful episcopate, the sacred core Christian traditions circulating in the churches, and the summarizing creeds of early Christianity. All three of these but others also played a pivotal role in the emergence of proto-orthodox Christianity including the lections read in church liturgies along with the hymns that reminded the participants of their core beliefs.

CHAPTER 4

Other Important Authorities and Guides: The Episcopate, Sacred Traditions, Core Creeds, and Hymns

1. INTRODUCTION

Von Campenhausen has rightly observed that despite the emerging challenges facing the churches and the multiple changes in church gatherings, expanding creeds, and traditions, "the development and advance that takes place in the Church is never such that the origins in Christ and the original faith of the apostles are fundamentally superseded and eliminated." He goes on to add, "Progress and development within the Church's history have always been on the lines of regrasping the original truth, of fresh interpretation, application, making actual what Christ once and for all has done and promised." He concludes, "For all Christian Churches, the tradition of the New Testament—understood and interpreted according to its spirit—always remains the standard" (Campenhausen 1968: 17–18). Later creedal formulations often reflect the historical and doctrinal concerns of churches and their authors regularly claimed that their new affirmations were clear "from the beginning," but despite the later additions they did not materially affect the initial New Testament (NT) core tradition and churches regularly cited it.

Although some scholars have posited a "Q" community of Jesus' followers that did not have a reference to the crucifixion of Jesus for sins or his resurrection, there is no indication that such a community ever existed. Those scholars regularly point to the second-century *Gospel of Thomas* as evidence for such a community, but its author's awareness of the Synoptic Gospels that all have the death and resurrection narratives in them suggests that the author of the *Gospel of Thomas* was aware of those traditions and also had a different agenda. The so-called Q Community hypothesis is contradicted by Paul's affirmation after stating the core tradition that "Christ died for our sins and that he was buried, and that he was raised on the third day ... and that he appeared" to his followers (1 Cor 15:3–8) and "so whether then it was I or they, so we proclaim and so you have come to believe" (1 Cor 15:11). Paul never distinguished his proclamation about the death and resurrection of Jesus from that of the apostles and other earliest followers of Jesus. This affirmation in creedal form was at the heart of the earliest Christian proclamation and is reflected in the earliest creeds (e.g., Rom 10:9) and the core beliefs of the early church. While that expanded over time, the core tradition was never lost.

2. FROM THE APOSTLES TO THE EPISCOPATE

Following the death of Jesus, the authority of the apostles was primary in churches, and it was widely believed that they faithfully transmitted the core sacred traditions of and about Jesus to the churches subsequently through the bishops of churches, and eventually and locally through the elders (presbyters) and deacons. The expanded leadership authorities, the first-century creeds, and citations of some of the NT writings were frequently appealed to in the church fathers' responses to doctrinal and "heretical" issues facing late first- and second-century Christianity.

Among the sacred traditions and early creeds cited in church gatherings, an important response to the threats facing the unity of the early churches and even their very existence was the empowerment of the bishop's office. This is seen especially in the letters of Ignatius whose interest focused mostly on dealing with heresy and unity in the churches (*Eph.* 2.2; 4.1; *Magn.* 6.1–2; 7.1–2; 13.2; *Trall.* 2.1; 3.1; 13.2; *Phld.* 2.1–2; 7.1–2; *Smyrn.* 8.1). The NT reflects several different forms of church governance (Acts 6:3–5; 13:1–3; 15:6–30; 1 Cor 5:1–6; 6:1–6; Phil 1:1; 1 Tim 3:1–13; 2 Tim 2:2, 14), but no organizational structure was commanded either by Jesus or by the apostles specifically on how to structure the churches. The NT writers regularly acknowledge some form of leadership in the churches beginning with apostles, prophets, teachers, elders, deacons, and bishops (e.g., Acts 6:1–7; 11:30; 15:1–6, 22–23; 1 Cor 6:1–7; Rom 16:1–3; Phil 1:1; 1 Tim 3:1–13; 1 Pet 5:1–5; Matt 18:15–20), but the precise structures of the organization are seldom clear.

Most NT letters were sent to churches without reference to specific leadership or structure and generally to a specific location (Rom 1:7; 1 Cor 1:2; 2 Cor 1:1; Gal 1:2; James 1:1; 1 Pet 1:1, passim), but Philippians is the exception that includes beside the church also the bishops and deacons. In none of these cases is a particular style of leadership admonished, though, in the case of the Corinthian church, the congregation is called upon to make a disciplinary decision (1 Cor 5:9–13; cf. also Matt 18:15–20). None of these passages have clear guidelines on church organization, though the Pastoral Epistles appear to have a more advanced order and organizational structure in the churches. It is likely that "hard times call for strong leadership" and the challenges the churches were facing led to the strengthening of the role of the bishop.

The church at Corinth ousted their leaders in an apparent power grab and Clement of Rome (*c.* 90) wrote *to the church* (1.1) to reverse that decision and to restore peace, unity, and not to violate the established rule of God's ministry under severe penalty (41.1–3) and appeals to Isa 60:17 to speak of "bishops and deacons" (42.4–5). Clement speaks of the bishops appointed by apostles and later of those approved who should succeed them (44.1–2), but some of the Corinthians removed them from their positions (44.4–6). He therefore calls on the church to reverse its decision to remove their appropriately appointed leaders (47–48). Clement's arguments assume an established order in the churches at the end of the first century and the order becomes clearer and is strengthened in the second century and thereafter.

We see in the NT that in the earlier churches variations can be seen in patterns of leadership, structure, practices of baptism, liturgy, structure, the Eucharist, ordination, discipline, and dealing with heresy in the churches. Von Campenhausen reminds us that the vitality of the church was not seen in its order but in its "fundamental principle of the Gospel," noting further that "order, like good works, always come in the second place, and can be rightly achieved only when what is first, the unique thing … is asserted and willed above all else" (Campenhausen 1968: 126). He posits that initially "the primitive Church started ... with, in almost every sphere of life, a multiplicity of forms and arrangements, to an extent embarrassing to Catholics, and indeed, astonishing even to us" (Campenhausen 1968: 131). Eventually many changes took place, but the role of the bishop emerged as the dominant voice in the late first- and second-century churches.

In the first decades of the second century CE, the office of "bishop" (earlier the title was likely interchangeable with that of "presbyter" or "elder") began to acquire more and more prominence and the recognized need for more organization, authority, and control in the church became apparent. The main three causes of this increased tendency toward a hierarchical organization were: (1) the death of the apostles that left a perceived vacuum of authority in churches; (2) the growth of heresy that threatened to splinter the churches; and (3) the rapidly growing and expanding number of churches with large distances separating them. The role of the wandering charismatic preachers or prophets in churches was already diminishing, perhaps because of their abuse of privilege that eventually gave way to the more stable role of the bishop and teachers. *Did.* 11–13 offers an interesting look at the problem of the wandering prophets and how to deal with those who inappropriately profited from the churches. The *Didache* offers specific details not only on how to welcome the prophets but also how to deal with those who acted inappropriately. Interestingly, the second-century satirist Lucian of Samosata (*c.* 120–190 CE) noted earlier described with mocking humor a Christian prophet who took advantage of simple and ignorant Christians (*Peregr.* 16). Such actions by some Christian prophets were dealt with in admonitions in *Did.* 11–13, and doubtless gave rise to the lower interest in the prophetic ministry in the second-century churches. The emphasis on that role returned during the charismatic Montanists at the end of the second and early third centuries but was dealt with harshly in the succeeding church fathers with the notable exception of Tertullian who joined the Montanists. Some of those prophetic individuals were believed to be deceitful and Christians were advised not to welcome or trust them (2 John 7–11; cf. also Matt 7:15; 24:11, 24), but some of those travelers acted more acceptably and were appropriately received (3 John 5–10).

By the end of the first and early second centuries, the belief arose that the best way to deal with emerging church divisions, false prophecy and bad behavior, including in churches facing persecution, was to increase the power of the local church officers and especially the role of the bishop. An improvement in the relations between the churches generally—though not always—resulted from having strong leaders or bishops over them. The later notion of a central, overarching bishop, such as the position later occupied by the Bishop of Rome, did not manifest itself in the early life of the church, but the idea of a powerful episcopate did take hold in Asia Minor, especially in the teaching and example of Ignatius of Antioch (died *c.* 115 CE). His major concerns were both for unity among the churches and dealing with heretics in the churches. By vesting power in the bishop or overseer of the congregation, authority was assigned to that role to deal with all matters affecting the churches. The emergence of a hierarchical structure appeared to work toward peace and harmony in the churches and helped them deal more effectively with the problems they were facing. This emerging structure cited as its authority the apostolic writings and creeds that emerged out of the "apostolic deposit" or teaching the apostles passed on in the churches (the *regula fidei*). This appeal to the authority of bishops enabled the churches to deal more effectively with threats to its unity and integrity as a community of followers of Jesus the Christ and Lord of the church.

Irenaeus, like Ignatius and later Cyprian, emphasized the role of the bishop in faithfully delivering the sacred traditions, the *regula fidei*, to the churches, and he also advocated a strong bishop and episcopate as Christians faced the threats of heresy and persecution (Bakke 2005: 397–408). Hans von Campenhausen observes that the increased power of bishops dealt not only with unity, heresy, and persecution but also with church structure and mission (Campenhausen 1969: 238–64). However, all of the organizational structure and authority issues were not completely settled in the second or even third centuries, despite an empowered episcopate. Von Campenhausen claims that the early churches did not at first focus on structures and governance, and hence there was considerable variety present in them, but since Jesus gave no clear command on how the church should organize, the major focus of the churches was on their mission. He concludes, "questions of Church order only gradually, as the occasion demanded, and in a quite secondary manner, claimed any considerable attention." He added that because of varied circumstances facing the early churches, their responses to issues such as structure, divorce, and various grievances also varied, and there was "no uniform constitution, no agreed canon, no one formula of confession" (Campenhausen 1968: 124). This variability can also be seen in fourth-century editions of the *Apostles' Creed* and with some of the differences in the *Nicene Creed* (Schaff 1980: 2.534–7).

The unity in the churches was also affected by their growth. The larger and more widespread the church became, the greater were the challenges in maintaining unity. The importance of strong leadership and more structured organization was recognized early on (late first and second century) and subsequent attempts to return to a simpler and less structured church were never fully achieved. The relationship between episcopal authority, church doctrine, and ecclesiastical and biblical canons became more clear in Irenaeus's notion of apostolic succession (Jenson 2010: 71–6; Frend 1984: 66–8). Philip Schaff concluded, "Tradition is thus intimately connected with the primitive episcopate. The latter was the vehicle of the former and both were looked upon as bulwarks against heresy." He added, "In the substance of its doctrine this apostolic tradition agrees with the holy scriptures, and though derived, as to its form, from the oral preaching of the apostles, is really, as to its contents, one and the same with those apostolic writings" (Schaff, 1980: 2:525, 528). For him, the traditions, episcopate, rules, creeds, and scriptures of the church are not contrary to one another but rather they complement and interpret one another.

3. SACRED TRADITION IN EARLY CHRISTIANITY

References to Christian tradition (παράδοσις) are frequently seen in the earliest NT writings, especially in Paul's letters (e.g., 1 Cor 7:10; 11:2, 6, 23; 15:1–11; 2 Thess 2:15; 3:6). For Paul, this tradition is the church's sacred truth and the Gospel that he proclaimed he believed was a "revelation" from God that was also handed on in the churches to Paul by those who preceded him (1 Cor 15:1–3; 8–11). The anonymous author who wrote to Diognetus, a possible teacher of Marcus Aurelius (c. 161–180 CE) and written perhaps by 150–200 or later, offers a criticism of the Jews and a summary of the Christian faith and the benefits of conversion, and claimed that he was a "disciple of the apostles" (*Ep. Diog.* 11.1) and that he would "administer worthily that which *has been handed* down (παραδοθέντα) to those who are becoming disciples of truth" (*Ep. Diog.* 11.1; LCL, emphasis added). The "truth" he was teaching appears to be both the Christian Gospel and proclamation of Jesus as the Lord of the church. He claims that this tradition comes from Jesus the Christ ("the Word") and was "proclaimed by the apostles and believed by the heathen" (11.3). He adds that this "truth" or "fear of the Law is sung, and the grace of the prophets known, the *faith of the Gospels is established, the tradition of the apostles* is *guarded,* and the grace of the church leaps for joy" (11.6, Ehrman, LCL, emphasis added). That "truth," he claims, was passed on to the apostles by Christ and then to their successors and he invites Diognetus to become a fellow believer (12.1).

Irenaeus admonishes those in every church "who may wish to see the truth, to contemplate clearly the *tradition of the apostles* manifested throughout the whole world" (*Ag. Haer.* 3.3.1, ANF, emphasis added). Soon afterward, he relates how the "church in Rome" dispatched "a most powerful letter to the Corinthians [1 Clement], exhorting them to peace, to renewing their faith and *to declaring the tradition which it had lately received from the apostles.*" Summarizing the apostolic faith, Irenaeus concludes that those who follow it can learn from "the apostolic tradition of the Church." He adds that through the succession of apostles, "the *ecclesiastical tradition from the apostles,* and the *preaching of the truth,* have come down to us" (3.3.3, ANF, emphasis added). The early church's sacred tradition formed its primary authority *before* there was a Christian scripture. Irenaeus asked where his readers would find the truth if the apostles "had not left us writings" and he answers, "Would it not be necessary to follow the course of *the tradition which they handed down to those to whom they did commit the churches*" (3.4.1 ANF, emphasis added).

The NT words for "tradition" (παραδίδωμι, or παραδοῦναι, and παράδοσις) are sometimes coupled with "receiving" tradition (παρέλαβον) as in 1 Cor 15:2–3. This terminology is used in reference to the church's sacred teachings that reflect its revelation or proclamation (compare Rom 6:17; 1 Cor 11:2 [παρέδωκα], 23 [παρέλαβον and παρέδωκα]; 15:2–3 [παρέδωκα]; 2 Pet 2:21 [παραδοθείσης] and cf. also Luke 1:2; Acts 16:4 [παρεδίδοσαν]) (Büchsel 1964: 2:171–3). The term in 1 Cor 15:2–3 states clearly that one's salvation depends on receiving the tradition in 15:1–8. Observe the order in this text of three emphases followed by one (15:3–5) and introduced by "that" (ὅτι) and the witnesses here are in a two-one sequence (e.g., he appeared to Cephas *then* (εἶτα) to the Twelve, *then* (ἔπειτα) to above five hundred brothers, *then* (ἔπειτα) to James, *then* (εἶτα) to the rest of the apostles, again, the two-one sequence with the "then" alternating, and last of all to Paul who was the last appearance that he added to the former without the "that" or "then.") This balance (3-1 and 2-1) made that tradition easily remembered in early churches. In the first half of the second century, it was mostly the traditions of Jesus' words, actions, and fate that formed the earliest and most important traditions circulating in the later churches (the *regula fidei*). Those traditions often included an appeal to an interpretation of the Hebrew scriptures, and eventually also by an appeal to the newly recognized Christian scriptures that in time eventuated into a fixed biblical canon.

Those who suggest that other expressions of early Christianity were more popular prior to the time of Constantine's influence over the church in the fourth century CE do not show familiarity with the earlier church, traditions and creeds circulating in the first-, second-, and third-century churches. Jenson rightly contends that there is an obvious connection between the creeds of the early church and its eventual NT canon (Jenson 2010). While there are some challenges in his arguments, he clearly argues for the often-overlooked relationship between creeds and the biblical canon of the church. The NT canon was not a late development that somehow emerged in the fourth century after the church then had power, money, and influence.

Several important responses from the second- and third-century churches to multiple arising crises they were facing had a major impact on later Christianity, including the expanded role of bishops, church order, clarification of the rules of faith (or church tradition), and the *recognition* of *Christian scriptures* that likely, following the Hellenistic model and the Jewish Hebrew Bible, later emerged as a fixed Christian biblical canon. For a more complete discussion of the Hellenistic influence on the formation of the Hebrew and Christian biblical canons, see McDonald (2013: 13–49).

4. EARLY AND LATER CHURCH CREEDS

The shorter NT creeds precede the later more formal and more strict wording in creeds like the *Old Roman Creed*, the *Apostles' Creed*, and the *Nicene Creed* that generally reflect not only the earliest teachings of the churches in the NT teachings but later issues facing the churches as well. We will first look at the earliest Christian creeds. These early creeds are generally focused on the identity and activity of Jesus as Lord of the church and are followed by several second-century creeds that overlap considerably with them but also address current issues or "heresies" facing the churches at that time. For example, including God as the "Father Almighty as creator of Heaven and earth" reflects a response to the Marcionite and Gnostic distinctions between the creator god (a *Demiurge* or "craftsman") and the God of Jesus. While divine creation is taught in the NT (e.g., 1 Cor 8:6; John 1:3; Col 1:15–16), it is not found in the more formal NT creeds. Given the church's Jewish ancestry and acceptance of the HB books, divine creation was assumed and not mentioned in creeds until later when divine creation was denied or challenged. The NT creeds focus almost exclusively on Jesus and his activity, but later they expanded to address current issues and without rejecting the earlier focus on Jesus' identity and activity.

A. NT Creeds

The early NT creeds generally include summaries of core Christian beliefs about Jesus (e.g., 1 Cor 15:3–8; Phil 2:6–11; see also Ignatius, *Trall.* 9 and Polycarp, *Phil.* 2). These focus mostly on Jesus' divine identity and special relationship to God, as well as his role in salvation. Eventually they also focused on divine creation, the Holy Spirit, Christian mission, and responsible Christian living. These early creedal formulations include but are not limited to Matt 16:16; 28:18–20; Mark 12:29–31 (likely also 10:45); John 1:1–3, 12–14; 1:49; 6:68–69; 20:28; Acts 2:22–36; 8:36–37; 16:31; Rom 1:3–4; 4:25; 10:9; 1 Cor 8:6; 11:2; 11:23–29; 12:3; Eph 1:3–14; Col 1:12–20; 2:9–15; 2 Thess 2:15; 3:6; 1 Tim 2:6; 3:16; 2 Tim 2:8; 1 Pet 3:18; 1 John 4:2. Luke Timothy Johnson observes that several of these texts are similar to and functioned like Israel's *Shema* (Deut 6:4, 5–8) (Johnson 2003: 10–11). Similar elements of the early Christian creedal formulations can also be seen in the sermons attributed to Peter and Paul in Acts.

Among the themes in *later* Christian creedal traditions is the regular reference to Jesus' humanity (1 John 4:2) along with his special relationship with God, but the most common elements in most of those earlier creeds are the identity of Jesus and the emphasis on the significance of his death and resurrection in the divine plan of salvation. From the end of the first century, most of the creeds of the church began to include an emphasis on the humanity of Jesus, that he was born of a woman, crucified under Pontius Pilate, raised from the dead, and will also be the judge of humanity at the soon end of the age. Jesus' humanity is also clear in the canonical Gospels but not emphasized in NT creeds as much as in later creeds, likely in response to the Docetic teaching. There can be no doubt about the considerable diversity of early Christianity, especially in the second and third centuries, but it is also nonetheless clear that the earliest surviving creedal summaries of the "Gospel" included Jesus' special relationship with God and the importance of his death and resurrection for the forgiveness of sins. As can be seen from the structure and summary elements in these early formulations, they were circulating *orally* from the earliest stages of the church and decades before any NT texts were written.

Most of the NT creeds are found in the writings of Paul and most were likely passed along in the churches orally before and during Paul's ministry. The NT creeds and traditions predate the NT writings themselves and focus generally on Jesus' identity, activity, and commands, but mostly on his death and resurrection that was central to the core message of the earliest churches. The affirmations in these creeds and traditions reflect the earliest Christian beliefs and practices and focus on Jesus' ministry and teachings, death and resurrection by the mid-30s CE.

The *Apostolic Tradition* followed by the *Apostles' Creed*, the *Nicene Creed*, and others include most of the same affirmations but also regularly include divine creation. The earlier second-century creeds were less strict in the wording and what was included in them, but they regularly reflect NT teachings. For more on this, see Kelley (1972: 88–99), Schaff (1978: 29–108), and Ferguson (2008: 427–35).

The earlier *regula fidei* affirmations were more flexible in wording and generally summarized the primary traditions and teachings circulating in the churches. The later creeds of the church, which date to late second century (Irenaeus, Tertullian) or early third (Hippolytus), but *mostly* in or after the fourth century, include the *Old Roman Creed*, on which the *Apostles' Creed* and the *Nicene Creed* appear to depend. These later creeds are more formal and stricter in wording and often reflect the heresies confronted by orthodox teachers at the time of their writing (Kelley 1972: 88–99). The later baptismal creeds eventually expanded to include a Trinitarian focus (Father, Son, Holy Spirit) and the Virgin Birth, the resurrection of the dead, the church, and life everlasting. The wording in the subsequent creeds was stricter and less flexible.

It appears that Hippolytus of Rome may have written or participated in writing parts of *The Apostolic Tradition* (ἡ ἀποστολικὴ παράδοσις) at the end of the second or early third century and that reflects the Roman baptismal confessions and perhaps also the Alexandrian baptismal affirmations. That creed was also Trinitarian in scope, though initially second-century creeds were more binitarian, focusing mostly on the Father (God) and Son (Jesus or Logos) that we see more clearly in Hippolytus (*Refutations* 10.28–30). Origen argued that strict adherence to the articles of the creed were for him essential "and saves the man who believes them." He claimed that *all* articles must be believed and otherwise "the man would be defective" in his faith (*In ev. Ioann* 32.16) (Kelley 1972: 88–99). The later creeds emphasize what was omitted or challenged earlier such as God as creator and Father of Jesus the Son, the Virgin Birth, the Holy Spirit, resurrection, and life everlasting. After Hippolytus, the inclusion of the Holy Spirit and these other issues were common in subsequent orthodox creeds.

Although the earliest NT creeds did not include references to the Virgin Birth, Ignatius (*c.* 115) later describes Jesus' virgin birth as an essential ingredient of Christian belief (Eph 7:2; cf. 18:2; but especially 19:1: "the virginity of Mary (ἡ παρθενία Μαρίας) and her giving birth"; cf. also *Magn.* 11). By the time of Irenaeus (*c.* 170–180) and thereafter, this was included in most church creeds as part of its core teachings (*Haer.* 1.10.1). He later emphasized the virgin birth, saying that Jesus was the "creator" who "condescended to be born of a virgin" (*Haer.* 3.4.2). His emphasis on God as "Father Almighty and maker of Heaven and earth" (*Haer.* 1.10.1) doubtless reflects the influence of Marcion and the Gnostics who rejected that the God of Jesus was the creator of earth.

The church's sacred traditions existed generations before the emergence of the NT writings and well before the major heresies affected churches in the second century and later. Generally, those traditions focus more on the identity of Jesus and his relationship with the Father and only briefly and summarily on the role of the Father and the Spirit. The later church councils that addressed the scope of the church's NT canon recognized those books that most clearly reflected the church's earliest traditions and those books that were not contrary to those traditions. Again, unless there was a widely accepted core of teachings about Jesus, it is difficult to see how a NT canon could have existed. It is also true that the NT writings are not the only early Christian documents that reflect those same sacred traditions that were pivotal in establishing a collection of sacred Christian scriptures. Clearly, other writings were also widely welcomed initially but later not included in the NT and nonetheless reflected the NT and early church sacred traditions and creeds noted above, for example, *1 Clement, Shepherd of Hermas, Didache, Epistle Barnabas*, and others.

There is no doubt that *some* traditions seldom mentioned in the NT were likely less known to post-Easter followers of Jesus, for example, the virgin birth and Jesus' descent into "hell" (1 Pet 3:19). However, after recognizing those writings in the Christian scriptures and in the NT canon, some of those items were later included in canons of faith and creedal formulations. By the late fourth century, Rufinus, and others after him, included some traditions in the *Roman Creed*, and also included in its well-known successor the *Apostles' Creed*. Those additional items were no doubt welcomed in some early churches but not by all despite being included in the later formulation of the orthodox creeds. It has been observed that the *Apostles' Creed* says very little about Jesus' humanity in it, except that he was "crucified under Pontius Pilate for our sins," which is more reflective of Paul's theology but not clearly stated in the Synoptic Gospels or Acts (except, e.g., Jesus' ransom for many in Mark 9:45). Broadly speaking, however, the identity of Jesus seen in the NT designations and the significance of his death, resurrection, glorification, and relation to God are all prominent in the much later creeds of the church and no doubt this "orthodoxy" played a role in the recognition of the writings that would later comprise the church's NT canon.

As suggested earlier, there is often little logic in the reception of some of the books of the NT canon (e.g., 2-3 John, Jude) and why others were not accepted as scripture (e.g., 1 Clement). Timothy Lim's discussion of the failure of having clearly stated posited criteria for the formation of the Old Testament (OT) or HB is also true regarding the NT canon. He concludes that there is no "criterial logic" that clearly identifies the rationale for the literature included in the biblical canon (Lim 2017: 12–24). He chooses instead "family resemblances," that is, "resemblances are shared among the books." It is also true that there are exceptions to the usual criteria used to argue for the NT canon, namely, apostolicity, antiquity, orthodoxy, and use, but what the NT books do have in common are family resemblances, namely, they reflect similar early traditions and the NT and later creeds. The later church's NT canon reflects the early church's sacred traditions and creedal formulations seen in the NT and the early church fathers.

While there are differences in emphases in the NT canon, at its core there is broad agreement in its many affirmations. That core is broadly reflected in Irenaeus' creedal formulations (*c.* 170) included above, which is an early proto-orthodox position that obtained widespread approval by the end of the third century and even before the conversion of Constantine. Those writings closest to the time of Jesus and his apostles (antiquity) alone are insufficient to account for canonicity, but their primary message is central to the formation of the biblical canon.

Elements of the NT traditions and creedal statements are reflected in many writings from the first and second centuries, but all views about Jesus in that period do not reflect the later orthodox views that gained priority in the church. For example, as noted previously, Hal Taussig's *The New New Testament* includes ten other writings that were not later included in the church's NT canon but likely did reflect some elements of early Christianity. However, as we saw in Moberley above, those additional writings included in Taussig's "new Bible" simply do not reflect the beliefs of a majority of churches in the second to fourth centuries (2017: 108–35). None of the commonly posted criteria makes completely clear the formation of the NT canon, or why *Didache, 1–2 Clement, Shepherd of Hermas,* and *Epistle of Barnabas, Letters of Ignatius,* and *Letter of Polycarp* were all excluded along with others. The traditions, creeds, and NT scriptures reflect the earliest stages of the church and those family elements, in Lim's words, that led to the creation of a NT canon, but the boundaries are not always clear nor why some books were included and others not. What is clear, however, is the connection between the early church traditions and creeds, especially those that reflected the core traditions of the church, and the books that likewise did so and were welcomed into the church's NT.

The authors of the second-century creeds often show familiarity with several (not all) NT writings, but they do not list those writings or include references to them in their creeds. Jaroslav Pelikan provides a helpful "Syndogmaticon," or listing of the most important ancient sources or reflections of the key elements in the church's early creedal statements and dating from the second century CE (Pelikan 2003: 542–70). He acknowledges that none of the early creeds or the early church councils resolve the problem of the apocrypha, and it was only finally resolved in the controversial confessions of the reformation (2003: 139). I would add that this is also true of the early churches' NT books well into the fourth century. Johnson claims that the church's creeds have their origin and parallels in the *Shema* (Deut 6:4–9) (Johnson 2003: 11–30), and both he and Pelikan clarify in their examination of the creeds and their historical contexts of the earliest traditions of the church (e.g., Rom 10:9–10; cf. 1 Cor 12:31; Cor 15:3–8). These traditions are at the heart of early Christianity and are found in the NT writings, the Apostolic Fathers, and second- and third-century church fathers who constructed the church's creeds. They were often constructed in the context of dealing with heresies as well as establishing more clearly what they believed were the church's sacred teachings and traditions. The church fathers recognized those scriptures that they believed best reflected its oldest traditions circulating in the early churches, despite their allowing for growth in the expansions of those creeds to address later challenges (heresies) facing the churches such as we later see in the Nicene Creed.

Bart Ehrman and David Dungan contend that the NT canon was finally decided by the orthodox Christians after they acquired power, money, and influence in the fourth century following the conversion of Constantine (Dungan 2007; Ehrman 2003), but their evidence for that position is not convincing. It is more likely that proto-orthodoxy and later orthodoxy won the day because its teachings reflected the earliest church traditions, creeds, and Christian writings circulating in *most* churches. That influence largely determined the scope of the later collection of NT scriptures. They argue that the NT canon is more of a reflection of the "orthodox" churches after they had received power following the conversion of Constantine, but that argument does not show awareness of the multiple parallels between the later creedal developments and the earliest church traditions, creeds, and the NT writings, all of which emerged long before the conversion of Constantine.

While it may be possible that some NT writings (Revelation) and orthodox teachings may have been influenced by Constantine's conversion and the church's subsequent enhanced power, that is a difficult argument to prove. It is more likely Irenaeus's argument that proto-orthodoxy was supported by apostolic succession that the apostles and subsequent leaders of the church passed on to their successors. That "apostolic deposit" remained the core of the church's rule of faith that carried the day in the fourth century. Orthodox Christianity was clearly the dominant expression of Christian faith in the fourth century and that faith was rooted in those earlier traditions, creeds, and Christian writings that were closest to the time of Jesus and were circulating in churches from their beginning.

B. Creeds Addressing the "Heresies"

By the end of the first and early second century, some Christians began to question Jesus' full humanity. As discussed earlier, they were known as docetics, that is, those who claimed that Jesus only appeared to have a human body. As a result, the church leaders emphasized Jesus' full humanity and that began to be included in early Christian statements about him (1 John 4:2; Ignatius, *Trall.* 9.1–2). It was especially seen in his crucifixion under Pontius Pilate. For example, in his *1 Apol.* 61, Justin (*c.* 150–155 CE) affirms Jesus' humanity during confessions at baptisms as follows: "And in the name of Jesus Christ, who was crucified under Pontius Pilate, and in the name of the Holy Spirit, who through the prophets foretold all things about Jesus, he who is illuminated is washed" (*1 Apol.* 61; *ANF* modified). See also his later *Dial.* 89–98 in which he argued at length that Jesus had to die and be buried.

Hippolytus (*c.* 170–236) wrote a treatise against Noetus (*Against the Heresy of Noetus*), who did not distinguish between the Father and Jesus and even claimed that the Father was born, suffered, and died. This led Hippolytus and other church fathers to condemn Noetus despite his affirmation of the humanity of Jesus and acknowledging that Jesus "suffered, and died even as he died, and rose again on the third day, and is at the right hand of the Father" (*ANF*; cf. Eusebius, *H.E.* 2.20.2). Jesus' humanity was regularly acknowledged in subsequent confessions of his suffering and crucifixion under Pontius Pilate. See, for example, in the *Apostles' Creed* (possibly *c.* 340 CE and its final form *c.* 700 CE) first mentioned by name *c.* 390. It appears to be an expansion of the earlier *Old Roman Creed* (perhaps *c.* third century and cited in Epiphanius, *Haer.* 72.3). It is more reflective of Western than Eastern Christianity. It was regularly cited and affirmed at Christian baptisms. Those creeds combine the divinity and humanity of Jesus by affirming his birth from the Virgin Mary but go on to state the only *historical* (human) part of that creed: "He suffered under Pontius Pilate, was crucified, died, and was buried." Similarly, the *Nicene Creed* affirms Jesus as "one in being" (*homoousios*) with the Father and "for our salvation." It states that Jesus "came down and became flesh, becoming human, [and] he suffered, and rose on the third day" (Johnson 2003: 54–5). The relationship of Jesus with the Father, his birth in Judea, and suffering and death, as well as triumph over death are regular elements in multiple creedal formulations of early Christianity and are reflective of various NT texts that later became the church's *Christian* scriptures and eventually its NT biblical canon. These so-called heresies were addressed in more detail above.

5. AN EXPANSION OF THE EARLY CREEDS

In the late first and second centuries, several church fathers began expanding but not changing the core elements of the earlier creeds from the first century. Some of these expansions are less formal and only stated as important or even essential by a church father, but by the end of the second century these expansions appear to be more formal and include the expansions such as affirming the virgin birth of Jesus as we saw less formerly in Ignatius but, as we will see, more formally later in Irenaeus and even critically important later in Origen. Essentially, in their expansions they reinforced the earlier traditions circulating in the churches. Clement of Rome, for example, appears to have begun the argument of apostolic succession when he challenged the Corinthian church's decision to depose its bishops who had received their teachings from the apostles. Speaking of the apostles, Ignatius later writes,

> Our apostles likewise knew, through our Lord Jesus Christ, that there would be strife over the bishop's office. For this reason, therefore, having received complete [perfect] foreknowledge, they appointed the leaders mentioned earlier and afterwards they gave the offices a permanent character; that is, if they should die, other approved men should succeed to their ministry. These, therefore, who were appointed by them or later on, by other reputable men with the consent of the whole church, and who have ministered to the flock of Christ have been well-spoken of by all—these we consider to be unjustly removed from their ministry. (*1 Clem.* 44.1–4; trans. Holmes 2007:102–5)

Irenaeus drew on Clement of Rome's argument that the church's sacred traditions came from the apostles and were passed on by them to the leaders (bishops) in the churches. He writes,

> Suppose there arose a dispute relative to some important question among us. Should we not be obliged to turn to the most ancient Churches with which the apostles had dialogue and learn from them what is certain and clear in regard to the present question? And what should we do if the apostles themselves had not left us writings? Would it not be necessary in that case to follow the course of the tradition that they handed down to those to whom they entrusted the leadership of the Churches? (*Haer.* 3.4.1 adapted from *ANF*; for a more detailed description of this, see his *Haer.* 3.3.3)

It is difficult to argue against his logic here and it had considerable value in his arguments against heretical writings (McDonald 2017: 2:68–73).

The emergence of "proto-orthodoxy" that both affirmed and also expanded the earlier NT writings and creedal formulations and preceded the later Nicene Creed affirmations is seen in the second- and third-century church fathers. In the following examples, there is faithfulness to the apostolic deposit (the church's traditions and "rule of faith") passing along in the churches. Irenaeus, in his *Against Heresies*, says in an authoritative manner, "as the apostle says" (Preface 1), and in citing Jesus' words in Matt 7:15 in reference to wolves in sheep's clothing, writes, "against whom the Lord has enjoined us to be on our guard" (Preface 2, *ANF*). Tertullian, promoting the "rule of faith" (*regula fidei*), urges readers to avoid darkness and rather to seek "our own." That is "only that which can become an object of inquiry without impairing the rule of faith" (*On Prescription Against Heretics* 12, adapted from *ANF*), and later states, "For whenever it shall be manifest that the true Christian rule and faith shall be, there will likewise be the true Scriptures and expositions thereof, and all the Christian tradition" (*On Prescription Against Heretics* 19, *ANF*). In his *Against Marcion*, Tertullian speaks against those who subvert "the rule of faith" (3.1; *ANF*); and clearly identifies this rule of faith with the apostolic deposit passed on in the churches, saying that what is to be followed comes from the apostles, such as that which Paul brought to the Galatians to correct them, namely, the "rule of faith" (4.5). Origen refers both to the rule of faith and, like Irenaeus and Clement of Rome before him, he affirms that the "teaching of the Church, transmitted in orderly succession from the apostles, and remaining in the Churches to the present day, is still preserved, and that alone is to be accepted as truth which differs in no respect from ecclesiastical and apostolical tradition" (*On First Principles*, Preface 2; *ANF*).

As the church fathers focused on the sacred tradition (*regula fidei*), summarized in the NT creeds, and supported by the church's *Christian* scriptures, it is interesting that none of the earliest creeds mention the church's scriptures or their scope. That is generally true also in the expanded creeds in the second century and later. While some of the later local church councils did identify the scriptures that could be read in churches, none of the ecumenical church councils listed or identified their sacred scriptures. Was that because of continuing disagreement over the scope of those collections or that the sacred traditions about the church's faith was deemed more important to the churches of those times? We cannot say for sure, but lists of the church's scriptures are strangely absent from the creeds and ecumenical councils and only found in *local* church councils beginning in the fourth century. While there was wide agreement on most of the church's scriptures, complete agreement on the scope of those collections took centuries to establish and mostly only for local councils as we will see later. The early church creeds focused mostly on Jesus and although they expanded later, as we will see, the core elements of the earliest creeds continued to focus on Jesus in most of the churches.

The short and simple NT creeds precede the later more formal and more strict expanded wording of creeds. The three best-known formal creeds that are still cited in churches include the following:

Old Roman Creed **(first seen in a baptismal creed in the 3rd century):**

I believe in God the Father almighty; and in Christ Jesus His only Son, our Lord, Who was born from the Holy Spirit and the Virgin Mary, Who under Pontius Pilate was crucified and buried, on the third day rose again from the dead, ascended to heaven, sits at the right hand of the Father, whence He will come to judge the living and the dead, and in the Holy Spirit, the holy Church, the remission of sins, the resurrection of the flesh, (the life everlasting). (See the text in Greek in http://en.wikipedia.org/wiki/Old_Roman_Symbol)

Nicene Creed **(issued in 325 CE at the Council of Nicea and later expanded):**

I believe in one God, the Father almighty, maker of heaven and earth and of all things visible and invisible. And in one Lord Jesus Christ, the only-begotten Son of God, begotten of the Father before all ages, God of God, Light of Light, very God of very God, begotten not made, being of one substance with the Father, through Whom all things were made: Who for us men and for our salvation came down from heaven, was incarnate by the Holy Spirit of the virgin Mary, and was made man: Who for us, too, was crucified under Pontius Pilate, suffered, and was buried: the third day He rose *according to the Scriptures*, ascended into heaven, and is seated on the right hand of the Father: He shall come again with glory to judge the living and the dead, and His kingdom shall have no end. And in the Holy Spirit, the Lord and Giver of life, Who proceeds from the Father and the Son: Who together with the Father and the Son is worshiped and glorified: *Who spoke by the prophets*. And I believe one holy, Christian, and apostolic Church. I acknowledge one baptism for the remission of sins, and I look for the resurrection of the dead and life of the age to come. Amen. (Emphasis added)

Apostles' Creed **(first mentioned in Ambrose,** *Ep.* **42.5,** *c.* **390 CE):**

I believe in God the Father Almighty, Maker of heaven and earth. And in Jesus Christ, His only Son, our Lord; Who was conceived by the Holy Spirit; Born of the Virgin Mary; Suffered under Pontius Pilate; Was crucified, dead and buried; He descended into Hell; The third day He rose again from the dead; He ascended into heaven; And sits on the right hand of God the Father Almighty; From thence He shall come to judge the living and the dead. I believe in the Holy Spirit; The Holy Christian Church, the Communion of Saints; The Forgiveness of sins; The Resurrection of the body; And the life everlasting. Amen.

It is interesting that only the *Nicene Creed* mentions the scriptures with the words "according to the Scriptures" in reference to the resurrection of Jesus and "Who spoke by the prophets," but there is no identity of those scriptures. None of the ancient creeds mention the scope or contents of the church's scriptures. The earlier creeds also do not mention the scriptures or their scope but rather focus primarily on Jesus. By the end of the second century the creeds expanded to include references to divine creation that is mentioned in the NT writings (e.g., John 1:3; Col 1:15–16; 1 Cor 8:6; Rev 4:11), but like Jewish tradition and teaching, divine creation was always assumed and is in the foundational book of the Torah (Gen 1–2). The inclusion of divine creation was undoubtedly in response to the teachings of Marcion and the Gnostics (noted earlier).

There are several important early traditions that focus on affirmations about Jesus' identity, his role in salvation, and Christian responsibility and living. These traditions include but are not limited to Matt 16:16; 28:18–20; Mark 10:45; 12:29–31; John 1:1–3, 12–14, 49; 6:68–69; 20:28; Acts 2:22–36; 8:36–37; 16:31; Rom 1:3–4; 4:25; 1 Cor 8:6; 11:2; 11:23–29; 12:3; Eph 1:3–14; Col 1:12–20; 2:9–15; 2 Thess 2:15; 3:6; 1 Tim 2:6; 3:16; 2 Tim 2:8; 1 Pet 3:18; 1 John 4:2. Besides these, see elements of the early Christian faith in the sermons attributed to Peter and Paul in Acts, and also in Rom 1:3–4; 10:9–10; 1 Cor 8:6; 1 Tim 2:5–6; 1 Pet 3:18–21 but also Phil 2:6–11 and the summaries in 1 Cor 15:3–8 and Phil 2:6–11; plus, some early-second-century creeds in Ignatius (*Trall.* 9 and Polycarp, *Phil.* 2). These became a part of the later core traditions of the churches and were often cited by the church fathers to support their affirmations of the identity and activity of Jesus (see also Kelley 1972: 88–99).

Like the later creeds, the NT creeds, with one exception (1 Cor 15:3–8) but otherwise do not mention or list the church's scriptures. The early creeds generally focused on the identity and activity of Jesus and that continued to be the case in second-century creeds that overlap considerably with NT creeds, but also address the current issues or "heresies" and challenges facing churches at the time. As noted earlier, it was important to the proto-orthodox churches in the second century to include the Father Almighty as creator of heaven and earth, reflecting the Marcionite and Gnostic beliefs that distinguished between the creator god (Demiurge) and the God of Jesus. The *Apostolic Tradition,* followed by the *Apostles' Creed,* and the *Nicene Creed* include most of the same affirmations. The earlier second-century creeds were less strict in their wording and what was included in them is often in NT teachings.

Von Campenhausen has observed that "Progress and development within the Church's history have always been on the lines of regrasping the original truth, of fresh interpretation, application, making actual what Christ once and for all has done and promised." He concludes, "For all Christian Churches, the tradition of the New Testament—understood and interpreted according to its spirit—always remains the standard" (Campenhausen 1968: 17–18). As we will see, later creedal formulations also reflect the historical and doctrinal concerns *from their time* and often their authors claimed that such new affirmations were clear "from the beginning." However, there was a core that remained unchanged despite later additions that were made to address current concerns from time to time that expanded that initial NT core. While divine creation was believed from the church's beginning, it did not need to be affirmed in early creedal affirmations until the time when it was challenged (Marcion and the Gnostics).

Among the themes included in *later* Christian creedal traditions is the regular reference to Jesus' humanity (1 John 4:2) along with his special relationship with God, but the most common and central elements in most of those early creeds are the identity of Jesus and the emphasis on and significance of his death and resurrection. By the end of the first century, most of the creeds of the church began to include an emphasis on the humanity of Jesus, namely, that he was born of a woman, crucified under Pontius Pilate, and continued earlier affirmations that he was raised from the dead, and also that he will be the judge of humanity at the end of the age. Jesus' humanity is clear in the canonical Gospels and never denied by any author of the NT writings.

As we saw earlier, there can be no doubt about the considerable diversity in early Christianity, especially in the second and third centuries, but it is also nonetheless clear that the earliest surviving creedal summaries of the "Gospel" included Jesus' special relationship with God and the importance of his humanity, death, and resurrection for the forgiveness of sins. For more discussions of this diversity, see Bauer (1971) and Koester (1971: 114–17). As can be seen from the structure and summary elements in these early creedal formulations, they were circulating *orally* from the earliest stages of the church and likely for decades before most of the NT texts were written. The NT creeds and traditions predate the NT writings themselves and focus generally on Jesus' identity, activity, and commands, but mostly on his death and resurrection that was central to the core message of the earliest churches. The affirmations in these creeds and traditions reflect the earliest Christian beliefs circulating in churches by the mid-30s CE.

Again, near the end of the first century, Jesus' full humanity began to be doubted by some Christian docetics who claimed that Jesus only appeared to have a human body. As a result, the church leaders regularly *emphasized* his full humanity (1 John 4:2; Ign. *Trall.* 9.1–2; Justin, *1 Apol.* 61 and his later *Dial.* 89–98; Hippolytus, *Against the Heresy of Noetus;* cf. Eusebius, *H.E.* 2.20.2). Jesus' humanity was regularly in the *Apostles' Creed* and the earlier *Old Roman Creed* cf. Epiphanius, *Haer.* 72.3). The *Nicene Creed* affirmed Jesus' nature as "one in being" (*homoousios*) with the Father and "for our salvation" and states that Jesus "came down and became flesh, becoming human, he suffered, and rose on the third day" (trans. by Johnson 2003: 54–5). The relationship of Jesus with the Father, his birth in Judea and suffering and death, as well as his triumph over death are all regular elements in various creedal formulations of early Christianity of the fourth century and reflect dependence on early church tradition and various NT texts that later became the NT biblical canon of early Christianity.

Again, from the late first century and following, several church fathers began expanding, *but not changing* the core elements of the earlier NT creeds.

6. THE CORE OF THE *REGULA FIDEI*

Tertullian, promoting the "rule of faith" (*regula fidei*), urges readers to avoid darkness and rather to seek "our own." That is "only that which can become an object of inquiry without impairing the rule of faith" (*On Prescription Against Heretics* 12, adapted from *ANF*), and later he states, "For whenever it shall be manifest that the true Christian rule and faith shall be, there will likewise be the true Scriptures and expositions thereof, and all the Christian tradition" (*On Prescription Against Heretics* 19, *ANF*). Tertullian often speaks against those who subvert "the rule of faith" (e.g., *Against Marcion* 3.1; ANF); and clearly identifies this rule of faith with the apostolic deposit passed on in the churches saying that what is to be followed comes from the apostles, such as that which Paul brought to the Galatians to correct them, namely the "rule of faith" (4.5). Finally, Origen refers both to the rule of faith, like Irenaeus and Clement of Rome before him and affirms that the "teaching of the Church, transmitted in orderly succession from the apostles, and remaining in the Churches to the present day, is still preserved, and that alone is to be accepted as truth which differs in no respect from ecclesiastical and apostolical tradition" (*On First Principles*, Preface 2; *ANF*).

Establishing the core identity of Jesus was essential before there could be a broad agreement on the church's earliest creeds. The creeds were the "rule of faith" (*regula fidei*) and have their roots in the earliest history of the church as we saw above in the NT, but this is also true in the early church fathers in the late first and second centuries. There could not have been a church without some agreement on the core beliefs about Jesus. As we have seen above, his followers agreed that he was in the form of God, took on human form, died on a cross, and was highly exalted (Phil 2:6–11). This affirmation is also the primary explanation for the origin of the church and was necessary before there could be a NT canon.

The most central authorities of the early followers of Jesus and the subsequent church fathers were the *words of Jesus* that were equivalent to a scriptural status (e.g., Acts 20:35; 1 Cor 7:10; 14:37; 1 Tim 5:18; see also *1 Clem* 13:1: "especially remembering the words of the Lord" (46:7). Those "words" of Jesus and the church's *First Scriptures*, the Jewish scriptures that had not yet been fully determined in the first century CE were the earliest authorities as argued earlier (see also McDonald 2017: 1:296–335). By the middle of the second century, this also included the apostolic *written* witness, namely if a teaching was believed to be the words of Jesus or to have come from an apostle, it was also authoritative in the churches. For example, in Justin's *Dial*. 100.1 he writes: "*it is written* in the Gospel" and a move toward the authority of the Gospels is in *2 Clement* 8:5 that cites Luke 16:10–12 with the introductory words: "For the Lord says *in the Gospel*." See also the author of the *Didache* (8:2) citing the Lord's prayer in Matt 6:9–13 and introduces it as follows: "as the Lord commanded *in his gospel*." Before Justin (c. 150), it was the "words of the Lord" in the apostolic writings (the Gospels) that were viewed as scripturally authoritative initially and not the sources where they were found. Justin is the first known early Christian writer to refer to the Gospels in a scriptural manner and refer to reading them alongside of or even instead of the "prophets" and using the designation *"it is written"* for the canonical Gospels. Also, the author of the *Epistle of Barnabas* 4:14 (*c.* 135–150) cites the words of Jesus in Matt 22:14 and introduces them with the scriptural designation: *"as it is written* [Greek = ὡς γέγραπται] many called, but few chosen." Scholars are well aware of the difficulty of dating the *Epistle of Barnabas*. The only clue allows either for shortly after the destruction of the temple in 70 CE or after the defeat of the Jewish Bar Kochba rebellion after 135. It is common to date it around 135–150 CE. Obviously, it was highly valued in the early churches and was included in Codex Sinaiticus (*c.* 375 CE).

It is also interesting that the pseudonymous writings attributed to the NT apostles began to emerge after the middle of the second century when apostolic *written* authority became more prominent in the churches. The use of pseudonymous names was a common way for pseudonymous authors to have recognized apostolic authority for their teachings.

It was essential to establish the identity of Jesus before there could be broad (never complete) agreement on the church's earliest creedal affirmations. The creeds were the "rule of faith" (*regula fidei*) that have their roots in the earliest history of the church as we saw above in the NT, but this is also true in the early church fathers in the late first and second centuries. There could not have been a church without some agreement on the core beliefs about Jesus. As we have seen above, his followers agreed that he was in the form of God, took on human form, died on a cross, and was highly exalted as Lord (Phil 2:6–11). This affirmation is both the primary explanation for the origin of the church and its development.

7. THE *REGULA FIDEI* AND CHRISTIAN SCRIPTURE

The identity of Jesus and his nature was at the heart of the church's *regula fidei* or canon of faith and that was threatened by Docetic, Marcionite, and Gnostic Christians and became a hotly contested issue in second- through the fourth-century churches. The division within the Christian community over these issues also threatened the unity of the Roman Empire and so Emperor Constantine *ordered* the bishops throughout the empire to gather in Nicea (*c.* 325) to find unity on these matters. At Nicea there was considerable but not complete agreement eventually on those matters. The aim, no doubt, was to attain some level of peace in the churches and because of Constantine's urging and insistence, some of that was achieved for most churches and the orthodox Christians appear to have won the day. After Nicea and the broader agreement on the identity of Jesus, various lists or catalogues of the church's Christian scriptures, the NT, began to appear. How could there be any agreement on the scope of the church's scriptures until there was considerable agreement on the identity of Jesus, the Lord of the church? While differences over his identity continued after Nicea, there was greater unity in the churches and that obviously provided greater opportunity for agreement on the scope of the church's NT canon. Broad agreement on the church's core sacred traditions and creedal formulations made it possible for greater clarity later in sorting out which Christian writings would be recognized as Christian scripture. We will see below that the surviving manuscripts and local council decisions also reflected the orthodox core beliefs and after that was well established it became possible to determine Christian scriptures, but these were determined largely by use and not by council decisions that generally reflected what was true in their local vicinities.

The "canon of faith" (the *regula fidei*) that emerged and found broader agreement in the churches is often called "proto-orthodoxy" in later second- and third-century Christianity, especially in the teachings of Irenaeus, Tertullian, Hippolytus, and Origen who recognized the orthodox teachings of most of the churches. As we will see in the next chapter, the second-century heresies were answered by an appeal to the "words of the Lord" (Jesus), the church's core traditions, its First scriptures (OT), and various NT texts (Sundberg 1964; 2002: 68–90; Hahneman 1992; Gamble 2002: 267–94; McDonald 2017: 2:274–304). The "canon of faith" they were defending and seeking to establish on firm grounds can be seen especially in Irenaeus whose summary of the Christian canon of faith reads:

> The Church, though dispersed throughout the whole world, even to the ends of the earth, has received from the apostles and their disciples this faith: It believes in one God, the Father Almighty, Maker of heaven, and earth and the sea and all things that are in them and in one Christ Jesus, the Son of God, who became incarnate for our salvation and in the Holy Spirit, who proclaimed through the prophets the dispensations of God, the advents, the birth from a virgin, the passion, the resurrection from the dead, and the ascension into heaven in the flesh of the beloved Christ Jesus, our Lord. He also *proclaimed through the prophets* his future manifestation from heaven in the glory of the Father "to gather all things in one," and to raise up anew all flesh of the whole human race. [This will take place] in order that to Christ Jesus, our Lord, God, Saviour, and King, according to the will of the invisible Father, "every knee should bow, of things in heaven, and things in earth, and things under the earth, and that every tongue should confess" him. And he will execute just judgment towards all sending into everlasting fire "spiritual wickednesses," and the angels who transgressed and became apostates, together with the ungodly, and unrighteous, and wicked, and profane among men. But he will, in the exercise of his grace, confer immortality on the righteous and holy, and those who have kept his commandments, and have persevered in his love, some from the beginning of their Christian course, and others from the time of their repentance. He will surround them with everlasting glory. (*Haer.* 1.10.1, *ANF*, emphasis added, and text adapted; cf. 3.4.2)

The second-century church fathers did not deal with emerging heresies by establishing a list of NT scriptures but rather by establishing a rule of faith that they believed derived from and is reflected in the earliest apostolic traditions as well as in the teachings of the NT. The apostolic community passed along these sacred traditions to the succeeding leadership in the churches. The recognition of these traditions is summarized in several second-, third-, and fourth-century creeds that formed the foundation for recognizing the later fixed collection of NT scriptures.

Despite the many challenges facing the early church, the core beliefs remained, namely Jesus' special relationship with God his Father, his humanity, death for sins, and resurrection or exaltation. By the sixth or seventh century when the *Apostles' Creed* was finally penned, the humanity of Jesus does not appear to have been a point of significant disagreement any longer in most churches in the East or West.

The early church did not have a Bible and the church existed before there was either a fixed OT or NT and even before any Christian scriptures were written, but they could not have existed long without their core traditions and beliefs about Jesus and the ability to transmit them to his followers. From its beginning, there was continual teaching about Jesus (Acts 2:29–36, 42) and that remained the case despite the early church's many challenges, whether with opposition or persecution. The growth and development in the later creeds understandably reflected current issues facing the churches. The early sacred traditions remained stable and central in the church's subsequent life, liturgical expressions, and its foundational creeds that expressed the core elements of its faith. It is difficult to believe that a widely accepted collection of Christian scriptures could have been adopted by the churches before there was considerable agreement on the identity of Jesus, the significance of his death and resurrection, and his role in the forgiveness of sins.

8. HYMNS, SONGS, AND THE EARLY CORE TRADITIONS

Besides the summary NT creeds and later creedal formulations observed above, often an overlooked area of influence in the transmission of the early core Christian traditions are the early Christian hymns and spiritual songs. Just like today and throughout the history of Christianity, the songs sung in various church liturgies have long advanced the transmission of the church's core beliefs. The churches' hymns and spiritual songs regularly affirmed the essence and significance of the Christian faith for most believers including for those who were illiterate. The same could also be said of much of the art employed in Christian buildings, monasteries, chapels, and the like. They too regularly told the story of the church's key teachings and events and they proved especially helpful for understanding the primary teachings of the church by those who could not read. Everyone could understand the images, both young and old, and the core message they intended to present, whether with symbols of the cross, a fish, a boat, or other well-known images of the church. With such images it was not long before nonliterate persons in the church could still understand the primary Christian teachings. I will only focus on the importance of hymns and spiritual songs in early Christianity here since we are dealing with clear affirmations in songs of core beliefs, but the focus on art in churches also has an interesting story in early Christianity.

At the heart of the early Christian faith was a proclamation primarily about the identity and significance of Jesus for bringing God's salvation to humanity and that was advanced by proclaiming a core collection of his teachings, actions (miracles), fate (death and resurrection), and their implications of that for Christian beliefs, their mission, and lifestyle. These beliefs were transmitted in the church's core traditions, creeds, and worship. Initially there was no settled HB or Christian OT or NT, but the early Christian beliefs can be seen not only in the NT writings and summarized in their early NT creeds but also in the church's hymns and spiritual songs. Of course, the church's songs were never on the same level of authority as the church's scriptures or ever equated with them, but most of those songs did transmit the central Christian beliefs in early church father writings. As we saw earlier, the early church beliefs and sacred traditions were circulated in churches orally well before there were any written NT writings, let alone a NT canon. Those early core beliefs and traditions were repeated in church teachings, hymns, spiritual songs, creeds, and regular readings of selected lections or texts accompanied by their interpretation and relevance for Christian faith and living, but they were also expressed regularly in their baptismal and eucharistic affirmations. The music accompanying these activities reaffirmed for church laity the core elements of their Christian faith.

From the church's beginning the means of communicating the core Christian proclamation was not limited to written texts or the proclamation or the teachings in church gatherings. As we see in several NT writings, as well as in early and later church gatherings, songs were sung again and again to familiar music that both inspired and educated the early Christians about their core beliefs. Along with the church's scriptures and regular practice of teaching its core beliefs, these songs had an important role in the church and all participants could share those core beliefs together through them. The hymns and spiritual songs, though not equated with the church's scriptures, nevertheless reinforced the church's primary teachings about the Christian faith even though not equated with the church's scriptures.

It is easy to forget the valuable function of music in the early church's worship gatherings and its value in transmitting the core elements of the Christian faith. While it is popular in many churches today to say that their core doctrine does not come from the hymn book but from the Bible, that was not initially the case when there was no Bible in any church. Along with a command for those filled with or led by the Spirit to proclaim and teach the essence of the Christian faith (Matt 28:20; Acts 6:42), the early Christians were also informed by their "singing psalms and hymns and spiritual songs among yourselves, singing and making melody to the Lord in your hearts" and "giving thanks to God at all times and for everything" (Eph 5:18–21; cf. also Col 3:16). Examples of songs of praise and affirmation of faith can be seen, for example, in Luke 1:46–55; Phil 2:6–11; and Rev 4:8, 11; 5:9–10, 12–13.

Singing in worshipful gatherings was not invented by the early Christians but was inherited from their Jewish siblings who regularly sang in their times of worship and various gatherings. See, for example, the spontaneous song in Exod 15:1–18 and Judg 5) or the lament in some of the songs sung. The Psalter was largely intended to be sung, though the melodies of many favorite Psalms have been lost (Pss 22, 45, 57–59, 75, 80; cf. also Pss 30 and 68), but those psalms continue to be sung but with different melodies and that has continued throughout the history of Judaism and Christianity. The HB/OT songs included both praise (Pss 8, 29, 33, 104, 111, 113) and lament (e.g., Pss 12, 44, 74, 79; cf. 2 Chron 35:25), supplication, and other occasions including the imprecatory psalms (e.g., Ps 109). Singing was very common in the HB/OT and there are many examples of praise noted above. Singers were always prominent in temple worship (1 Chron 15:16–28) and responsible for both instruments and vocal praise (2 Chron 5:13). When the Jews returned from Babylon, the singers were with them (Ezra 2:41; cf. Neh 7:1; 12:27–47). The additional song later inserted between Dan 3:24 and 25 was also well known in antiquity despite not being included in the HB but only in the LXX.

As a result of this long-standing history and tradition of singing in Jewish gatherings (especially synagogue and temple), it is not surprising that singing was also a common feature of early Christian gatherings along with the teaching and preaching ministries in each local congregation. Back then and throughout church history singing was a normal and common way of transmitting the core traditions of the Christian faith. An important Jewish-Christian collection of some forty-two hymns is the *Odes of Solomon*, the oldest known collection of some forty-two Christian songs (*c.* 100–125 CE) and perhaps originating from the same milieu where the Gospel of John was written (Charlesworth 1985: 2:725–771). Interestingly, these songs were even cited as scripture for a time in the early churches. The last church father to cite the collection as scripture was Lactantius in the early fourth century (*Divine Institutes* 19.6; cf. also 4.12.3). *Odes* 1, 5, 6, 22, and 25 were translated in the Gnostic text, *Pistis Sophia*, causing some to suggest that it was a Gnostic collection of odes and citing parallels in *Odes* 11, 24, 30, 34, and 39, but in the *Odes* there is no denying the role of God in creation, it also affirms the humility of Christ (Ode 41.11–16), the humanity and incarnation of the Messiah (Ode 33.5–11), that he was crucified (27.1–3; 42.1–2), and was raised from the dead (8.5–6; 41.12; 42.11–13) (McDonald 2014: 108–36, especially note 115). The important point here, of course, is that having songs listed among a scriptural collection was not unusual in early Christianity before there was a Bible. For example, in P^{72} (*c.* late third or fourth century), *Ode* 11 of the *Odes of Solomon* is included in a collection of NT scriptures with other Christian writings. Also, an eleventh- or twelfth-century discovery at the Laura Monastery on Mt Athos contains besides the NT books a collection of psalms and odes (ms Gregory 1505). See also Pliny's letter to Trajan asking what he should do with Christians and mentions "they met regularly before dawn on a fixed day to *chant verses* [singing] alternatively among themselves in honor of Christ as if to a god" (Pliny the Younger, *Letter* 10.96.7).

Likely most of the early Christians were illiterate and could not read but they obtained and transmitted the Christian message that they learned not only in the preaching and teaching in their churches but also from what they learned in their singing of songs and hymns that celebrated what God had done for them in Christ. Again, that is certainly true today and though most in the Western world can read, many still do not study their scriptures like biblical or theological scholars, but they are regularly inspired and informed in their faith by the singing of hymns and odes or spiritual songs that have been constantly written and passed on in churches from their beginning. It is obvious all hymns or spiritual songs, ancient or contemporary, are not of equal value, but they have long been influential in the formation of the churches and in their propagating their core Christian messages.

Although today it is true that churches do not establish their doctrinal beliefs from their hymnbooks, the singing in the churches has always been an important way of communicating essential Christian theology and the church's core teachings. That also was one of several means of communicating the church's core teachings in antiquity *before there was a Bible* and before many could read the church's scriptures and before the scriptures were produced. We saw this in Lactantius who also saw those texts as scripture. While preaching and teaching were the most important means of communicating those core teachings, it is also true that the use of Christian hymns and spiritual songs was a common way of transmitting the core traditions of the Christian faith in churches from their beginning. An obvious note here that should bring some pause in how we affirm what we sing in churches is that there was a time when the church's songs were often well informed by its teachers and theologians but now that is not always true. I have often thought how helpful to us it would be if more song writers would have some connection with some of those who are more skilled in teaching the church's core beliefs (some are, but many are not). Nevertheless, spiritual songs and hymns have had and continue to have an important role in the history of early Christianity beginning long before there was a Bible. For example, the well-known Christmas carols have informed the church's faith about the significance of the birth of Jesus and the Advent for centuries and often for those who could not read but could remember the essence of the story of Jesus' Advent before they could read those stories in the scriptures.

While most of the early Christians were illiterate, they learned and even transmitted the Christian message not only by what they learned in the teachings of the churches but also in their songs and hymns that they learned from repetition and memory that celebrated what God had done for them in Christ. That is certainly true today not only in the Western world churches but also in several third world countries where many still cannot read or study their Bibles like the literate leaders that served the early churches. They are inspired nevertheless by the singing that has been a constant in the churches from their beginning and it regularly conveys the core teachings of the church.

The earliest known description of a Christian worship service outside of the NT is found in Justin Martyr's *Apology* (*c.* AD 160). Its geographical setting is Rome, and Justin describes what usually took place when the Christians gathered for worship:

> After these [services] we constantly remind each other of these things. Those who have more come to the aid of those who lack, and we are constantly together. Overall that we receive we bless the Maker of all things through his Son Jesus Christ and through the Holy Spirit. And on the day called Sunday there is a meeting in one place of those who live in cities or the country, and *the memoirs of the apostles* [the Gospels] *or the writings of the prophets* [perhaps all or most of what we now call the Old Testament] *are read as long as time permits.* When the reader has finished, the president in a discourse urges and invites [us] to the imitation of these noble things. Then we all stand up together and offer prayers. And, as said before, when we have finished the prayer, bread is brought, and wine and water, and the president similarly sends up prayers and thanksgivings to the best of his ability, and the congregation assents, saying the Amen; the distribution, and reception of the consecrated [elements] by each one, takes place and they are sent to the absent by the deacons. Those who prosper, and who so wish, contribute, each one as much as he chooses to. What is collected is deposited with the president, and he takes care of orphans and widows, and those who are in want on account of sickness or any other cause, and those who are in bonds, and the strangers who are sojourners among [us], and, briefly, he is the protector of all those in need. We all hold this common gathering on Sunday, since it is the first day, on which God transforming darkness and matter made the universe, *and Jesus Christ our Saviour rose from the dead on the same day. For they crucified him on the day before Saturday, and on the day after Saturday, he appeared to his apostles and disciples and taught them these things which I have passed on to you also for your serious consideration.* (Justin, 1 *Apol.* 67; *ANF*, emphasis added)

While today churches do not establish church doctrine from hymn books, it is likely that many illiterate early Christians learned some, if not many, of their beliefs from the songs that were sung in their church gatherings, and some of those songs were treated like scripture, that is, believed, even if not called scripture. As noted above, Lactantius in early fourth century treated the *Odes of Solomon* as scripture, but more than that, both ancient Judaism and some early Christians welcomed multiple hymns and spiritual songs among their scriptural collections.

On a personal observation, I regularly attend and participate in multiple church denomination's worship services whether in "high" services (traditional with more liturgy) or "low" (more contemporary music with less liturgy and more worship choruses or songs) type services. Recently I attended a church service with worship that had blended music (contemporary and traditional) including the use of organ, piano, and stinged instruments, including drums, guitars, and a keyboard and a couple of brass instruments. I was thinking throughout the service that the core elements of the Christian faith were being presented in every part of that service beginning with the music and inspirational singing of both familiar hymns and newer worship choruses. I also observed the reading of several scriptures, the offering of prayers, and a sermon focused on the implications of several biblical texts for Christian faith, living, and mission. The primary focus was on God's love for humanity in the Gospel of John and was extended to how Christ showed God's love by dying on the cross and how that has implications for how Christians are also called to love others by paying whatever price that love may require to care for those in need of our love and God's love. It was a very moving service, but I also noticed throughout that I did not need to know how to read to follow what was taking place in the church services. The scriptures were read aloud in churches along with many of the familiar songs reflecting their core church beliefs.

When I began going to church as a teenager many years ago, I remember that some older church members could not read or write, but they carried a Bible to church even when they could not read it, they regularly expressed their faith in ways not unlike the other Christians there who could read and write. They offered where possible deeds of love and service in the church's ministries. Some served communion, visited the sick and needy, and openly shared their faith in the churches. This was probably not unlike many persons in the early churches. Singing the core Christian traditions was a valuable tool in early Christianity to transmit the church's sacred traditions and beliefs. Any songs that do not reflect the church's core beliefs seldom last long in church worship. While the songs are not considered sacred scripture, they regularly transmit the core authoritative traditions and beliefs of the church. (For helpful summaries of the role of hymns and spiritual songs in early Christianity, see Martin 1982: 2:788–90; Bichel 1992: 3:350–51 and his 2005: 814–17; for more detailed research see Roberts 2008: 628–40; McGuckin 2008: 641–56; Brock 2008: 656–71; Wellesz 1949; and Lattke 1991; Ferguson 1997: 1:748–51; Delling 1972: 8:489–93; Charlesworth 1977; Church and Mulry 1988; and McGuckin 1995.)

In the next chapter I will focus on several major challenges *facing* early Christianity including several developing "heretical" challenges from within the churches and how they were addressed by various church fathers. These challenges include, of course, not only Roman persecutions against the Christians but also the multiple doctrinal variants that threatened the existence of the church and core Christian beliefs that many of proto-orthodoxy adherents believed were foundational for understanding and proclaiming the church's identity and mission.

CHAPTER 5

The Lectionaries, Manuscripts, and Their Texts

1. INTRODUCTION

The surviving early Christian lectionaries, manuscripts, and their texts are very important for understanding authorities in early Christianity before there was a Bible. They reflect the actual or *operative* scriptures of the early churches that functioned as authorities for those churches. They let us know what writings were actually circulating in churches and informing the faith of Christians in antiquity. While the canon lists are very important indicators of what informed church leaders and their decisions about the scope of the church's scriptures, they tell us what church's leaders and scholars believed should be read in the churches, but they do not tell the whole story. The local churches that had lectionaries and copies of the church's scriptures sometimes tell a different story. That will be the focus in this chapter. The lists, lectionaries, and some of the larger biblical manuscripts generally emerged roughly at the same time, and all are important for understanding the operative authorities in the early churches.

The date, location where the manuscripts were discovered, and the extent where possible to know who produced them are very important for determining their significance, origin, and influence. The surviving manuscripts are largely from the dry climate regions, especially Egypt and the Jordan Valley, and they let us know not only what was read to the people in churches in those regions but sometimes also what was read in churches that was not recognized by those who constructed the canon lists or catalogues. Because of the translocal movement of texts in the Roman Empire, some texts could have been sent from one part of the Empire to another in just a matter of weeks, it is likely that what was read in churches in Egypt might well have been read also in Rome or Antioch. I have earlier observed that some texts that were later rejected as scripture in the fourth- and fifth-century catalogues were still being read by some Christians in their churches well into the eighth and ninth centuries and even later, so some church leaders considered it important to condemn them some four or five centuries later after councils had rejected them as we saw earlier in the mid ninth century *Stichometry of Nicephorus* (McDonald 2017: 2:313–14; Collins, Evans, and McDonald 2020: 79). I will also examine some of the uncial or majuscule manuscripts that let us know what writings were being read in some churches well into the fourth and fifth centuries before the Bible was fully formed for the churches.

I will begin with a focus on writing and writing materials used to produce the church's scriptures and their relevance for understanding the transmission of the church's scriptures in antiquity.

2. THE ACT OF WRITING

In the ancient world, the act of writing often carried with it the implication of something very important was transmitted and occasionally something with considerable authority, and occasionally even having divine authority. The very words "it is written" had special meaning and was often used to identify sacred texts. "As the scripture says" is literally "as the writing says" and therefore the implication is that it must be taken seriously. Because writing materials were quite expensive in antiquity and often inaccessible to many, most of what was written was considered quite significant. Important communications were sometimes etched in stone or on ostraca (broken potsherds) or in other more permanent media (inscriptions on stone) and put on public display. The familiar words "it is written in stone" have long roots in the thinking about written materials in antiquity. Certainly not everything written was considered divine, but the average person took the words "it is written" or "it is etched in stone" to be very important and often also not to be taken lightly. For a careful description of writing among the Jews in antiquity, see M. Bar-Ilan (1988: 28–38).

At first, ancient writings were inscribed on walls or on stone, wood, beaten metal, and eventually on clay tablets (*c*. 3100 BCE and following). Some important writings were etched in stone (Exod 31:18) or painted on walls (Dan 5:5–9), or even placed on flattened metal (chiefly copper, such as the *Copper Scroll* among the Dead Sea Scrolls) or silver (sheets hammered to a smooth surface), and potsherds. Around the turn of the Common Era, flat wooden blocks were bound together with leather strings to make tablets (codices) with wax inside and a stylus that allowed a writer to make several notes and subsequently erase them and use the same wax in the codex again. Sometimes codices included several papyrus pages sewn together and were often used for nonliterary documents such as bills of sale and personal correspondence, while more important writings were placed in a more literary format such as scrolls of papyrus sheets or animal skins sewn together and circulated in rolls. By far papyrus (plural papyri; cf. from which the word "paper" derives) and animal skins were the most common writing materials employed during the time of Jesus and later. In the last decade of the first century, the author of Revelation spoke of a scroll with seven seals that was progressively unsealed to reveal its contents (Rev 5:1–8:5). Scrolls occasionally were written on both sides (possibly the meaning of Rev 5:2) and that reflects not only the value of the manuscript's contents but also the value of the material employed in the transmission.

Papyrus manuscripts were cheaper to produce and among the most common writing material in antiquity. The papyrus plant grew in abundance along the banks of the Nile River in Egypt and was harvested and made into writing materials. The material was often called *byblos* because large quantities of this material were shipped out of the Syrian harbor city of Byblos. Our word Bible comes from the plural *biblia* of the Greek word *biblion* ("book"). Papyrus sheets were often pasted together end to end to form a lengthy roll or scroll. With the development of the codex, papyrus sheets were often combined with other sheets, folded, and sewn at the middle edge to hold the pages together. The number of sheets that were combined to make a quire varied, but seldom more than eight sheets that once folded produced sixteen pages on which one could write on both the front and back (recto and verso) of each page. Over time multiple quires were sewn together allowing for longer documents to be combined and sewn together in one codex.

By the fourth century CE scrolls and codices made of animal skins became the standard writing vehicles in churches for transmitting their scriptures, but most of the Christian scriptures (*c.* 70 percent) were written on papyrus sheets folded and sewn together to form a codex (cf. 2 Tim 4:13) and sometimes a roll (perhaps about 30 percent of the time). The surviving manuscripts let us know that few churches had all four Gospels or all the New Testament (NT) *even if* they knew they existed. Before the fourth century, due to the possible sizes of the codex, the manuscripts of that time seldom contained more than one or more of the Gospels along with a few other NT writings. By the end of the second century the advanced technology for producing codices made it possible to include all four Gospels and Acts in one codex (P^{45}), but very few manuscripts have all four Gospels until much later. Another papyrus manuscript from about the same time (P^{46}) contains most of Paul's letters (approximately two hundred pages). Other combinations of multiple Christian texts were produced in the third century, for example, P^{72} that contains besides Jude, and 1–2 Peter also *Nativity of Mary*, *3 Corinthians*, Melito's *Homily*, a hymn, the *Apology of Phileas*, and Psalms 33 and 34.

The use of parchment manuscripts (both rolls or scrolls and codices) first developed in ancient Pergamum and soon the technology spread from there to the whole empire and allowed for larger collections as the technology advanced. The value of using parchment was that it was easier to write on and easier to erase when mistakes were made or when a writer wanted to reuse the same writing material for a different purpose (palimpsests). Because of the considerable expense of writing materials, it was common to erase by rubbing the parchment documents entirely and use them again for other purposes. Some biblical manuscripts are on reused parchment manuscripts and some earlier biblical manuscripts were erased and used for other purposes.

Before and during the first century CE, the roll or scroll was used for almost all literary documents as we see in the Dead Sea Scrolls. The opening of the scroll is also a part of the literary convention known to the author of the book of Revelation in Rev 5:1–5 speaking of the scrolls and seals in 6:1–8:1. See also how the author refers to his own writing as "this book" in Rev 22:18–19. Informal writings were sometimes put in notebooks (tablets or handbooks, that is, codices) and those writings often had more informality and abbreviations in them. The Jews regularly used scrolls when copying their sacred scriptures and the codex for other documents. Jewish scribes only began using codices in the fourth century for producing their scriptures. At first single books were copied in the scrolls, and later major sections of the Hebrew Bible (HB) were placed on one scroll with individual sheets sewn together to make a long scroll as we see in the lengthy famed scroll of Isaiah found at Qumran among the Dead Sea Scrolls. When the technology advanced sufficiently so that the whole of the HB could be placed on a single scroll (fourth century CE), the Jews continued to separate the Pentateuch from the rest of the Jewish scriptures and place it on its own scroll that was more than seventy feet in length. This practice meant that each of the three groupings of the HB writings was eventually transmitted together on separate scrolls devoted to Law, Prophets, and Writings.

In the third century CE, the codex was used in approximately 50 percent of Roman literary documents. In the fourth century, the codex had gained parity with the roll or scroll among the Romans for literary documents, primarily with the use of parchment rather than the traditional papyri sheets. According to Gamble, those who produced codex documents for use in Christian churches were generally aware that they were producing second-class books, or handbooks, and not formal literary writings. Gamble cites E. G. Turner in this regard, saying that "scribes who copied on a codex of papyrus in a single column were aware that they were writing a second-class book" (Gamble 1995:70). He also has a helpful discussion of the origins of the codex and its widespread use in the early churches, including arguments that suggest Paul's use of them is the background for the church's acceptance and continuation of their use (Gamble 1995: 49–61). This suggests that initially the early churches may not have received NT literature as sacred scripture but rather as informal teaching materials for the church. Gamble observes that the "fine bookhand" normally seen in literary documents is only rarely seen in Christian texts before the fourth century. They are more typically produced in the less formal round type letters often referred to as a "reformed documentary" type of writing (Gamble 1995: 66–71).

The predominant use of the codex in the early Christian communities (*c.* 70 percent of the time) may well have its roots in the way that Paul circulated his letters. Early tradition points to Paul's use of the codex for letter writing to churches. For instance, the Latin term *membranai*, transliterated into Greek as μεμβράνας, in 2 Tim 4:13 is sometimes translated as "parchments," but the term likely refer to codices (Gamble 1995: 50–5). Hurtado discusses this possibility and while he is generally sympathetic to Gamble, he nevertheless is not convinced that Paul either carried with him a collection of books (codices) or whether early church history supports this interpretation, but he agrees that it is "perfectly possible" that someone in the middle of the first century could have used codices or books (Hurtado 2006: 76–9).

Gamble suggests that the early tradition that Paul wrote to seven churches fits well with the writings regularly attributed to him, namely Romans, 1–2 Corinthians, Galatians, 1–2 Thessalonians, Philippians, Ephesians, Colossians—which included Philemon, and this accounts for ten letters attributed to Paul. I am aware of scholarly doubts about Paul's authorship of Ephesians, Colossians, and 2 Thessalonians, but that will not be a part of the discussion here. The earliest collections of Paul's writings that we have do include Ephesians, Colossians, and 2 Thessalonians (P[46], *Codex Vaticanus*, and *Codex Sinaiticus*). I am also aware of the arguments against Pauline authorship of 2 Thessalonians and the Pastorals and addressed them earlier. Circulation of Paul's writings to these *seven* churches may have inspired a similar pattern of letters to seven churches in the Apocalypse of John (Rev 2–3) and for the seven *Letters* of Ignatius of Antioch to churches in the early second century. The number itself suggests completeness. The circulation of Paul's writings to *seven* churches may imply their completeness and later believed to have usefulness for all churches. Despite the many items in them that focused on specific matters related to local churches, the letters proved quite useful to many churches in subsequent generations.

For our purposes, it is interesting that the ten letters to these seven churches (Romans, 1–2 Corinthians, Galatians, Ephesians, Philippians, Colossians, 1–2 Thessalonians, with Philemon) fit reasonably well on the normal length of a single quire of a codex of approximately 200–220 pages but not on a scroll or roll. Gamble notes that these ten letters of Paul would occupy some eighty feet on a roll or scroll manuscript, which is more than double the maximum length of most scrolls in antiquity and three times the average size. On the other hand, the single codex with one quire could accommodate in one volume all the letters of Paul to the seven churches (= ten letters). Because Paul's letters were generally placed in order beginning with the largest (Romans) and descending to the smallest (Philemon), a volume with all these letters to the seven churches, and in a descending sequence, only made sense if they were placed in one volume rather than in separate rolls or scrolls. The sequence, Gamble claims, would be lost if the letters had circulated in separate rolls and it is unlikely that the tradition of seven churches used in Rev 2–3 and the seven *Letters* of Ignatius to churches would have emerged had Paul's letters not circulated together. The length of a single quire codex is also the approximate length of the P^{46} that contains the earliest collection of Paul's writings without the Pastoral Epistles and Philemon but with the book of Hebrews inserted between Romans and 1 Corinthians (Gamble 1995: 58–66).

By the fourth century CE, following considerable advances in the technology of producing larger codices and the production of majuscule or uncial manuscripts on parchment, there was sufficient capacity to include all the books of the Christian Old Testament (OT) and NT in one codex or volume that could expand to some 1,600 parchment manuscript pages. When discussions of the scope of the biblical canon began to take place in antiquity, they centered only on the *books* that comprised the sacred collections and not on their *text* or *translation*, or even the space available to include them in such collections. None of the earliest scrolls (rolls) or codices employed in transmitting the books of the NT had sufficient capacity to include all the NT writings, though by the early third century the four Gospels and Acts could be included in one codex of roughly 200–220 pages, as we see in the fragmented P^{45} and P^{46}. Initially (i.e., for the church's first 150 years or so), only a few NT books at most could reasonably fit into a single codex or even a scroll. The *current* 128 NT papyrus manuscripts (and still growing in number) are listed in the Nestle-Aland *Novum Testamentum Graece* 28th edition and the UBS *Greek New Testament,* 5th edition). These and other more recent editions (Holmes SBL edition) list the earliest known collections of NT manuscripts, but in the first four centuries only fourteen manuscripts contain more than one book and of those only a handful have more than two documents. The recent *Greek New Testament* published by Tyndale House, Cambridge, UK, in 2017 includes three additional papyrus manuscripts (P^{29}, P^{30}, and P^{35}). However, the number of surviving papyrus NT manuscripts will doubtless increase to around 140 in future editions since other texts have been found and after their assessment and cataloguing, they will be added to the collection.

With advances in the size of the codex by the fourth century, one codex volume could include all the church's scriptures, both OT and NT in one large volume. It remains a question whether the initial capacity of the codices had any effect on the contours or shape of the Bible.

It was common in the second and third centuries for biblical manuscripts to contain limited portions of our current NT canon such as one or more gospels and a few epistles at best with a few notable exceptions. Further, the earliest surviving manuscripts do not always have *the same* text in them despite their considerable overlap. For canon formation purposes, the fourth century and later uncial or majuscule manuscripts are of particular interest for canon studies because they had a greater space capacity that allowed for the inclusion of all the church's scriptures. These issues—the books included, the text of those books, their transmission, and translation—and other issues related to ancient literary artifacts have a direct bearing on issues related to the authority and biblical text today.

As noted above, most of the early copies of the NT scriptures were produced on papyrus in rolls or scrolls until the early second century they were mostly (70 percent) copied in codices in capital letters (uncial or majuscule) without spaces between the words, possibly to conserve space on expensive writing materials. The generally nonprofessional materials and the codex used in the early stages of transmitting Christian writings may reflect an earlier nonscriptural view of the materials such as Paul's letters (cf. 2 Tim 4:13) that were *ad hoc* addresses to local congregations discussing specific issues affecting them. By the middle to late fourth century, Christian professional scribes began producing manuscripts on parchment in the codices with both considerably higher quality and greater capacity or volume, yet still, perhaps because of cost or custom, those manuscripts also had no spaces between words for several more centuries.

By the eighth century, scribes began to insert spaces between words and write mostly in lowercase letters (*minuscule* manuscripts). These manuscripts are commonly called "cursive" (from Latin, *cursivus*, "to run") because of the practice of writing all the letters of a word without lifting the pen from the page (i.e., a running hand) but with spaces between the words. Until Gutenberg invented moveable type and the printing press (1454) and published the whole Bible (1456), all biblical texts were produced by hand. After the seventh or eighth centuries they were produced in lowercase lettering often with colorful imagery (i.e., decorative letters and illustrations) especially at the beginning of books and chapters. For more information on the practice of writing and the materials used for writings in the ancient world, see Wegner (1999), Hurtado (2006: 43–93), Porter (2013: 77–146), and Richards (2004 and 2013: 345–66, 200).

We now turn to the content of the Christian manuscripts from antiquity beginning with the lectionaries.

3. THE LECTIONARIES

Lectionaries are among the most overlooked entities that transmitted the church's scriptures in antiquity. They were selections from longer books that were read in churches in their liturgies. Such selected reading from longer books was also practiced in the synagogues and continued in the early churches. These recognized scriptural texts were regularly read in churches from their beginning but their contents are clearer and more specific from around the middle to the end of the fourth century, especially in Constantinople and other churches in the East. A helpful summary of these valuable resources is in Rouwhorst (2013: 822–42). The evidence for scripture reading in churches is limited initially, but doubtless goes back to the church's earliest beginnings that are rooted in Jewish practices in the synagogues in which the earliest Christians came and participated regularly. For examples of reading scriptures in the synagogues in the first century CE see, for example, Luke 4:16–21; Acts 13:15; 2 Cor 3:15, and the common practice of reading Christian texts in churches is everywhere assumed in the letters addressed to the churches from Paul, James, Peter, and John. However, the evidence for what specifically was read besides the NT letters is seldom as clear until the fourth and fifth centuries as in the case of the readings during the church's Eucharist observances and at baptisms.

The church's roots in Judaism make it understandable that early Christians would have followed their Jewish siblings' practice of reading scripture in the synagogue gatherings on the Sabbath and their interpretation and implications as those present were able to interpret them. This practice was less common in Temple worship that focused mostly on sacrifice and the singing of psalms. The practice of a regular reading of Torah or Pentateuchal texts and the *haftarah* (a conclusion of a biblical lesson), the practice of including a pericope from the Prophets, was common in the synagogues on the Sabbath in the time of Jesus (Acts 13:15; Luke 4:16–21; cf. also Philo, *Spec. Laws* 2.60–62; Josephus *J.W.* 2.289–92; *m. Meg.* 3.6). Because the early Christians followed the pattern of the synagogue in their gatherings, it is likely that they also read texts of scriptures. As noted, evidence of reading NT texts in Christian gatherings can be seen in the NT letters that were addressed to churches as we see in Col 4:16. Those letters regularly cite multiple Hebrew scriptures mostly from the LXX and there is no defense presented for citing those sacred texts, but rather they are read as justification for what the authors were saying. It was not as if they were introducing something new to the people whom they were addressing, but rather the authors assume their readers will also recognize the scripture texts introduced with the usual scriptural designations, "as it is written" or "as the scripture says," or even without those designations when the authors are "writing with scripture" as noted earlier.

Justin in the mid-second century described a typical gathering of Christians on the Sunday and listed the activities that regularly took place in their meetings. That description was provided in the previous chapter but for here it mentions the regular reading of the "memoirs of the apostles" (the Gospels) "or" the writings of the prophets (the Hebrew scriptures/OT writings) as long as time allows or permits, noting that they do not read all of them on one occasion but rather like the Jews reading a selection in the synagogues from Moses (Torah) and a *haftarah* (portion of the prophets). There are multiple examples of reading of selections of the scriptures in synagogues in late Second Temple Judaism and useful summaries of these are in L. Levine (2005: 135–51) and those in early Christianity are summarized in Gerard Rouwhorst (2013: 825–7) and A. J. Levine (2017: 249–50, 759–63). In synagogues regular readings from the Pentateuch ("Moses") with some readings of the Prophets were common in the first century, as we see from Luke 4:16–21 and Acts 13:15.

The more familiar Christian liturgical readings in ancient churches, like those that are more contemporary, often included readings from the Law, Prophets and/or Psalms, Gospels, and Epistles. More is known about the lectionary contents from the fourth century and later, although readings from the Gospels are quite early in Christian worship as we saw earlier in Justin mentioning the Gospels ("memoirs of the apostles") or "prophets" (= all the HB/OT scriptures). This is seen also in Tertullian, Cyprian, and Augustine. While sometimes whole books were read, especially the smaller letters or minor prophets, most often the lectionaries were selections from the Law (Pentateuch), Prophets, Gospels, and Epistles. Interestingly, *Did.* 8–10 (*c.* 90–100 CE) focuses on how to pray, observe fasting days and the Eucharist, but with no references to scripture reading while observing them. The author's reference to the example of Jesus "in his gospel" that cites his prayer (the Lord's Prayer) as a model to follow in Matt 6:9–13 suggests the readers were familiar with that Gospel. The author also admonishes readers to avoid reprimanding one another but to admonish in peace "as you have learned from the gospel and similarly to say prayers, offer charity," and "engage in all your activities as you have learned in the gospel of our Lord" (15.3–4, LCL). The author assumes that readers are familiar with the Gospels of Matthew and Mark and that most likely means their familiarity came from a liturgical reading of the Gospels in their church gatherings. It is highly unlikely that all of those hearing the *Didache* read to them would have had their own copies of it or the Gospels so they could check it out. *Did.* 16 has several parallels from the Gospels of Mark and Matthew. Clearly, scriptures were read in church gatherings, but the specific texts are generally uncertain until the fourth century and thereafter.

Miller has observed that the scriptures known to the Orthodox Christians in the East were almost completely lections in the liturgies that were read in the churches. He observes that of the 1,500 surviving Septuagint (LXX) manuscripts employed in the preparation of Rahlfs's and Frenkel's *Verzeichnisder griechischen Handschriften des Alten Testaments* (2004) only seventeen manuscripts have a full OT. He goes on to say that the common persons in churches knew their OT only partially and mostly through the church's OT lectionaries that he calls the "Prophetologion." He contends that the whole OT was seldom known to all the churches throughout the whole Byzantine period and that "the Prophetologion was the Old Testament of Byzantine Christianity." He adds that this selective core of the OT "is reducible to a strictly textual core" (Miller 2010: 55–8). This was likely for three reasons: (1) the difficulty and cost of producing a complete collection of the OT scriptures that "ensured that few exemplars of such scope were produced in antiquity;" (2) low literacy rates would have prevented most of the people from being familiar with the church's scriptures; and (3) the familiarity and accessibility of a complete OT would not have been possible to most since the circulation of such longer texts would have been prohibitive and did not circulate freely in antiquity. This is similar in the surviving NT manuscripts, namely, there is little evidence that the scope of the OT and NT was widely known throughout the Byzantium period and certainly those few copies of both Testaments in the fourth and fifth centuries (Sinaiticus, Vaticanus, and Alexandrinus) were not widely circulated or even known in many if not most churches as the surviving manuscripts show.

Only a small group of NT manuscripts (now over 5,740) contain all the NT books and none of them contain all the NT books and *only* those books before around 1000 and possibly even as late as 1116 CE as in the case of a Mt Athos manuscript (Gregory 922; cf. Schmidt 2002: 475–9). The lectionaries that were circulating in the churches largely from the fourth century are the best representatives of the sacred books known in most of the ancient churches. Unfortunately, little attention has been paid to the role that lectionaries had in the formation of the church's scriptures (Schmidt 2002: 55–76; Scanlin 1996: 300–12). What Miller says about the Orthodox churches in the East is most likely also true for most churches in the West. The church's scholars might well have known and had accessibility to all the books that now comprise the church's OT canon, but certainly not the average minister or priest let alone layperson.

By the fourth century and thereafter churches began to prepare lections for Eucharist observances and baptisms as well as for festive occasions in churches. The evidence for complete Bibles for churches in the East and West was rare in antiquity and for many centuries. As a result, the selection of lections was especially valuable for church worship and other special occasions. Hopefully scholars will give more attention to lections as they consider the multiple influences that gave rise subsequently to the church's Bibles.

4. THE MANUSCRIPTS AND CHRISTIAN SCRIPTURE

One of the peculiarities of the early Christian community is its preference for the codex by no later than 100 CE. The codex undoubtedly appealed to Christians because of its portability and convenience and possibly also its greater affordability. Later improvements in the production of the codex allowed multiple books to be included in a single codex. By the middle of the fourth century when all the church's sacred books could be included in a single volume, this also began the emergence of multiple fixed biblical multiple canon lists. The technology of producing books and the increased capacity of the codex eventually made it possible to contain the whole Bible in one volume, but as noted earlier, the cost of the materials and professional copiers made it difficult or even impossible for most churches to have a complete collection of the church's scriptures. Besides the cost of hundreds of animals and the salary of a qualified scribe, the average of more than two years per copy made it very costly for a church to own a complete copy of the scriptures it recognized. Again, as the capacity of the codex increased, so also did the number of books included in it along with occasionally other books not later included in the church's Bible.

It is interesting that no manuscript includes all the books of the NT until the middle to late fourth century as we see in *Codex Sinaiticus*, but it also includes the *Epistle of Barnabas* and the *Shepherd of Hermas*. As noted earlier no known manuscript contains all the NT books *and no others* until around 1116 CE (Gregory 922; see Schmidt 2002: 476–7; see further discussion of this manuscript below). Some manuscripts as late as the fourteenth century contain books not later included in church Bibles. Most early churches did not have access to all the OT and NT books and sometimes their sacred collections included noncanonical books such as *the Shepherd of Hermas, the Epistle of Barnabas, the Didache, 1 and 2 Clement*, the *Letters* of Ignatius, and occasionally other gospels, letters, and apocalypses. If the capacity of codices was able to accept more texts in it before the fourth century, we can only imagine what else might have been in them and how they might have affected subsequent church history.

In 367 CE when Athanasius sent out his annual *Festal letters* to let churches know when to celebrate Easter, he often added considerably more in them than the date to celebrate Easter. In his *Thirty-Ninth Festal Letter* he advised churches on which sacred books to read in the churches, which to read privately, and which to avoid altogether. His OT is similar to the HB, and he also adds Baruch and the Epistle of Jeremiah but omits Esther. He allowed private reading of several non-HB books and non-NT books, but rejected the reading of those he believed were pseudonymous or heretical that he identified as "apocryphal" that should not be read at all.

The ancient manuscripts occasionally include noncanonical writings among the scripture collections and they often omit some NT books as well. An example of this is in *Codex Vaticanus* that along with P^{46} omits the Pastoral Letters, though possibly because both are fragmented texts, which may not have been the case in *Codex Vaticanus*. One cannot be sure here, since they are absent from the two oldest manuscript collections of Paul's writings P^{46} and Marcion's collection. The current Greek NTs do not indicate that the Pastoral Epistles are absent from *Codex Vaticanus* or P^{46}. Unfortunately, much of the significant information about the full contents of the NT manuscripts must be found elsewhere than in the introductions of the Greek NTs. Daryl Schmidt and Eldon Epp provide a valuable service reminding us of the many omissions in the available biblical apparatuses but also what all of this means for understanding the Bible in its early formative period (Epp 2002; Schmidt 2002). They acknowledge that the manuscripts functioned authoritatively in the communities that had them (and that produced them), and some manuscripts also contain nonbiblical books.

They also note that the scriptural text in these manuscripts also often varies. Many unintentional errors and intentional changes were included in the early manuscripts, and along with their multiple variants they served as authoritative texts that welcomed and read them. Epp rightly concludes, "Most if not all such competing variants were held to be canonical, wittingly or not, at various times and places in real-life Christian contexts, requiring the disquieting conclusion that canonicity of readings has virtually the same degree of multiformity as do the meaningful competing variants in a variation unit" (Epp 2002: 515). In many instances the term "canonical" no longer applies to only one variant reading and therefore no longer to only a single text of NT writings (Epp 2002: 515).

Sanders, speaking about textual variations in the book of Psalms, agrees substantially with Epp and writes, "There were probably as many canons as there were communities." He explains that the problem of fluidity in the books and texts in the collections of books that various communities possessed brings "attention to the question of literature considered authoritative—that is, functionally canonical—by one Jewish or Christian community but not by another" (Sanders 1999: 316–33, 1995: 56–63, here esp. 58; and 1991: 203–17). This is an important factor that is seldom understood or focused on by biblical scholars.

Epp shows that the canon manuscripts from the fourth and fifth centuries represent more the scriptural texts of the Christian communities up to that time. They show more accurately the situations in the local churches than do the canon lists or the books listed by councils or synods that served the churches. While there is considerable overlap in the contents of the biblical manuscripts and the canon lists, there are also considerable variations in them (Epp 2002: 495–6; and Sanders 1999: 316–33; and his 1991: 203–17). He supports this point by noting that textual and biblical scholars tend only to discuss the *biblical* books found at Oxyrhynchus but not the noncanonical books that were also discovered there (2004: 14–17). For example, the manuscripts discovered at the Egyptian Oxyrhynchus site also include

> seven copies of the Shepherd of Hermas
> three copies of the Gospel of Thomas
> two copies of the Gospel of Mary
> one copy of the Acts of Peter
> one copy of the Acts of John
> one copy of the Acts of Paul
> one copy of the Didache
> one copy of the Sophia of Jesus Christ
> two copies of the Gospel of Peter
> single copies of three unknown gospels/sayings of Jesus
> one copy of the Acts of Paul and Thecla
> one copy of the Protevangelium of James
> one copy of the Letter of Abgar to Jesus. (see Eusebius, *Hist. eccl.* 1.13)

While many early NT books were also found at Oxyrhynchus, we cannot overlook that the above apocryphal books and some unknown gospel-like writings were also found there (Epp, 2004: 18–20). Epp further notes that in the discovery at Oxyrhynchus there was one Old Latin and twenty-three Greek manuscripts of the LXX that included portions of Wisdom of Solomon, Tobit, Apocalypse of Baruch, and 1 Enoch. For more information on the Egyptian manuscript discoveries and their contents, see more detailed information in McDonald (2017: 2:237–94).

The point here is that the scriptural collections varied from time to time and place to place in the formative period before there was a recognized Bible. It is likely from Epp's and Schmidt's investigations that all the biblical and noncanonical writings discovered in the ancient world functioned as scripture for some Christians in the communities where those books were found. This, of course, relies on careful examinations of the contents of the ancient biblical manuscripts because they aid considerably in our understanding of scriptures that informed the faith of the ancient Christians.

Despite widespread illiteracy in the Greco-Roman world in the first century and thereafter, there is no doubt that sacred texts significantly informed the faith of the followers of Jesus from the church's beginning. Hurtado rightly observes that from its beginning early Christianity was a "bookish" religion and reminds us that, even in the NT, Paul admonishes his readers to read his letter to other congregations (Col 4:16). Paul regularly wrote to individuals as well as to congregations and expected his writings to be read to the people *in those churches* (Gal 1:2) (Hurtado 2016: 105–41). By all accounts, the Gospels circulated in churches from their beginnings along with a collection of Paul's writings, some of which were in Rome and known by Marcion. Several of them were known in churches in the late first and early second centuries and were cited by several early church fathers. This can be seen in the frequent citations of them in the second century and thereafter (McDonald 2017: 2:247–54).

The NT writers base their arguments about Jesus in their interpretation of many preexisting Jewish religious texts that had gained widespread approval as scripture before the time of Jesus, most of which were later included in the church's OT canon. The discovery of the Dead Sea Scrolls noted earlier supports arguments that a broader collection of religious texts than those included in the later HB and Christian OT were circulating in Palestine and informed segments of late Second Temple Judaism and later early Christianity. From earliest times, the reading of sacred texts in Christian gatherings shaped the early congregations. As we saw earlier, the synagogue was the primary antecedent to the practices of worship and teaching in the early churches and they included regular readings of sacred texts and prayers that were also important aspects of Christian liturgical services.

5. MAJUSCULE/UNCIAL MANUSCRIPTS FROM THE SECOND TO FIFTH CENTURIES

Because of the greater capacity to include all the churches' scriptures in one very large volume by the middle to late fourth century, it is important to see what was in those pandect codices that can help us to see what religious texts were informing Christian faith at that time. In them we will see several writings not later included in Christian Bibles but were considered at one time scripture for some Christians. Some noncanonical books are occasionally included in church father citations, various translations, and manuscripts; and sometimes canonical writings were omitted. The following list of the fourth century and later uncial manuscripts not only have considerable overlap but also several differences. They show both the considerable overlap in most of the texts accepted by Christians as scripture in the fourth to the thirteenth century, as well as variations in some of the "fringe" books not welcomed by all in Eastern and Western churches. Primary examples include the following:

1. Greek—*Codex Vaticanus* (B, *c.* 350–375): The OT includes Esther *with additions*, 1–2 Esdras, Wisdom, Sirach, Judith, Tobit, 1 Baruch, Epistle of Jeremiah, Susannah, Bel and the Dragon. The NT is fragmentary and breaks off in the middle of Heb 9:14. Later hands added the rest of the NT books including 1–2 Timothy, Titus, Philemon, and Revelation.
2. Greek—*Codex Sinaiticus* (Aleph or ℵ, *c.* 375–380): 1–2 Esdras, Tobias, Judith, 1 and 4 Maccabees, Wisdom, Sirach, Esther with additions, 1 Baruch, Epistle of Jeremiah. It includes all the NT books and also the Epistle of Barnabas and Shepherd of Hermas.
3. Greek—*Codex Alexandrinus* (A, *c.* early to mid-fifth century): Additions to Esther, 1 Baruch, Epistle of Jeremiah, Tobit, Judith, 1–2 Esdras, 1, 2, 3, 4 Maccabees, Wisdom, Sirach, Psalms of Solomon, Prayer of Manasseh, Psalms of

Solomon, Psalm 151, and 14 Odes. It includes all the NT books in a different order *plus* 1 and 2 Clement and possibly Psalms of Solomon listed in the table of contents.
4. Greek—*Codex Claromontanus* (D; likely fifth to sixth century): Wisdom, Sirach, 1–3 Maccabees, Esdras, Judith, and Tobit. Its NT inserted text in Latin and Greek = Matthew, Mark, Luke, John; Paul includes Romans, 1–2 Corinthians, Galatians Ephesians, 1–2 Tim. Titus, Col. Phlm., 1–2 Peter, James, 1–3 John, Jude, Hebrews, Ep. Barn., Revelations, Acts, Shepherd, Acts of Paul, *Revelations of Peter* (missing Philippians and 1–2 Thessalonians).
5. Greek—*Codex Venetus* (fifth and eighth centuries): Additions to Esther, 1–2 Esdras, Wisdom, Sirach, Baruch, Epistle of Jeremiah, Susanna, Bel and the Dragon, Tobit, Judith, 1, 2, 3, 4 Maccabees.
6. Syriac—*Codex Ambrosianus*, 7a1 (seventh century): Wisdom, Epistle of Jeremiah, 1–2 Baruch, Susanna, Bel and the Dragon (Dan 13–14), Judith, Sirach, Apocalypse of Baruch, 4 Ezra, 1–4 Maccabees, Josephus, *War* VI.
7. Latin—*Codex Sangermanensis* (D[abs1] or 0319, *c.* ninth or tenth centuries): Includes Odes, plus OT Apocrypha, 2 Esdras, and the NT including Shepherd of Hermas (see Houghton 2016: 213–14).
8. Latin—Cassiodorus' pandect (complete Tanak/OT) is a nine-volume Bible (late sixth century): Wisdom of Solomon, Sirach, Tobit, Judith, 1–2 Maccabees, additions to Esther, and the additions to Daniel (Hymn of the Three Young Men [Dan 3:24–90]), plus Susanna, Bel and the Dragon (Dan 13–14; see Houghton 2016: 58–9, 206–7.)
9. Latin—*Codex Amiatinus* (early eighth century): Wisdom of Solomon, Sirach, Daniel additions (Hymn of the Three Young Men = Dan 3:24–90; Susanna and Bel and the Dragon = Dan 13 and 14 in Catholic Bibles), additions to Esther, Tobit, Judith, and 1–2 Maccabees. Baruch and Epistle of Jeremiah are missing (Gallagher and Meade 2017: 254–5).
10. Latin—The Alcuin Bible (*c.* 800): the Tanak/OT and 2 Esdras (= 3 Esdras), Tobit, Judith, Wisdom, Sirach, Baruch, and 1–2 Maccabees.
11. Latin—The Paris Bibles (early thirteenth century onwards): They generally follow the Alcuin Bible. 2 Esdras (= 3 Esdras), Tobit, Judith, Wisdom, Sirach, Baruch, 1–2 Maccabees (Houghton 2016: 105–9, 189–91).

6. THE TEXTUAL VARIANTS AND THEIR IMPORTANCE

With few exceptions (Origen and Augustine are the primary exceptions), the ancient church fathers focused mostly on the *books* that comprised their OT and NT canons and not on their specific texts. Both HB/OT and NT scholars today are aware of the considerable variants in the HB/OT/NT manuscripts of the biblical books. Scholars debate over whether there were only a few hundred of them, but others (especially Emanuel Tov) contend that there are some 900,000 variants in the surviving HB/OT manuscripts and many scholars contend that there are between 200,000 and 350,000 variants in the surviving NT manuscripts, which is more than the words in the NT. Whatever the case, it is clear there are no two manuscripts that are exactly the same until the invention of the printing press and moveable type. While the initial aim of textual critics was to establish the original text of the biblical books by examining, comparing, and contrasting the texts in the surviving manuscripts and account for those variants, that goal of establishing the original text of the church's scriptures is still elusive despite being much closer than was possible years ago. Consequently, many textual critics had given up on arriving at the original text of the biblical books and seek to find what the manuscripts reflect of the sociohistorical context in which they were found and how the language is used in the various manuscripts. Most of the variants in the manuscripts are quickly resolved, but some are not, and some were intentional changes to the manuscripts by those who produced or copied them. This leaves open many questions about the text of the church's scriptures for today. Most textual scholars agree that they have likely gotten as close to the original text of the Bible as they can unless another batch of ancient manuscripts is found.

Nevertheless, the primary responsibility of textual critics and biblical interpreters is to determine as precisely as possible what the author of a biblical book wrote. In this sense, the primary goal of biblical textual criticism is still to establish the best and most original wording of a biblical text insofar as it can be determined. Since no autographs (so-called "original manuscripts") have survived antiquity, textual scholars sift through and evaluate a myriad of ancient manuscripts that often are different in their texts to determine the most plausible wording of a biblical book. That goal of determining the original text of the biblical books is seldom easy, but most textual critics agree that they are much closer than before, and, as Epp has concluded, unless a major newly discovered collection of biblical manuscripts emerges in some cave, garbage dump (as at Oxyrhynchus, Egypt), or found in an unidentified container in a museum or library, they are about as close to the originals as they can get. Indeed, Epp concludes that the original text is becoming more elusive as new manuscripts are discovered and other factors such as determining deliberate or intentional changes are acknowledged and factored into consideration (Epp 2002: 71–2).

The freedom with which some earlier copiers altered the scriptural texts contributes to the difficulty in trying to recover original texts of those manuscripts. Most NT scholars today agree that Matthew and Luke made use of Mark's Gospel adding corrections, and acknowledge that the parallels in Matthew and Luke that are not found in Mark generally come from other sources with their own modifications of it. It is often referred to as Q (German: *Quelle* or "Source"). The differences in the wording and sequence in those common parallel texts reflect the freedom to make changes in Q to fit their own narratives, for example, the Sermon on the Mount (Matt 5–7) is in large measure the Sermon on the Plain in Luke 6 and elsewhere in Luke, where the wording is often similar but often not the same. It is not certain whether Matthew and Luke had the same version of Mark or Q before them when they wrote their Gospels.

Textual critics are helpful in showing, for instance, that Mark 16:9–20 (a source for many sermons on missions) was not the original ending of that Gospel. Modern translators typically put these verses in a footnote or in brackets with explanations indicating that those verses lack textual support. John 21 (also a source of many sermons on two NT words for love: *agapē* and *philia*) is well attested in Gospel manuscripts, but it was also most likely added to John's Gospel prior to the end of the second century when the textual history of that Gospel begins to be more certain.

In the case of John 21, its authenticity is determined not as much by textual evidence as by the context and internal evidence of the Gospel of John and chapter 21 itself. For example, in John 20, Jesus appeared to the disciples, imparted the Holy Spirit to them, and commissioned them for ministry, but in John 21, they are back in Galilee fishing and do not recognize him when he comes to them even though in John 20, they saw him. Jesus' interaction with Peter about his love for him clearly seems to deal with Peter's threefold denial of Jesus and the death of John rather than focusing on the differences in the two words for love in the passage in 21:15–17. The oldest translations of this passage (Syriac Peshitta and Old Latin) do not have two different words for love but one. Be that as it may, John 21:24 clearly reflects other hands involved in this chapter. Stanley Porter's contribution to my festschrift on this matter urges that John 21 is an original part of John's Gospel (Porter 2007: 55–73), but at present those who make this claim do not have convincing arguments. Porter, however, does reflect how scholars can often disagree on such matters and yet still work together as friends.

An important question naturally arises when discussing textual variants, namely, did many of them arise because early copiers often had little hesitation about changing the texts they copied? Sometimes differences arise in the manuscripts because copiers used different copies of the same biblical books circulating in churches. Sometimes the copiers made deliberate changes in the texts they were using as exemplars and most often to clarify the text or support emerging church doctrine (as in 1 John 5:7–8). Many of the variants of biblical texts continued to be copied by other copiers in subsequent transmissions of those texts. Aland and Aland acknowledge that some variants in the texts may not be due to scribal error but to "its [the biblical text's] character as a 'living text'" (1989: 69). This means that the copies of Mark that Matthew and Luke used may already have included changes earlier copiers thought important for the current churches that were using them. While most textual changes are admittedly due to scribal error, intentional changes were often made based on the copier's theological perspective, or simply because copiers intended to clarify the texts for their churches and changed them to "in other words" to clarify what they understood. Language regularly changes over time and later copiers and the readers may not have understood the older wording in a new context. That same problem continues in all translations and editions of the biblical texts.

Ehrman contends that because the books of the emerging Christian scriptures were circulating in manuscript form in the fourth century and were copied by hand, we should expect both intentional and unintentional changes. He concludes that the biblical texts were never inviolable and contends that while most of the changes were "the result of scribal ineptitude, carelessness, or fatigue, others were intentional, and reflect the controversial milieu within which they were produced." He points to examples where the current Christological focus of the churches led many copiers to make changes to bring out the clarity of those views as they were copying and transmitting the church's scriptures. He claims that the scribes occasionally altered the words of the text by putting them in "other words." In such instances, they were textual *interpreters* and not copiers only. At the same time, by altering the words, they did something quite different that is not to be minimized. Although other scholars challenge several of Ehrman's conclusions, he is probably correct that the fluidity (variants) in the texts of the NT manuscripts continued well into the third and fourth centuries and even beyond (Ehrman 1993: 274–80). Aland and Aland speak of "the tenacity of the New Testament textual tradition," concluding that "some 10 to 20 percent of the Greek manuscripts have preserved faithfully the different text types of their various exemplars, even in the latest period when the dominance of the Byzantine Imperial text became so thoroughly pervasive. This is what makes it possible to retrace the original text of the New Testament through a broad range of witnesses" (1989: 69–70).

It appears that initially the NT writings were not treated as sacred or inviolable scriptural texts, and since we know that some copiers made changes in the biblical texts for both practical reasons such as to clarify language because they knew that language changes over time they made appropriate adjustments, but sometimes changes were made for theological reasons (John 3:13b and 1 John 5:7–8 as noted earlier) to correct what they thought was an error in the manuscript that they were using to prepare another one or to advance a cause special to them. This, of course, complicates the task of textual criticism to recover the earliest and most reliable biblical text. Epp clarifies the problem when he asks, "If it is plausible that the Gospel of Mark, used by Matthew, differed from the Mark used by Luke, then which is the original Mark? And if it is plausible that our present Mark differed from Matthew's Mark, and Luke's Mark, then do we not have three possible originals?" (Epp 2002: 73–4). Changes in the text occurred early on and the frequency of such changes creates a challenge for interpreters today who want to establish the earliest text of Mark or other ancient NT texts. This leads us back to a discussion of earlier notions of text types in the surviving manuscripts.

Because of the significant expense involved in securing the services of professional scribes, and the costs of the expensive materials, the early Christians were generally unable to produce carefully prepared professional literary copies of biblical books. Professional scribes in the ancient world were paid well, namely some 750 *denarii* per year plus the scribes' regular maintenance (a residence and related provisions, etc.). That amount was more than double and sometimes triple what the average skilled workman received. The early churches were generally not able to employ the best scribes who had the best technical skills to produce careful copies of their sacred scriptures. As a result, they sometimes had to make use of what Metzger called "literate amateurs" to prepare copies of the churches' scriptures and this amateurish quality of manuscript preparation is reflected in many of the earliest manuscripts of the NT. No doubt because of this, many of the errors and changes in the NT writings emerged early on and were passed along in subsequent copies, and later still other changes were introduced.

The care taken in copying NT manuscripts generally improved by the fourth century when it became more common for churches, for a time, to use professional scribes to produce copies of their scriptures. The cost of copying the OT and NT books by professional scribes in the fourth century including the materials was approximately 30,000 *denarii*, or roughly four years' salary for a legionary some 100 years earlier. Kurt and Barbara Aland have noted that by the fourth century those manuscripts prepared on parchment or animal skins, mostly sheep or goatskins, replaced most of the papyrus manuscripts. One sheep or goat normally provided two double folios, namely only four folios of a finished manuscript. Copying the whole of the NT required between 200 and 250 folios to complete the entire project. This means that at least fifty to sixty sheep were needed to produce a volume or codex containing *only* the NT books. The Alands' rightly conclude that only the upper classes could afford such an expensive undertaking, but that was not characteristic of the typical Christians and their churches (Aland and Aland 1989: 76–7).

The commercial centers for literary productions were called *scriptoria*, and greater care was taken in the *scriptoria* to produce copies of the Christian scriptures. In the later Byzantine era, however, the task of producing copies of the scriptures was often given to monks in monasteries who produced copies of the scriptures in their private cells and often with less precision than copies produced by the professional *scriptoria*.

Accidental and even intentional changes continued to appear in biblical manuscripts, until the invention of moveable type and the printing press in the mid-fifteenth century when exact copies could be produced, but even then, variations continued and multiple editions of the Greek and Latin Bibles continued, though with far less frequency than was true in the earlier centuries. Difficulties in transcription were compounded by the weariness of posture necessary to make such copies often in uncomfortable places. With the use of an ink pen, such copying required a fresh dip in the ink well after every four to six letters. One can imagine the difficulty involved in producing large manuscripts and the sheer effort in maintaining alert attention to the details of a manuscript while at the same time sitting in cramped positions that strained many of the muscles of the body! As the body wearied and became tired unintentional errors crept into the copies whether they were prepared in the scriptorium or in the cell of a monastery (Metzger and Ehrman 2005: 25–7). There is a greater stabilization in the biblical text after around 850 CE and the variants decline, but they were never fully eliminated (Metzger and Ehrman 2005: 275).

The estimated fluidity of the text in its initial stages makes the task of textual critics formidable. In several cases it is possible to determine that a text was changed for theological reasons as we saw in 1 John 5:7–8, but often it is not so apparent. Could a corrector of a text have returned it to its original state or simply tried to clarify it for later readers? Intentional alterations of biblical texts, whether for theological, historical, stylistic, or other reasons, were behind Epp's use of the designations of "multivalence" of the "original text" (Epp 2002: 74–5). He suggests that rather than seeking an original text, textual scholars are now more likely to be looking for "several layers, levels, or meanings" of the text, though he prefers to call them "dimensions of originality."

When the books of the NT were first written, preserved, reproduced, and circulated in the churches, they were hand copied. Over time and depending on the amount of use of the manuscripts, they wore out and were discarded or stored in a variety of ways, but before they were retired, new copies of earlier copies were made. We should remember that, as Evans has noted, some manuscripts depending on the amount of use could have lasted for twenty to thirty years and some more than a hundred years (Evans 2015). In the last 120 years or so, thousands of Greek manuscripts and fragments of manuscripts of the OT and NT writings have been discovered and many continue to be investigated. In terms of the NT manuscripts, roughly only 8 percent of these cover most of the NT writings and the vast majority contain only small portions of the NT writings and most of them exist only in fragmentary form.

In 1994 the official registry of biblical manuscripts, the Institute for New Testament Textual Research at Münster, Germany, listed over five thousand Greek manuscripts of the NT: 115 papyri, 306 uncial manuscripts, 2,812 minuscule manuscripts, and 2,281 lectionaries (Schnabel 2004: 59–75). These numbers change almost yearly as new manuscripts are recovered and the database therefore must also change. In 2003, the Institute for New Testament Textual Research listed 5,735 Greek manuscripts of the NT, but now it is over 5,740 and possibly up to 5,750 manuscripts, and it is likely that even more will soon be added to that number. I am told by some textual critics that there are manuscripts or fragments of manuscripts that have yet to be catalogued and will likely soon see the light of day and the total number is expected to increase. The latest published number of NT papyrus manuscripts (the earliest collection of manuscripts dating from the second to the seventh century) now stands at 128, and that number will surely grow.

The number of majuscule–uncial manuscripts or capital lettered manuscripts without spaces between the words (the collection dating roughly from the fourth to the tenth centuries) now stands at 310. There are some 2,877 minuscule or lowercase manuscripts with running letters (roughly from the ninth to the fifteenth centuries), and some 2,432 Greek lectionaries (selected portions of scriptures that were read in churches) that are occasionally listed in the multiple readings in support of a text but are seldom considered in textual evidence of readings, even though some of them may date earlier than some continuous manuscripts. These numbers are listed in the most recent edition of Metzger and Ehrman (2005: 50), but they change almost annually as more manuscripts are found and placed in the public domain. By the time this book is published, it is likely that the number of biblical papyri manuscripts will be even larger! The numbers will continue to change as more investigations of collections in European museums and libraries are catalogued and examined by competent scholars. In personal communication, Stanley Porter, a prominent papyrus and NT scholar, told me about containers of manuscripts in European libraries and museums that have not yet been catalogued, examined, and evaluated.

Eventually these will doubtless come to light, be catalogued, and published. According to Epp's analysis of the surviving continuous text manuscripts, 2,361 contain one or more gospels, 792 of Paul's letters, 662 of Acts and the Catholic or General Epistles, and 287 of the Book of Revelation (Epp 2002: 505). These numbers also reflect the popularity of the Gospels and less interest in the book of Revelation. The emerging principles of textual criticism are incorporated not only into the more recent critical editions of the Greek NT but also in newer translations of the Bible such as the recent editions of the *New Revised Standard Version, Revised English Bible, New International Version*, and the *New Jerusalem Bible* and the *ESV*.

Readers generally understand accidental changes in the biblical texts because of the difficulties involved in making copies by hand and often in difficult or uncomfortable circumstances. These were often accompanied by dim light and eye strain, but intentional changes in Christian biblical manuscripts present a greater challenge. As already observed, most of those changes or variants are easily identified by comparison with multiple manuscripts and they are easily corrected. Some scribal corrections were at times simply attempts to harmonize apparently contradictory passages. Most intentional changes were introduced to bring clarity to contemporary theological issues facing churches and to support various orthodox positions of the church. Ehrman cites a number of these deliberate changes in the second to the fourth centuries that reveal the orthodox tendencies to deal with the various heresies that were present in churches. As we briefly noted above, the well-known corruption of the biblical text for Christological purposes is the *Comma Johanna* (or the "Johannine Comma") in 1 John 5:7–8 where a Trinitarian addition was introduced into the text of 1 John. This change is not found in any known Greek manuscript, but Erasmus likely translated it from the Latin Sistine [SIXT]-Clementine edition of the Latin Vulgate and inserted it under pressure from his contemporaries into the second edition of his Greek NT. The *Johannine Comma* includes the words: "For there are three who bear witness in heaven, the Father, the Word, and the Holy Spirit, and these three are one. And there are three who bear witness on earth, the spirit and the water and the blood, and these three are one." This addition, of course, was intended to support the church's understanding of the Trinity, but it has no Greek manuscript textual support. Cyprian in the third century may have known of this addition and it may have originated in North Africa, but that is speculation. Ehrman describes the colorful history of this passage in the Christian Bible (1993:91–9). For another brief discussion of this passage, see Schnackenburg (1992: 44–6). Desiderius Erasmus (1469–1536) added the

Comma in his second edition of the NT Greek text because he was under pressure to do so, but it did not have adequate Greek antecedents.

Likewise, there are several additions to the end of Mark's Gospel following 16:8 that indicate that there was widespread belief that the original gospel did not end with the words "for they were afraid" (Mark 16:8; Greek: ἐφοβουντο γάρ). As we saw above, a later scribe added 16:9–20, which is largely, though not completely, a summary of the conclusions of the other three canonical gospels. It is likely that a well-intentioned scribe added what was believed to be a more appropriate conclusion to a gospel about good news (compare the beginning to Mark 1:1) instead of ending the story of Jesus on a note of fear. How Mark concluded his Gospel continues to bother many scholars today. Interestingly, *Codex Vaticanus* ends the gospel in 16:8 in the middle of a column with scribal marks in the margins, suggesting some question about the text, but uncharacteristically it also leaves a complete blank column (the third column, or right-hand column of the page) following the ending of that gospel. Leaving a whole column blank in the *Vaticanus* manuscript is rare. It appears that the copier may have known or believed that something else was needed to complete Mark, but was unsure what it was and simply left room for a later hand to include it. Currently most NT scholars, unlike earlier, do not believe that 16:8 is the way the original Gospel ended and the original ending appears to have been lost. John 7:53–8:11 also has an uncertain textual history and most textual scholars acknowledge that it was not an original part of John's Gospel, but some argue that it nevertheless fits well in the first century time and context of the Gospel of John. Evans observes that Luke 22:43–44 (compare with Matt 26:36–46; Mark 14:32–42; cf. with Luke 22:39–46) focuses on the prayer of Jesus with an insertion into the text of an angel appearing from heaven with Jesus sweating as if it were drops of blood. These verses are not in the oldest manuscripts, but it seems clear that a scribe wanted to insert them into the text early on to enhance the drama and experience of Jesus (Evans 2011: 161–72).

There are also some twenty variations in the NT texts on marriage and divorce issues in the Synoptic Gospels. The early churches had a considerable stake in this issue and many additions or changes were introduced into the NT texts to clarify an issue for current and subsequent generations of Christians dealing with that issue. The variants in the surviving manuscripts were welcomed as scripture in the communities that received them (Epp 2002: 514–15; Parker 1997: 78–93). Similarly, the role of women in the church was clearly another area of contention for some churches as we see in the variants in the texts that mention Priscilla (or Prisca) who is sometimes diminished in stature in the ancient texts. Similarly, the reference to Andronicus and Junia, who were "prominent among the apostles" (Rom 16:7), is challenged in several *later* Greek texts and the name is changed to Junias, a male name, even though all known church fathers up to the eighth century agreed that Junia, a female, occupied the role of apostle. One can also see this in the problematic texts of 1 Cor 14:34–35 and 1 Tim 2:8–15 that led some early churches to marginalize the role of women in their ministries (for Priscilla, see Kurek-Chomycz 2006: 107–28; Epp 2005). In his discussion of 1 Cor 14:34–35, Epp calls our attention to the two dots (or *"distigme"* = two marks) in the left margin of this text in *Codex Vaticanus* that point to the doubts the copier had about this text. He also notes that the relocation of these verses after 14:40 in several ancient texts adds to their uncertainty (2005: 14–20).

It is likely that Paul never wrote these verses since it would be rather difficult for women to pray or prophecy, not only with their heads covered (1 Cor 11:5) but also with their mouths shut (14:34–35)! In the case of 1 Tim 2:8–15 text, many NT scholars rightly do not think that this is a Pauline text but rather that it was written by a later hand in the name of Paul. This view has been challenged by Philip B. Payne (2009: 217–67), who offers one of the best discussions of 14:34–35 available with both the internal and external evidence and concludes with Epp that this passage is clearly an interpolation that interrupts the flow of the argument that Paul is making in the passage. He adds that it is a non-Pauline interpolation and also notes that 1 Tim 2:12 is the "only verse in the Bible alleged to explicitly prohibit women from teaching or having authority over men" and says that it was never intended to be a universal rule in Paul (Payne 2009: 337–97).

While most biblical manuscripts functioned authoritatively or canonically in the churches that possessed and read them and there was considerable overlap in their contents, the texts of those manuscripts were still fluid. Epp aptly concludes, "Our multiplicities of texts may all have been canonical (that is, authoritative) at some time and place" (Epp 1999: 245–81). It is likely that many of the textual variants in the NT manuscripts occurred *before* 200, that is, before their scriptural status was broadly recognized. That may suggest that the later understanding of the inspiration and inviolability of sacred NT texts were also not yet in place. The presence of the many variants in the NT texts may also suggest that the prohibitions against changing the texts were simply a common convention of the time and not a reality. We can see that in the widespread changes in all textual transmissions (Koester 1989: 37). Koester contends that the second century was the period of the most intense changes in the biblical texts, perhaps because at that time their sacred status had not yet been fully established (Koester 1990: 275–6, 295–302).

As we saw earlier in reference to the Gospels, the texts of the NT were treated like scripture before they were called scripture, but the initial lack of that recognition may have contributed to many of the changes during the formative period. Ehrman has understood the seriousness of this problem and observes that the overwhelming number of variants in the NT manuscripts outnumbers the words in the NT (2005: 84–9)! While there is considerable agreement on most of the texts, there remain many unsolved issues regarding the original NT texts. Epp discusses the problem of determining an original text of the NT and draws attention to several important implications of that inquiry (Epp 2005: *Perspectives*, 551–81, esp. 561).

This problem is also paralleled in the surviving OT manuscripts as noted above. In his "Prologue to the Hebrew Bible: A Critical Edition," Hendel acknowledges that an examination of the variants in the HB manuscripts (essentially those from Qumran, the Masoretic Text [MT], the Samaritan Pentateuch [SP], and the Septuagint [LXX]), that is, looking for a perfect original text of the Hebrew Bible, is only a dream. He begins with two citations: "The concept of the 'definitive text' corresponds only to religion or exhaustion" from Jorge Luis Borges in his "The Homeric Versions," followed by a brief citation from Bernard Cerquiglini stating that "Every edition is a theory" in his *In Praise of the Variant* (Hendel 2016: 15).

Hendel acknowledges that an analysis of the Qumran texts (the Dead Sea Scrolls) in relation to the other surviving major textual variants in the Masoretic Text, the Samaritan Pentateuch, and the Septuagint, "has made it clear that many books of the Hebrew Bible circulated in multiple editions during the Second Temple period" (2016: 17). He shows from the parallel and multiple attempts to establish a "master text" of Shakespeare's works that the conclusions were essentially the same as with the HB. He cites Stephen Greenblatt's "The Dream of the Master Text" that also had the same initial goal of establishing only what Shakespeare wrote, but had to conclude after all of their examinations of the multiple texts of Shakespeare that "the careful weighing of alternative readings, the production of a textual apparatus, the writing of notes and glosses ... all make inescapably apparent the fact that we do not have and never will have any direct, unmediated access to Shakespeare's imagination" (Hendel 2016: 38–9). Following his study of the research of other HB/OT textual critics, Hendel wisely concludes,

> In the case of the Hebrew Bible, we are not even dreaming of access to a single author, since the texts are multiauthored and editorially complex. But there is a similar realization of the nontransparency of a critical edition. We cannot have unmediated access to the master [original] text; it is beyond our evidence and our capabilities. The dream of a perfect text is unreal, counterfactual. The best we can do is to make a critically responsible text, a useful and innovative edition, one that takes account of the evidence we have and the acumen we can muster.

Hendel's words are also appropriate for trying to determine the original words of the NT texts. The surviving manuscripts reflect not only multiple variants in them but also, and not infrequently, multiple authorial hands, sometimes called pseudonymous insertions into the NT writings.

Even though *some* copyists of the NT manuscripts were careful in their transmission of the biblical texts, they all nevertheless made mistakes, and those who copied their works made mistakes as well. Some of the many variants were major when adding or omitting letters, words, or skipping lines or making corrective or explanatory changes in the texts. Aland and Aland offer a helpful discussion of the types of scribal errors that may be found in the NT texts (1989: 282–316; cf. also Metzger 2005: 300–343).

Initially the copiers of the church's NT and other Christian writings were probably unaware that they were copying scriptural documents, and, because of insufficient funds to produce quality professional copies, as we saw earlier, churches occasionally used less than qualified copiers to produce copies of their cherished texts. As a result, mistakes and deliberate changes were made in the production of biblical manuscripts. The lack of good literary skill in the transmission of the NT writings noted above is often seen in the earlier papyrus manuscripts (Metzger 1992: 15). Even when churches were able to pay professional scribes to transcribe their sacred texts, some errors or variants continued. Apparently, few attempts were made to stop or correct the variants until the middle to late fourth century and thereafter because professional scribes were employed. Even then, inadvertent, and sometimes deliberate, changes were made in the manuscripts that were produced and copies of those were passed on to churches often *for centuries*.

The written tradition in some instances may have been hastily prepared and quickly circulated in multiple copies. For example, in the case of Paul's letter to the Romans, presumably delivered to the Roman Christians by Phoebe (Rom 16:1–2), multiple copies of that letter could have been produced for the various churches in that region and all from the same exemplar or even multiple exemplars. There were likely at least five house churches in Rome at that time, but possibly dozens, and it is likely that several church leaders would have wanted copies of that letter for their own congregations. Consequently, several "initial" copies of that letter could have been circulating in and around Rome in the first century and possibly made by different copiers (so argues Epp 2014: 58; cf. also Jewett 2007: 942–8). Since no two copies of any surviving ancient document are exactly alike, it is quite possible that while there was considerable overlap in these copies, variants in them would have been passed on in subsequent transmissions of the letter for other churches or even in the same churches. The only question here is whether there were *substantial* changes made in these copies but not whether changes were made. In the early churches some copiers of the text of the NT writings apparently thought it helpful to add clarity to the NT texts they copied to make them more useful to subsequent generations of Christians.

Interestingly, Parker challenges the notion that all copiers were mindful of or even focused on the textual details in their copying of the early Christian manuscripts. With all that they had to do to select, prepare, and use the writing materials and their involvement in the final format of the manuscript, he suggests that the text itself may not have been the highest item on the copiers' agenda (Parker 2014: 29–30). This lack of attention to detail among many copiers may have led to the many ancient warnings against changing the texts being copied. It appears that this warning or strong admonition against changing a sacred text (Deut 4:2; Rev 22:18–19) was also likely a convention that reflected the authoritative nature and importance of a text in question but also was added to discourage a common practice among copiers who not infrequently make changes in the texts they copied.

Since no known autographs ("original" texts) of either the OT or NT scriptures have survived antiquity, biblical scholars rely on the work of text-critical scholars and their analysis of multiple textual traditions and individual texts to make informed decisions about the earliest possible and most reliable biblical text. Discerning the earliest possible text through an assessment and comparison of many ancient manuscripts is not an exact science but is occasionally called an art. What contributes to challenges text scholars face is that they do not always agree on the criteria they employ in the task of discerning the most reliable text of the NT scriptures (Epp 2002: 17–76; and his 2014: 79–114). Holmes, for instance, concludes his investigation of several texts and raises questions about the viability of the traditional established text-critical criteria, asking whether "they help only to authenticate decisions made on other grounds, and if so, how do we acknowledge and account for them?" (Holmes 2014: 11–24, here 24).

The number of textual variants in the manuscripts varies with the scholars who examine them, but they are plentiful and Ehrman notes that in 1550, John Mill, fellow of Queens College, Oxford, surveyed some one hundred NT manuscripts, along with patristic citations and versions of the NT, and made the disturbing discovery of some 30,000 variants in them (Ehrman 2005: 83–8, 89–90). Eckhard J. Schnabel (2004: 59) suggests that of the known NT manuscripts he wrote, there were approximately 9,000 versional manuscripts and probably some 300,000 variant readings in them! Such numbers pose considerable challenges for those involved in textual criticism. For example, in the well-known Greek *Codex Sinaiticus* (*c.* 350–375 CE), Parker has noted that it alone contains over 27,000 corrections made in its text, "yet in spite of this number it is almost as remarkable to us how many things [in that text] stand uncorrected" (2014: 31). For purposes of this inquiry, such investigations and knowledge of these variants in the NT writings raise questions about which text of the Bible is authoritative for translators and for churches today. As we observed earlier, the church initially was not focused on the text of their scriptures so much as on the books that comprised their NT. The considerable diversity among the ancient texts, though not unlike the diversity in transmission of other ancient documents, is nonetheless evidence that for centuries the church's primary interest had to do with the *books* that were included in the church's sacred scriptures and not their *texts*, even though, as we will see, the diversity in the scriptural texts did not go unnoticed in antiquity.

Modern scholars have produced Greek texts that are sometimes referred to as "eclectic" or selective texts that depend on a variety of texts from the traditional text types to construct the best and most reliable NT text. This perspective is now represented in the UBS[5], Nestle-Aland[28] texts, and in Michael W. Holmes, *The Greek New Testament: SBL Edition* (2010), and the recent *Tyndale Greek New Testament*.

Despite the diversity in the ancient texts, most, if not all of them, were considered canonical scripture in the churches that had them and used them in worship, instruction, and Christian living. What brought these texts—and their variety of changes and interpretations—into a manageable collection? The level of diversity in the texts was always held in some check by the church's *regula fidei*. For example, in the details in the story of the Prodigal Son (Luke 15:11–32), the early Christians could allow for some variation in a few minor details of wording, but they would never have accepted changes that led the father to reject the returning son or whether the elder brother welcomed him home. There were limitations to the diversity allowable in *most* cases. Also, most of the changes in the texts favored the orthodox traditions circulating in the churches. They did not tend toward the so-called heretical movements in the second and third centuries and despite some acceptable diversity in the churches' scriptures, there was a tradition-imposed limitation on the amount of diversity that could be tolerated. The church's vigorous defense against heresy in the second through the fourth centuries testifies to the kinds of limits that were acceptable before there was a Bible.

Ehrman's conclusion, based on his examination of multiple ancient manuscripts, is that "the texts of these [NT] books were by no means inviolable; to the contrary, they were altered with relative ease and alarming frequency," while "most of the changes were accidental, the result of scribal ineptitude, carelessness, or fatigue. Others were intentional and reflect the controversial milieu within which they were produced." Ehrman contends that many of the debates over Christology affected the accuracy of the transcription of the NT manuscripts (1993: 274–80; see also Metzger and Ehrman 2005: 250–71).

Swanson addresses the many intentional changes in the biblical texts even after their scriptural status had been determined. He claims that these changes in the text demonstrated the

> freedom scribes exercised in the transcription of the text. Evidently there were scribes who did not have a concept of the inviolable nature of the text of scripture. They exercised their freedom to innovate and to express in their own language what a passage of scripture meant to them ... The living character of the tradition is perhaps the most possible explanation to account for the marked changes that took place in the sources over the centuries. (Swanson 2001: xv)

Some of the variants in the ancient manuscripts make the work of text-critical scholars quite challenging and in several instances their conclusions about the original text are admittedly educated guesses. Metzger and Ehrman offer the sobering conclusion:

> Although in very many cases the textual critic is able to ascertain without residual doubt which reading must have stood in the original, there are not a few other cases where only a tentative decision can be reached, based on an equivocal balancing of probabilities ... In textual criticism, as in other areas of historical research, one must seek not only to learn what can be known but also to become aware of what, because of conflicting witnesses, cannot be known. (Metzger and Ehrman 2005: 343)

We stated earlier that Helmut Koester claims that many of the significant corruptions of the NT Gospel texts came during the first and second centuries (Koester 1989: 37), but for some textual critics the evidence for this is not as compelling as supposed and it is mostly inferential based on the lack of a fixed collection of Christian scriptures throughout most of the second century. The variety and number of variants in the third- and fourth-century manuscripts, however, suggest that Koester may well be right. Kruger challenges Helmut Koester and others, including this writer, who point to the many textual variants in the manuscripts, including the intentional variants in the earliest surviving NT manuscripts (Kruger 2014: 63–80). These variants are evidence for a fluid period of scriptural identification and transmission in the early churches. No one doubts the existence of textual variants, but I contend that they also reflect that most (not all) of the copies of the NT manuscripts initially were prepared by amateur copiers whose major concerns did not include textual consistency nor were the texts always or at least initially viewed as scripture. That accounts for some of the many variants but not the intentional ones that were either added for clarification or to add support to current theological issues and concerns facing later churches.

The above observance of textual variants complies with the fact that while several NT writings were read and cited in the second-century churches, initially they generally were not yet called "scripture" before the middle to end of that century. *Minor* changes in these texts would not likely have caused much concern *at that time*. Radical changes that denied the church's most important core traditions about Jesus or the early churches, however, would not have been welcomed or continued in textual variants or textual transmission. The evidence from the second century is meager since only two small fragments of the Gospel of John (P^{52} and P^{90}) can be dated that early along with a few citations from early church fathers. Consequently, it is best to be cautious about the number of changes to the biblical texts in the second and third centuries. Some early copies of manuscripts of NT texts were produced in a responsible and careful manner (e.g., P^{66}, late second century and P^{75}, early to middle third century) and likely others.

Some early copiers of the NT texts display skill in their attention to the details of the texts that they copied. Michael Holmes, in a personal correspondence to me, reminded me that "the scribe of P^{75} is one of the best workmen ever to copy a biblical text" but adds that unlike this copier, the later "scribe of Beza—quite apart from the character of the text he was copying—is not a careful workman." Larry Hurtado, also in personal correspondence on September 29, 2006, offered similar qualifications about the quality of transmission of texts in the early churches, adding that while some copiers of early biblical literature may have been "amateurs," it may be better to say that *some* of the earliest biblical manuscripts produced in the early churches "seem largely to be by skilled scribes, but apparently not of formal book hand quality," which, he says, is "likely a reflection of the socio-economic level of most Christians: able to afford a skilled copyist, but not able to afford the luxury trade."

All ancient biblical manuscripts were copied from earlier copies and the changes in them multiplied in transmission over many centuries. The trained eye readily identifies most of the accidental and even most of the intentional changes, but what accounts for them is not always clear. Swanson is aware of the daunting challenges before text-critics in establishing the earliest and most reliable NT texts. He also makes the point that despite the many differences in the texts, each manuscript, regardless of the textual changes made by the copiers, was scripture in an early Christian community (Swanson 2001: xxv–xxxi).

7. ANCIENT ACKNOWLEDGMENT OF TEXTUAL VARIANTS

Metzger and Ehrman cite Augustine, who wistfully reflected on the frequent mistakes in translating the biblical manuscripts and wrote, "anyone who happened to gain possession of a Greek manuscript and fancied that he had some ability in both Latin and Greek, however slight that might be, dared to make a translation" (*De doctrina Christiana*, 2.11.16). Several ancient church fathers commented on the diversity and errors in the NT texts that were circulating in the churches, but overall, *little was done* to correct them. Irenaeus (*c.* 170), when discussing the number 666 in Rev 13:18, acknowledged the problem of errors among copies of existing manuscripts as well as the lack of original texts to correct them. He concluded that the evidence supports the number 666, but then adds, "I do not know how it is that some have erred following the ordinary mode of speech and have vitiated the middle number [6] in the name." He goes on to say that he is "inclined to think that this occurred through the fault of copyists, *as is wont to happen*, since numbers are also expressed by letters; so that the Greek letter which expresses the number of sixty was easily expanded into the letter Iota of the Greeks." After explaining how changes may have happened, Irenaeus warns those who deliberately change the sacred texts, adding that "there shall be no light punishment [inflicted] upon him *who either adds or subtracts anything from the Scripture*" (Irenaeus, *Against Heresies* 5.30.1, ANF. Emphasis added). Eusebius notes that Irenaeus also warned those who would later copy his own work that they take diligent care not to change his treatise. For example, Eusebius reports the conclusion of Irenaeus's closing comment about his text *On the Ogdoad*. It reads,

> I adjure you, who shall copy out this book, by our Lord Jesus Christ, by his glorious advent when he comes to judge the living and the dead, that you compare what you will transcribe and correct it with this copy that you are transcribing, with all care, and you shall likewise transcribe this oath and put it in the copy. (*Hist. eccl.* 5.20.2, LCL, adapted)

Parker indicates that this passage not only shows Irenaeus's attempt to make sure that copiers of his book make careful use of his exemplar but also shows his awareness that editorial changes of texts were quite common in antiquity, hence a warning meted out by God (2014: 25–6). Not only were those who made copies of the NT writings admonished in the name of God to be careful in making copies of these texts and not to make any changes in it, so also were other writers of antiquity. Making changes in the texts that transcribers were copying was not uncommon in antiquity and the vast number of variants in the NT writings suggests that in several instances those who copied the NT writings may not have been as careful as some have argued. Ancient authors knew that what they wrote could and often would be wrongly copied or intentionally changed.

Origen's knowledge of such errors in the church's scriptural texts is seen in his concern for eliminating them in his comparison of the leading texts of the HB of the Jews and of the OT of the church in his *Hexapla* (or Six-Columned OT) in the third century. He included critical marks in his text to say what he thought should be omitted and what he thought should be included in his attempt to revise and correct the Septuagint (LXX) (Metzger 1963: 78–95; cf. Holmes 1991: 101–34). The notion of an inviolable text, as noted earlier perhaps a convention of the times, still points to the importance of a text that must go unchanged. Jerome was also aware of the deliberate and accidental changes in the biblical texts and was commissioned by Pope Damasus in 384 to produce a Latin text of the scriptures that eliminated these errors in the earlier Latin scriptures. Jerome's Latin Vulgate was initially challenged, but eventually it was received with wide acclaim in the church. It is apparent that others did not share Jerome's concern over the errors in the biblical manuscripts and only rarely did the early churches take steps to deal with them. The above notwithstanding, until the time of Erasmus in the sixteenth century, it appears that no significant effort was given to stabilizing the NT Greek texts or dealing with the many errors present in them. For more detail on this, see Metzger (1979: 179–90).

The early church fathers were clearly aware of textual variants in the biblical scriptures circulating among churches in the ancient world. Some copyists saw that other antecedent manuscripts differed from the ones they knew, and occasionally some of them made what they thought were corrective changes to get back to what they believed was the original text of scripture—or at least to clarify its meaning. Differences or variants in the manuscripts circulating in churches were well known to several early church fathers, but with the exceptions of Origen and Augustine, only a few tried to do something about them (especially Irenaeus). Numerous questions about the original text of the Bible persist among scholars, and there is no doubt that the variants are plentiful in the surviving manuscripts.

Scholars disagree over whether these variants reflect a different attitude toward the NT texts in their early transmission. Kruger has listed several of the early church fathers' responses to the willful changes in the NT manuscripts and concludes that while the variants were there, there was regularly an attempt to correct them and bring them in line with what was believed to be true and correct or original text (Kruger 2014: 69–80). He draws attention to the early church fathers' reflections on Deut 4:2 that warned against changing sacred texts (deleting or adding to them) but is aware of the challenge of multiple variants in the NT manuscripts. He acknowledges that "it seems evident that two historical realities *coexisted* within early Christianity: early Christians, as a whole, valued their texts as scripture and did not view unbridled textual changes as acceptable, and at the same time, some Christians changed the New Testament text and altered its wording (and sometimes in substantive ways)" (Kruger 2014: 79). His article challenges my conclusions about the earliest transmissions of the NT texts, namely that they were not initially viewed as sacred scripture, but he is careful not to deny what is obvious—that the variants in the texts are sometimes significant and occasionally intentional. Whether Deut 4:2 was simply a convention used by ancient authors who wanted to make sure that no one changed what they wrote is not clear, but it is apparent from the enormous number of variants in the NT texts that the admonition in Deut 4:2 was seldom followed.

Hull makes a compelling argument for the proto-orthodox focus of most of the intentional changes to the biblical text. He draws attention to scribal errors that needed correction and the necessary changes to clarify the meaning of the text for Christians in a later generation (Hull 2011: 84–5). The many variants in the NT manuscripts, and the early church fathers' awareness of them and displeasure because of them, suggest that there were efforts to correct them or find ways to eliminate the changes, but finding those attempts is challenging. Kruger correctly draws attention to several examples of the early church fathers' concern about the variants and changes in the texts of the NT scriptures (Kruger 2014: 75–9), but he is also aware that those concerns did not eliminate the remarkable number of the variants. The lack of care with which some manuscripts were copied did not go unnoticed, but there were some early examples of well-copied manuscripts, as mentioned above in P⁷⁵, and many other manuscripts in the Alexandrian family of biblical manuscripts.

The bottom line is that the accidental errors were still present even among the best prepared manuscripts in the fourth century and later well-intentioned and well-trained scribes were also susceptible to a careless moment. The quality of transmission of ancient biblical manuscripts varies from one manuscript to another in greater or lesser degrees, and the variations in the biblical texts, patristic citations, and lectionaries are considerable.

8. A STABILIZED GREEK TEXT

Erasmus of Rotterdam, noted above, produced the first published Greek text of the NT in 1516 and it was based primarily on two twelfth-century minuscule manuscripts that he found at the university at Basle, Switzerland. In his subsequent editions, he included five or six additional Greek manuscripts, but none of them dated before the tenth century. His Greek text also included a correction of several Latin translations in Jerome's Vulgate, as well as texts from a late edition of the Vulgate that he translated into Greek when he found the Greek text lacking it, as in the final six verses of Revelation and the Johannine *Comma* (1 John 5:7-8). His edition of the Greek Text was revised four more times in 1519, 1522, 1527, and 1535. The first edition contained hundreds of typographical errors that reveal the haste in which he prepared his text. Theodore Beza finally revised it again and produced his own Greek text relying heavily on Erasmus' text. This became the textual basis for the NT in the *King James Version* of the Bible (Metzger and Ehrman 2005: 142-9). Beza's Greek text was eventually called the *textus receptu*s or the "received text" because for generations biblical scholars based their translations and exegesis of the NT on it. Ehrman (2005: 78-83) notes that the origins of the term "received text" (*Textus Receptus*) comes from Abraham and Bonaventure Elzevir who produced an edition of the Greek NT in 1633 and told their readers "You now have the text that is *received by all*, in which we have given nothing changed or corrupted" (Ehrman 2005: 82, emphasis added). While there is little substantial theology lost by using the King James translation, and little of significant theological matter changed by it, it is nonetheless an inferior translation in that it does not generally reflect the earliest and most reliable text tradition of the Greek NT. It includes many additions to the biblical text, most notably John 3:13b; 7:53-8:11; Mark 16:9-20; and 1 John 5:7-8. The more equivocal texts, such as 1 Cor 14:34-35, when seen in the earlier manuscripts such as *Codex Vaticanus* with the *distigme* dots in the margin of the text noted above along with the internal flow of the passage, suggest that the passage has a questionable status in that context. These dots, however, are absent in the later *textual receptus*.

All translators and interpreters of NT text know the importance of discerning the most reliable biblical text. They are especially concerned with the evidence that supports authenticity and they generally rely heavily on the most recent editions of the Greek NT, namely the Nestle-Aland 28th edition (N/A²⁸) of *Novum Testamentum Graece* and the United Bible Society's 5th edition (UBS⁵) of *The Greek New Testament*. I would add that Michael Holmes's *The Greek New Testament* (SBL Edition, 2010) has some 500 differences in his text from the N/A²⁸ and UBS⁵ editions (which essentially have the same text but with different footnotes) and Holmes's text is arguably based on a careful evaluation of the texts in multiple manuscripts, for example, Mark 1:1; and the division between Eph 5:21 and 22. The editors and managers of these major editions know well that many factors are involved in establishing a reliable Greek text, including discerning not only the earliest text but also the most reliable text. It is also quite possible to produce a very good translation of an inferior early Greek text as well as a poor translation of a very reliable text! Most textual scholars today prefer those texts that have been identified as Alexandrian texts to the Western and Byzantine texts (the so-called *Textus Receptus* or "received text"), with some exceptions as noted above.

The diversity in the ancient NT *texts* is evidence that for centuries the church's primary focus was on *books* of the Bible and not on the integrity of the biblical text in them. Clarke recognizes this and shows that there is no single ecclesiastical form of the NT text that was established in antiquity despite awareness of the diversity of textual variants (Clarke 1999: 321–2). Given the large number of variants in the ancient NT texts, is it yet possible to produce a universally approved text of the church's Bible? Undoubtedly church traditions, councils, and orthodoxy influenced which books we have and to some extent limited the scope of the intentional changes in these ancient texts. The church's canon of faith, or the *regula fidei*, was clearly operative during the transmission of these texts and Ehrman is no doubt correct when he observes that loyalty to orthodoxy often affected textual transmission. The early church's vigorous defense against what it called heresy in the second through the fourth centuries and even later testifies to the limits of diversity that was acceptable in the ancient churches. This tendency toward orthodoxy in the textual changes is also attested in the NT manuscripts.

So, which text of the NT is authoritative for the church today? This question has not gone unnoticed by biblical scholars. While there is considerable agreement on most of the texts, there remain unsolved issues in the NT texts (Ehrman 2005: 84–9).

9. FINAL REMARKS AND CONCLUSION

Most of the NT papyrus manuscripts date from the third and fourth centuries and a few more up to the seventh century. The kinds of texts that preceded these surviving manuscripts a hundred years earlier are unknown, but we can suggest that in some instances those texts may have been something quite like the eclectic texts in the recent editions of the Greek NT, that is, some of them may have been the product of several hands. Again, most intense changes to the NT texts more likely took place in the late first and second centuries before the NT writings were widely acknowledged as sacred scripture. Since intentional changes were also introduced *after* these texts were received as sacred scripture, we can only imagine what the situation of transmission of the NT writings was like *before* their scriptural recognition began.

It may be worth noting that throughout history most churches have carried on their ministries and established their doctrines *without* appeal to the use of the elusive *original* manuscripts of the NT or the eclectic texts of modern construct. The copies of their scriptures were not perfect, but remarkably they functioned as sacred texts and informed the churches of their core beliefs and traditions from their beginning. Often, they possessed only some of their scriptures. Although no known ancient or modern translations are based on the elusive "original manuscripts," their absence has not hindered the current churches from using the only biblical texts they possess in their worship, instruction, and mission, namely the eclectic constructs that exist today. In other words, while the biblical texts that informed the early Christians contained many transcriptional and intentional alterations, they nevertheless functioned as scripture for those who had them.

The same is true of the books in the ancient manuscripts. While they sometimes contain other books, they generally overlap in their inclusion of the most cited NT books (the Gospels and most of the Pauline epistles, Acts, 1 Peter, and 1 John). We do not know of a time when *all* original texts of the NT informed the faith of all or even most of the earliest churches. Copies were certainly made of most of them in the first century to allow greater circulation and it is most likely that none of them were exact copies. The first copiers of the NT writings also likely made changes in what they were copying to clarify for their readers what the authors of the Gospels intended or what they thought Paul intended to say. I do not think they made changes to obscure the meaning of the authors of those early texts produced in the apostolic period. We know that some of the early Christian writings and several Jewish religious texts were not eventually recognized as Christian scripture after several centuries of use as scripture, but they were recognized and circulated as authoritative texts in the churches much earlier.

The loss of the original texts of the biblical literature eventually occurred whether in the generation in which they were produced by their authors or much later as we saw in Evans's suggestion above. It is interesting that no early church father complained about not having any original "perfect" manuscripts of the church's scriptural texts. They welcomed what was passed on to them and even when some church fathers often saw errors in their copies of the scriptural texts, they simply tried to correct them and move on. All early and subsequent copies of the church's scriptural texts were produced by hand initially for centuries by persons with various writing skills unlike those of the later professional scribes who produced the more attractive and professional copies in the fourth and fifth centuries when it was possible for some churches to obtain professional help in producing their scriptural manuscripts when some larger churches had more to make use of professional scribes or copiers.

All this raises, of course, questions about the views of some theologians who propose an original perfect scriptural text as the basis for inspired scripture. Even if such a perfect text once existed, it has been lost and the church has existed for almost 2,000 years without it. Despite multiple doubtful texts that still exist in current eclectic NT Greek texts, the church continues to grow and what it has continues to encourage and give guidance to the churches for their beliefs and mission in the world. In other words, and more boldly, there is no evidence that a perfect biblical text ever informed any ancient or modern church despite how often some theologians appeal to it. Also, there is no example of an ancient manuscript that looks exactly like the current eclectic Greek text that is used today to produce the translations used in churches around the world. The same is also true of the current eclectic texts of the Hebrew scriptures or the church's OT. No two handwritten copies were the same until the invention of the printing press and moveable type, so which one was the one most churches followed? Likewise, as we saw above, the surviving manuscripts reflect the scriptures of the churches that possessed those manuscripts and read them. The surviving manuscripts and those that were at one time lost functioned as their sacred scriptures both before and after the churches developed a Bible, and even though some manuscripts include different books than the ones listed in the ancient biblical canon catalogues, the writings the ancients had still functioned as scripture and gave guidance to them. The manuscripts from antiquity and their texts, despite sometimes containing different books and multiple variants in the texts, were important factors in the life of churches before there was a Bible.

The next chapter will focus on several important artifacts of history, namely the *nomina sacra* (sacred names), translations, and church councils that functioned in early Christianity before there was a Bible.

CHAPTER 6

The Ancient Artifacts: *Nomina Sacra*, Translations, and the Councils

1. THE LITERARY ARTIFACTS OF ANTIQUITY AND THEIR IMPORTANCE

The literary artifacts of antiquity transmitted or reflected the literary authorities of early Christianity. The oral traditions of the churches continued to be circulated in the second century as we saw earlier in the example of Papias, but as memory was fading in time and the early eyewitnesses had died, the most important artifact for the transmission of the church's sacred writings was in ancient manuscripts. Some of those manuscripts lasted perhaps up to two hundred years depending on the amount of use they had. Earlier it was assumed that most of them lasted not more than twenty to thirty years, but that has recently been challenged in a recent article where Evans shares his investigations of the use of ancient manuscripts and concludes that they likely lasted and functioned in churches much longer. He challenges the earlier arguments about manuscripts lasting about one generation at best and concludes that some of them may have lasted well over two hundred years (Evans 2020: 1–31). After his survey of the length of time that ancient manuscripts were used in the Greco-Roman world, he concludes, "Given that there is no evidence that early Christian scribal practices differed from pagan practices, we may rightly ask if early Christian writings, such as the autographs and first copies of the books that eventually would be recognized as canonical scripture, also remained in use for one hundred years or more." This statement came to me in personal correspondence with Professor Evans, who sent to me not only his summary but subsequently also a copy of his published paper (2015: 23–37; see also his 2020: 75–97). If correct, his findings could be quite significant since it would be possible that some of the oldest surviving copies of New Testament (NT) writings that date from the second and third centuries, and possibly later, may depend on autographs or original documents. While this is possible, there is no way currently to demonstrate whether any of the current earliest known surviving manuscripts of NT writings are copies of the original biblical manuscripts. It is also difficult to establish precisely how often those manuscripts were used and regular use would, of course, affect the longevity of their use in ancient churches.

At some point, as the autographs ("original" handwritten manuscripts) of the NT writings were wearing out, and because their high value in the life of the church was recognized, churches had literate individuals in their congregations, sometimes known as "literate amateurs," who made copies of these valuable texts so they could continue to be circulated in the churches and inform their faith. Some of those manuscripts were copied more carefully than others and by more capable copiers with more advanced skills. The earliest manuscripts eventually wore out, were lost, or destroyed in persecutions, or even stored in undisclosed and unknown locations. There are arguments for each of these possibilities. An important question here, of course, is how faithful the copiers were to the manuscripts they used to produce newer copies. Few, if any, of the earlier copiers were professional scribes before the fourth century, but there were several exceptions where careful copies were produced (e.g., P^{75}). Because of the significant numbers of Old Testament (OT) and NT texts that have survived antiquity—in the vicinity of some 9,000 OT manuscripts or fragments and some 5,750 NT manuscripts whether partial or complete—it is now possible for textual critics to compare and assess the surviving manuscripts and arrive at reasonable estimates of the original text. As we saw earlier, those estimates were sometimes "best guesses" of what was in the original texts because of some uncertainties that still exist.

The surviving biblical manuscripts tell us broadly what writings informed the life of many early churches. Because so many of those manuscripts have been lost (Hurtado 2006), there doubtless will remain several gaps in our understanding, but what remains in the surviving artifacts often reveals important information about what texts and beliefs were of importance for the early Christians who welcomed writings that were included among the church's scriptures.

Soon after the birth of the early church, and probably by the end of the first century, the early church showed considerable preference for the codex or book format for transmitting its Christian writings, though not exclusively since some biblical manuscripts were still in rolls or scrolls (Hurtado 2006: 43–89, 90–3, and 209–26). The Apostle Paul himself, perhaps knowing of Roman use of this form of writing material, *may* have initiated the church's use of the codex (2 Tim 4:13), but whatever the case by the early second century the use of the codex was the more common means of transmitting Christian writings (over 70 percent of the time).

The Romans are credited with the invention of the codex and were the first to use it for nonliterary documents such as one finds in contracts, bills of sale, personal notebooks, school texts, and other such items. Pliny the Elder gives a description of the manufacture of papyrus sheets (*Nat.* 13.74–82), which replaced the wood and wax used in the earlier manufacture of the codex. By the end of the first century CE, the use of the codex expanded considerably. The Roman poet Martial (*c.* 82–84 CE), for example, encouraged his readers for the sake of convenience to use small codices to transport his epigrams or poems (*Epigr.* 1.2). Later he indicated that other writer's works had also been placed in this format, namely the works of Homer (14.184) Virgil (14.186), Cicero (14.190), Livy (14.190), and Ovid (14.192). At the end of that century, about 20 percent of the Roman writings were circulated in the codex, but the majority of learned writings continued to be published in the roll or scroll format.

2. THE CHRISTIAN USE OF *NOMINA SACRA*

The nonliterary style of Paul's letters to churches characterizes the earliest NT writings as *ad hoc* texts to address specific issues in the churches that suggests a reason for their reproduction in a codex format. In the initial stages of transmission, abbreviations for special "holy words" (God, Lord, Jesus, Christ, and sometimes Spirit) are the most common such abbreviations that normally use the first and last letters of a word (or the first, second, and last letters of a word) with a line over the top of the letters. They are regularly used in the NT manuscripts and in time other terms were added to this and most commonly there are fifteen such designations found in NT manuscripts. Hurtado identifies the most frequently used abbreviations or *nomina sacra*. After the most common names—Jesus, God, Lord, and Christ, the others include spirit, man, son, father, David, cross, mother, savior, Israel, Jerusalem, and heaven. He also lists the Greek words and their abbreviations in this collection (Hurtado 2006: 134). Tomas Bokedal also lists these abbreviated words according to frequency. This practice likely had its origins in the Jewish use of the Tetragrammaton (YHWH) to identify the divine name of God (Yahweh) (Bokedal 2014: 84–123). When the Jewish scriptures were translated into Greek, it appears that some contractions of God (Grk. *theos*) and Lord (Grk. *kurios*) were used to identify those sacred names.

The relatively recent term, *nomina sacra*, for this ancient practice of abbreviating special terms in documented hand manuscripts came from Ludwig Traube, who coined it in his 1907 book (*Nomina sacra. Versuch einer Geschichte der christlichen Kürzung*. Quellen und Untersuchungen zur lateinischen Philologie des Mittelalters 2; München: Beck, 1907). Traube's designation caught on and has been used ever since to identify the ancient Christian contractions (or suspensions). A suspended *nomina sacra* example is the first and second letters in a word with a line over the top. These designations have received considerable attention in recent years in text-critical studies as well as among those who examine Christian literary manuscripts. For a discussion of these designations, see C. M. Tuckett (2003: 444–6), Hurtado (2006: 95–134, 1998: 655–73), and Bokedal (2014: 83–123). Scholars have debated their origins (whether Jewish or Christian) and studied their forms (regular and derivate) and their theological implications. All scholars who have written about this practice agree that the reverence of the name of God is Jewish, but the debate persists about whether these abbreviations have any explanatory significance. What is commonly accepted by most who examine these abbreviations is summarized by Tuckett who lists the five agreements as follows:

(a) the practice is well-established and consistently applied in the earliest Christian MSS we possess (and hence must go back earlier still, (b) that it is *not* a simple space-saving device, (c) it is probably a *Christian* innovation, (d) it represents an attempt to reflect the *sacred*, religiously "special" nature of the referents of the nouns being abbreviated in this way: hence the description "*nomina sacra*," (e) such sacredness is probably to be related to the reverence shown in Judaism to the divine name. (Tuckett 2003: 432)

The early Christians identified Jesus with *kurios* and *christos*, but other distinct designations eventually grew in number to include several terms common in the early church's traditions, some of which were not in themselves sacred terms, for example, *man, king, mother, father*, and several others. The list of the fifteen most common abbreviations in Christian texts, beginning with the most common, includes the following Bokedal (2014: 89–90).

The most cited group includes:

Θεος = Θς (God)   Χριστος = Χρ, Χρς, Χς (Christ)
Ιησους = Ιη, Ιης, Ις (Jesus)   Κυριος = Κς (Lord)

The second most cited group includes:

σταυρος = στς, στρς, (cross)   Πνευμα = Πνα (Spirit)

The third most cited group includes:

σταυροω = στω (crucify)   Πατηρ = Πρα (father)
ανqρωπος = ανος (man, human being)   Ιερουσαλημ = Ιλημ (Jerusalem)
Υιος = Υς (son)   Ισραηλ = Ισλ (Israel)
Πνευματικος = Πνκς (spiritual)

The fourth most cited group includes:

ουρανος = ουνος (heaven)   μητηρ = μηρ (mother)
Δαυιδ = δυδ (David)   σωτηρ = σηρ (savior)

It is quite possible that initially several of these so-called *nomina sacra* reflect the nonliterary or documentary hand style of communication in early Christian writings since abbreviations were seldom used in literary texts. However, that changed later and soon they were used in all kinds of Christian texts. That practice continued, including in sacred, literary, and personal correspondence. These abbreviations that normally included the first and last letter of the Greek word, occasionally with a middle letter and a short line over the top of the abbreviation, are in abundance not only in ancient Christian biblical manuscripts but also elsewhere in other Christian texts. Their presence in a manuscript identifies the text as Christian, however, that does not mean that all ancient texts using them were identified as scripture.

Hurtado and Bokedal place considerable emphasis on the role of *nomina sacra* in identifying Christian sacred scripture, but Tuckett challenges whether they were all Christian designations or were invented by the Christians, perhaps copying the Jewish practice of using the Tetragrammaton for the name of God (Yahweh), or that they were all found in NT or OT texts. He points to several exceptions that Bokedal appears to ignore or believes that they are unsustainable. For example, he observes several exceptions to the notion that they reflect the biblical canon or scriptural books (POxy 3.407, P[52]), a fragment of that does not contract *kurie* in the *Gospel of Mary*, though ἄνθρωπος ("man" or "human being") is abbreviated; a Michigan papyrus manuscript (PMich. 130) of *Shepherd of Hermas* that does not abbreviate God (θεῷ); POxy 4.656 with parts of Genesis in which God (θεός) is uncontracted; in P[72] three times κύριος is unabbreviated (1 Pet 3:12; 2 Pet 1:2; 2:9; cf. also 2 Pet 2:20) (Tuckett 2003: 436–42). Perhaps more importantly, Tuckett makes three important claims, arguing that the phenomenon of these abbreviations is not confined to Christian texts and positing (1) that some were possibly produced by Jewish scribes and others by non-Christian scribes; (2) this phenomenon is attested across both canonical and noncanonical literature (e.g., Shepherd of Hermas, Gospel of Thomas, Gospel of Mary, and Egerton Papyrus 2), and (3) he concludes that the practice of abbreviations in texts is not in itself a *Christian* phenomenon (Tuckett 2003: 442–3).

Tuckett doubts whether the abbreviations were initially sacred designations, certainly not all of those listed above, and points out that Moses, Isaiah, and others in themselves were not sacred, even in the biblical text (Tuckett 2003: 445–6). He suggests instead that the names were abbreviated to highlight an emphasis for a reader as aids when the lector read the sacred writings to a congregation (Tuckett 2003: 431–58). Hurtado concedes some of Tuckett's points, especially that some of the *nomina sacra* were not all sacred designations and that others besides the Christians used such designations, but he contends nevertheless that the four primary designations in question—God, Lord, Jesus, and Christ—do identify *Christian* manuscripts and are the places of the greatest consistency of use. His summary of these designations is helpful: (1) there is greater consistency in the use of these four primary designations than in any of the others and these antedate the other such designations; (2) there is greater consistency in use when these four terms are in reference to God and Jesus, showing that these four emerged as reflections of Christian reverence for Jesus and God; (3) *nomina sacra* forms are characteristic of Christian texts, but less regularly and consistently used in private letters, magical texts, prayer and liturgical texts; (4) in both biblical and nonbiblical texts some Christian scribes are more consistent than others, but the dominant pattern is clear and reflects a practice that was both impressively and quickly appropriated (Hurtado 2006: 109–33).

AnneMarie Luijendijk has observed that the *nomina sacra* were used in nonliterary texts, such as inscriptions and papyrus letters, as well as in the early Christian NT texts, and that this phenomenon has not yet received adequate discussion. While concluding that scholars still debate over the origin of these abbreviations and why they were used, she observes that they all agree that the *Christian* abbreviations employed by scribes do point to manuscripts produced by Christians. She writes,

> Although the origins of the writing of *nomina sacra* remain under discussion, no one any longer disputes the Christian character of these contractions. As a matter of fact, scholars always interpret the presence of *nomina sacra* in literary manuscripts as an indicator that a Christian scribe has copied the manuscript, and apply this principle both for literary manuscripts and for epigraphical and papyrological sources. (Luijendijk 2008; and her 2010: 217–54)

Most of the NT and other Christian writings, possibly except for the Gospels, were initially produced for small groups of Christians and a formal literary style was not required. The use of *nomina sacra* does not necessarily mean that all texts that included them were viewed *as sacred scripture*, but rather they show that the text was likely produced or copied by a Christian when the four most common *nomina sacra* were used. Clearly the NT manuscripts include them, but they are not restricted to the NT manuscripts. Bokedal's arguments for the Christian manuscripts identified by the *nomina sacra* appear to ignore or not seriously consider the exceptions presented in Tuckett and Luijendijk. Bokedal claims that the *nomina sacra* "are important for the understanding of the Christian Scripture as Scripture," adding that "ritually as well as textually the *nomina sacra* set the Scriptures apart as Christian Scriptures" (Bokedal 2014: 241–2). He strangely argues against Ulrich's view that "the books that came to be the Bible did not start off as books of the Bible" (Ulrich 2002: 35), claiming instead, "On the contrary, I would argue, in corporate worship it is precisely, or at least as a rule, the biblical books are read out aloud as part of the common scriptural reading" (Bokedal 2014: 243). He concludes from the *nomina sacra* that "the books that came to be the Bible started, at least in part, as books with a unique status." Since the early Christian writings were read in churches, he concludes that they must also have been recognized as scripture. He seems unconvinced by the fact that the *nomina sacra* were used not only in biblical manuscripts but also in other Christian documents such as we see in Irenaeus and Tertullian. No one has ever suggested that they were scripture.

3. EARLY TRANSLATIONS OF THE CHURCH'S SCRIPTURES

Approximately 9,000 manuscripts of versions or translations of the NT texts have survived antiquity, yet their contents, namely the books in them and the reliability of the translations in which they are found, have received little attention from biblical scholars. These and other translations provide an important lesson in the history of the origin of the Bible. While some early translations have been lost, the ones that survive are an important source for letting us know what literature the recipients and their translators believed was sacred and they aid textual critics in piecing together the earliest possible text of the NT. The early Christians freely translated their scriptures into several languages including Syriac, especially the Syriac Peshitta, Old Latin, the Armenian translations, and others.

At the end of the second century several Latin translations of LXX manuscripts were produced and Tertullian regularly cited or quoted them. The early Latin translations were often inaccurate and they included with the Hebrew Bible (HB) texts several disputed books. At the end of the fourth century Augustine expressed his disappointment with the quality of many of the Latin translations by would-be but inferior translators as follows:

> Those who translated the Scriptures from Hebrew into Greek can be counted, but the Latin translators are out of all number. For in the early days of the faith, everyone who happened to gain possession of a Greek manuscript and thought he had any facility in both languages, however slight that might have been, attempted to make a translation. (Augustine, *De doctrina christiana* 2.11.16.36)

Given the complexity and expense of producing a translation, it is generally assumed that when the NT books began to be translated, those writings were highly valued and recognized for their liturgical, catechetical, and missional value for the churches. In other words, we are saying that they were likely recognized as authoritative texts that functioned like Christian scripture, or at the least that those texts were well on their way toward that recognition. The early Christian translations of both their OT and NT scriptures are a primary resource on what the translators and churches thought was sacred literature. Because of the universal focus of their mission, Christians freely translated their sacred texts into several languages. The earliest translations of the NT were in the Old Latin, Syriac (especially the Peshitta), and Armenian, which date mostly from the early third century to the fifth centuries and later. The new translations prepared for various early Christian communities formed a collection of sacred texts, that is, a scriptural canon on a local basis.

Early Christian translations of OT books show which books were circulating as scripture in the second and later centuries and the fluidity of early Christian OT canons. The following early translations have considerable significance for an understanding of the development of the Christians' Bible (Metzger 2001: 25–51).

1. *Syrian Versions.* For several centuries the NT did not include the so-called Minor NT Epistles (2 Peter, 2–3 John, and Jude) and Revelation, but Tatian's *Diatessaron* (or *Gospel of the Mixed*) and *3 Corinthians* were included in their scriptural collections. Eventually, after several centuries, as the Greek texts had greater influence in Syria

and the *Diatessaron* and *3 Corinthians* were excluded, and the Minor NT epistles were eventually added. It took longer, however, to include Revelation (seventh to eighth century). The surviving ancient manuscripts have an interesting history and reflect diversity for centuries.

  a. The *Old Syriac* version. Although only the four canonical Gospels are preserved in two fragmented manuscripts of this translation that dates from the fourth or fifth centuries, the original translation probably dates from the end of the second or beginning of the third century. The Eastern church fathers who used this translation often also refer to Acts and the letters of Paul. By the end of the second century CE some Jews had translated the Hebrew scriptures into Syriac and it became known as the Syriac Peshitta ("common") translation. After their conversion to the Christian faith, the translators of the Peshitta also included the NT writings (Metzger 2001: 26–9; Weitzman 1999: 1). The Syriac OT translations generally included all the Tanak books with an unusual order and the Book of the Women containing Ruth, Esther, Judith, and Susanna.
  b. Eventually there were six versions of the Syriac scriptures translated from the LXX in Origin's Hexapla as well as in a Christian Aramaic version. The most important surviving Greek translations (Milan, Paris, Florence, and Cambridge) include most of the disputed texts and other texts as well. Ancient Syrian Christianity appears quite open to "inclusiveness" (Rompay 2020: 136–65).
  c. The Peshitta (or *Syriac Vulgate*, designated Syr^p) likely comes from the beginning of the fifth century and contains twenty-two NT books (it omits 2 Peter, 2 and 3 John, Jude, and Revelation).
  d. The *Philoxenian* version, perhaps produced in the early sixth century, was also known as the *Harclean Version* because of a later revision by Thomas of Harkel in the early seventh century. For the first time in this translation the Catholic Epistles and Revelation were added to the Syrian churches' collection of scriptures.
  e. The *Palestinian Syriac* version (*c*. fifth century). Only a few fragments of these translations still exist, and they include the Gospels, Acts, and several (not all) of the letters of Paul.
2. *Latin Versions*. By the end of the second century, several Latin translations of LXX manuscripts were produced and Tertullian regularly cited or quoted them. The early Latin translations were often inaccurate and included, with the HB texts, several disputed books (Metzger 2001: 30).

The following additional list does not include all the omitted or disputed or deuterocanonical and readable texts, but simply notes the variety of books besides the HB books in the Latin translations. Because of considerable confusion in existing Latin translations, in his new translation, Jerome with others translated the OT scriptures *from the Hebrew* (*c*. 390–404) and not the Greek LXX, but he himself did not recognize the scriptural status of the disputed or deuterocanonical books. After that *Codex Amiatinus* (*c*. 700 CE), the pandect Latin Bible, and most other translations following it, included several but not all the disputed deuterocanonical books (van Liere 2014: 4–15).

  1. The *Old Latin* versions (perhaps late second to early third century). There were several Old Latin manuscripts produced during the third century and later that fall generally into two categories: African and European versions. In the surviving fragments, portions of the four canonical Gospels, Acts, and portions of Paul's

letters survive, along with a few fragments of Revelation. It may be that Tatian (*c.* 170) used an Old Latin version of the Gospels for his *Diatessaron*, but he may also have used a Greek text that was translated into Syriac.

2. The *Latin Vulgate* version produced by Jerome in the late fourth and likely early fifth centuries in Palestine (Bethlehem). There are a good number of surviving copies of this version containing the whole Bible but, besides the NT writings, there are two codices (*Codex Dublinensis*, *c.* eighth century and *Codex Fuldensis*, *c.* sixth century) that also contain the apocryphal letter of Paul to the *Laodiceans*.

3. *Coptic Versions*. Around the late third or beginning of the fourth century, Coptic translations began appearing that included some six dialects (Sahidic, Boharic, Achmimic, sub-Achmimic, Middle Egyptian or Oxyrhynchite dialect, and Fayyumic). Most Tanak books were included along with several disputed books. In the beginning of the third century, the Coptic versions in the Sahidic and Bohairic dialects are the most important among the various manuscripts that have survived, and the contents of these versions include the four Gospels, Acts, and the Pauline Letters.

4. *The Gothic Versions* (*c.* middle to end of the fourth century). The earliest manuscripts of this version include four Gospels, some Pauline letters, and a portion of Neh 5–7.

5. *The Armenian Versions* (late fourth and early fifth centuries). The fifteen hundred or more copies that have survived date from the eighth century and later and some have all of the NT writings, but others are missing various NT books. It is interesting that *3 Corinthians* is also in this version of the NT writings. Gregory the Illuminator (*c.* 257–331) introduced Christianity into Armenia near the end of the third century. He was able to convert Tirides I, king of Armenia, who called on all of his subjects to adopt Christian faith. By the fifth century, the OT and NT were translated from the Syriac translations. The Armenian OT scriptures included several of the disputed books in question including *History of Joseph and Asenath*, *Testaments of the Twelve Patriarchs*, *The Book of Adam*, *The History of Moses*, *The Deaths of the Prophets*, *Concerning King Solomon*, *A Short History of the Prophet Elias*, *Concerning the Prophet Jeremiah*, *the Vision of Enoch the Just*, and *The Third Book of Esdras* (= chapters 3–14 of 4 Ezra) (Hovhanessian 2013: 1–6, 63–87).

6. *The Georgian Version*. It is possible that the origin of this version goes back to the fourth or fifth century, but its oldest surviving manuscripts date from the ninth century. It contains the four Gospels, Acts, and the Catholic Epistles. Near the end of the tenth century, the book of Revelation was translated and added to the collection.

7. *The Ethiopic Version* (now in the Ge'ez language *c.* as early as the fourth or as late as the seventh century). Most of the surviving manuscripts of this version date after the thirteenth century and currently it is not possible to know how much of the NT was initially translated into this language in the earliest stages of the translation since only partial manuscripts have been discovered. This version is the largest known Bible containing more than eighty books and its NT included not only the twenty-seven books of the NT but also *Sinodos*, *1 Clement*, the *Book of the Covenant*, and *Didascalia*. Rufinus noted that the mission to Ethiopia began during the reign of Constantine (*Hist. eccl.* 11.9), but the contents of the Ethiopian Bible are puzzling since the eighty-one books that comprise it show considerable fluidity in the books in the surviving manuscripts. It is difficult to find the same eighty-one books in each. Ethiopian Christians were isolated from the rest of Christendom for

almost a thousand years and their OT may date from the fourth and fifth centuries and reflect an early Syrian canon. Besides the Tanak books, their OT includes Prayer of Manasseh, Jubilees, 1 Enoch, 2 Ezra and Ezra Sutuel, Tobit, Judith, Esther with additions, 1–3 Maccabees, Psalm 151, Daniel with additions, Baruch, Epistle of Jeremiah, Wisdom, Sirach, and Pseudo-Josephus. The orders of these books vary in the surviving collections and Bibles (Metzger 2001).

There were several other translations, but the above reflect the fluidity of books included in the early and even later Christian translations. The examples in canon lists, citations, manuscripts, and the translations agree on the continuing fluidity for centuries. The ancient OT translations regularly included the Tanak books but often differed in the books included in them (Metzger 2001: 38–51).

Other later and less important translations for our purposes include the Arabic versions from the eighth century to the nineteenth century, the Sogdian (or Middle Iranian) version, which dates from the ninth to the eleventh century, and the Old Church Slavonic version during the ninth century that was important especially for the Bulgarians, the Serbians, Croats, and Eastern Slavs. In the late third to early fourth centuries, some churches were planted in Nubia, but when the Arabs to the north essentially cut them off from the rest of Christendom, they declined numerically and eventually disappeared. There was considerable growth in that church during the sixth century and it is likely that a vernacular Nubian version was produced between the third to the sixth century, but it is not clear exactly when it was translated or what was included in it at that time (Metzger 2001: 50–1).

An obvious point here is that these translations do not contain the same books though they often overlap considerably in terms of the Gospels and letters of Paul, but also include several other NT writings. Only one of the translations contains all of the NT books but it contains other writings besides. Except for Jerome's *Latin Vulgate*, none of the translations appear to have been well prepared, and Jerome did not improve on the translations of the apocryphal or deuterocanonical texts in his translation, nor did he think highly of several of the NT writings in his translation of them. His Vulgate is not an even treatment of all of the books in his translation. Some of the difficulties with these early translations had to do with the problem of translating the many nuances of the Greek into other languages. Metzger and Ehrman explain that not only were incompetent translators involved in the preparation of many of these translations, but they also show that there were features of the Greek syntax that are not easily transferred to another language. For example, they explain, "Latin [unlike the Greek] has no definite article; Syriac cannot distinguish between the Greek Aorist and perfect tenses; Coptic lacks the passive voice and must use a circumlocution. In some cases, therefore, the testimony of these versions is ambiguous" (Metzger and Ehrman 2005: 95).

These various ancient translations let us know which books were received as authoritative scriptures at various times and places as well as something about the beliefs of the churches that used and transmitted them. None of the translations before the fourth century include all of the NT books and very few after that do until much later. There is much that we do not know about the contents of these translations since some exist only in fragments and only a few of them have been studied adequately. Nevertheless, most of the early versions contain *some* of the books of the NT, especially the Gospels and Paul, but not all of those writings and some of them contain other books besides the biblical books. In time, *some* of these versions expanded to include more of the canonical books, but the earliest versions often omit several NT books. The same can be said of some of the earliest Greek NT manuscripts. The NT portion of *Codex Sinaiticus*, for example, contains a complete collection of the NT books, but it also contains some noncanonical books (the *Epistle of Barnabas* and a fragment of the *Shepherd of Hermas*). The various churches that received the early translations generally did not have the whole Bible in their translations and often included *only* the NT books that were useful in their worship and instruction.

The implications of this survey of the early translations are considerable. The greater church in antiquity never claimed that only the Greek translation of the Hebrew scriptures or that the Greek alone was the inspired text of the NT and that all others were uninspired. The Syriac Peshitta was surely scripture to Syrian-speaking Christians who welcomed and used the Peshitta in their worship and instruction in their churches. They did not conclude that their scriptures were less inspired than those used by Greek-speaking Christians. The Ethiopian and Coptic Christians had their own translations of their scriptures and both recognized them as divinely inspired. This is not unlike Christians today who welcome as scripture popular new translations and read them in local churches. The variations in the quality of these modern translations are obvious to scholars and all of them are clearly not produced with equal skill.

The Latin Vulgate translation eventually, though not initially, came close to being *the* translation for Western churches, but that was not the case in most of the Eastern churches that stayed with the Greek texts. Except in the case of the LXX, no early church father made unique claims for the authority of only one translation over many others that were produced. Unlike rabbinic Jews, the early Christians were anxious to translate their sacred scriptures into the languages of the people they had evangelized. Some church fathers (Irenaeus, Origen, Augustine, Jerome) noted the poor quality of several translations, but that did not deter the ancient churches from authorizing and accepting new translations of their scriptures in multiple languages of the people.

Most Christians today cannot read their Bibles in the biblical languages of Hebrew, Aramaic, and Greek, but they nonetheless receive what they have in their native tongues as inspired sacred texts. This is not unlike what occurred in antiquity. Does the authority and inspiration of the biblical text relate only to the original language(s), or does it transcend the Hebrew, Aramaic, and Greek texts in which they were first produced? Is the authority and inspiration of the scriptures of both Testaments the same in the large number of translations of the biblical texts available today? The OT scriptures of most of the early Christians was not the HB, but rather the Greek translation of the Hebrew scriptures. The notion that the authority of the scriptures did not transfer to the LXX does not appear in early Christianity—even though there are considerable differences between the Hebrew and the LXX texts as we saw earlier and in other translations.

What bearing does the concept of translation have on inspiration? Does the notion of inspiration apply only to the autographs or original texts of the Bible (which we no longer have)? Does inspiration apply to copies of the biblical manuscripts, all of which contain mistakes of one sort or another or at least variants within the manuscripts? That raises questions also about current translations of the Bible that are based on an eclectic text of the scriptures that does not exist in any of the surviving manuscripts of antiquity that have numerous variants in them. This is not an argument to abandon any views on the sacredness of the biblical books. On the contrary, historically churches have affirmed the Bible and that God continues to speak to the followers of Jesus in a variety of translations. However, some of those translations are clearly better than others.

Historically, the church has not spoken with a single voice on the above matters, even though from the beginning of the church portions of the teachings of Jesus that were included in canonical Gospels were translated from Aramaic (most probably) into Greek and subsequently into different languages. For example, see the Papias reference above that refers to Matthew producing a collection of sayings of Jesus (*ta logia*) in Hebrew and later others interpreting (translating) them (Eusebius, *Hist. eccl.* 3.39.16). The church has never chosen only one translation of the Bible, though there were moves in this direction (i.e., with Jerome's Latin Vulgate). Some modern Christians still argue for the sacredness of the King James Bible (only) but that does not address the needs of those who speak German, French, Chinese, Arabic, or French or any other language. As is true today, so it appears to be the case in antiquity. There was no distinction understood in their translations and all were considered inspired by God by those who had them. Certainly, some translations are of better quality than others. The early church fathers never said that only one translation was inspired and acceptable for reading in the churches.

Craig D. Allert discusses this issue and rightly concludes that inspiration is not locked into any one translation (Allert 1999: 85–113). He calls for a redefinition of inspiration that more ably reflects the phenomena of scripture and reflects better that inspiration is more appropriately related to the *function* of scripture rather than to its specific words as we see in 2 Tim 3:16–17. He concludes that translations can in fact be inspired, "because the community views them as accurately reflecting what the community as a whole believes is the will of God in them. This reflection is preserved in the biblical canon and is authoritative for the historic orthodox community of faith today" (Allert 1999: 112). That also appears to be the position of the early Christians who heard or read the scriptures in a different language, although there was no perceived distinction in the level of inspiration in translations of the church's scriptures, and the distinctions between many of them are *generally* minimal though with some exceptions. Most of the early NT translations reliably told the same story of Jesus. Remarkably, the notion of the authority of scripture was not significantly affected in most churches despite fluidity in the texts of the NT with the challenges associated with translating them.

By the early seventh century, the scriptures of the church existed in Greek, Old Latin, Gothic, Syriac, Coptic, Armenian, Georgian, Ethiopic, and Sogdian (Metzger 2001: 8–9). The early translations were often of poor quality and none of them included all the books of current Bibles or *only* those books.

The use of translations has been a part of the church almost from its beginning. When Jesus spoke, it is generally agreed that he spoke in Aramaic and probably also Hebrew, but he likely also had some facility in Greek, as many scholars now contend. All four of the canonical Gospels were written in Greek and the words Jesus originally spoke to his disciples were first translated into Greek from Hebrew or Aramaic or both. Although the Gospels were written in Greek, many of the traditions in them were initially based on Aramaic and Hebrew sources, whether oral or written, and subsequently translated into Greek. This is the first known translation activity in the early churches and that perhaps was the source and motivation for subsequent translations. Evans suggests that Jesus himself did not privilege the Hebrew but was open to translation and rewording the scriptural texts (Evans 2020: 427–49).

One of the oldest traditions about Matthew, according to Papias of Hierapolis (60–130 CE), is that he collected "oracles" of Jesus in the Hebrew language, and "each teacher interpreted [or translated] them as best he could" (Eusebius, *Hist. eccl.* 3.39.16). However, the Gospel of Matthew as we now have it was written in Greek and it is difficult to say what was gained or lost in an initial translation of Jesus' sayings into Greek, but the early Christians took their gospel about Jesus to various places *in Greek*, the most common language in the Greco-Roman world at that time, and there is no indication that they thought they were taking something with them that was second rate or inferior because it was a translation. The following discussion focuses on the use, significance, and contents of early translations of the NT writings.

Perhaps the first known translation was the Syriac Peshitta and subsequent translations included several of the disputed or deuterocanonical books in the OT books. In the earliest Syriac manuscripts, the NT included all the NT books except the Minor or 'Pococke' Epistles (2 Peter, 2–3 John, Jude) and Revelation, but they also initially included Tatian's *Diatessaron* (c. 150–160) that he harmonized and often changed their scriptural texts to be more in tune with the LXX as in the case of John the Baptist's diet. Also, that collection eventually included *3 Corinthians* (c. 150–165). The *Diatessaron* harmony of the four canonical Gospels was popular well into the fifth century in Syria along with *3 Corinthians* that was written in Paul's name to address the Gnostic threats to the proto-orthodox Christians and introduced into Syrian churches most likely in the third century and likely also welcomed as Christian scripture. A commentary was written on *3 Corinthians* and that signals its high esteem and function as scripture in the Syrian communities as well as elsewhere as in Armenia where it continued to be included among the scriptures there until well into the 1800s. Besides the Tanak books, the Armenian versions included several of the disputed books in question as well as *History of Joseph and Asenath*, *Testaments of the Twelve Patriarchs*, *The Book of Adam*, *The History of Moses*, *The Deaths of the Prophets*, *Concerning King Solomon*, *A Short History of the Prophet Elias*, *Concerning the Prophet Jeremiah*, the *Vision of Enoch the Just*, and *The Third Book of Esdras* (= chapters 3–14 of 4 Ezra). Their NT also included *3 Corinthians* and the *Repose of the Blessed Disciple* (John) well into the nineteenth century (Hovhanessian 2012: 1–6, 63–87). For the most relevant sources here, see Metzger 1987: 176, 182, 219, 223; Houghton 2016: 170, 194–6, 246, 266; Klugkist and Reinink 1999: 51–4 (who say 3 Corinthians has only a light footprint in the Latin mss B [Vg^s B], also including *Laodiceans*, and placed after Hebrews, plus ms VL 86 and its table of contents that 3 Cor was removed from its original text); see also Verheyden (2013: 389–411); Elliott (2013: 469–70); and Williams (2013: 527–35).

In regard to the OT scriptures, Augustine's Latin collection (*de Doctrina* 2.8.26–28) does not list all the disputed or deuterocanonical or "readable" texts but simply notes the variety of books besides the HB books in the Latin translations. His OT collection includes besides the Tanak books but also Tobias, Judith, 1–2 Maccabees, 1–2 Esdras, Wisdom, and Sirach. He includes all twenty-seven NT books/letters.

Jerome's Latin version of the OT did not willingly accept the "deuterocanonical" books but was pressured to accept them from the churches. That collection, as noted earlier, after being identified at the Council of Trent is for the first time identified as "deuterocanonical" texts by Sixtus of Siena in 1566 in his *Bibliotheca Sancta*. He called the Tanak/HB books "protocanonical" (*Protocanonicos*). Jerome included most of them in his Latin Translation, though he only translated two of them (Tobias and Judith) but did not accept them as sacred scripture. His OT list *generally* followed the Tanak order, as we see in his *Preface to Samuel and Kings*, but broadly follows the common Christian order (see his *Epistle* 53). He accepted all and only the twenty-seven NT books and labels the deuterocanonicals as "apocrypha" in his *Prologus Galeatus* (c. 390–396 CE; see also his *Epistle* 53 and *Epistle* 107).

The Coptic versions included all of the NT books, but the Catholic books are in a different sequence beginning with 1–2 Peter, 1–2–3 John, Jude, and Revelation, but some lists also include 1–2 Clement (Metzger 1987: 224–5).

Finally, besides the Tanak/HB books, the Ethiopic version includes the *Prayer of Manasseh*, *Jubilees*, *Enoch*, 2 Ezra and *Ezra Sutuel*, Tobit, Judith, Esther with additions, 1–3 Maccabees, Psalm 151, Daniel with additions, Baruch, Epistle of Jeremiah, Wisdom, Sirach, and *Pseudo-Josephus*. The orders or sequences of these books vary in their surviving collections and Bibles. Their NT includes besides the usual twenty-seven NT books *Sinodos* (four sections), Clement, *Book of the Covenant* (two sections), and *Didascalia* (Metzger 1987: 224).

4. LOCAL COUNCIL DECISIONS AND THE CHURCH'S SCRIPTURES

Church councils were common from the beginning of the early church and its leaders deliberated current issues affecting the churches. The first church council took place in Jerusalem to decide whether and how to welcome the Gentiles into the church (Acts 15). There were several *local* church councils that came after that, but the decisions were all local and many of their decisions are not known. No general or ecumenical councils ever discussed the scope of the Christian scriptures. While the Council of Trent (1546) is sometimes cited as evidence that an ecumenical council did deliberate on the scope of the church's scriptures, it did not include either the Orthodox in the East or the Protestants in the West. Only the local councils or synods produced lists of scriptural texts that could be read in churches, and the earliest records of those decisions come from the middle to late fourth century. It appears that for the most part, the twenty-seven books in the NT that are now approved by all three church branches (Orthodox, Catholic, and Protestant) come from the fourth century at the earliest with some disagreement then on several OT and NT books (for more detailed information on this, see McDonald 2017: 2:265–318).

The popularity of some texts may have influenced the inclusion of some disputed books for readability in public or in private. Also, some doubtful HB/Tanak books, for example, Esther, Song of Songs, and Ecclesiastes, were eventually welcomed but not without some question. Included in the table below are some of the non-HB books that were accepted by church councils and remained in Western and Eastern churches. These council decisions reflect both agreement and disagreement on the scope of the church's OT scriptures but also a difference in setting forth fixed scripture collections. Unlike Catholics and Protestants, Orthodox Christians did not have a council decision on the scope of their scriptures though in practice they have not added more books to their collection and the fluidity of that collection is mostly in their ancient collections but not in new ones.

Although Tertullian mentions earlier church councils deliberating and rejecting the *Shepherd of Hermas* (see below), he may be speaking of the regular church councils in Hippo and Carthage near his home. It is difficult to find evidence for any decision elsewhere to reject that book at that time since it continued to have a long life of use for centuries and by some church fathers and was included in later surviving manuscripts. No one should suggest that what Tertullian had in mind was true for all churches in the Greco-Roman world in his generation. Several local church councils later list the books that had greater receptivity and approval circulating among churches in the regions represented at the councils. None of the first seven *ecumenical* councils deliberated the scope of the church's scriptures.

The evidence from church council decisions listing the books in the church's scriptures generally appear in the fourth century and later, though Tertullian (*c.* 200) indicated that "every church council" rejected the *Shepherd of Hermas* calling it an "adulterous" book because it allowed forgiveness after repentance and baptism (*De Pudicitia* 10 and for similar focus on adultery and immorality, see also *De Pudicitia* 20 and *De orat.* 16). Tertullian's broader text, focusing on repeated repentance after adultery, attacks the Shepherd of Hermas as follows:

> I would yield my ground to you, if the scripture of "the Shepherd," which is the only one which favors adulterers, had deserved to find a place in the Divine canon; if it had not been habitually judged by every council of Churches (even your own) among apocryphal and false (writings); itself adulterous and hence a patroness of its comrades; from which in other respects, too, you derive initiation; to which, perchance, that "Shepherd" will play the patron whom you depict upon your (sacramental) chalice, (depict, I say, as) himself withal a prostitutor of the Christian sacrament. ... I, however, imbibe the Scriptures of that Shepherd who cannot be broken. ... But, even if pardon is rather the "fruit of repentance," even pardon cannot co-exist without the cessation from sin. So if the cessation from sin the root of pardon, that pardon may be the fruit of repentance. (*De Pudicitia* 10)

It is interesting that he indicates that the *Shepherd* was already called "scripture" before by several church fathers. His concern over repeated repentance and pardon that he believes is allowed in the *Shepherd* is likely not only a statement in his post-Montanist conversion perspective but also a recognition that it was widely welcomed despite his assertion that it was determined by every church council to be among apocryphal and false writings. It is not clear which councils he has in view (Montanist or otherwise?). Since there are no surviving records of those church councils that clarify what was welcomed and what was not among the Christian scriptures, it may be unwarranted to guess what their decisions might have been. There is no other evidence that the Shepherd was rejected by that time (not even the Muratorian Fragment (MF) as argued elsewhere, see McDonald 2017: 2: 274–305). No evidence exists for church interest in deliberating those choices at this early date.

Interestingly, Tertullian accepted the scriptural status of *1 Enoch* because it was cited by Jude that he accepted as scripture (see Jude 14 and Tertullian, *On the Apparel of Women* 1.3). One can only wonder about what other books were deliberated at that time and what decisions came from the council decisions, if any. To support his argument against the *Shepherd*, Tertullian acknowledges that some early councils supported his rejection of its scriptural status, but again, what those councils in the early third century decided is unclear and no record of their decisions has survived. It may be that Tertullian was speaking with hyperbole or perhaps he was speaking about decisions made at Carthage that had regular (almost annual) church councils. Tertullian likely welcomed the *Shepherd* as scripture before his Montanus conversion and because of the strictness in morality promoted by the Montanists, he rejected it because it appeared to him to offer forgiveness or pardon of sins after the initial repentance of sins and baptism (*Shepherd* 31:2–7). Because of this, Tertullian concluded that it "favors adulterers." For a more detailed discussion of the use and recognition of the Shepherd in early Christianity, see Osiek (1999: 1–7).

Hill has argued that evidence for this frequently neglected reference to church councils excluding the Shepherd supports his conclusion that the Muratorian Fragment (MF) canon list was produced at such a council around the time of Tertullian (2016: 56–69). The problem with that position, of course, is that no records of any local church councils at that time exist that dealt with the scope of the church's scriptures, and the most recent dating of the MF places it in the middle to late fourth century. For arguments in favor of a late-fourth- or early-fifth-century dating of the MF see Rothschild (2018: 55–82; and her 2021 volume).

Finally, it would be strange if the *Shepherd* had been widely rejected by the time of Tertullian since other church fathers from approximately the same time had welcomed it as scripture. For example, Clement of Alexandria regularly cites it as scripture (e.g., *Stromata* 2.1; 2.9; 2.12; 4.9; 6.15 more than seventeen times). The *Shepherd* was introduced and cited as scripture also by Irenaeus as "Truly, then, the Scripture declared ..." (*Haer.* 4.20.2 citing *Shepherd*, 2. *Sim.* 1, using γραφή; cf. *Haer* 2.20.2; cf. *Mand* 1.1). Origen (see *On Prin.* 1.3.3 and 4.1.11) acknowledges the *Shepherd* as scripture but does acknowledge that some despise it. He describes it as "divinely inspired" and connected its author with the Hermas mentioned in Rom 16:14. While it was later excluded from scriptural or canonical lists, as in the case of Athanasius' *Thirty-Ninth Festal Letter* in 367, it was nevertheless allowed to be read in private. The *Shepherd of Hermas* was later included in the late-fourth-century *Codex Sinaiticus* and it was also included in the Latin list inserted in *Codex Claromontanus* (D^p), along with *Acts of Paul* and *Revelation of Peter*. There is an obelus posted beside these books, which could mean that those texts may not have been in the initial listing or that they were not considered scriptural and only allowed for private reading. The *Shepherd* was also included in the fifth-century *Codex Alexandrinus* along with 1–2 Clement. This is relevant because Hill and others cite Tertullian's rejection of the *Shepherd* as evidence for a second-century dating of the MF and NT canon consciousness in the late second century (Hill 2016: 56–69). There is no clear evidence that councils made any decisions about the scope of the church's scriptures and Tertullian does not say anything about a council determining the full scope of the church's scriptures at that time, only its doubts about the *Shepherd*. The following church council canon lists reflect the Hebrew and Greek books that were included among the Christian scriptures. The most notable church councils that specifically dealt with the scope of the biblical canon for the churches include the following:

1. Council of Laodicea, canons 59–60 (*c.* 360, but possibly later in origin): Canon 60 was most likely inserted later. It does not accept Revelation.
   These are all the books of OT appointed to be read: (1) Genesis of the world; (2) The Exodus from Egypt; (3) Leviticus; (4) Numbers; (5) Deuteronomy; (6) Joshua, the son of Nun; (7) Judges, Ruth; (8) Esther; (9) Of the Kings, First and Second; (10) Of the Kings, Third and Fourth; (11) Chronicles, First and Second; (12) Esdras, First and Second; (13) The Book of Psalms; (14) The Proverbs of Solomon; (15) Ecclesiastes; (16) The Song of Songs; (17) Job; (18) The Twelve Prophets;(19) Isaiah; (20) Jeremiah, and Baruch, the Lamentations, and the Epistle; (21) Ezekiel; (22) Daniel.
   And these are the books of the NT: Four Gospels, according to Matthew, Mark, Luke, and John; The Acts of the Apostles; Seven Catholic Epistles, to wit, one of James, two of Peter, three of John, one of Jude; Fourteen Epistles of Paul, one to the Romans, two to the Corinthians, one to the Galatians, one to the Ephesians,

one to the Philippians, one to the Colossians, two to the Thessalonians, one to the Hebrews, two to Timothy, one to Titus, and one to Philemon.

2. Council of Rome (382) that is repeated in the *Decretum Gelasianum* (496): includes Wisdom, Sirach, 1–2 Esdras, Tobit Judith, and 1–2 Maccabees, probably also additions to Daniel and Esther, but Baruch and Epistle of Jeremiah are missing. It reads as follows:

Likewise, it has been said: Now indeed we must treat of the divine scriptures, what the universal Catholic Church accepts and what she ought to shun. The order of the Old Testament begins here: Genesis one book, Exodus one book, Leviticus one book, Numbers one book, Deuteronomy one book, Josue Nave [Joshua] one book, Judges one book, Ruth one book, Kings four books, Paralipomenon [i.e., Chronicles] two books, Psalms one book, Solomon three books, Proverbs one book, Ecclesiastes one book, Canticle of Canticles one book, likewise Wisdom one book, Ecclesiasticus [i.e., Sirach] one book. Likewise, the order of the Prophets. Isaiah one book, Jeremiah one book, with his Lamentations, Ezekiel one book, Daniel one book, Hosea one book, Amos one book, Micah one book, Joel one book, Obadiah, one book, Jonah one book, Nahum one book, Habakkuk one book, Zephaniah one book, Haggai one book, Zechariah one book, Malachias one book. Likewise, the order of the histories. Job one book, Tobias one book, Esdras two books [i.e., Ezra & Nehemiah], Esther one book, Judith one book, Maccabees two books.

Likewise, the order of the writings of the New and Eternal Testament, which only the holy and Catholic Church supports. Of the Gospels, according to Matthew one book, according to Mark one book, according to Luke one book, according to John one book. The Epistles of Paul the Apostle in number fourteen. To the Romans one, to the Corinthians two, to the Ephesians one, to the Thessalonians two, to the Galatians one, to the Philippians one, to the Colossians one, to Timothy two, to Titus one, to Philemon one, to the Hebrews one. Likewise, the Apocalypse of John, one book. And the Acts of the Apostles one book. Likewise, the canonical epistles in number seven. Of Peter the Apostle two epistles, of James the Apostle one epistle, of John the Apostle one epistle, of another John, the presbyter, two epistles, of Jude the Zealot, the Apostle one epistle.

—This Decree of the Council of Rome (AD 382) on the Canon of scripture took place during the reign of Pope Damasus I (AD 366–384)

3. Councils of Hippo and Carthage (393, 397):

It was also determined that besides the Canonical scriptures nothing be read in the church under the title of divine scriptures. The Canonical scriptures are these: Genesis, Exodus, Leviticus, Numbers, Deuteronomy, Joshua the son of Nun, Judges, Ruth, four books of Kings, two books of Paraleipomena, Job, the Psalter, five books of Solomon, the books of the twelve prophets, Isaiah, Jeremiah, Ezechiel, Daniel, Tobit, Judith, Esther, two books of Esdras, two books of the Maccabees.

Of the NT: four books of the Gospels, one book of the Acts of the Apostles, thirteen Epistles of the Apostle Paul, one epistle of the same (writer) to the Hebrews, two Epistles of the Apostle Peter, three of John, one of James, one of Jude, one book of the Apocalypse of John. (Note: the 419 council added Hebrews to Paul's letters making it fourteen. Earlier in 397 there was some doubt about its author and Hebrews was separated from the thirteen letters attributed to Paul).

Let this be made known also to our brother and fellow-priest Boniface, or to other bishops of those parts, for the purpose of confirming that Canon. Because we have received from our fathers those books must be read in the church. Let it also be allowed that the Passions of Martyrs be read when their festivals are kept.

4. Trullan Synod (691) and Seventh Ecumenical Council (787): affirmed earlier Eastern canons of local synods that welcomed the disputed books. They did not mention Cyril of Jerusalem who rejected the deuterocanonical books. None of the ecumenical church councils made any decisions on the scope of the church's scriptures.

5. Council of Trent (1546): 1–2 Esdras, Tobias, Judith, Wisdom, Sirach, Baruch, and 1–2 Maccabees, plus additions in Daniel and Esther. No known ecumenical council addressed the issue of the books that were in either the OT or NT or specifically which could be read in the churches. Its OT and NT include:

Of the OT, the five books of Moses, namely, Genesis, Exodus, Leviticus, Numbers, Deuteronomy; Joshua, Judges, Ruth, the four books of Kings (Samuels and Kings), two of Paralipomenon (Chronicles), the first and second of Esdras, the latter of which is called Nehemiah, Tobias, Judith, Esther, Job, the Davidic Psalter of 150 Psalms, Proverbs, Ecclesiastes, the Canticle of Canticles, Wisdom (of Solomon), Ecclesiasticus (Sirach), Isaiah, Jeremiah, with Baruch, Ezechiel, Daniel, the twelve minor Prophets, namely, Hosea, Joel, Amos, Obadiah, Jonah, Micah, Nahum, Habakkuk, Zephaniah, Haggai, Zechariah, Malachi; two books of Machabees [sic.], the first and second.

Of the NT, the four Gospels, according to Matthew, Mark, Luke, and John; the Acts of the Apostles written by Luke the Evangelist; fourteen Epistles of Paul the Apostle, to the Romans, two to the Corinthians, to the Galatians, to the Ephesians, to the Philippians, to the Colossians, two to the Thessalonians, two to Timothy, to Titus, to Philemon, to the Hebrews; two of Peter the Apostle, three of John the Apostle, one of James the Apostle, one of Jude the Apostle, and the Apocalypse of John the Apostle.

If anyone does not accept as sacred and canonical the aforesaid books in their entirety and with all their parts, as they have been accustomed to be read in the Catholic Church and as they are contained in the old Latin Vulgate Edition, and knowingly and deliberately rejects the aforesaid traditions, let him be anathema. "Let all understand, therefore, in what order and manner the council, after having laid the foundation of the confession of faith, will proceed, and who are the chief witnesses and supports to whom it will appeal in conforming dogmas and in restoring morals in the Church."

5. THE EMERGENCE OF CHRISTIAN SCRIPTURAL CANON LISTS

The following is a summary of the contents and importance of some of the early church council decisions on the scope of the Christian scriptures. I have argued elsewhere that the multiple lists of allowable scriptures to be read in churches began to appear after the Council of Nicea (325) in the fourth and fifth centuries (McDonald 2017: vol. 2:265–319), which are very important for understanding how the churches at that time acknowledged the books that eventually formed their Bible. The following tables do not list the Tanak/HB books unless they are *not* included in the collections, but they do include the deuterocanonical books in the LXX and occasionally others. Some of these lists omit some NT books but sometimes exclude others. A more complete collection of these lists along with helpful comments is in Gallagher and Meade (2017) and a smaller collection in McDonald (2017: 1:491–9 and 2:361–9). Some noncanonical books are occasionally included in church father citations, various translations, and manuscripts. The following reflects both the considerable overlap in contents as well as the continuing fluidity in early Christianity on the scope of its scriptures in both the East and West. Much of the information below comes from Gallagher and Meade (2017) and McDonald (2017: 1:491–9 and 2:361–9). I should say in advance that the notion of a Christian "Bible" was present largely in the middle to late fourth century and thereafter when decisions were made at local council levels about which books the constituent church in those locations could read in churches and in private. However, the notion of a Bible or fixed collection of books was not fully possible for centuries later when pandect collections of the church's scriptures was possible and made more available to pastors as well as professors and many local churches. That is when that collection became known as the "Holy Books," that is, "Holy Bible."

A. OT and/or NT Canon Lists from the East

1. Bryennios (*c*. 100–150): order varies in Pentateuch, not clear on Lamentations, Baruch or Epistle of Jeremiah, or Esther, but includes 1–2 Esdras.
2. Melito of Sardis (*c*. 170): OT only, excludes Esther and likely includes Wisdom of Solomon.
3. Origen (*c*. fl. 210–253): OT = includes 1–2 Esdras, Epistle of Jeremiah, *possibly* 1–2 Maccabees, but also Susanna and other deuterocanonical books that he defended. The Twelve Minor Prophets are likely accidently omitted. His NT may exclude 2 Peter and possibly but not clear 2–3 John and Revelation. See his *Selectae in Psalmos* 1 where he says there are "twenty-two encovenanted books according to the Hebrew tradition;" *Comm. on Matt.* 1 preserved in Eusebius, *Hist. eccl.* 6.25.3–6; *Comm. on John* 5; *Homil. on Josuam* 7.1). But this may not be his own view of what books are sacred.
4. Eusebius (*c*. 320–339): His OT apparently follows Origen's list that he includes in his *Hist. eccl.* 6.25.1–14. His NT books = "Recognized" (ὁμολογουμένοις—ὁμολογουμένως) = four Gospels, Acts, letters of Paul (identity not given), 1 John, 1 Peter, possibly Revelation. "Disputed" (ἀντιλεγομένων—ἀντιλεγομένος) = James Jude, 2 Peter, 2–3 John, and possibly Revelation and Gospel according to the Hebrews. "Spurious" (νόθοις—νόθος) = Acts of Paul, Shepherd, Apocalypse of Peter, Epistle of Barnabas, Didache. "Heretical" (= the αἱρετικῶν—αἱρετικός) = Gospels of Peter, Thomas, Matthias and other Gospels, Acts of Andrew, Acts of John, and other Acts—all of which are "shunned altogether."
5. Cyril of Jerusalem (*c*. fl. 350–87): Jeremiah includes Baruch and Epistle of Jeremiah, Daniel including Susanna and Bel and the Dragon, but excludes Revelation. See his *On the Divine Scriptures* in *NPNF*. All NT writings except Revelation.
6. Athanasius of Alexandria (*c*. 367): In his 39th *Festal Letter*, the OT includes in Jeremiah Baruch, Lamentations, and Epistle of Jeremiah. Daniel includes Susanna and possibly Bel and the Dragon. Athanasius excludes Esther. The whole NT is present. "Readable" books (= some deuterocanonical books) include Wisdom, Sirach, Esther, Judith, Tobit, Didache, Shepherd. Rejected books = "Apocrypha" (that he says are "invented by the heretics") and include *Enoch*, possibly *Ascension*

of *Isaiah*, *Testament of Moses*, and *Apocalypse of Elijah*. He includes the whole NT canon.
7. Synod of Laodicea, Canons 59–60 (*c.* 360–380): The OT includes Baruch and Epistle of Jeremiah and 1–2 Esdras. The whole NT except Revelation.
8. *Apostolic Canons* 85 (*c.* 375–380): The OT includes 1–2 Esdras, Judith, 1–4 Maccabees, Psalm 151, Wisdom and likely also Sirach. The NT includes 1–2 Clement, not Revelation. He (Clement?) adds eight books of the Constitutions for bishops.
9. Gregory of Nazianzus (*c.* 330–391): OT likely includes in Jeremiah both Epistle of Baruch and Epistle of Jeremiah, but no other disputed or deuterocanonical texts. His NT questions but still includes Revelation (see his *Iambi ad Seleucum*, lines 251–320).
10. Amphilocius of Iconium (*c.* 380): His OT raises questions about Esther and includes the Epistle of Baruch and likely Epistle of Jeremiah in the book of Jeremiah. His NT includes most of the NT books, but like Syrian churches also raises questions about 2 Peter, 2–3 John, Jude, and Revelation.
11. Epiphanius of Salamis (*c.* 315–402): His three lists of OT writings number them as twenty-seven instead of twenty-two or twenty-four and in all three he includes 1–2 Esdras, and the Epistles of Jeremiah and Baruch (*Panarion* 8.6.1–4; *De mensuris et ponderibus* 4–5 and 22–23). After listing the complete NT, he adds Wisdom and Sirach (see *Panarion* 76.22.5).

B. OT and NT Canon Lists from the West

1. Muratorian Fragment (*c.* 375–400): The current *fragment* includes most of the NT books but does not include Hebrews, 2 Peter, or James and strangely includes Wisdom of Solomon at the end of the NT list, much like Epiphanius above. The MF rejects the public reading of Shepherd but encourages its private reading. The author also rejects reading texts by Arsinous, Valentinus, and Miltiades, along with two pseudonymous texts in Paul's name (Laodiceans and Alexandrians). Its references to Pius as the brother of Hermas, Miltiades as heretical, the Cataphrygians instead of Montanists, and the lack of parallels of NT canon lists before the fourth century date it in the middle to late fourth century.
2. *Codex Claromontanus* (*c.* mid-sixth century): A Greek manuscript with a Latin insertion between Philemon and Hebrews listing OT and NT books. The OT includes Wisdom, Sirach, likely the additions to Jeremiah, 1-2-3-4 Maccabees, Judith, and Tobit. The complete NT is included along with *Epistle of Barnabas*, *Shepherd of Hermas*, *Acts of Paul*, and *Revelation of Peter*.
3. Mommsen or Cheltenham List (*c.* 365): The OT includes 1–2 Maccabees, Tobit, Judith, Psalm 151, and likely Wisdom and Sirach (based on the number of lines listed for Solomon). Ezra is not included. The NT canon but with questions about 2 Peter, 2–3 John, and likely only affirms 1 Peter and 1 John since after noting that there were two letters of Peter, the author inserts "*una sola*" ("only one") and after noting three letters of John also adds "*una sola*." This NT list does not include Hebrews, James, or Jude.
4. Hilary of Poitiers (*c.* 310–367): OT includes Epistle of Jeremiah and indicates that *some* add Tobit and Judith making a twenty-four-book OT. No NT canon is listed. See his *Instructio Psalmorum* 15.

5. Jerome of Stridon and Bethlehem (*c.* 347–420): His OT includes Tanak books and mostly in that order adopting the Hebrew twenty-two-book canon *at that time* with its usual combinations (Ruth with Judges, Ezra-Nehemiah, 1–2 Samuel, 1–2 Kings, 1–2 Chronicles, the Twelve [Minor Prophets]). The NT canon includes all the NT books, though Jerome expresses some doubts about Hebrews. Some noncanonical books could be read in church, but not to settle doctrinal issues. These include Wisdom, Sirach, Judith, Tobit, 1–2 Maccabees, and the Christian *Shepherd of Hermas*. Sources: see *Prologus Galeatus*, *Epistle 53*, *Epistle* 107.
6. Rufinus of Aquileia (*c.* 345–410, here 404): The OT includes all the Tanak books and possibly Baruch and Epistle of Jeremiah. His "ecclesiastical" category encourages *reading* several non-Tanak/HB and non-NT texts, but not as scripture. These books include Wisdom, Sirach, Tobit, Judith, 1–2 Maccabees. The Christian "ecclesiastical" texts for reading include *Shepherd of Hermas*, *Two Ways* (= *Didache*), and *Judgment of Peter*. Source: his *Commentary on The Apostles' Creed*.
7. Hippo Council (*c.* 393 report): The canonical OT established by this council includes Tanak plus also Wisdom, Sirach, Tobit, Judith, and 1–2 Maccabees. This Hippo council's NT includes all and only the NT books, but also as readable in the church the *Passion of the Martyrs*. Source: *Breviarium of Hipponense* 36.
8. Augustine of Hippo (*c.* 354–430): OT includes all Tanak books but did not mention Lamentations, Baruch *or* Epistle of Jeremiah, but also Esdras A and B, Tobit, Judith, 1–2 Maccabees, Wisdom, Sirach. The NT includes all and only the NT books. Source: his *On Christian Teaching* 2.8.12.24–13.29.
9. Pope/Bishop of Rome Innocent I (*c.* 402–417): OT includes Tanak books and Wisdom, Sirach, Tobit, Judith, 1–2 Esdras, and 1–2 Maccabees. His NT includes all and only the NT books. Source: Innocent, Epistle 6 *ad Exsuperium Tolosanum* (*c.* 405).

The above lists reflect early notions of what should comprise the church's scriptures, but again the presence of largely fixed Bibles circulating in churches is centuries later and the notion of "holy books" or "Holy Bible" does not come into prominence in churches until after the wider distribution of pandect collections of the church's scriptures. Jerome may be credited with speaking of "holy books" in the early fifth century in reference to the church's collection of scriptures, but that was not a widely known or used designation in churches until centuries later (for more on this see McDonald 2020: 141–2).

6. CONCLUSION

The NT scriptures of the earliest Christian churches differ in several respects from the NT that most Christians use today, in terms of the books contained in it, the texts of those books, and also the translations of them. Some early Christian communities produced copies and translations of the NT books from weaker textual traditions circulating among their churches and initially they either did not know or they did not use all of the books that currently make up our NT canon. Some of the Christians may have adopted something like a "canon within a canon" by teaching and preaching only those books that had more relevance for their communities of faith, but it is more likely that many early churches simply did not have access to all of the books in the current biblical canon whether in the OT or NT. In other cases, some early churches also accepted for centuries other books that are now considered noncanonical writings. Eventually those books, especially *Shepherd of Hermas*, *Epistle of Barnabas*, *1* and *2 Clement*, and the *Didache*, were excluded from various sacred collections and later they did not obtain canonical status. This suggests something akin to "decanonization" for some in the early churches. Both inclusion and rejection of some early Christian writings were present in various stages of the ancient churches' development of a biblical canon.

There appears to be little logic in why the early church fathers included some books in a collection of texts to be read in churches, but other equally orthodox books were not included, for example, *1 Clement*, *Shepherd of Hermas*, and *Didache*. The usual criteria for establishing the NT canon, namely apostolicity, antiquity, orthodoxy, and use, are helpful, but they are modern arguments based on a limited collection of comments in the church fathers and various council decisions, and there are exceptions to each of these criteria as I have noted earlier (McDonald 2017: 2:320–48). The later church's NT canon reflects the early church's sacred traditions and creedal formulations seen in the NT and the early church fathers, but no one in antiquity gave a clear rationale for which NT books would inform Christian faith, though in a broad sense the decisions of the Council of Nicea (325) made it clear that some books would not be accepted that rejected the majority views on the identity of Jesus. That said, as we saw above, other books not welcomed also agreed with the majority on the orthodox issues. While there are differences in emphases in the NT canon, at its core there is broad agreements and parallels in its many affirmations. That core Christian tradition that is at the heart of the Christian movement is broadly reflected in the Irenaeus creedal formulations *c*. 170 listed above, which is an early proto-orthodox position that obtained widespread approval by the end of the third century even before the conversion of Constantine. Those writings closest to the time of Jesus and his apostles (antiquity) alone are insufficient to account for canonicity, but their primary message (orthodoxy) was an important factor, namely the content of the books selected, but most importantly widespread use.

It appears that the churches that had their scriptures in translation (from the Greek) *generally* had fewer books available to them than those that had their scriptures in Greek, but even those collections did not for centuries include all the twenty-seven books in their collections. In several instances, they also had some extra-canonical books in their collections. As we saw, there are no NT manuscripts that contain all of the books of the NT *and no others* until around the year 1000. In all cases, however, there is no ancient view of inspiration that distinguished the translations of the NT books from those written in the Greek language. Those Christians who received their scriptures in translation also believed that God had inspired their scriptures. Remarkably, the church's oldest theological beliefs were often developed without the aid of a full or complete and carefully translated NT. Their beliefs were largely dependent on the oral and written traditions circulating in churches in the first couple of centuries and the partial collections of the NT scriptures.

The early churches with translated scriptures made use of them in their worship, instruction, and mission, even though the translations were not uniform in quality or in the specific books included in them, though most included one or more of the Gospels and several of the letters of Paul. Those translated collections of scriptures did not have *all* the same books and the quality of some of the translations was often inferior to other translations. Nevertheless, the churches with their scriptures in translations accepted what they had as inspired by God, and they established their doctrine, worship, and mission on the basis of these translations. How significant is this? Had all early Christians owned and used a complete set of the NT books *and no others*, and if their NT books all had the same or a similar biblical text, would that have made any difference in the theology and life of the churches? If so, what would that difference be?

On another note, what might be gained if Christians were informed by the same texts that informed the faith of many ancient Christians but were not finally included in the current Greek NTs? Swanson has raised this question and offers in a highly readable format the various readings of the NT books and indicates that ancient manuscripts with those texts were all read as scripture in the communities that had them. What difference in the church's theology would some of those readings make today? Swanson suggests that it might well be interesting to pursue that inquiry by comparing the various texts that he cites in his work, both canonical and noncanonical, and what the theological implications that the intentional changes to the biblical text might make (see Swanson 2003). What difference would it make if the sacred books that informed the early Christians left behind also informed the faith and understanding of Christians today? This is not a call to reform the current Bible whether its OT or NT, but only that familiarity with the books that informed the early Christians, or some of them, need not be held at arms distance and that we may be able to learn something from them. We should also observe that none of the earliest church creeds or any of the ecumenical church councils speak of the scope of the church's scriptures or a fixed biblical canon.

The next chapter will examine both the interesting and challenging issues related to origin, function, and circulation of pseudonymous writings in antiquity and whether they still exist in Christian Bibles and if so the implications for Christian faith.

CHAPTER 7

Pseudepigrapha and Apocrypha in Early Christianity

1. INTRODUCTION

It is well known that pseudepigraphal writings by pseudonymous authors were quite common in the ancient world and also in early Christianity and many critical questions related to its production, use, and reception in early Christianity will be our focus here. Was it authoritative in the churches that had it and were its early readers aware of its pseudonymous character? Finally, was some of it included in the Bible and if so, how can that be dealt with today? Does it or should it impact current notions of inspiration and authority for the church? These are among the most important questions we will examine below.

The modern rejection of the practice of forgery and production of pseudonymous texts is not always the same as it was in antiquity. Then it was not illegal even if found disappointing by many ancient authors. If pseudonymous texts were welcomed among the sacred and authoritative writings in the early churches, how were they perceived and used in churches to advance their mission? How did some pseudonymous writings gain the status of "temporary scriptures" in some early churches? Further, were all such writings cut from the same piece of cloth, namely, were they all written to deceive readers as some scholars contend, or were they all promoting heretical teachings as some suggest, or could there be another explanation for their production and use in early Christianity? It is important to recognize that many of the pseudonymous writings did serve as an authority for a time in some early churches and some of them still do.

Scholars presently debate whether such writings were deemed as sacred scripture for a time and further whether such writings remain in both the Old Testament (OT) and New Testament (NT). As a result of many inquiries over many years, several significant and pivotal studies have emerged recently that address these and other related issues. An important question that is raised by the study of the production and use of pseudonymous writings in early Christianity is whether a work that involves a fraud, whether pious or not, can be regarded as compatible with the character of a message from God. Metzger is right when he says that such questions are easier to raise than to resolve to everyone's satisfaction (Metzger 1972: 3–24).

Since its production and use was common in churches in their early centuries, one must ask whether ancient pseudonymous texts were an acceptable literary device *at that time* and to what extent was their value and sacredness connected to their authorship? Foucault raises this question and its importance (1984: 101–20) and I will return to it below. Were all pseudonymous texts perceived as deceitful and was all of it eventually removed from the sacred scripture collections when detected? Finally, did some pseudonymous writings remain in the church's scriptures? Of course, all such questions have implications for the understanding of scripture in antiquity and how important authorship was; or was the message in such writings more important than questions of authorship? These and other questions will be the focus below.

The designations "apocrypha" and "pseudepigrapha" are often difficult to distinguish since some of the writings in both collections were produced in a pseudonymous name. It appears that the distinctions could be as simple as saying that the difference is that pseudepigrapha is essentially what was not included in the so-called apocrypha collection. That is not far from the definition of R. H. Charles' well-known two-volume work, namely, it appears that whatever he did not include among the apocrypha was included in the second volume titled pseudepigrapha. The designation "apocrypha" is sometimes employed in antiquity to identify either heretical writings or religious texts falsely produced in the names of well-known persons from the biblical tradition. Initially "apocrypha" (ἀπόκρυφα) essentially had to do with what was called "secret" or "hidden" texts that would be revealed later at an appropriate time and often revealed only to a few (e.g., the "wise"). It is similar to ἀπόρρητον ("not to be spoken") and neither designation initially had negative connotations as we see in Dan 12:4; 4 Ezra 12–14; cf. Rev 5:1–5; 10:4–11, and elsewhere, but by the end of the second century CE, it began to have pejorative connotations among some church fathers and by the fourth century it was regularly used as a negative designation that referred to fraudulent (pseudonymous) or heretical writings (McDonald 2021: 24–51). This is similar in Origen (see ΒΕΠΕΣ = [Βιβλιοθήκη Ελλήνων Πατέρων και Εκκλησιαστικών Συγγραφέων] 16.355.5–6 and 16.329.26–28). It is not altogether clear why "apocrypha" came to be used for questionable or rejected texts nor why what was "hidden" came to be identified as rejected works, but that begins to emerge in the late second century and is common in the fourth century.

2. THE ORIGIN AND MEANING OF PSEUDEPIGRAPHAL WRITINGS

Pseudonymous writings were well known in antiquity and the designation "pseudepigrapha" likely originated with Dionysius of Halicarnassus (*c.* 30 BCE) who wrote about the speeches reportedly written by Dinarchus (a metic speech writer in Athens, *c.* 360–290 BCE). In his *On Dinarchus* 11, Dionysius attempted to distinguish the speeches written by Dinarchus from those falsely written in his name and was apparently the first to use the designation *pseudepigraphoi* (Greek = ψευδεπίγραφοι "falsely attributed writings") for those texts written in his name (see especially *In Din.* 4, but 2, 3, and 9). (This source is cited in Najman and Peirano.) Some of it could go back to legal codes attributed to the Babylonian king, Hammurabi (*c.* 1792–1750 BCE; see Rist 1972: 75). The production of pseudonymous texts in ancient Greco-Roman literature was largely from the fourth and third century BCE and onward falsely produced in the names of famous writers and sold for personal gain to the museums of Alexandria (perhaps as early as 283–246 BCE) and Pergamum (197–159 BCE) as well as for multiple other motives (Metzger 1972: 5–12; Rist 1972: 75–80).

Pseudonymous writings were quite common in the ancient world going back at least to the Babylonian era, and more so later in the Greco-Roman world. As noted above, well before the emergence of early Christianity the production of literature falsely written in the names of earlier ideal or well-known persons was well known. Multiple examples of this practice in the ancient world are notable and some are also later than the NT era but not as relevant for our purposes, namely Iamblichus (*c.* 250–330; *Life of Pythagoras* 31), Olympiodorus (*c.* 380–425; *Prolegomenon* 13.4–14.4), and Elias (500–550; *In Porphyrii Isagogen et Aristotelis Categorias Commentaria* 128.1–22). These are cited by Ehrman (2011: 131–3, 282), but they could also include many earlier classical writers who had pseudonymous writings published in their names, as in the cases of Lysias, Galen, Apollonius, Plato, Pythagoras, Socrates, Xenophon, and others (see more listed in Metzger 1972 and Rist 1972).

The modern focus on pseudepigrapha examines mostly that which was forged or misattributed, but that is not always the way they are viewed in antiquity. Not all pseudepigrapha is pseudonymous and that makes it more difficult to find a suitable name for the phenomena that we are describing. The practice of writing in another's name, commonly known as pseudonymity and its product as pseudepigrapha, was widespread in antiquity. As we will see, it is difficult to define that literature since it also overlaps with early Christian "apocrypha" that is also difficult to define and not all of it now so identified was pseudonymous. It is more commonly understood as literature written with the intent to deceive readers, or as religious writings not included in the Bible. Some of these texts are not the same as those included in current lists of OT apocrypha. Earlier distinctions are difficult to maintain in current research that focuses on a much wider collection of texts in both of those categories with the challenge of knowing when and how to limit such collections since date, genres, and names often vary. Several careful summaries of OT pseudepigrapha and its understanding of Second Temple Judaism are found in Flint (1999: 2:24–66), Reed (2008: 467–89), Stuckenbruck (2010: 143–62; Tuckett (2015: 2–12), and Collins, Evans, and McDonald (2020).

Multiple examples of Greco-Roman and Jewish production and use of pseudonymous texts are similar to those produced in and commonly welcomed in early Christianity (Clarke 2002: 440–68; Metzger 1972; Rist 1972). That is well established, but the motive for its production is where scholars are divided and also whether it was discerned by the early church fathers. Was it written as something like a pen name to hide one's identity for sake of security, or to honor one's esteemed ideal model or teacher, or as an act of humility as in the case of Silvan that Metzger identifies, or to deceive readers to advance theological positions? Metzger, Clarke, and Rist list possibilities for several motives, but broadly agree that most of it was written to deceive readers.

According to Donelson (1986), it appears that the modern investigation of *Christian* pseudonymous writings in biblical literature began with Friedrich Schleiermacher in 1807 and subsequently F. C. Baur (1835) who focused mainly on the Pastoral Epistles (1 Timothy, 2 Timothy, and Titus). Baur argued that the production of pseudonymous texts in antiquity was intended to deceive readers and several conservative scholars agreed with that assessment but denied its presence in biblical literature claiming that it was always rejected in the early church (e.g., C. L. Mitton, Donald Guthrie, J. S. Candlish). More recently scholars of such investigations have waded through much of the considerable literature and conclude that many of the earlier defenses against its use in the early churches are based more on theological arguments than on careful investigations or exegesis, namely, how could a book inspired by God and focused on divine truth originate in a lie or forgery (Ehrman)?

Since Schleiermacher and Baur, there has been an emerging acknowledgment that some biblical books or texts in the Bible are pseudonymous and questions about their continuing presence in it have involved multiple reexaminations of biblical texts often resulting in speculations about their production and use in antiquity. The most common question in those studies focused on whether pseudonymous texts were included in the church's NT and often focusing on the Pastoral Epistles but now on others also. Marshall has rejected Paul's authorship of the Pastoral Epistles *in their current condition*—especially 1 Timothy and Titus, but nevertheless thinks there is sufficient authentic Pauline material in 2 Timothy to suggest that Timothy or Titus was the final author/editor of the corpus. Instead of using the term "pseudonymity" to describe authorship, he prefers "allonymity" and "allepigraphy," by which he argues that the anonymous writer continued (lengthened or completed) what Paul had intended to say (Marshall 1999: 79–89). He makes a strong case for the authenticity of the Pastorals and affirms their presence in the biblical canon. The question that emerges, however, is whether the ancients focused mostly on authorship as the final criterion for canonicity or the content.

In their as yet unpublished article on pseudepigrapha in antiquity, "Pseudepigrapha as an Interpretive Construct," Hindy Najman and Irene Peirano (2019) offer an alternative possibility, namely that it was consciously used in antiquity not always as forgery but rather "as a reading practice which is fundamentally interpretive," that is, as a means of continuing the teaching of an earlier famed teacher when the issue of authorial origin was not as important as it later became. They agree that this was not always the motivation for producing some pseudonymous writings, namely forgery and deception. They insist that modern scholars often impose contemporary notions anachronistically on ancient writings with the result that modern understandings of authenticity have obscured the dynamics of how such texts were viewed and welcomed in antiquity. They disagree with Ehrman and contend that the distinctions between canonical and noncanonical writings that have been influenced by modern notions of pseudonymous writings do not reflect all uses of pseudepigrapha in antiquity. They cite multiple examples from classical, Jewish, and Christian documents to support their view that such writings were not initially considered forgeries when they were written. By way of example, they also cite Iamblichus (Neoplatonist philosopher and student of Porphyry, *c*. 245–325 CE) who approved of such activity regarding writings produced in the name of the famed Pythagoras saying:

> It was a fine thing that they [authors of pseudepigraphal texts] even attributed and assigned everything to Pythagoras and did not keep as their own any doctrines among those that they discovered except in rare cases; for there are in fact altogether very few people whose works are circulated with their own name attached to them. (Iamblichus, *De vita Pythagoras* 198.9)

According to Najman and Peirano, it has always been the case that humans imitate admired exemplars, writings attributed to or written in names of exemplars by refinement and extension of what the unknown authors believed was at the heart of the exemplar's intention. They conclude that pseudepigraphy "is not a practice of transgression but one of ethical formation." They argue that attributing later writings to an earlier figure is a way of extending and transforming that earlier person "through the application and extension of that past" and "at the same time is about re-invigorating a new present. This is catapulted into a new future which is revised and transformed interpretive extension of that past." While not all scholars understand pseudepigrapha this way, the understanding of how some of that literature was produced offers another possibility of how it should be considered by modern interpreters of that tradition. They argue that it is "imperative that we look at pseudepigrapha outside of the disciplinary and intellectual limits inherited from post-enlightenment scholarly discourses."

I define "pseudepigrapha" here essentially and broadly as writings produced under a false name. A pseudonym is a fictitious name or an assumed name, normally used by authors who, for various reasons, choose to hide their identity to advance an unpopular perspective or to publish under the name of a well-known person to ensure its reception or for personal security or other reasons as we will see below. The practice of writing under a false name was common from the late fourth or early third century BC, though likely even earlier in Jewish scriptures, extending well into the early Christian era, for example, Deuteronomy and some Psalms and Proverbs.

Many scholars have addressed the problem of finding consistent designations of the literature identified as pseudepigrapha and distinguishing those texts from what is usually called apocrypha, especially Metzger, Rist, Stuckenbruck, Rist, Tuckett, and Flint (see Bibliography). The history of use of both terms in classical Greco-Roman literature as well as in ancient Jewish and Christian literature shows its widespread use and the variations in how the terms were used for centuries (Adler 2002: 211–28 and his 2019: 287–303).

Stuckenbruck acknowledges the difficulty of adequately defining and distinguishing both "apocrypha" and "pseudepigrapha" in antiquity and shows how both considerably overlap in their nature and contents. He seeks a better and more clear way of identifying the literature in question and how it relates to current biblical literature. Stuckenbruck and Tuckett acknowledge the difficulty of defining "apocrypha" consistently since its original meaning changed over time and without ancient agreement over the scope of the literature included in those overlapping designations (see J. K. Elliott 2013: 1:455–78; Frey 2019: 1–43; Stuckenbruck 2010; Tuckett 2015: 3–12).

As noted above, "apocrypha" initially had to do with prophetic individuals receiving secret or hidden texts that were sealed until a later appropriate time (e.g., Dan 8:18–26; 12:2–9; see also 4 Ezra 12–14 and Bar 6). A NT parallel may be discerned in Jesus speaking in parables preventing their meaning to others (unbelievers?) but openly to his disciples (Mark 4:10–12 citing Isa 6:9–10 LXX and 4:33–34 //'s in Matt 13:1–17 and cf. Luke 10:23–24). In current perspectives, the designation *usually* refers to texts in the LXX but not in the Hebrew Bible (HB)/Tanak that Catholics identify as "deuterocanonicals." However, that is not precise and further explanation is needed since not all of the "apocryphal" or "deuterocanonical" texts are pseudonymous. Again, the technical definition of a "pseudepigraphon" is the practice of attributing one's words to another author, but an "apocryphon" is not necessarily a pseudonymous text as Tuckett has shown. Recent scholarship focuses considerably on the origin and function of pseudepigraphy in antiquity (see Elliot 2011: 1:60–69 and 2013: 1:455–78; Stuckenbruck 2010: 143–62). Metzger (1972: 3–4) also acknowledges the difficulty of defining all pseudepigrapha as "literary forgeries" and says a "literary forgery is essentially a piece of work created or modified with the intention to deceive." In other words, it wrongly attributes a work to a false author, but Metzger concludes that all pseudepigrapha may not be literary forgeries, that is, works wrongly attributed to well-known authors. He contends that a "genuine forgery" is one that has a "calculated attempt to deceive" (Metzger 1972: 3–4; see also Adler 2002: 211–28). An "apocryphon" is not necessarily a pseudonymous text as Tuckett has shown, but some of them are. The Wisdom of Solomon was not written by Solomon and the same is also true of the additions to Daniel and Esther, yet they were attributed to the original authors of Daniel and Esther.

Metzger questions whether all ancient pseudonymous texts were written with the intent to deceive. He lists nine possible motives for pseudepigraphy in antiquity in classical history, Judaism of Late Antiquity, and early Christianity. These include: (1) Such texts were produced for financial gain as in the cases of the libraries at Pergamum and Alexandria paying for what they considered were acquired texts from earlier famed writers but some persons were rewarded for producing pseudonymous copies in the names of famous authors. (2) He observes that some pseudepigrapha were produced out of malice and lists several examples. (3) He claims that some of it was produced out of love and respect for a venerable author or teacher from whom they had been taught or learned much. Metzger cites here James Moffatt saying that this was "innocent admiration and naïve sympathy" from a student wanting to honor his teacher. (4) The fourth motive was alleged or real modesty that led to attributing a work to someone better than the author or to God as in the famed case of Salvian writing to honor God in the name of Timothy, which means "honor of God." (5) This includes spurious writings in the name of famed Attic writers modeling something after their works and generally creating fictitious works. (6) Among various genres available, creating epistolary texts attributed to famous persons was very popular, not only in classical names but also in famed Jewish names (e.g., Epistle of Jeremiah) and Christian pseudonymous letters (*3 Corinthians*). (7) Erroneous attribution of texts to the wrong author, sometimes the name of the author was the same as a more familiar person (homonyms). (8) Those pseudepigraphal texts by literary frauds that were attributed to important persons (e.g., Lucian of Samosata and John Chrysostom) for diverse reasons, in classical authors as in the case of Strabo to provide support for the Athenians' possession of the Island of Salamis and in the latter case to advance various theological positions. (9) He concludes that production of various religio-philosophical treatises in mythical personages such as Orpheus, the Sibyl, and Hermes were written not only by Greco-Roman pseudonymous authors but also both Jewish and Christian authors in the names of Sibyls (Metzger 1972: 5–12).

Aune lists four common explanations for the existence of pseudonymous texts in ancient literature: (1) it arose at a time when the biblical canon was already closed and well-known names were used to secure acceptance; (2) it was used to protect the identity of a writer who might be in danger if his or her true identity were known; (3) apocalyptic visionaries may have had visions from those figures to whom they attributed their work; and (4) the writer may have identified with a person of the past and written as his representative (1983: 109). He suggests that the first of these options is the most likely, but not without qualifications. As a device to legitimize a piece of literature Aune adds that pseudonymous authorship was intended to accord the writing in question the esteem and prestige given to the earlier well-known figure. He concludes that "pseudonymity is functional only if readers accept the false attribution" (1983: 110).

Charlesworth lists seven possible categories of *Christian* pseudonymous literature. His list includes: (1) works not by the named author but probably containing some of the reputed author's own thoughts (Ephesians and Colossians; 2 Timothy and Titus); (2) documents by someone influenced by another person to whom the work is ascribed (1 Peter and maybe James); (3) compositions influenced by earlier works of an author to whom they are assigned (1 Timothy, 2 Timothy, Titus); (4) Gospels (eventually) attributed to an apostle but deriving from later circles or schools of learned individuals (Matthew and John); (5) Christian writings attributed by their authors to an OT personality (*Testament of Adam, Odes of Solomon, Apocalypse of Elijah, Ascension of Isaiah*); (6) once-anonymous works (perhaps Mark, Luke, and Acts) now correctly or incorrectly credited to some familiar NT persons such as attributing Hebrews to Paul); (7) compositions that intentionally try to deceive the reader into thinking that the author is someone famous (2 Peter 3:1) (Charlesworth 1992: 5:540–1 and 1997: 2:768–75). Clarke lists eleven possible motives for writing pseudonymous writings (Clarke 2002: 450–65).

In Protestant Bibles that include the apocrypha (or deuterocanonical texts) these writings are almost completely the additional books or portions thereof that are in the LXX but not in the HB and, following the example of Martin Luther, placed between the Protestant OT and NT. Many of those texts are pseudonymous texts written under a false name, for example, Wisdom of Solomon, Psalms of Solomon, 2 Esdras, and others. From mostly the fourth century CE "apocrypha" was regularly used of doctrinally "heretical" or spurious texts. We should also observe that several of the OT pseudepigrapha were either produced or rewritten and used by Christians. Given the presence of such writings among their Jewish siblings, it should not be surprising that some Christians also produced pseudonymous writings. Pseudonymous texts in the ancient Greco-Roman society as well as in Judaism and early Christianity are well known and its widespread use may have its origin, as suggested above, from the Greek era when it was practiced by those wanting to sell books in the names of famous authors to kings wanting to establish libraries as in the cases of Pergamum and Alexandria of Egypt (Elliott 1993; Metzger 1972; Rist 1972). I will focus initially on the production and use of pseudonymous writings in Judaism because of its likely influence on its production and use in early Christianity.

3. JEWISH PRODUCTION AND USE OF PSEUDEPIGRAPHA

The Jewish practice of producing and using pseudonymous texts may have begun even earlier with the Deuteronomistic history in the latter part of the seventh century BCE when scribes of Josiah discovered or produced the book of Deuteronomy in the name of Moses (Collins 2018: 163–81). The same can be said about some of the Psalms attributed to David or Proverbs attributed to Solomon. Pseudepigraphy is well represented in the famed nonsectarian scrolls in the Dead Sea Scrolls, with most of it dating from roughly 200 BCE and circulating in Palestine in the time of Jesus, and it continued mostly until around 200 CE among the Jews. The production of Jewish apocalyptic texts in the name of a well-known predecessor was quite common in late Second Temple Judaism. Some texts now called "rewritten Bible" or more appropriately "rewritten Scriptures," such as the author of Jubilees rewriting Genesis and his supposed revelation of the Law to Moses during his forty days on Mount Sinai (Exod 24:18), were also common in antiquity. Was the production of pseudonymous texts a common and widely acceptable practice in antiquity? Mroczek carefully and helpfully addresses this issue (2016: 118–55).

The collection of Dead Sea Scrolls has provided multiple examples of Jewish pseudonymous texts that were brought to Qumran by their Essene residents. Some of those are regularly called "rewritten scriptures" that transformed earlier scriptural documents in the Hebrew scriptures. These include, for example, the *Rewritten Pentateuch*, *Jubilees* rewriting Genesis, the *Temple Scroll*, *1 Enoch*, *Testaments of the Twelve Patriarchs* (T12P), and others. These "rewritten" texts led readers to assume that the authors listed in the rewritten works were the authentic authors of those documents. Some Christians also rewrote portions of existing texts, as in 2 Esdras (4 Ezra) and *Ascension of Isaiah*, to transform them into texts that supported their own Christian claims. For a helpful discussion of the "rewritten" texts at Qumran, see especially Sidnie White Crawford (2019: 208) and James Charlesworth (1985 and 2002) who focus on the canonical and noncanonical writings in the Dead Sea Scrolls collections.

Pseudonymous writings were commonly produced in late Second Temple Jewish writings and in early Christianity, and, as noted, some may be in the ancient Hebrew writings, perhaps as early as the late seventh century BCE as in the case of the production of Deuteronomy attributed to Moses. Did Moses write Deuteronomy or was it someone or others after him? The Jewish practice of producing pseudonymous texts likely began with the Deuteronomistic history in the latter part of the seventh century BCE when scribes of Josiah produced or discovered the "book of the law" (likely Deuteronomy; see 2 Kings 22:8–13). It was later affirmed that Moses wrote it (2 Chron 34:14; Deut 1:1; see Collins 2018: 63–181). There are also other examples of it, likely Isa 24–27, as well as the later insertions in Daniel and Esther, some psalms attributed to David and including proverbs attributed to Solomon.

This ancient practice of writing pseudonymously is usually not always the same as when a writer uses a pen name, as in the case of the well-known Mark Twain (born Samuel Clemens), but rather when we refer to cases in which a separate writer produces a document in the name of a known person (famous or influential) under a false name. Was this practice always or often intended to deceive readers? Of course, the motivation *may* have been to deceive readers in order to have a wider distribution for the pseudonymous authors' views, but some such writings may have stemmed from a desire to honor a renowned leader, for example, when an author attempted to express a celebrated figure's views or to indicate that the pseudonymous author's views are in keeping with the views of a well-known person. A useful list of the OT pseudepigraphal texts is in Charlesworth (1985: 836–40), and more recently in Bauckham, Davila, and Panayotov (2013) and a recent careful discussion of it in Najman and Peirano (2019) noted above.

Because pseudonymous Jewish religious writings were widespread among Jewish communities in late Second Temple Judaism, it is important initially to focus on examples in that community before and during the time of Jesus and his earliest followers. As noted, pseudonymous writings were discovered at Qumran among the Dead Sea Scrolls including 1 Enoch. Several of those were also circulating among some early Christians and presumed to be scripture. By the fourth century Athanasius set forth in his *Thirty-Ninth Festal Letter* (*c.* 367) the books could be read in the churches. His OT included all the books in the HB/Tanak except Esther, but he also included Baruch and the Epistle of Jeremiah. He not only classified those books that were readable in churches as "canonical" scripture, but also listed a few others that were not canonical but were quite popular and he identified them as "readable" (Greek = ἀναγιγνωσκόμενα) texts for private use to advance piety only because he thought they were also helpful for new converts. This contrasts with those he classified as "nonreadable" (Greek = μὴ ἀναγιγνωσκόμενα), that is, they were "apocryphal" and heretical, spurious, or fraudulent books. Catholics later adopted a larger collection of those readable books that they later classified as "deuterocanonical" texts as noted earlier and these largely were those additional books circulating in the LXX, but not in the HB. Most Protestants regularly designate the deuterocanonical texts as "apocrypha" and exclude them from their Bibles, but some of the Protestant ecumenical Bibles do include them and place them, following Luther's example, between the OT and NT.

Because of its considerable relevance and later influence, I attach here a portion of Brakke's updated translation of Athanasius's *Thirty-Ninth Festal Letter* with its list of all the books he considered canonical, then the readable books, and finally the rejected books:

> As I begin to mention these things, in order to commend my audacity, I will employ the example of Luke the evangelist and say myself: *Inasmuch as certain people have attempted to set in order for themselves the so-called apocryphal books and to mix these with the divinely inspired Scripture,* about which we are convinced it is just as those who were eyewitnesses from the beginning and assistants of the Word handed down to our ancestors, it seemed good to me, because I have been urged by genuine brothers and sisters and instructed from the beginning, *to set forth in order the books that are canonized, transmitted, and believed to be divine,* so that those who have been deceived might condemn the persons who led them astray, and those who have remained pure might rejoice to be reminded (of these things). (Emphasis added)

> 17. There are, then, belonging to the Old Testament in number a total of twenty-two, for, as I have heard, it has been handed down that this is the number of the letters in the Hebrew alphabet. In order and by name they are as follows: first, Genesis; then Exodus; then Leviticus; and after this, Numbers; and finally, Deuteronomy. After these is Joshua, the son of Nun; and Judges; and after this, Ruth; and again, next four books of Kings, the first and second of these being reckoned as one book, and the third and fourth likewise being one. After these are First and Second Chronicles, likewise, reckoned as one book; then First and Second Esdras, likewise as one. After these is the book of Psalms; and then Proverbs; then Ecclesiastes and the Song of Songs. After these is Job; and finally, the Prophets, the twelve being reckoned as one book; then Isaiah; Jeremiah *and with it, Baruch*; Lamentations *and the Letter* [= *Letter of Jeremiah*]; and after it, Ezekiel and Daniel. To this point are the books of the Old Testament. [*Note*: Esther is not included.]

> 18. Again, one should not hesitate to name the books of the New Testament. For these are the four Gospels, Matthew, Mark, Luke, and John; than after these, Acts of the Apostles and seven letters, called catholic, by the apostles, namely: one by James; two by Peter; then three by John; and after these, one by Jude. After these there are fourteen letters by Paul, written in this order: first to the Romans; then two to the Corinthians; and after these, to the Galatians; and next to the Ephesians; then to the Philippians and to the Colossians; and after these, two to the Thessalonians; and that to the Hebrews; and additionally, two to Timothy, one to Titus, and finally that to Philemon. And besides, the Revelation of John. [Note: this is the first time 2 Peter is included in a NT list.]

> 19. These are the springs of salvation, so that someone who thirsts may be satisfied by the words they contain. *In these books alone the teaching of piety is proclaimed. Let no one add to or subtract from them.* Concerning them the Lord put the Sadducees to shame when he said, "You err because you do not know the Scriptures or their meaning," and he reproved the Jews, "Search the Scriptures, for it is they that testify to me." (Emphasis added)

> 20. But for the sake of greater accuracy, I add this, writing from necessity. There are other books, in addition to the preceding, *which have not been canonized*, but have been appointed by the ancestors *to be read to those who newly join us* and want to be instructed in the word of piety: the *Wisdom of Solomon, the Wisdom of Sirach,*

Esther, Judith, Tobit, the book called Teaching of the Apostles, and the Shepherd. (Emphasis added)

21. Nevertheless, beloved, the former books are canonized; the latter are (only) read; and there is no mention of the apocryphal books. Rather, (the category of apocrypha) is an invention of heretics, who write these books whenever they want and then generously add time to them, *so that, by publishing them as if they were ancient, they might have a pretext for deceiving the simple folk.* Great is the hardheartedness of those who do this and who do not fear the word that is written: "You shall not add to the word that I commanded you, nor shall you subtract from it." Who has made the simple folk believe that those books belong to Enoch even though no Scripture existed before Moses? On what basis will they say that there is an apocryphal book of Isaiah? He preaches openly on the high mountain and says, "I did not speak in secret or in a dark land." How could Moses have an apocryphal book? He is the one who published Deuteronomy with heaven and earth as witnesses. (Trans. Brakke 2010: 61; emphasis added; also see his translation and comment in 2010: 60–6. See also Brakke's 1994 and 1995 articles)[1]

Athanasius's *Festal Letter* was highly influential in churches in the east, but not all churches at that time accepted his list of OT or NT canonical books. Many Syrian churches, as we saw earlier, did not welcome the minor (or "Pocoke") NT Epistles (2 Peter, 2–3 John, and Jude) and Revelation until centuries later. The task of establishing the identity and scope of the so-called OT apocrypha or deuterocanonical books has been long and challenging. This collection of Jewish religious texts dates *mostly* from 200 BCE to 100 CE.

Some pseudonymous texts were cited in the second and third centuries as or like scripture by some early church fathers. 1 Enoch, for example, was cited as scripture by Tertullian, *Idol.* 4.2–3 citing *1 En.* 19.1, 99.6–7 and *1 En.* 8.1 in *Cult. fem.* 1.3 and 2.10; Clement of Alexandria, *Strom.* 1.1.13; cf. *Ecl.* 2.1 citing *1 En.* 19.3; Irenaeus, *adv. Haer.* 1.1.1; Origen cited in Eusebius, *Hist. eccl.* 6.24–25 who quotes *1 En.* 19.3 and 21.1 in *Prin.* 4.4.8; *1 En.* 6.6 in *Comm. John* 6.25; cf. *c. Cels.* 5.52–55; and Rufinus, *Exp. Symb.* 36–38 in which he welcomes the reading of apocryphal writings and the opportunity to learn from them. Other examples of the authoritative citations of pseudonymous texts in antiquity are in Reed (2008: 467–90 and fnn 15–17 on 471); for an overview of the history of the recognition of pseudepigrapha, see also Reed (2009: 403–36). For multiple examples of the use of pseudepigrapha in antiquity beginning with Origen, but including others as well, see also Adler (2019: 287–308).

Interestingly, as Athanasius was speaking about *1 Enoch*, he admits that it was circulating as scripture as late as the mid-fourth century but claims that only simple folks acknowledge it as scripture since no scripture existed before Moses and concludes saying, "the testimony from the apocryphal books *is superfluous because it is unfounded*—for the Scripture is perfect in every way" (trans. Brakke 2010). It is generally acknowledged that some of the deuterocanonicals are also pseudonymously produced texts, for example, Wisdom of Solomon, the additions to Daniel and Esther, likely also Tobit and Judith, and others, and in its current condition likely also the book of Daniel. While

---

[1] I have omitted Braake's footnotes, but they generally list the scriptures cited in the text. The standard earlier translation by R. Payne-Smith, from *Nicene and Post-Nicene Fathers*, Second Series, Vol. 4. Edited by Philip Schaff and Henry Wace (Buffalo, NY: Christian Literature Publishing, 1892), is still useful and especially its revision for *New Advent* by Kevin Knight. http://www.newadvent.org/fathers/2806039.htm.

the pseudonymously written texts were *generally* excluded from the church's canonical scriptures from the fourth century and later, we will see below whether that was always the case.

4. CHRISTIAN PRODUCTION AND USE OF PSEUDEPIGRAPHA

Like late Second Temple Judaism, the production and use of pseudonymous writings was quite common in early Christianity, and the primary question is whether it was intended to deceive readers or if there might have been other motives for it. By way of example and in reference to the NT writings, Najman and Peirano point to Origen who denied that Paul wrote Hebrews (written anonymously) but nevertheless welcomed it because he thought "the thoughts are those of the apostle [Paul], but the diction and phraseology are those of someone who remembered the apostolic teachings and wrote down what had been said by his teacher" (Eusebius, *Hist. eccl.* 6.25.13). They also observe Jerome's response to Porphyry, the well-known critic of early Christianity (*c.* 232–303 CE), who denied Daniel was the author of the biblical book attributed to him based on his argument that it was written after Antiochus IV in the second century BCE (see Jerome, *In Dan. Prologue* = fr. 43).

This shows, of course, that date and context were obviously used to discredit the authenticity of a writing believed to be pseudonymous and to challenge the early Christians' appeal to Daniel to make their case that Jesus was the Messiah. As we saw above, they conclude that all pseudonymous literature is not cut from the same piece of cloth and that some of it was sometimes used as "creative acts of interpretation" of well-known predecessors or teachers. In part their argument is based on the Jewish use of Targum, Pesher, *Rewritten Pentateuch*, *Jubilees*, the *Genesis Apocryphon* that tries to justify Abram's giving up his sister to Pharaoh, 4 Ezra (2 Esdras), and they also conclude that some of these texts were "entirely new compositions that reused and implemented biblical traditions." Najman and Peirano argue that some of these ancient texts were more imitation than false attribution through which the mimetic self-effacing practices of imitating exemplary figures played an important role as spiritual discipline.

Cases have been made for and against the origin and use of ancient pseudonymous texts as innocent texts either under a pen name or to honor a past hero or teacher by students/ authors (so Baur, Guthrie, Mitton), but many if not most of those texts were written to deceive their readers (Donelson 1986: 9–23). Donelson contends that the author(s) of the Pastorals "conform beautifully" to the pseudepigraphic letter genre current in the author's generation that are unlike the widely recognized authentic letters of Paul (Donelson 1986: 54–66, 69–90). He and others argue that early Christian pseudepigraphal texts were also inserted in several biblical books reflecting pseudonymous authors portraying their own writings in the names of earlier well-known apostolic writings. They claim that some of these include *at the least* Mark 1:1b; 16:9–20; John 3:13b; 7:53 – 8:11; John 21; Rom 16:25–27; 1 Cor 14:33b–36; 1 John 5:7–8, and others as well. These insertions were not originally a part of the NT writings but were inserted later by copiers or scribes *generally* to advance later orthodox doctrinal positions (Hull 2011: 84–5). Several pseudonymous books circulated in churches for a time and were produced in the typical genres in the present NT, namely gospels, Acts, Epistles, and apocalypses and mostly in the names of well-known church leaders (apostles, especially Peter, James, John, and

Paul), but in some cases in the names of familiar OT figures as in the case of the *Ascension of Isaiah* and portions of 2 Esdras (4 Ezra). For the characteristics of apocryphal texts and books compared to canonical writings, see Jörg Frey (2019: 1–43) who lists parallels in genre, but generally with distinctions, using first-person, expanded narratives, and filling in lacunae missing in the canonical texts. He also focuses on the authorial aspect of these writings adding to or correcting differences in biblical texts (e.g., Chronicles vs. Kings and Matthew and Luke vs. Mark).

Again, the production and use of pseudonymous writings were also quite common in early Christianity well into the Medieval Period and is currently listed variously under the designations of pseudepigrapha and apocrypha. Multiple collections and introductions of most of that literature are available to modern readers (see Bibliography). In terms of *Christian* pseudepigrapha, there are more than eighty known *Christian* pseudonymous writings (Evans 2005: 256–7), often referred to as "New Testament Apocrypha," (Schneemelcher 1991-2) or "Apocryphal New Testament" (Elliott 1993), or "Early Christian Apocrypha" (Gregory and Tuckett 2015) and "New Testament Apocrypha" (Burke and Landau 2016: vol. 1; and Burke 2020: vol. 2).

Generally, pseudonymous texts were written in the names of celebrated NT figures (e.g., Peter, John, Paul, James, and Andrew) and *mostly* written from the second to fourth centuries and in similar genres as those in the NT, namely, gospels, epistles, acts, and apocalypses. After a brief introduction, I will not only focus on the question of whether some of it remains in the NT but also acknowledge that multiple insertions within the texts of several NT books also exist and those insertions are passed along as the text of the original authors of those books. Rist has observed that both orthodox and so-called heretical Christian groups inserted those additional texts to promote their later specific views and teachings and suggests that modern ethical implications and sensitivities toward such practices are not evidenced like today despite accusing their opponents of making those insertions (Rist 1972: 90–1).

Remarkably, when Rufinus translated Origen's work he openly acknowledged that he sometimes changed it to make it cohere with the orthodoxy he thought was appropriate and to make Origen's writings more acceptable to his community. Interestingly, Origen himself welcomed several pseudonymous writings, which may provide an argument for the inclusion of the Pastorals in the church's NT canon. He accepted them not because of their authorship but because of their content (e.g., Susanna and others). By the mid- to late fourth century that argument began to change in favor of a rejection of known pseudonymous texts but by then the widespread use and popularity of some texts later determined to be pseudonymous became difficult to exclude, especially 2 Peter, Hebrews, James, 2–3 John, Jude, Revelation, and likely some aspects of the Pastorals. Some pseudonymous texts continued to be welcomed by some church fathers longer than others as in the cases of the *Epistle of Barnabas* and *Shepherd of Hermas* included in *Codex Sinaiticus*. For many centuries other later texts such as the *Acts of Paul and Thecla*, and *3 Corinthians* continued to be read in some churches.

Most biblical scholars now reject Pauline authorship of the Pastoral Epistles though some acknowledge that authentic Pauline texts may be in them (e.g., perhaps 2 Tim 1:15–18; 4:5–21). Some scholars defend the practice of pseudonymous writing in the first century (Meade 1986; Dunn 1987:65–85; Aland 1961: 39–49). Since there are likely authentic Pauline traditions in the Pastorals, namely the rejection of Paul in Asia Minor (2 Tim 1:15–18), the manner of the apostle's death (2 Tim 4:6–8), and many of the closing comments to colleagues in 2 Tim 4:14–22 also appear to be genuine Paul. Also, his words to Titus may have a touch of Paul in them as well (Tit 1:5–16). It would be easy to draw that conclusion. We might ask whether 2 Timothy and Titus should be separated from 1 Timothy that does not have much that is familiar from Paul in his acknowledged letters. If the author(s) of the Pastoral Epistles simply wanted apostolic sanction for Paul's views on organization and discipline in churches, and therefore attached Paul's name to his own writings, what conclusion(s) should we draw about the Pastorals? Can they be sacred scripture for the church if there was deceptive intention in their construction? Since most of the important theological issues in the universally acknowledged letters of Paul (Romans, 1–2 Corinthians, Galatians, Philippians, 1 Thessalonians, and Philemon) are absent in the Pastoral Epistles (reconciliation, eschatology, "in Christ," justification by faith, the prominent role of the Holy Spirit, and a simple church organizational structure), can a case be made that the Pastoral Epistles in their current form were not originally written by Paul? Did someone who followed Paul perhaps write what he (she) thought was what Paul would have said to address the current issues facing the churches later?

Some scholars agree that pseudonymous writings are deceptive literature but deny its presence in the NT (e.g., Guthrie 1965: 15–39; Porter 1995:105–23). Others are convinced that it was present not only in early Christianity but that some of it remains in the NT itself. Other scholars have asked whether there might be better explanations for its presence in antiquity and possibly in the NT (Metzger 1972).

By the fourth century it appears that most of the *known* or suspected deceptive pseudepigraphic writings were dismissed as forgeries, but were the church fathers at that time able to discern through their examinations all the early Christian pseudonymous writings? Did they have access to all of Paul's other writings?

Scholars acknowledge that some unknown copiers of the biblical texts inserted a number of texts into both OT and NT writings as they made their copies for various purposes (e.g., Isa 24–27 and also Second and Third Isaiah, Daniel and its later additions, Esther and its later additions, and Jeremiah that is shorter in the LXX [and sometimes the copiers included Baruch and the Epistle of Jeremiah in it], but the same is true in regard to NT writings as we see noted earlier in Mark 16:9–20; John 3:13b; 7:53–8:11; 1 John 5:7–8; possibly 2 Thess 2:1–3; the end of Rom 16:25–27; and others). Most of the later textual insertions in NT texts were supportive of orthodox positions when the texts were copied.

Currently several scholars agree that several pseudonymous texts are in the biblical literature, and some (especially Ehrman) suggest that only nine of the twenty-seven NT books were written by those whose names are on them. However, that likely exceeds reasonable assessments of the NT writings, and such conclusions are regularly contested in scholarly essays. Nevertheless, several scholars continue to acknowledge that both the OT and NT contain pseudonymous writings (Clarke 2002; Flint 1999; Metzger 1972), and the primary question is how to identify and deal with it. While the early Christians did not invent this practice, they certainly produced and made use of it. So, if discovered, should it remain in the Bible?

The importance of apostolic authority is found especially in the beginning of Paul's letters, and he often appeals to his own apostolic authority in his apostleship, for example, 1 Cor 9:1–2; 12:28; 15:3–8, 11; Rom 16:7; see also Acts 1:12–26. That authority was *not focused on apostolic writing*, however, until later in the second century (e.g., Justin, *1 Apol.* 64–67). That emerging apostolic authority was soon attached to writings believed to come from apostles or their disciples (Mark and Luke) who were close to the time of Jesus and the ministry of the apostles. Apostolic authority was attached to the canonical Gospels likely from the beginning of their circulation in churches (Evans 2020: 2–11), but no later than the early second century, and to other NT writings that eventually all were believed to have been written not only by prominent NT apostles, especially Peter, John, and Paul, but by others also from the apostolic community. As recognition of the authority for apostolic authorship of written texts began to emerge, about mid-second century, many pseudonymous writings with apostolic names began to appear in churches and some were initially and unwittingly welcomed like sacred scripture in some churches (e.g., the church at Rhossus that was reading the *Gospel of Peter*, cf. Eusebius, *Hist. eccl.* 6.12.3–6). The act of attaching apostolic names to the writings enhanced their reception as church's Christian scriptures.

The issue of authorship, or apostolic authorship in particular, does not appear to have been a significant factor after the deaths of the apostles and until well into the second century when attributing apostolic authorship to pseudonymous writings began to emerge. The earliest references to the individual gospels, as we saw earlier, are few until well into the second century and initially the citation of gospel texts focused primarily on the words and actions of Jesus in them and not on their authors. While the sayings of Jesus in the Gospels were frequently cited by the second- and third-century church fathers, especially and more frequently in Matthew, the identity of the Gospels was not an important factor until later in the second century, beginning largely with Justin's *1 Apology* (*c.* 150–155). The composition of pseudonymous texts in apostolic names began to appear when early copiers and scribes began transmitting Christian writings in apostolic names. The question remains whether the authors of those pseudonymous texts intended to deceive readers by writing in the names of well-known prophetic figures (e.g., Enoch, Isaiah) or apostolic figures (Paul, Peter, John, James, Andrew, and others)?

The presence of pseudonymous texts in biblical collections is, of course, the more controversial aspect of our study and the question of why it was so widespread in early Christianity for centuries is less clear. If it was intended to deceive, how could it still have been used or read in churches? The question rightly emerges with the prevalence of pseudonymous writings in early Christianity and whether they were written by orthodox writers or so-called heretical authors. That raises the question of the importance of authorship initially in the early churches or whether the content of a writing was more important to early readers. They may not have had the ability to discern authorship issues and welcomed a text attributed to an apostle as an apostolic document.

It appears that the core teaching of the churches was circulating in the churches before there were written texts that advanced it and writings that cohered with those early traditions were welcomed without regard to authorship initially or the ability to discern apostolic authorship. The proclamation or Gospel was the church's earliest tradition circulating in churches and over time was central to the selection of the books that would be included in the church's scriptures. Those teachings expanded from time to time to address emerging issues facing the churches, but they were not radically changed and that *regula fidei* was essential in the selection of books in the biblical canon. The criterion of orthodoxy, that is, the core tradition of the churches, determined which books would be acceptable despite disputed authorship. Most of the rejections over authorship were focused on the heretical teachings in those documents, for example, the *Gospel of Judas* mentioned earlier in Irenaeus.

While the use of the term "apocrypha" began to change in the Greek-speaking Christian communities to refer to heretical or pseudonymous writings from the late second century and regularly in the fourth century, even then there was no full agreement on what was "apocryphal" beyond saying that it was not "canonical" or sacred scripture. It appears that by the fourth century CE whenever a text was determined to be pseudonymous it was regularly excluded from the church's sacred scriptures, but most of the time it was so declared because it was believed to be heretical (Athanasius, Jerome, Rufinus). By the fourth century whatever was believed to be pseudonymous was also rejected by the church fathers, but did the church fathers recognize all of the pseudonymous writings that were circulating in the churches? Were some pseudonymous writings initially included into the church's Bible and wrongly believed to be authentic apostolic texts, but wrongly remained in it? Modern scholarship has generally acknowledged that some pseudonymous texts were not recognized as such and were included wittingly or unwittingly in the church's sacred scriptures. Some of it was undetected in antiquity although there were questions raised about many of the texts that were initially questioned and later rejected, but some of the disputed texts at that time (e.g., James, 2 Peter, 2–3 John, Jude, Hebrews, Revelation) were eventually welcomed as we saw earlier in Eusebius (*Hist. eccl.* 3.25). It is interesting that after citing Dionysius's questions about the authorship of Revelation (Eusebius, *Hist. eccl.* 7.25) and Origen (Eusebius, *Hist. eccl.* 6.25,13) questioning the authorship of Hebrews, both books were included in the church's NT scriptures. Most scholars agree that Moses did not write Deuteronomy nor did Daniel the prophet write the biblical text attributed to him and Paul did not write Hebrews, but they were all welcomed into the church's Bible.

The anonymous texts, namely the Gospels, Acts, and Hebrews, 1, 2, 3, John, perhaps should not be considered here since they do not claim apostolic authorship. However, despite not knowing or emphasizing their authorship, all were included in the Christian scriptures. Regarding Revelation, of course, we see in the opening verses that it was written by "John," and the book is not necessarily a pseudonymous text since "John" was a popular name in the first century; there were several others also named John in antiquity, but the text was welcomed as a text by the Apostle John being the author of Revelation. Interestingly, as we saw above that Dionysius denied that John the Apostle wrote Revelation, but he did not reject its scriptural status and the only question for him was about its authorship and evidently not its content.

It is common currently to ask whether pseudepigraphy was a suitable venue for advancing Christian beliefs and whether such writings, if discovered in the biblical canon, should be excluded. It appears clear that some texts whose authorship was unknown or disputed remained in the church's scriptures because they had gained what Stuckenbruck called an "irresistible momentum" because they were widely popular and long welcomed by many churches so excluding them later was no longer possible (2010: 143–62).

The primary purpose of pseudonymous writing appears to have been twofold, namely filling in gaps not included in the biblical texts and to advance theological positions mostly orthodox (e.g., 1 John 5:7–8; John 3:13b, and others) but also non-orthodox ("heretical") positions. Both motivations, of course, are deceptive. Most Christian pseudonymous religious texts in names of apostolic figures appear to have been intended to present anachronistically earlier (first-century?) thinking in later documents and for later communities. Establishing authoritative beliefs in later churches doubtless was a motivation for some to produce such texts. Again, there is considerable evidence that shows that when such pseudonymous writings were detected they were generally rejected by most church fathers and not included in their sacred scriptures. That appears to be the case especially from the fourth century and thereafter, but it is also likely that the church fathers were not always aware that the writings they attributed to well-known persons were pseudonymous texts. It may also be that some pseudonymous texts were so popular among large numbers of Christians—and they were orthodox in their content—that they were welcomed, used, and cited by so many, that it was not feasible to delete them from the emerging Christian biblical canons as in the cases of the Pastoral Epistles in their current form, 2 Peter, and likely others.

Nijay Gupta's recent *RBL Review* of C. R. Hutson's commentary on *First and Second Timothy and Titus* (Gupta 2021) offers a more balanced approach to the Pastoral Epistles suggesting that their final form appears to have been produced in the second century. Some of the content, such as 2 Tim 4, appears to be Paul, but the ecclesiology appears to be second century. Likewise, the central themes of Paul's theology such as justification by faith, reconciliation, and the role of the Spirit are absent in the Pastorals, but that does not mean that some of their content may reflect authentic Pauline tradition (1 Tim 1:15) that surely would not have been put on Paul's lips or pen by an adoring student of Paul. So also, 2 Tim 1:15 and 4:6–18 appear to be authentic Paul.

Again, all scholars agree that the practice of producing and circulating pseudonymous texts in antiquity was widespread even in Christian communities and this raises the question again of whether some of those pseudonymous texts were included in the church's Bible. There is little doubt that pseudonymous texts were inserted in multiple biblical manuscripts whether OT or NT. That is well established, but what about some of the books? If anonymous or pseudonymous insertions were inserted into the OT or NT writings, why would it be surprising if whole books also were produced pseudonymously? Again, were any pseudonymous writings included in the biblical canon? The answer appears to be yes.

Apart from Irenaeus, Origen, and Augustine, there was very little focus on an authentic text of those books or attempts to correct them. Athanasius's distinction between canonical and some of the so-called noncanonical ("readable") texts that could be read in private shows that both categories were welcomed though some were read in public and the others in private. For the Eastern churches, following Athanasius, only the former HB books were acknowledged as sacred scripture and used to establish church doctrine, but the noncanonical "readable" books (deuterocanonicals) still could be read for instruction and inspiration. In other words, both categories were deemed to be within the orthodox tradition and not heretical. Not all churches agreed on the scope of the "readable" writings, as we see in the canonical lists earlier and often the canonical lists that include sacred writings do not include the same books.

Given the above, does one welcome a book as scripture based on its authorship or was its content also a factor in the acceptance? Some anonymous texts were likely welcomed based on their contents, for example, the Gospels, Hebrews, 1, 2, 3 John, and Revelation written by John, but not likely the Apostle John. It appears that some NT books were welcomed into the biblical canon because of a belief in their apostolic authorship (Pastorals, 2 Peter, Hebrews, Revelation, 2–3 John, and likely others). Some were welcomed likely because of their popularity among the churches despite questions about their questionable authorship (Pastorals, Hebrews, 2 Peter, Revelation, and others). Eusebius acknowledges the widespread disputes over some NT books (*Hist. eccl.* 3.25), but despite Hebrews' questionable authorship it is likely that its valued content made it have an "irresistible momentum" (Origen and others) noted above, but eventually it was attributed to Paul likely to avoid its rejection. There were initial questions about the authorship of Hebrews in the 393 and 397 church councils at Hippo and Carthage, but by the 419 council at Carthage doubts were removed and Hebrews was attributed to Paul as that canon list suggests. Clearly, the insertion of apostolic names not only was useful in establishing the NT canon but it was also important in advancing the use of pseudonymous texts in the ancient churches. The use of apostolic names to advance "heretical" positions is noted in Tertullian, Athanasius, and the MF (late fourth century), which itself is pseudonymous, along with *Apostolic Constitutions* that reject pseudonymous texts but is itself pseudonymous! As we saw above Rufinus openly admits that he changed what Origen wrote to make it more acceptable to his readers.

When the early church fathers began using the term "Apocrypha" it was not *consistently* in reference to heretical texts, so much as a reference to more esoteric and even some prophetic texts that we saw earlier in the seventy other books that were mentioned in 4 Ezra 14:19–47. The references to pseudonymous and therefore "apocryphal" heretical books are clearly seen in Athanasius above, but also in Cyril of Jerusalem and Jerome in the late fourth and fifth centuries. Eventually, by the late fourth and fifth centuries, the known or perceived pseudonymous writings came to be viewed as disputed or heretical ("apocryphal") and were generally rejected by subsequent church fathers except in the cases noted earlier that had widespread approval in churches.

The evidence of disputes among churches over the scope of their scriptures is reflected in the surviving biblical manuscripts, canon lists, and lectionaries (orthodox churches). That which kept most of the disputes manageable in the churches is the early broad agreement on the core of what was believed about Jesus and learned from his teachings that were passed on in the churches from its beginning. Later that was limited for some to what Eusebius calls the "Holy Tetrad" (Eusebius, *Hist. eccl.* 3.25.1). Some early Christians also welcomed the *Gospel of Hebrews*, the *Gospel of Alexandrians*, the *Gospel of Peter*, the *Apocalypse of Peter*, and others. Later these were all rejected when it was believed that they did not transmit the church's core sacred traditions about Jesus, or that they were not faithfully transmitted, or were pseudonymous.

The core sacred teachings that focused on the identity of Jesus (Christology), his primary teachings, and his activity (miracles) and fate (death and resurrection) were all transmitted both orally and in writing by some church fathers *before* there was a Bible. Those traditions were familiar in the church's teachings, preaching, singing, baptismal confessions, and eucharistic affirmations from their beginning and they provided the boundaries of what was acceptable in the emerging scriptural canon. However, there was a continual production of pseudonymous texts in the second to the fourth centuries mostly and written in the names of well-known apostolic figures that some churches likely unwittingly welcomed as apostolic. The following is a listing of some of the most prominent Christian pseudonymous writings in the names of well-known persons and in NT genres.

1. Gospels:

    The Protoevangelium of James
    The Infancy Gospel of Thomas
    The Gospel of Peter
    The Gospel of Nicodemus
    The Gospel of the Nazoreans
    The Gospel of the Ebionites
    The Gospel of the Hebrews
    The Gospel of the Egyptians

The Gospel of Thomas
The Gospel of Philip
The Gospel of Mary

2. Acts (the first five of these are called the "Leucian Acts" and sometimes were circulated together):

The Acts of John
The Acts of Peter
The Acts of Paul
The Acts of Andrew
The Acts of Thomas
The Acts of Andrew and Matthias
The Acts of Philip
The Acts of Thaddaeus
The Acts of Peter and Paul
The Acts of Peter and Andrew
The Martyrdom of Matthew
The Slavonic Acts of Peter
The Acts of Peter and the Twelve Apostles

3. Epistles:

Third Corinthians
The Epistle to the Laodiceans
The Letters of Paul and Seneca
The Letters of Jesus and Abgar
The Letter of Lentulus
The Epistle of Titus

4. Apocalypses:[2]

The Apocalypse of Peter
The Coptic Apocalypse of Paul
The First Apocalypse of James
The Second Apocalypse of James
The Apocryphon of John

---

[2]"Apocalypse" is a transliteration of the Greek *apokalypsis* ("revelation" or "disclosure"). Aune defines this literary genre as

> a form of revelatory literature in which the author narrates both the visions he has purportedly experienced and their meaning, usually elicited through a dialogue between the seer and an interpreting angel. The substance of these revelatory visions is the imminent intervention of God into human affairs to bring the present evil world system to an end and to replace it with an ideal one. This transformation is accompanied by the punishment of the wicked and the reward of the righteous. (Aune 1983: 108)

The Sophia of Jesus Christ
The Letter of Peter to Philip
The Apocalypse of Mary

Also, multiple extraneous pseudonymous *texts* inserted into the biblical texts were commonplace especially in the second and third centuries, many of which are well-known to biblical scholars who address them in current critical commentaries. Some of these widely acknowledged inserted pseudonymous texts were noted earlier and some of them include several OT inserted texts as in the Daniel insertions and Esther insertions; likely Isa 24–27) and many others noted earlier. For more NT Apocrypha, see Burke and Landau (2016: vol. 1) and Burke (2020: vol. 2).

Koch observes that the most popular names attached to pseudonymous literature attracted entire genres. For example, divine law came from Moses, wisdom from Solomon, and church regulations were produced in apostolic names—or groups, as in the case of the *Didache* (or *Teaching of the Twelve Apostles*) and the *Apostolic Constitutions* (Koch, "Pseudonymous Writing," 712–13). A common justification for pseudonymous literature is that many of these writings imply on the part of their authors a consciousness that "association with a tradition confers legitimacy." Koch adds that in some cases the authors to whom the writings are ascribed are considered as alive in heaven and therefore still effective in the present. To this extent the attribution of authorship to men of God is the same as ascribing it to God, Christ, or angels. Since what is involved in such literature is not the conscious use of an inaccurate name, the designation "pseudonymous" should be used only with reservations. Charlesworth agrees and cautions against calling all such literature "forgeries" (Charlesworth 1997: 768–75). All pseudonymous literature should not be painted with the same brush, although much of it was undoubtedly intended to deceive readers and some of it may have been intended to attribute writings to one who had inspired the authors and mentored them.

5. CANONICAL PSEUDONYMOUS LITERATURE

The question of whether pseudonymous writings, if discovered, should remain in the Bible continues to have scholarly debate. The arguments often begin from theological preference rather than historical inquiry. How can forgeries or fraudulent documents remain in the inspired Bible? The biggest question has to do with whether pseudonymous authors intended to deceive. Metzger holds out that some of the authors may not have intended to deceive, but rather to honor the one in whose name the author added teachings supposedly from that earlier famed antecedent (Metzger 1972).

We have seen that the usual candidates include the Pastoral Epistles, Ephesians, Colossians, 2 Thessalonians, James, 2 Peter, and possibly also Jude and 1 Peter. In the case of 1 Peter, the question has to do with the letter's remarkably good Greek and style—uncommon among working-class persons from Galilee, but others respond that 1 Peter was written through a skilled secretary, namely, Silvanus (5:12), like in antiquity, as in the case of Dionysius of Alexandria and his assessment of the book of Revelation and Origen's assessment of Hebrews. Revelation is an interesting case because it makes no claim to have been written by the Apostle John, though its author does name himself as "John" (Rev 1:9). It is likely that Revelation was included in the biblical canon over its competitors, namely the *Apocalypse of Peter* and *Shepherd of Hermas*, because it was believed by a majority that the author identified as John was indeed the Apostle John.

From antiquity the book of Revelation had a difficult time being received into the biblical canon and even today the orthodox who finally welcomed it in their NT between the seventh and eighth centuries do not read it in their liturgies. That, of course, rightly raises the question recently posed that if it is not read in church, how can it be considered scripture or a part of the church's NT canon (Scanlin 1996: 300–12)? Today, as with Dionysius noted earlier, we recognize that the style, content, and vocabulary of Revelation are considerably different from other writings attributed to John the Apostle—Gospel of John or 1 John or even 2–3 John and it is seldom read in any liturgical texts in churches whether in the East or West. The Gospels, Acts, Hebrews, and 1–3 John were all written *anonymously* and not under a pseudonym, and the names that we now use for those works were later attached to them in the second century when apostolic scribal authority became more important following the deaths of the apostles and those near them.

Donelson may be right when he claims that no acknowledged pseudonymous writing was consciously accepted in any collection of approved writings in the ancient Greco-Roman world—Jewish, Christian, or secular (1986: 11). However, it is possible that despite their intentions, some pseudonymous or anonymous writings were welcomed by church leaders (e.g., 2 Peter and the Pastoral Epistles, Hebrews).

We should also remember that it was not illegal to write pseudonymous texts in antiquity, but in practice when it became known they were generally despised and rejected especially in the fourth and fifth centuries CE when the major contours of the biblical canon were largely shaped, especially if their contents were deemed to be heretical.

For several centuries, both Jews and Christians accepted as scripture many writings now identified as pseudonymous texts, but by the fourth century at the latest it began to change, but not initially (McDonald 2006: 190–214, 230–32; and 2017: 2:164–72, 327–35). Much of this literature was shaped and inspired by the language, metaphors, and symbols of the OT or by the writings earlier attributed to pivotal early Christian leaders (apostles). The authorship attributed to OT figures included names such as Enoch, Abraham, Shem, Moses, David, Solomon, Levi, and other Hebrew patriarchs, but also Christian writings were attributed to early apostolic leaders such as Peter, John, Paul, and James but others as well who were in the apostolic community.

Were *all* pseudonymous writings from antiquity intended to deceive readers? Bart Ehrman says "yes" and contends that those who suggest other, more honorable motives in its production can show no evidence for their position (Ehrman, 2011: 115–42). Interestingly, he acknowledges that some pseudonymous writings could have been written by authors with good intentions but concludes that they nevertheless lied and that in such matters they should have been more honest (2011: 262–5). But again, he contends that several biblical authors falsely claimed to be someone they were not, namely, celebrated apostolic or other biblical figures. He rejects the notion that pseudonymity was widely acceptable in antiquity and even questions how such writings could be the Word of God if they are deceitful. He bluntly concludes that those who wrote in another's name were liars and deceitful, and he recognizes that this conclusion has serious implications for those who look on the Bible as an infallible and authoritative guide to the truth of God (2011: 1–32). I would counter that such notions that are present today were not likely present initially when "secret" documents were produced in the names of famous persons and Christian pseudonymous texts were commonly welcomed (e.g., *Ep. Barn.*, *Didache*). From the fourth century on, however, pseudonymous writings were widely rejected as scripture if they were believed to be pseudonymous. Earlier we observed in the comments from Charles Hill that Origen was fully aware of errors and pseudonymous writings but welcomed some of them anyway (Hill 2016: 43–88). Perhaps the ethically loaded terms Ehrman uses, namely, "liars" and "forgeries," should be softened to "well-intentioned" or such like. The production of pseudonymous writings, while unacceptable to our generation, was a common and a widely accepted practice in antiquity and for a time some of their authors may not have been consciously aware of doing something inappropriate.

By the fourth century many church fathers began questioning the legitimacy of including such texts in their scripture collections and in the various canon lists (Gallagher and Meade 2017 and McDonald 2017: 1:491–9 and 2:361–9). Again, it is important to ask whether it is appropriate to judge ancient writings by modern standards. Do instances exist where unethical motivations were present in the production of pseudonymous writings? Perhaps in the Muratorian Fragment that wanted late fourth-century readers to think his (her?) text was from the second century. It seems that some authors of that literature may have thought what they were doing was okay and appropriate to advance the church's mission. Yet by the fourth century, most church leaders decided that such writings could not be welcomed among the church's sacred scriptures. Nevertheless, for several centuries there was a dispute over accepting some popular pseudonymous writings such as *1 Enoch*, *Epistle of Barnabas*, *Didache*. That also raises the question of whether some writings could legitimately and *rightly* be accepted in the biblical canon because of their content despite their falsely attributed authorship.

Metzger is no doubt right to observe that there were many ways to view pseudepigraphy in antiquity and, as we saw earlier, offers nine examples from ancient literature, whether classical, Jewish, or Christian, to make his point when he speaks of the difficulty of establishing compelling arguments for any criteria for either OT or NT writings. He is joined in that assessment by Peirano and Najman cited earlier (Najman 2007 and Najman and Peirano 2019). Metzger concludes that there were multiple ways of viewing pseudonymous writings primarily because there were many different motives that led to its production and concludes that "no strictly consistent policy or pattern can be discerned either in the selection of the OT or the NT books or in the rejection of other books" (1972: 5–15).

A current example of the difficulty of leaving behind a beloved text that does not reflect the earliest church traditions is, of course, the continuing use of the King James Version (KJV) of the Bible that now is outdated and is based largely on manuscripts dating almost a thousand years later than what we now have for both the OT and NT scriptures. The popularity of the KJV in some English-speaking countries continues despite the more accurate translations available for reading and study today.

Many popular ancient Christian writings outside the NT are now generally acknowledged as pseudonymous works, including *Didache*, *2 Clement*, the *Apostolic Constitutions*, the *Epistle of Barnabas*, the *Gospel of Thomas*, and many others. By the fourth century, as we see in the writings of Eusebius, the writings that were believed to be pseudonymous or heretical were regularly rejected (*Eccl. Hist.* 3.25.4–7). Discussions of why such texts are rejected are rare before the fourth century, except when they were considered heretical documents, and several eminent early church fathers accepted pseudepigraphal books as sacred scripture. As we saw above, Tertullian cited *1 Enoch* as scripture when dealing with women's attire (*Apparel* 1.3). It is remarkable, then, that the pseudonymous *Apostolic Constitutions* document (*c.* mid-fourth century) was itself written falsely in the names of the apostles, but nonetheless warns Christians against reading pseudepigraphal literature! Notice first how its author claims to be reflecting the words of the apostles:

> On whose account also *we*, who are now assembled in one place,—Peter and Andrew; James and John, sons of Zebedee; Philip and Bartholomew; Thomas and Matthew; James the son of Alphaeus; Simon the Canaanite, and Matthias, who instead of Judas was numbered with us; and James the brother of the Lord and bishop of Jerusalem, and Paul the teacher of the Gentiles, the chosen vessel, *having all met together, have written to you this Catholic doctrine* for the confirmation of you, to whom the oversight of the universal Church is committed. (6.14, ANF 7:456; emphasis added)

Two chapters later the author writes,

> We have sent all things to you, that you may know our opinion, what it is; *and that you may not receive those books which obtain in our name but are written by the ungodly. For you are not to attend to the names of the apostles, but to the nature of the things, and their settled opinions.* For we know that Simon and Cleobius, and their followers, have compiled poisonous books under the name of Christ and of His disciples, and do carry them about in order to deceive you who love Christ, and us his servants. And among the ancients also some have written apocryphal books of Moses, and Enoch, and Adam, and Isaiah, and David, and Elijah, and of the three patriarchs, pernicious and repugnant to the truth. The same things even now have the wicked heretics done, reproaching the creation, marriage, providence, the begetting of children, the law, and the prophets; inscribing certain barbarous names, and as they think, of angels, but to speak the truth, of demons, which suggest things to them. (6.16, ANF 7:457, emphasis added)

Apparently, by the middle of the fourth century, *known* pseudonymous writings were no longer held in high esteem in the churches, even if such documents continued to be produced in apostolic names.

6. THE IMPORTANCE OF PSEUDONYMOUS WRITINGS

Scholars today widely understand the value of the study of the so-called apocryphal and pseudepigraphal literature. This literature provides important social portraits of the life and thought of the early churches at various junctures after its first century and it also reflects some of the challenges that churches were facing when that literature was produced. Without these writings we do not have a complete understanding of the emergence and growth of early Christianity and are left without a full understanding of some important terms and issues such as "Son of Man," the notion of apocalyptic eschatology, the meaning of kingdom of God, messianic expectations, and many other topics of special interest that are common in the pseudepigraphal writings. Interpreters of early Christianity know the immense value of this literature for informing our understanding of the broader context of early Christianity before the orthodox triumph of the fourth century. This is true not only of the OT apocrypha and pseudepigrapha but also of the so-called NT apocryphal writings. The earliest churches did not draw a fine line between church tradition and their Christian scriptures, nor did they initially make precise decisions on the scope of their sacred texts and some texts that were later rejected. They were helpful to some communities because of their useful content and not because the authorship question was settled for them.

7. CONCLUSION

No one seriously denies the presence and influence of pseudonymous writings in antiquity. Its production and use were especially common in the Greco-Roman world, late Second Temple Judaism and early Christianity. Jews and Christians produced and used such texts and, in some cases, considered some of them as sacred scripture. What also appears obvious now is that the ancient world did not have the same standards that moderns have regarding its production or use, at least in the early stages of its production and circulation in churches. Rist acknowledges that "There is little evidence that the early Christians were sensitive to the ethical implications of pseudepigraphy, literary deception, save as they accused their opponents of using this misleading artifice" (Rist 1972: 90). He adds that the early Christians, "whether 'orthodox' or 'heretical' used pseudepigraphy frequently and for the most part unashamedly to promote their special views and doctrines" (Rist 1972: 91). It may be that modern scholarship is imposing current ethical standards on early Christianity when the early Christians were not as aware that such activity was as unethical as we consider it today. As we saw above, Tertullian clearly denounced it, and that may be evidenced in letters attributed to Paul (2 Thess 2:2–3; 3:17) and Peter (2 Pet 1:18; 2:1–3), but there were multiple examples of it in late Second Temple Judaism, and concern about authorship does not appear as apparently central to them as it became so in the thinking of much later Christians. Some of the NT writings made use of several pseudonymous texts that they believed were scripture (e.g., Heb 1:2–3—Wis 7:25; Jude 14—*1 En.* 1:9), and did so whether knowing that it was pseudonymous or not.

It appears from the use and familiarity with Jewish pseudonymous texts that the primary question for the earliest Christians was whether the document was useful in their local communities for teaching and proclamation and whether it advanced their beliefs and sacred traditions. The content of some of the pseudonymous writings was carefully monitored in churches and sifted through the church's core traditions, creeds, worship, teachings, baptisms, and eucharistic meals. In other words, content, usefulness, and coherence with community beliefs apparently took priority over authorship until the larger church later made decisions about scripture based on authorship and content (Augustine). By the fourth century *most* known pseudonymous writings were rejected.

Porter has argued that if a text was deemed pseudonymous then it must be rejected, and he believes that the early church did so and defends the traditional accepted authorship of the NT writings (Porter 1995: 105–23, 1996: 136). Such writings could not be used as sacred scripture, he argues, if a text was not written by its reputed author. He rightly says that an anonymous text on which a later pseudonymous name was added does not qualify here, but it is not clear if he thinks those texts that were not written by apostles, but were so attributed, should be kept in the biblical canon, namely Hebrews, and John who wrote the Apocalypse. Clarke argues against Porter's position and is more open on the matter and is not willing to throw out the Pastorals even if Paul did not write them as we now have them (Clarke 2002: 441–64).

Even though fourth- and fifth-century church councils regularly rejected pseudonymous writings, there is little evidence that all the local churches did the same or were even aware of the texts with false authorship. Since by the fourth century it appears clear that church councils rejected pseudonymous texts, it is not clear that the local churches fully agreed with or were even familiar with the council decisions on such matters, and they continued to read in their churches what had been rejected at council meetings even centuries earlier (Stichometry of Nicephorus). Some texts with questionable authorship had obtained what

Stuckenbruck called "irresistible momentum" and they continued to be read as scripture in many churches. I pointed out earlier that the later *Stichometry of Nicephorus* (ninth century) continued to reject writings that had been rejected four-hundred or more years earlier. Why continue rejecting them if no one was still reading them? It also appears likely that a text that had complied with the church's sacred traditions and was useful to many local churches continued to be welcomed among the local churches' sacred scriptures for centuries. That would also include 3 *Corinthians* in some Western as well as Syrian and later Armenian churches for centuries along with the *Diatessaron.* Some pseudonymous texts had a short life, that is, a "temporary scriptural status," but others that were likely pseudonymous had widespread use in churches and were not rejected except in the case of perceived heretical teachings.

We saw earlier that Origen acknowledged the value of Hebrews, an anonymous text, but said that only God knows who its author was and he welcomed it. He also welcomed Susanna that was not written by the original author of Daniel. Hebrews was likely finally approved because it was attributed to Paul, but one must ask whether its valued message had reached "irresistible momentum" and so Paul's name was attached to it to ensure its acceptance.

In the second century there was little focus on authorship until toward the end of that century when the Gospels were more beginning to be cited by name, but initially, they were generally not cited by author but rather by the sayings or activities of Jesus in them that were cited. They began being cited as "memoirs of the apostles" by Justin (*1 Apol.* 64–67) and not by name even then until Irenaeus (*c.* 170–180). By the fourth century when more focus was on authorship and even date (as in the case of the *Shepherd of Hermas* as scripture in the Muratorian Fragment) it became more common to dismiss texts considered pseudonymous. Some texts were dismissed earlier as in the cases of Tertullian rejecting the *Acts of Paul* and Irenaeus rejecting the *Gospel of Judas* or later Serapion finally rejecting the *Gospel of Peter* after closer scrutiny of its content, not primarily authorship. However, because its content was unacceptable, so was its authorship. Similarly, if the content of a disputed writing was popular and widely accepted, it likely survived later decisions about rejecting pseudonymous texts. It is important for modern scholars to revisit the unfounded notion that all authors of pseudonymous writings had unethical intentions to deceive their readers or to promote either orthodox or heretical teachings. While that may have been true in some cases, it is not likely true in all cases.

I will proceed now to summarize what we have examined along with some of the implications of our study for today but were present in early Christianity before there was a Bible.

CHAPTER 8

Final Thoughts and Conclusions

Both before and after the Christian separation from Judaism (mostly from the mid-60s to c. 135 CE), many of the earliest Christians recognized the sacredness of most if not all of the Hebrew Bible (HB)/Tanak books but also several disputed books that were likely included in the LXX. Many Christians continued to read some of the disputed or deuterocanonical and even pseudepigraphal religious texts, but for some Christians, especially in the East, those books were read privately. Several early church councils affirmed the scriptural status of several disputed or deuterocanonical books, but they did not agree on what to call them, namely whether they were "ecclesiastical" or "antilegomena" or "apocryphal" or "scriptural" books or also which writings to include in their liturgies (Oikonomos 1991: 24–30). While later Protestant Reformation leaders began to reject the scriptural status of the deuterocanonical books, many Protestant churches continued to read them in their worship. While Martin Luther rejected their scriptural status, he recognized the value of some of them and also because of pressure from his churches, he retained them but placed them between his OT and NT translation. He followed Epiphanius's positive view toward some of these books (*De mensuris et ponderibus* 4; PG 43:244) and favored Baruch, Epistle of Jeremiah, Wisdom, and Sirach, but not as scripture (deSilva 2018; Fricke 1991: 46–87).

Some Protestants regularly included the deuterocanonical books in their Bibles until around 1850; they were reintroduced in some modern Protestant Bibles in the 1950s, but following Luther's example they placed them between the OT and NT. Most of the Protestant objections to those books had to do with praying for the forgiveness of sins for the dead (2 Macc 12:39–42), advocating meritorious works that contribute to one's salvation (Tob 4:10; 12:9; 14:10–11), the practice of exorcism (Tob 6:7–11), and giving of alms to atone for sin (Sir 3:30).

Long ago Reuss acknowledged the fluidity of the biblical canon and observed that Origen did not put an end to uncertainty about the scope and order of LXX books (see *Selecta in Psalmos*; cf. Eusebius, *Hist. eccl.* 6.25; Reuss 1891: 130–1). Despite awareness of the limited Hebrew canon, Origen accepted several disputed LXX books and defended his use of *Bel and the Dragon*, *Song of the Three Children*, the additions to Esther, and Judith in his letter to Julius Africanus (*ad Africanum* 13). Elsewhere he positively quoted the Wisdom of Solomon and Sirach (*Homily* 18 in *Numer.*) and called "Maccabees" (presumably 1–2 Maccabees) "the Scriptures, the Word of God" (*Princ.* 2.1.5; see more in McDonald 2017: 1:310–14; Grant 1965: 44).

While the LXX was for the most part the early Christians' First scriptures, what went into that collection is unclear and was never formally fixed or uniformly approved by all churches. Stendebach rightly concludes, "The church Fathers did not treat as canonical what they found in the Septuagint" but rather "what they treated as canonical came into the Septuagint" (Stendebach 1991: 3–4). It is difficult to establish which additional books were originally included in the LXX that are not in the HB because Christians have produced the only *surviving* copies and they likely introduced many changes in it. However, it is most likely that the LXX included several non-Tanak texts before the earliest Christians separated from Judaism. There is no evidence that the Christian LXX OT got bigger with time, and it is reasonable to assume that churches welcomed only the additional OT books in their LXX. Other books could have been added to an "original" collection of the LXX books such as the Prayer of Manasseh or 4 Ezra and others, but also some may have been deleted that were no longer found useful for the churches or for Judaism. Many studies have been made on the twenty-two or twenty-six "lost" books mentioned in the OT or Hebrew scriptures. They may have been lost in the destruction of Jerusalem in 597–596, but that is uncertain.

The Eastern Church fathers chose to read in their churches mostly those texts in the HB/Tanak, but they did not place them in the Tanak order (McDonald 2019: 397–413). Their scripture citations and canon lists reflect fluidity especially regarding Baruch, Epistle of Jeremiah, the additions to Daniel and Esther, and the Maccabees (McDonald 2021: Orthodox Christianity). Western churches generally followed the lead of Augustine who included many of the disputed writings. It is not clear why churches accepted the disputed deuterocanonical books and rejected the pseudepigrapha since initially Jesus and his followers were aware of some of the books from both collections and occasionally cited them or showed awareness of some of them (see Lewis 1991: 182; McDonald 2017a: 299–309). Only the Ethiopians included some of the pseudepigraphal books, especially *Jubilees* and *1 Enoch*, among their scriptures. Although some Eastern Church fathers rejected the scriptural status of the deuterocanonical books, most encouraged the people to read some of them. Western churches (Catholic) generally welcomed them among their scriptural collections.

The scope of the additional books in the current LXX is not necessarily what was in the earliest copies of the LXX manuscripts, but there is little evidence to support only the books in the current 2006 Rahlfs-Hanhart edition of the LXX. That collection comes from a broad variety of surviving manuscripts of the LXX, but not necessarily all that was initially included in it. Few now doubt the value of these disputed texts for knowing the religious perspectives of those who received and read them and the historical context of late Second Temple Judaism and early Christianity. Many also recognize their inspiration for homilies, meditations, liturgical forms, and their influence on poets, dramatists, composers, and artists (deSilva 2018: 31; Metzger 1987: xvi–xviii). The influence of this literature can be seen in present widespread belief in their sacredness and inclusion in most Christian Bibles (Orthodox, Catholic, Ethiopian, and now some Protestant Bibles as well) despite the fluidity in their contents and text.

In sum, I have argued that from the church's beginning, the primary authority and focus was on Jesus who was believed to be the anticipated Messiah. For most, he was the Lord of the church, and his words and fate were at the heart of all early Christian proclamations. Secondarily, the Jewish scriptures that later formed the HB were a major authority for the earliest followers of Jesus as they were for him. They were largely interpreted Christologically and eschatologically and those texts were among the scriptures circulating among the first-century Jews. The scope of the Jewish scriptures with its later HB and the church's OT scriptures were not settled for most churches until several centuries after the church began and some books were questioned not only by some rabbinic sages in the second and later centuries but also by early church fathers.

Early Christianity did not have a Bible or even a complete OT when the church was born, but there were collections of sacred texts that informed their faith. Although the early followers of Jesus accepted the Hebrew scriptures as their scriptures, the scope of those scriptures was still fluid for both the Jews and early Christians, but many of those scriptures were well known and cited frequently in Jewish and Christian literature in the late Second Temple period and later. As the church began, the NT, of course, had not yet been written and its production and recognition as scripture took much longer. In some cases, doubts about some NT books took centuries to resolve at the local church councils, but even later in the operative scriptures of the churches, namely the manuscripts that contained their Christian scriptures.

In the church's first two centuries, no one was thinking of a "Bible" or a fixed collection of sacred books. The origin of the church's Bible took centuries to develop after the various texts included in it were written. No NT writings were called "scripture" soon after they were written and nothing in them called for a limited collection of Christian scriptures. Interestingly also, no early Christian creed includes a listing of biblical books that were prescribed or rejected. No single copy or manuscript of all the NT books, *and only those books*, existed before the tenth or eleventh century. Also, the notion of a "Holy Bible" or "holy books" became more common by the ninth century although Jerome earlier had mentioned "the holy books" in reference to the church's scriptures. The current notion of a Bible as a complete collection of books without addition or subtraction took a long time to be popular in churches, but it became more common after the production of the pandect Paris Bibles and more so after printed Bibles became a reality.

Besides Jesus and the First scriptures of the early Christians, the third significant authority in early Christianity was apostolic authority that was often appealed to, certainly by Paul on multiple occasions (e.g., 1 Cor 9:1; Gal 1:1, passim), and by Peter with the selection of one to take the place of Judas and the focus on apostolic teaching (Acts 1:12–26; 2:42). However, at the heart of the beliefs in early Christianity was its core traditions, that is, its Gospel, and that gave the church not only its understanding of the identity of Jesus but also its own identity, mission, and guide for living. This tradition was passed on summarily in its earlier and later creeds, and through its songs, hymns, and affirmations in its baptisms, eucharists, preaching, teaching, and in the interpretations of the scriptural lections read in churches.

The creeds initially focused mostly on the identity and activity of Jesus and they grew and expanded over time to continue to address new issues churches were facing such as whether God was creator, or the creator was a Demiurge. Although there is nothing in the early Christian writings that leads one to say that the initial church was interested in forming a Christian OT or NT, eventually *some* of those initial writings were recognized as *Christian* scriptures and circulated in churches. Those writings *functioned* like scripture and were often cited in the second-century churches *like* scripture *before* they began to be *called* scripture mostly by the end of the second century, and most of those writings eventually formed most of the current NT. Although the notion of *Christian* scriptures was not present initially, by the end of the second century after considerable use and function like scripture in the churches several NT writings began to be called "scripture," but not all of them. It took several centuries longer for some of the NT writings to be called scripture.

After the Council of Nicea (325) when the identity of Jesus was settled for most churches, scripture lists began to appear in church fathers (especially Athanasius) and local church councils from the council of Laodicea in 360 CE and later, but the books in those canon lists varied on the fringes for centuries regarding several NT books, for example, the so-called "Pocoke" or "Minor" NT Epistles (= 2 Peter, 2–3 John, Jude), and Revelation, but also for others such as the Pastoral Epistles. By the mid- to late fourth century, some church leaders began to acknowledge a fixed biblical canon without complete agreement on its scope. As noted, none of the ecumenical councils ever dealt with the scope of the church's scriptures, but the multiple lists beginning before the formation of the Bible and continuing for centuries reflected differences over some of the biblical books. Some writings were included for a time but were excluded later over questions related to authorship and date. Others, whose authorship was questioned, were eventually welcomed as sacred scripture because they had achieved an "irresistible momentum" that persisted and was not reversable (Hebrews, Pastorals, and others).

Often overlooked artifacts of church history include the hymns, lectionaries, baptismal and eucharistic affirmations. They all affirmed traditions from the first century and in subsequent generations. Early Christian hymns also circulated from the first century and enhanced and enabled the transmission of the church's core beliefs and offered some control on variations or expansions in the core beliefs that were historically transmitted in the churches. The ancient lectionaries or selected shorter scriptural readings circulating in churches often reflect the scriptures that were welcomed in the churches. Few churches would have had the ability to possess or even read all their scriptures that the larger and more influential churches possessed. The manuscripts, canon lists, lectionaries, and citations all reflect not only considerable overlap in the recognized Christian authorities but also the fluidity in those collections for centuries.

Some church fathers rejected or ignored for centuries some of the NT writings, but eventually all of them were accepted, even Revelation the most disputed of the NT books. For a while additional "temporary scriptural" texts were added (*Shepherd of Hermas, Didache, Epistle of Barnabas*, and even 3 *Corinthians, Odes of Solomon*, and 1 Clement), but in time all of those were eventually excluded.

Although much of the thinking and beliefs of early Christianity developed, grew, and sharpened over the centuries, its core beliefs reflected in the NT remained largely unchanged. From its beginning, Jesus' special relationship to God was affirmed along with his crucifixion by the order of Pontius Pilate, that he died for the sins of humanity and was raised from the dead, and eventually that God was the creator of all things in heaven and earth emphasized in the NT but not in the early creeds, and that Jesus the Christ will return. The early followers of Jesus were Jews whose religious traditions have parallels with common practices and beliefs in many of the first-century Jewish practices along with their varied OT collections and later NT literature. Early Christian traditions are primarily seen in the NT writings and the early church fathers all show how the followers of Jesus met, worshipped, initially organized, and adapted from their Jewish siblings several of their practices such as their eucharists and baptisms. As the church became more Gentile, other characteristics also were included, but Gentiles were welcomed without the Jewish Christians abandoning their initial core beliefs, identity, and mission of the church along with much of their Jewish heritage. Jews did not have to cease being Jews to become followers of Jesus. Conversely, from the early years of the Christian movement, Gentiles did not have to become Jews to become followers of Jesus. Paul, of course, was highly instrumental in making that happen.

These all are important factors that functioned as authorities or guides in various ways before there was a Bible and they were also instrumental in the eventual formation of the Bible and early Christianity itself. While many challenges and changes emerged in the history of the church, its core beliefs that emerged early on have remained despite additions to those beliefs and clarifications over many centuries. Hopefully this volume will be helpful in encouraging further examination of those critical years that preceded the formation of the Bible and still have relevance today.

BIBLIOGRAPHY

Abegg, M. G. (2001). "4QMMT, Paul, and 'Works of the Law'," in *The Bible at Qumran: Text, Shape, and Interpretation*, edited by P. W. Flint. Grand Rapids, MI: Eerdmans, pp. 203–16.

Adler, W. (2002). "The Pseudepigrapha in the Early Church," in *The Canon Debate*, edited by L. M. McDonald and J. A. Sanders. Grand Rapids, MI: Baker, pp. 211–28.

Adler, W. (2019). "Origen and the Old Testament Apocrypha: The Creation of a Category," in *The Old Testament Pseudepigrapha: Fifty Years of the Pseudepigrapha Section at the SBL*, edited by M. Henze and L. Ingeborg. Early Judaism and Its Literature 50. Atlanta, GA: SBL Press, pp. 287–308.

Aland, K. (1961). "The Problem of Anonymity and Pseudonymity in Christian Literature of the First Two Centuries," *Journal of Theological Studies* 12: 39–49.

Aland, K., and Barbara Aland (1989). *The Text of the New Testament*. Translated by E. F. Rhodes. Grand Rapids, MI: Eerdmans.

Allert, C. D. (1999). "Is Translation Inspired? The Problems of Verbal Inspiration for a Translation and a Proposed Solution," in *Translating the Bible*, edited by S. E. Porter and R. S. Hess. JSNTS 173. London: UNKNO, pp. 85–113.

Allert, C. D. (2002). *Revelation, Truth, Canon and Interpretation: Studies in Justin Martyr's Dialogue with Trypho*. VCS 64. Leiden: Brill.

Anderson, P. N. (2001). "John and Mark—the Bi-optic Gospels," in *Jesus in Johannine Tradition*, edited by R. Fortuna and T. Thatcher. Philadelphia, PA: Westminster/John Knox, pp. 175–90.

Anderson, P. N. (2006). "Aspects of Historicity in the Gospel of John: Implications for Investigations of Jesus and Archaeology," in *Jesus and Archaeology*, edited by J. H. Charlesworth. Grand Rapids, MI: Eerdmans, pp. 587–618.

Antony, D. (2016). *Entangled Christianities*. Newcastle upon Tyne: Cambridge Scholars.

Armstrong, J. J. (2008). "Victorinus of Pettau as the Author of the Canon Muratori," *Vigiliae Christianae* 62: 1–34.

Aune, D. E. (1983). *Prophecy in Early Christianity and the Ancient Mediterranean World*. Grand Rapids, MI: Eerdmans.

Aune, D. E. (1987). *The New Testament in Its Literary Environment*. LEC. Philadelphia, PA: Westminster.

Bakke, O. M. (2005). "The Episcopal Ministry and Unity of the Church from the Apostolic Fathers to Cyprian," in *The Formation of the Early Church*, edited by J. Adna. WUNT 183. Tübingen: Mohr Siebeck, pp. 379–408.

Balch, D. L., E. Ferguson, and W. A. Meeks (eds.) (1990). *Greeks, Romans, and Christians: Essays in Honor of A. J. Malherbe*. Minneapolis, MN: Fortress Press.

Barber, M. P. (2011). "'The Yoke of Servitude': Christian Non-Observance of the Law's Cultic Precepts in Patristic Sources," *Letter & Spirit* 7: 67–90.

Bar-Ilan, M. (1988). "Scribes and Books in the Late Second Commonwealth and Rabbinic Period," in *Mikra: Text, Translation, Reading and Interpretation of the Hebrew Bible in*

Ancient Judaism and Early Christianity, edited by M. J. Mulder and H. Sysling. CRINT. Assen: Van Gorcum. Minneapolis, MN: Fortress Press, pp. 21–38.

Barnstone, W. (ed.) (1984). *The Other Bible*. New York: Harper & Row.

Barr, J. (1983). *Holy Scripture: Canon, Authority, Criticism*. Philadelphia, PA: Westminster Press.

Barrett, C. K. (1987). *The New Testament Background: Selected Documents*. 2nd ed. New York: Harper & Row.

Bartchy, S. S. (1973). *First-Century Slavery and 1 Corinthians 7:21*. SBLDS 11. Atlanta, GA: Scholars Press.

Barton, J. (1986). *Oracles of God: Perceptions of Ancient Prophecy in Israel after the Exile*. Oxford: Oxford University Press.

Barton, J. (1988). *People of the Book? The Authority of the Bible in Christianity*. Louisville, KY: Westminster John Knox.

Barton, J. (1997). *Holy Writings, Sacred Text: The Canon in Early Christianity*. Louisville, KY: Westminster John Knox.

Barton, J. (2002). "Marcion Revisited," in *The Canon Debate*, edited by L. M. McDonald and J. A. Sanders. Grand Rapids, MI: Baker, pp. 341–54.

Barton, J. (2012). "The Old Testament Canons," in *The New Cambridge History of the Bible: From 600–1450*, edited by J. C. Paget and J. Schaper. Cambridge: Cambridge University Press, pp. 145–64.

Bauckham, R. (2005). "Hymns," in *Oxford Dictionary of the Christian Church*, 3rd ed., edited by F. L. Cross and E. A. Livingstone. Oxford: Oxford University Press, pp. 814–17.

Bauckham, R. (2006). *Jesus and the Eyewitnesses: The Gospels as Eyewitness Testimony*. Grand Rapids, MI: Eerdmans.

Bauckham, R., J. R. Davila, and A. Panayotov (eds.) (2013). *Old Testament Pseudepigrapha: More Noncanonical Scriptures*. Vol. 1. Grand Rapids, MI: Eerdmans.

Bauer, W. ([1934] 1971). *Orthodoxy and Heresy in Earliest Christianity*. Edited by R. Kraft and G. Krodel. Philadelphia, PA: Fortress Press.

Beckwith, R. T. (1985). *The Old Testament Canon of the New Testament Church*. Grand Rapids, MI: Eerdmans.

Beckwith, R. T. (1993). "Canon of the Hebrew Bible and the Old Testament," in *The Oxford Companion to the Bible*, edited by B. M. Metzger and M. D. Coogan. New York: Oxford University Press, pp. 100–2.

BeDuhn, J. D. (2013). *The First New Testament: Marcion's Scriptural Canon*. Salem, OR: Polebridge Press.

Benko, S. (1984). *Pagan Rome and the Early Christians*. Bloomington: Indiana University Press.

Beyer, H. W. (1964–76). "Κανών," in *Theological Dictionary of the New Testament*, edited by G. Kittel and G. Friedrich and translated by G. W. Bromiley. Grand Rapids, MI: Eerdmans, pp. 3:596–602.

Bichel, M. A. (1992). "Hymns, Early Christian," in *Anchor Bible Dictionary*, editor-in-chief, D. N. Freedman. Garden City, NY: Doubleday, pp. 3:350–1.

Blackman, E. C. (1948). *Marcion and His Influence*. London: SPCK.

Boccaccini, G. (1991). *Middle Judaism: Jewish Thought, 300 BCE to 200 CE*. Minneapolis, MN: Fortress Press.

Boccaccini, G. (ed.) (2005). *Enoch and Qumran Origins: New Light on a Forgotten Connection*. Grand Rapids, MI: Eerdmans.

Bogaert, P.-M. (2012). "The Latin Bible, c. 600–c. 900," in *The New Cambridge History of the Bible: From 600–1450*, edited by R. Marsden and E. A. Matter. Cambridge: Cambridge University Press, pp. 69–92.

Bogaert, P.-M. (2013). "The Latin Bible," in *The Cambridge History of the Bible: From the Beginnings to 600*, edited by J. C. Paget and J. Schaper. Cambridge: Cambridge University Press, pp. 505–26.

Bohak, G. (1996). *Joseph and Aseneth and the Jewish Temple in Heliopolis*. Society of Biblical Literature. Early Judaism and Its Literature 10. Atlanta, GA: Scholars Press.

Bokedal, T. (2014). *The Formation and Significance of the Christian Biblical Canon: A Study in Text, Ritual and Interpretation*. London: Bloomsbury T&T Clark.

Bovon, F. (2002). "Canonical Structure of Gospel and Apostle," in *The Canon Debate*, edited by L. M. McDonald and J. A. Sanders. Peabody, MA: Hendrickson, pp. 516–27.

Bovon, F. (2012). "Beyond the Canonical and the Apocryphal Books, the Presence of a Third Category: The Books Useful for the Soul," *HTR* 105: 125–37.

Bovon, F. (2015). "'Useful for the Soul': Christian Apocrypha and Christian Spirituality," in *Oxford Handbook of Early Christian Apocrypha*, edited by A. Gregory and C. Tuckett. Oxford: Oxford University Press, pp. 185–95.

Brakke, D. (1994). "Canon Formation and Social Conflict in Fourth-Century Egypt: Athanasius of Alexandria's Thirty-Ninth Festal Letter," *HTR* 87: 395–419.

Brakke, D. (1995). *Athanasius and the Politics of Asceticism*. Oxford: Clarendon.

Brakke, D. (2010). "A New Fragment of Athanasius' Thirty-Ninth Festal Letter: Heresy, Apocrypha, and the Canon," *HTR* 103: 47–66.

Brock, A. G. (2000). "Early Christian Apocrypha," in *Eerdmans Dictionary of the Bible*, edited by D. N. Freedman. Grand Rapids, MI: Eerdmans, pp. 75–7.

Brock, S. (2006). *The Bible in the Syriac Tradition*. Revised ed. Gorgias Handbooks. River Road, NJ: Gorgias Press.

Brock, S. (2008). "Poetry and Hymnography (3): Syriac," in *The Oxford Handbook on Early Christian Studies*, edited by S. A. Harvey and D. G. Hunter. London: Oxford University Press, pp. 656–71.

Brooke, G. J. (2005). "Between Authority and Canon: The Significance of Reworking the Bible for Understanding the Canonical Process," in *Reworking the Bible: Apocryphal and Related Texts at Qumran*, edited by E. G. Chazon, D. Dimant and R. A. Clements. Leiden: Brill, pp. 97–114.

Brown, M. P. (2006). "Spreading the Word: The Single-Volume Bible," in *In the Beginning: Bibles before the Year 1000*, edited by M. P. Brown. Washington, DC: Smithsonian, pp. 176–203.

Brown, R. (1994). *The Death of the Messiah: From Gethsemane to the Grave: A Commentary on the Passion Narrative of the Gospels*. ABRL. 2 vols. Garden City, NY: Doubleday.

Brown, R. (1997). "The Babylonian Talmud on the Execution of Jesus," *NTS* 43: 158–9.

Brox, N. (1994). *A History of the Early Church*. London: SCM.

Bruce, F. F. (1971). *New Testament History*. Garden City, NY: Doubleday.

Bruce, F. F. (1988). *The Canon of Scripture*. Downers Grove, IL: InterVarsity

Büchsel, F. (1964–76). "Παραδοσις," Vol. 2, edited by Kittel and G. Friedrich and translated by G. W. Bromiley. Grand Rapids, MI: Eerdmans, pp. 171–3.

Burke, T. (2015). "Early Christian Apocrypha in Contemporary Theological Discourse," in *Oxford Handbook of Early Christian Apocrypha*, edited by A. Gregory and C. Tuckett. Oxford: Oxford University Press, pp. 441–57.

Burke, T. (ed.) (2020). *New Testament Apocrypha: More Noncanonical Scriptures*. Vol. 2. Grand Rapids, MI: Eerdmans.

Burke, T., and B. Landau (eds.) (2016). *New Testament Apocrypha: More Noncanonical Scriptures*. Vol. 1. Grand Rapids, MI: Eerdmans.

Caird, G. B. (1955). *The Apostolic Age*. London: Duckworth.
Callan, T. (1986). *Forgetting the Root: The Emergence of Christianity from Judaism*. New York: Paulist.
Callan, T. (1994). *The Origins of Christian Faith*. New York: Paulist Press.
Cameron, R. (1982). *The Other Gospels: Non-Canonical Gospel Texts*. Philadelphia, PA: Westminster.
Campbell, R. A. (1994). *The Elders: Seniority within Earliest Christianity*. Studies of the New Testament World and Its World. Edinburgh: T&T Clark.
Campenhausen, Hans von (1968). *Tradition and Life in the Church: Essays and Lectures in Church History*. Translated by A. V. Littledale. London: Collins.
Campenhausen, Hans von (1969). *Ecclesiastical Authority and Spiritual Power in the Church of the First Three Centuries*. Translated by J. A. Baker. London: Adam & Charles Black; German: *Kirchliches Amt und Geistliche Vollmacht*, J. C. B. Mohr, 1953.
Campenhausen, Hans von (1972). The *Formation of the Christian Bible*. Translated by A. Baker. Philadelphia, PA: Fortress Press.
Candlish, J. S. (1891). "Om the Moral Character of Pseudonymous Books," *Exp* 4: 91–107.
Cassey, R. (1938). "The Armenian Marcionites and the Diatessaron," *JBL* 57: 185–92.
Chadwick, H. (1990). "The Early Christian Community," in *The Oxford Illustrated History of Christianity*, edited by J. McManners. Oxford: Oxford University Press, pp. 21–61.
Chadwick, H. (1993). *The Early Church*. Pelican History of the Church. London: Pelican Books. Revised, from 1967 edition.
Charles, R. H. (1913). *The Apocrypha and Pseudepigrapha of the Old Testament*. 2 vols. Oxford: Oxford University Press.
Charlesworth, J. H. (1977). *Odes of Solomon*. Missoula, MT: Scholars Press.
Charlesworth, J. H. (1985). *Old Testament Pseudepigrapha and the New Testament*. 2 Vols. Cambridge: Cambridge University Press.
Charlesworth, J. H. (1988). *Jesus within Judaism: New Light from Exciting Archaeological Discoveries*. Garden City, NY: Doubleday, pp. 103–30.
Charlesworth, J. H. (1992). "Pseudepigrapha," in *Anchor Bible Dictionary*, gen. editor D. N. Freedman. Garden City, NY: Doubleday, pp. 5:540–1.
Charlesworth, J. H. (1995). *The Beloved Disciple: Whose Witness Validates the Gospel of John?* Valley Forge: Trinity Press International.
Charlesworth, J. H. (1997). "Pseudepigraphy," in *Encyclopedia of Early Christianity*, edited by E. Ferguson. New York: Garland Press, pp. 2:768–75.
Charlesworth, J. H. (2002). *The Pesharim and Qumran History: Chaos or Consensus?* Grand Rapids, MI: Eerdmans.
Charlesworth, J. H. (2005). "The Books of Enoch or 1 Enoch Matters: New Paradigms for Understanding Pre-70 Judaism," in *Enoch and Qumran Origins: New Light on a Forgotten Connection*, edited by G. Boccaccini. Grand Rapids, MI: Eerdmans, pp. 436–54.
Charlesworth, J. H. (2013). "Foreword: The Fundamental Importance of an Expansive Collection of 'Old Testament Pseudepigrapha,'" in *Old Testament Pseudepigrapha: More Noncanonical Scriptures*, edited by R. Bauckham, J. R. Davila, and A. Panayotov. Vol. 1. Grand Rapids, MI: Eerdmans, pp. xi–xvi.
Charlesworth, J. H., and C. A. Evans (1994). "Jesus in the Agrapha and Apocryphal Gospels," in *Studying the Historical Jesus: Evaluations of the State of Current Research*, edited by B. Chilton and C. Evans. NTTS 19. Leiden: Brill, pp. 479–533.
Chilton, B., and J. Neusner (1999). *Types of Authority in Formative Christianity and Judaism*. London: Routledge.

Church, F. F., and T. J. Mulry (1988). *The Macmillan Book of Earliest Christian Hymns.* New York: Macmillan.

Clabeaux, J. J. (1992). "Marcionite Prologues to Paul," in *Anchor Bible Dictionary*, general edited by D. N. Freedman. Garden City, NY: Doubleday, pp. 4:520–1.

Clarke, K. D. (1999). "Original Text or Canonical Text? Questioning the Shape of the New Testament Text we Translate," in *Translating the Bible: Problems and Prospects*, edited by S. E. Porter and R. S. Hess. JSNTS 173. Sheffield: Sheffield Academic Press, pp. 321–2.

Clarke, K. D. (2002). "The Problem of Pseudonymity in Biblical Literature and Its Implications for Canon Formation," in *The Canon Debate*, edited by L. M. McDonald and J. A. Sanders. Peabody, MA: Hendrickson, pp. 440–68.

Cohen, S. J. D. (1979). *Josephus in Galilee and Rome: His Vita and Development as a Historian.* Columbia Studies in the Classical Tradition 8. Leiden: Brill.

Cohen, S. J. D. (1987). *From Maccabees to the Mishnah.* LEC. Philadelphia, PA: Westminster.

Collins, J. J. (2012). "The 'Apocryphal' Old Testament," in *The New Cambridge History of the Bible: From the Beginnings to 600*, edited by J. C. Paget and J. Schaper. Cambridge: Cambridge University Press, pp. 165–89.

Collins, J. J. (2014). "The Penumbra of the Canon. What Do the Deuterocanonical Books Represent?" in *Canonicity, Setting, Wisdom in the Deuterocanonicals*, edited by G. G. Xeravits, J. Zsengellér, and X. Szabó. Deuterocanonical and Cognate Literature Studies 22. Berlin: de Gruyter, pp. 1–17.

Collins, J. J. (2018). *Introduction to the Hebrew Bible.* 3rd ed. Minneapolis, MN: Fortress Press.

Collins, J. J. (2020). "The Penumbra of the Canon: What Do the Deuterocanonical Books Represent," "Beyond the Canon: The Recovery of the Pseudepigrapha," and "Nonbiblical Literature in the Dead Sea Scrolls," in *Ancient Jewish and Christian Scriptures: New Developments in Canon Controversy*, edited by J. J. Collins, C. A. Evans, and L.M. McDonald. Louisville, KY: Westminster John Knox Press, pp. 7–48.

Collins, R. (1983). *Introduction to the New Testament.* Garden City, NY: Doubleday.

Comfort Philip, W., and D. P. Barrett (eds.) (2001). *The Text of the Earliest New Testament Manuscripts.* Revised ed. Chicago: Tyndale.

Constantinou Eugenia Scarvelis (2012). "Banned from the Lectionary: Excluding the Apocalypse of John from the Orthodox New Testament Canon," in *The Canon of the Bible and the Apocrypha in the Churches of the East*, edited by V. S. Hovhanessian. Bible *in the Christian Orthodox Tradition.* New York: Peter Lang, 2:51–61, here 52.

Conzelmann, H. (1973). *History of Primitive Christianity.* Translated by J. E. Steely. Nashville, TN: Abingdon.

Cowley, R. W. (1974). "The Biblical Canon of the Ethiopian Church Today," *Ostkirchliche Studien* 23: 318–23.

Crawford, S. W. (2008). *Rewriting Scripture in Second Temple Times: Studies in the Dead Sea Scrolls and Related Literature.* Grand Rapids, MI: Eerdmans.

Crawford, S. W. (2019). *Scribes and Scrolls at Qumran.* Grand Rapids, MI: Eerdmans.

Crehan, F. J. (1975). "The Bible in the Roman Catholic Church from Trent to the Present Day," in *The Cambridge History of the Bible: The West from the Reformation to the Present Day*, edited by S. Greenslade. Cambridge: Cambridge University Press, pp. 3:199–237.

Croy, N. C. (2003). *The Mutilation of Mark's Gospel.* Nashville, TN: Abingdon.

Dahl, N. A. (1978). "The Origin of the Earliest Prologues to the Pauline Letters," *Semeia* 12: 233–77.

Danielou, J. (1964). *The Theology of Jewish Christianity*. A History of Early Christian Doctrine before the Council of Nicaea. Vol. 1 of 3. London: Darton, Longman & Todd, 1964.

Daube, D. ([1956] 1998). *The New Testament and Rabbinic Judaism*. London: Oxford University Press. Reprinted by Hendrickson.

Davies, A. T. (1979). *Anti-Semitism and the Foundations of Christianity*. New York: Paulist.

Delamarter, S. (2002). *A Scripture Index to Charlesworth's The Old Testament Pseudepigrapha*. Sheffield: Sheffield Academic Press.

Delling, G. (1972). "*Hymnos*," in *TDNT*, edited by Gerhard Friedrich. Grand Rapids, MI: Eerdmans, pp. 8:489–93.

deSilva, D. A. (2011). "Pseudepigrapha," in *The Oxford Encyclopedia of the Books of the Bible*, edited by M. D. Coogan. Oxford New York: Oxford University Press. Pp. 2:212–28.

deSilva, D. A. (2012). *The Jewish Teachers of Jesus, James, and Jude: What Earliest Christianity Learned from the Apocrypha and Pseudepigrapha*. Oxford: Oxford University Press.

deSilva, D. A. (2018). *Introducing the Apocrypha: Message, Context, and Significance*. 2nd ed. Waco, TX: Baylor University Press.

Dibelius, M. (1982). *From Tradition to Gospel*. Cambridge: James Clarke.

Donelson, L. R. (1986). *Pseudepigraphy and Ethical Argument in the Pastoral Epistles*. HUT 22. Tübingen: Mohr Siebeck.

Dormandy, M. (2018). "How the Books Became the Bible: The Evidence for Canon Formation from Work-Combination in Manuscripts," *TC: A Journal of Biblical Textual Criticism* 23: 1–39.

Duff, J. (1999). "A Reconsideration of Pseudepigraphy in Early Christianity," *Tyndale Bulletin* 50(2).

Dungan, D. L. (2007). *Constantine's Bible: Politics and the Making of the New Testament*. Minneapolis, MN: Fortress Press.

Dunn, J. D. G. (1987). "The Problem of Pseudonymity," in *The Living Word*, edited by J. D. G. Dunn. Philadelphia, PA: Fortress Press, pp. 65–85.

Dunn, J. D. G. (1991). *The Parting of the Ways between Christianity and Judaism and Their Significance for the Character of Christianity*. Philadelphia, PA: Trinity Press International.

Dunn, J. D. G. (1997). "Pseudepigraphy," in *Dictionary of the Later New Testament and its Development*, edited by R. P. Martin and P. H. Davids. Downers Grove, IL: InterVarsity Press, pp. 977–84.

Dunn, J. D. G. (2003). *Jesus Remembered*. Vol. 1 of *Christianity in the Making*. Grand Rapids, MI: Eerdmans.

Dunn, J. D. G. (2005). *A New Perspective on Jesus: What the Quest for the Historical Jesus Missed*. Acadia Studies in Bible and Theology. Grand Rapids, MI: Baker Academic.

Dunn, J. D. G. (2013). "The Rise and Expansion of Christianity in the First Three Centuries: Why and How Did Embryonic Christianity Expand beyond the Jewish People?" in *The Rise and Expansion of Christianity in the First Three Centuries of the Common Era*, edited by C. K. Rothschild and J. Schröter. WUNT 301. Tübingen: Mohr Siebeck, pp. 197–203.

Dunne, J. A. (2014). *Esther and Her Elusive God*. Eugene, OR: Wipf & Stock.

Edrei, A., and D. Mendels (2007). "A Split Jewish Diaspora: Its Dramatic Consequences," *JSP* 16(2): 91–137.

Ehrman, B. D. (1993). *The Orthodox Corruption of Scripture: The Effect of Early Christological Controversies on the Text of the New Testament*. New York: Oxford University Press.

Ehrman, B. D. (2003a). *Lost Christianities: The Battles for Scripture and the Faiths We Never Knew*. New York: Oxford University Press.

Ehrman, B. D. (2003b). *Lost Scriptures: Books That Did Not Make It into the New Testament.* Oxford: Oxford University Press.

Ehrman, B. D. (2005). *Misquoting Jesus: The Story Behind Who Changed the Bible and Why.* San Francisco, CA: HarperSanFrancisco.

Ehrman, B. D. (2011). *Forged: Writing in the Name of God—Why the Bible's Authors Are Not Who We Think They Are.* New York: HarperCollins.

Ehrman, B. D., and M. W. Holmes (eds.) (2014). *The Text of the New Testament in Contemporary Research: Essays on the Status Quaestionis.* 2nd ed. Leiden: Brill.

Ehrman, B. D., and Z. Plese (2011). *The Apocryphal Gospels: Texts and Translations.* Oxford: Oxford University Press.

Elliott, J. K. (ed.) (1993). *The Apocryphal New Testament: A Collection of Apocryphal Christian Literature in an English Translation Based on M. R. James.* Oxford: Clarendon.

Elliott, J. K. (2011). "Apocrypha, New Testament," in *The Oxford Encyclopedia of the Books of the Bible*, edited by M. D. Coogan. Oxford: Oxford University Press, pp. 1:60–9.

Elliott, J. K. (2012). "The 'Apocryphal' New Testament," in *The New Cambridge History of the Bible: From Beginnings to 600*, edited by J. C. Paget and J. Schaper. Cambridge: Cambridge University Press, pp. 1:455–78.

Ellis, E. E. (1991a). *The Old Testament in Early Christianity.* WUNT 1/54. Tübingen.

Epp, E. (1997a). "The Codex and Literacy in Early Christianity and at Oxyrhynchus: Issues Raised by Harry Y. Gamble's Books and Readers in the Early Church," *Critical Review of Books in Religion* 10: 15–37.

Epp, E. (1997b). "Textual Criticism in the Exegesis of the New Testament, with an Excursus on Canon," in *Handbook to Exegesis of the New Testament*, edited by S. E. Porter. New Testament Tools and Studies 25. Leiden: Brill, pp. 73–91.

Epp, E. (1999). "The Multivalence of the Term 'Original Text' in New Testament Textual Criticism," *Harvard Theological Review* 92: 245–81.

Epp, E. (2002a). "Issues in New Testament Textual Criticism," in *Rethinking New Testament Textual Criticism*, edited by D. A. Black. Grand Rapids, MI: Baker, pp. 17–76.

Epp, E. (2002b). "Issues in the Interrelation of New Testament Textual Criticism and Canon," in *The Canon Debate*, edited by L. M. McDonald and J. A. Sanders. Peabody: Hendrickson, pp. 485–515.

Epp, E. (2004). "The Oxyrhynchus New Testament Papyri: 'Not without Honor Except in Their Hometown'?" *Journal of Biblical Literature* 123: 5–55.

Epp, E. (2005a). *Junia: The First Woman Apostle.* Minneapolis, MN: Fortress Press.

Epp, E. (2005b). *Perspectives on New Testament Textual Criticism: Collected Essays, 1962–2004.* Supplements to Novum Testamentum 116. Leiden: Brill.

Epp, E. (2011a). "Textual Criticism and New Testament Interpretation," in *Method and Meaning: Essays on New Testament Interpretation in Honor of Harold W. Attridge*, edited by A. B. McGowan and K. H. Richards. Atlanta, GA: SBL Press, pp. 79–105.

Epp, E. (2011b). "Traditional 'Canons' of New Testament Textual Criticism: Their Value, Validity, and Viability—or Lack Thereof," in *The Textual History of the Greek New Testament: Changing Views in Contemporary Research*, edited by K. Wachtel and M. W. Holmes. SBL 8. Atlanta, GA: SBL Press, pp. 79–127.

Epp, E. (2013a). "Textual Clusters: Their Past and Future in New Testament Textual Criticism," in *The Text of the New Testament in Contemporary Research: Essays on the* Status Quaestionis, 2nd ed., edited by B. D. Ehrman and M. W. Holmes. Leiden: Brill, pp. 519–77.

Epp, E. (2013b). "The Papyrus Manuscripts of the New Testament," in *The Text of the New Testament in Contemporary Research: Essays on the Status Quaestionis*, 2nd ed., edited by B. D. Ehrman and M. W. Holmes. Leiden: Brill, pp. 1–39.

Epp, E. (2014a). "In the Beginning Was the New Testament Text, but Which Text? A Consideration of 'Ausgangstext' and 'Initial Text,'" in *Texts and Traditions: Essays in Honour of J. Keith Elliott*, edited by P. Doble and J. Kloha. NTTSD 47. Leiden: Brill.

Epp, E. (2014b). "Textual Clusters: Their Past and Future in New Testament Textual Criticism," in *The Text of the New Testament in Contemporary Research: Essays on the Status Quaestionis*, 2nd ed., edited by B. D. Ehrman and M. W. Holmes. Leiden: Brill, pp. 519–79.

Evans, C. A. (2001). "The Dead Sea Scrolls and the Canon of Scripture in the Time of Jesus," in *The Bible at Qumran: Text, Shape, and Interpretation*, edited by P. W. Flint. Grand Rapids, MI: Eerdmans, pp. 67–79.

Evans, C. A. (2002). "The Scriptures of Jesus and His Earliest Followers," in *The Canon Debate*, edited by L. M. McDonald and J. A. Sanders. Peabody, MA: Hendrickson, pp. 185–95.

Evans, C. A. (2005). *Ancient Texts for New Testament Studies: A Guide to the Background Literature*. Peabody, MA: Hendrickson.

Evans, C. A. (2011). "Textual Criticism and Textual Confidence: How Reliable Is Scripture?" in *The Reliability of the New Testament: Bart D. Ehrman and Daniel B. Wallace in Dialogue*, edited by R. B. Stewart. Minneapolis, MN: Fortress Press, pp. 161–72.

Evans, C. A. (2015). "How Long Were Late Antique Books in Use? Possible Implications for New Testament Textual Criticism," *BBR* 25(1): 23–37.

Evans, C. A. (2017). "Jesus and the Beginnings of the Christian Canon," in *When Texts Are Canonized*, edited by T. H. Lim. RJS 359. Providence: Brown Judaic Studies, pp. 95–107.

Evans, C. A. (2020). *Jesus and the Manuscripts: What We Can Learn from the Oldest Texts*. Peabody, MA: Hendrickson.

Evans, C. A., and D. A. Hagner (eds.) (1993). *Anti-Semitism and Early Christianity: Issues of Polemic and Faith*. Minneapolis, MN: Fortress Press.

Ferguson, E. (1997). "Hymns," in *Encyclopedia of Early Christianity*, 2nd ed. New York: Garland Press, pp. 1:748–51.

Ferguson, E. (2003). *Backgrounds of Early Christianity*. 3rd ed. Grand Rapids, MI: Eerdmans.

Ferguson, E. (2006). "Baptism," in *NIBD*, edited by K. D. Sakenfeld, general editor. Nashville, TN: Abingdon, pp. 1:390–5.

Ferguson, E. (2008). "Creeds, Councils, and Canons," in *Oxford Handbook of Early Christian Studies*, edited by S. A. Harvey and D. G. Hunter. Oxford: Oxford University Press, pp. 427–45.

Ferguson, E. (2009). *Baptism in the Early Church: History, Theology, and Liturgy in the First Five Centuries*. Grand Rapids, MI: Eerdmans.

Filoramo, G. (1990). *A History of Gnosticism*. Cambridge: Blackwell.

Flint, P. W. (1999). "'Apocrypha,' Other Previously Known Writings, and 'Pseudepigrapha' in the Dead Sea Scrolls," in *The Dead Sea Scrolls after Fifty Years*, edited by P. W. Flint and J. C. VanderKam. Leiden: Brill, pp. 2:24–66.

Flusser, D. (1988). *Judaism and the Origins of Christianity*. Jerusalem: Magnes Press.

Foucault, M. (1984). "What Is an Author?" in *The Foucault Reader*, edited by P. Rabinow. New York: Random House, pp. 101–20.

Fox, R. L. (1987). *Pagans and Christians*. Perennial Library. New York: Harper & Row.

France, R. (1971). *Jesus and the Old Testament*. London: Tyndale.

Frend, W. H. C. (1982). *The Early Church*. Philadelphia, PA: Fortress Press.

Frend, W. H. C. (1984). *The Rise of Christianity*. Philadelphia, PA: Fortress Press.
Frey, J. (2019). "From Canonical to Apocryphal Texts: The Quest for Processes of 'Apocryphication' in Early Jewish and Early Christian Literature," in *Between Canonical and Apocrypha Texts: Processes of Reception, Rewriting, and Interpretation in Early Judaism and Early Christianity*, edited by Jorg Roder and Jörg Frey. WUNT 419. Leiden: Brill, pp. 1–43.
Fricke, K. D. (1991). "The Apocrypha in the Luther Bible," in *The Apocrypha in Ecumenical Perspective*, edited by S. Meuer. UBS Monograph Series No. 6. New York: United Bible Societies, pp. 46–87.
Gager, J. (1983). *The Origins of Anti-Semitism: Attitudes toward Judaism in Pagan and Christian Antiquity*. New York: Oxford University Press.
Gallagher, E. L. (2012). *Hebrew Scripture in Patristic Biblical Theory: Canon, Language, Text*. VCS 14. Leiden: Brill.
Gallagher, E. L. (2014). "Writings Labeled 'Apocrypha' in Latin Patristic Sources," in *Sacra Scriptura: How "Non-Canonical" Texts Functioned in Early Judaism and Early Christianity*, edited by J. H. Charlesworth and L. M. McDonald. London: Bloomsbury T&T Clark, pp. 1–14.
Gallagher, E. L. (2016). "Origen via Rufinus on the New Testament Canon," *NTS* 62(3): 461–76.
Gallagher, E. L., and J. Meade (2017). *The Biblical Canon Lists from Early Christianity: Texts and Analysis*. Oxford: Oxford University Press.
Gamble, H. Y. (1995). *Books and Readers in the Early Church: A History of Early Christian Texts*. New Haven, CT: Yale University Press.
Gamble, H. Y. (2002). "The New Testament Canon: Recent Research and the Status Quaestionis," in *The Canon Debate*, edited by L. M. McDonald and J. A. Sanders. Peabody, MA: Hendrickson, pp. 267–94.
Ganz, D. (2012). "Carolingian Bibles," in *The Cambridge History of the Bible: From 600–1450*, edited by R. Marsden and E. Ann Matter. Cambridge: Cambridge University Press, pp. 325–37.
Gathercole, S. (2015). "Other Apocryphal Gospels and the Historical Jesus," in *Oxford Handbook of Early Christian Apocrypha*, edited by A. Gregory and C. Tuckett. Oxford: Oxford University Press, pp. 250–68.
Gathercole, S. (2018). "The Alleged Anonymity of the Canonical Gospels," *JTS* 1 October.
Geer, T. C. Thomas C. Geer Jr. revised by Jean-François. "Analyzing and Categorizing New Testament Greek Manuscripts," pp. 497–518.
Gerhardsson, B. (1998). *Memory and Manuscript: Oral Tradition and Written Transmission in Rabbinic Judaism and Early Christianity* with *Tradition and Transmission in Early Christianity*. The Biblical Resource Series. Grand Rapids, MI: Eerdmans.
Gerhardsson, B. (2001). *The Reliability of the Gospel Tradition*. Peabody, MA: Hendrickson.
Goppelt, L. (1962, trans. 1970). *Apostolic and Post-Apostolic Times*. Translated by R. A. Guelich. London: Adam & Charles Black.
Grant, R. M. (1941). "The Oldest Gospel Prologues," *Anglican Theological Review* 23: 231–45.
Grant, R. M. (1961). *Gnosticism: A Source Book of Heretical Writings from the Early Christian Period*. New York: Harper.
Grant, R. M. (1965). *The Formation of the New Testament*. New York: Harper & Row.
Grant, R. M. (1970). "The New Testament Canon," in *The Cambridge History of the Bible*, Vol. 1: *From the Beginnings to Jerome*, edited by P. R. Ackroyd and C. F. Evans. Cambridge: Cambridge Univeristy Press, p. 284–308.

Grant, R. M. (1972). *A Historical Introduction to the New Testament*. New York: Simon & Schuster.

Grant, R. M. (1977). *Early Christianity and Society*. New York: Harper & Row.

Guignard, C. (2015). "The Original Language of the Muratorian Fragment," *Journal of Theological Studies* 66(2): 596–624.

Gupta, N. (2021). *RBL Review* of Christopher R. Hutson, *First and Second Timothy and Titus*. Grand Rapids, MI: Baker.

Guthrie, D. (1965). "The Development of the Idea of Canonical Pseudepigrapha in New Testament Criticism," in *The Authorship and Integrity of the New Testament*, edited by K. Aland. London: SPCK, pp. 15–39. Originally published in *Vox Evangelica* 1 (1962): 43–59.

Hahneman, G. M. (1992). *The Muratorian Fragment and the Development of the Canon*. Oxford Theological Monographs. Oxford: Clarendon.

Harnack, A. von (1908). *The Mission and Expansion of Christianity in the First Three Centuries*. Translated by J. Moffatt. London: Williams and Norgate.

Harnack, A. von (1925). *The Origin of the New Testament and the Most Important Consequences of the New Creation*. Translated by J. R. Wilkinson. New York: Macmillan.

Harrington, D. J. (2002). "The Old Testament Apocrypha in the Early Church and Today," in *The Canon Debate*, edited by L. M. McDonald and J. A. Sanders. Peabody, MA: Hendrickson, pp. 196–210.

Harrison, E. F. (1985). *The Apostolic Church*. Grand Rapids, MI: Eerdmans.

Heemstra, M. (2010). *The Fiscus Judaicus and the Parting of the Ways*. XIII. WUNT 2.241. Tübingen: Mohr Siebeck.

Hendel, R. (2016). "Prologue to The Hebrew Bible: A Critical Edition," in *Steps to a New Edition of the Hebrew Bible*, edited by Ron Hendel. Atlanta, GA: SBL Press, pp. 15–39.

Hengel, M. (1974). *Judaism and Hellenism: Studies in Their Encounter in Palestine during the Early Hellenistic Period*. 2 vols. Translated by J. Bowden. Philadelphia, PA: Fortress Press.

Hengel, M. (2002). *The Septuagint as Christian Scripture: Its Prehistory and the Problem of Its Canon*. Translated by R. Hanhart. Grand Rapids, MI: Baker.

Henze, M. and L. I. Lied (eds.) (2019). *The Old Testament Pseudepigrapha: Fifty Years of the Pseudepigrapha Section at the SBL*. EJL. Atlanta, GA: SBL Press.

Herford, R. T. (2003). *Christianity in Talmud and Midrash*. London: Williams & Norgate, 1903; reprinted in Eugene, Oregon by Wipf & Stock.

Heron, A. I. C. (2005). "Doctrine of the Canon," in *The Encyclopedia of Christianity*, edited by E. Fahlbusch, J. Milic, J. Mbiti, translated by G. W. Bromiley. Grand Rapids, MI: Eerdmans, pp. 1:344–5.

Hill, C. E. (2016). "'The Truth Above All Demonstration': Scripture in the Patristic Period to Augustine," in *The Enduring Authority of the Christian Scriptures*, edited by D. A. Carson. Grand Rapids, MI: Eerdmans, pp. 43–88.

Hofius, O. (1992). "Isolated Sayings of Jesus," in *New Testament Apocrypha*, edited by W. Schneemelcher and translated by R. M. Wilson. Revised ed. Louisville, KY: Westminster John Knox, pp. 1:88–91.

Holmes, M. (1981). "Origen and the Inerrancy of Scriptures," *JETS* 24: 221–31.

Holmes, M. (1991). "Textual Criticism," in *New Testament Criticism & Interpretation*, edited by D. A. Black and D. S. Dockery. Grand Rapids, MI: Zondervan, pp. 101–34.

Holmes, M. (2014). "When Criteria Conflict," in *Texts and Traditions: Essays in Honour of J. Keith Elliott*, edited by P. Noble and J. Kloha. DNTTSD 47. Leiden: Brill, pp. 11–24.

Horsley, G. H. R. (ed.) (1981). *New Documents Illustrating Early Christianity: A Review of the Greek Inscriptions and Papyri in 1977*. North Ryde, N. S. W., Australia: Ancient History Documentary Research Centre, Macquarie University.

Horst, van der P. W. (1994). *Hellenism–Judaism–Christianity: Essays on Their Interaction*. Kampen: Kok Pharos.

Houghton, A. G. (2016). *The Latin New Testament: A Guide to Its Early History, Texts, and Manuscripts*. Oxford: Oxford University Press.

Hovhanessian, V. S. (ed.) (2011). *The Canon of the Bible and the Apocrypha in the Churches of the East*. Reviewed by L. M. McDonald in *RBL*, September 27, 2013. http://www.bookreviews.org/bookdetail.asp?TitleId=8951.

Hovhanessian, V. S. (ed.) (2012b). "The Canon of Scripture in the Orthodox Church," pp. 1–6, and "New Testament Apocrypha and the Armenian Version of the Bible," pp. 63–87, in V. S. Hovhanessian, *The Canon of the Bible and the Apocrypha in the Churches of the East. Bible in the Christian Orthodox Tradition*. New York: Peter Lang.

Hull, R. F. (2011). *The Story of the New Testament Text: Movers, Materials, Methods, and Models*. SBL 58. Atlanta, GA: Society of Biblical Literature.

Hultgren, A. J., and S. Haggmark (1996). *The Earliest Christian Heretics: Readings from Their Opponents*. Minneapolis, MN: Fortress Press.

Hurtado, L. W. (1998). "The Origins of the *Nomina Sacra*: A Proposal," *Journal of Biblical Literature* 117: 655–73.

Hurtado, L. W. (2003). *Lord Jesus Christ: Devotion to Jesus in Earliest Christianity*. Grand Rapids, MI: Eerdmans.

Hurtado, L. W. (2005). *How on Earth Did Jesus Become a God?* Grand Rapids, MI: Eerdmans.

Hurtado, L. W. (2006). *The Earliest Christian Artifacts: Manuscripts and Christian Origins*. Grand Rapids, MI: Eerdmans.

Hurtado, L. W. (2016). *Destroyer of the Gods: Early Christian Distinctiveness in the Roman World*. Waco, TX: Baylor University Press.

Hurtado, L. W. (2018). *Honoring the Son: Jesus in Earliest Christian Devotional Practice*. Bellingham: Lexham, 2018.

Isaac, E. (2012). "The Bible in Ethiopic," in *The New Cambridge History of the Bible: From 600–1450*, edited by R. Marsden and E. Ann Matter. Cambridge: Cambridge University Press, pp. 110–22.

Jenson, R. W. (2010). *Canon and Creed Interpretation*. Louisville, KY: Westminster John Knox Press. See McDonald review in *RBL* review in: http://www.bookreviews.org (2011).

Jeremias, J. (1964). *The Unknown Sayings of Jesus*. 2nd ed. London: SPCK.

Jeremias, J. (1969). *Jerusalem in the Time of Jesus*. Translated by F. H. Cave and C. H. Cave. Philadelphia, PA: Fortress Press.

Jergens, W. (1979). *Faith of the Early Fathers*. 3 vols. Collegeville, Minnesota: Liturgical Press.

Jewett, R. (2007). *Romans: A Commentary*. Hermeneia. Minneapolis, MN: Fortress Press.

Johnson, L. T. (1989). "The New Testament's Anti-Jewish Slander and Conventions of Ancient Polemic," *JBL* 108: 419–41.

Johnson, L. T. (2003). *The Creed: What Christians Believe and Why It Matters*. Garden City, NY: Doubleday.

Jonas, H. (1963). *The Gnostic Religion*. Boston, MA: Beacon.

Kalin, E. R. (1967). "Argument from Inspiration in the Canonization of the New Testament." ThD diss., Harvard University.

Kalin, E. R. (1971). "The Inspired Community: A Glance at Canon History," *Concordia Theological Monthly* 42: 541–49.

Kealy, S. F. (1979). "The Canon: An African Contribution," *Biblical Theology Bulletin* 9: 13–26.
Kelley, J. N. D. (1972). *Early Christian Creeds*. 3rd ed. London: Longman.
Kelley, J. N. D. (1978). *Early Christian Doctrines*. New York: Harper & Row.
King, K. (2003a). *What Is Gnosticism?* Cambridge, MA: Harvard University Press.
King, K. (2003b). *The Gospel of Mary*. Santa Rosa: Polebridge Press.
King, K. (2013). "Theologies and Mission Practices among the so-called 'Heretics'," in *The Rise and Expansion of Christianity in the First Three Centuries of the Common Era*, edited by C. K. Rothschild and J. Schröter. WUNT 301. Tübingen: Mohr Siebeck, pp. 441–55.
Klassen, W. (1986). "Anti-Judaism in Early Christianity: The State of the Question," in *Anti-Judaism in Early Christianity*. I. *Paul and the Gospels*, edited by P. Richardson and D. Granskou. Waterloo, ON: Wilfrid Laurier University Press, pp. 5–12.
Klijn, A. F. J., and G. J. Reinink (1973). *Patristic Evidence for Jewish Christian Sects*. Leiden: Brill, pp. 1–31.
Klugkist, A. C., and G. L. Reinink (1999). *After Bardaisan*: *Studies on Continuity and Change*. Syriac Christianity in Honour of Professor Han. J. W. Drijvers (Orientalia Lovaniensia Analecta). Leuven: Peeters.
Knibb, M. A. (2006). "Language, Translation, Versions, and Text of the Apocrypha," in *The Oxford Handbook of Biblical Studies*, edited by J. W. Rogerson and J. M. Lieu. Oxford: Oxford University Press, pp. 159–83.
Koester, H. (1957). *Synoptische Überlieferung bei den apostolischen Vätern*. Berlin: Academie Verlag, diss. Marburg, 1953; *Texte und Untersuchungen*, 65. Berlin.
Koester, H. (1971). "GNOMAI DIAPHOROI: The Origin and Nature of Diversification in the History of Early Christianity," in *Trajectories through Early Christianity*, edited by J. M. Robisnon and H. Koester, Philadelphia, PA: Fortress Press, pp. 114–57.
Koester, H. (1982). *Introduction to the New Testament*. 2 vols. Philadelphia, PA: Fortress Press.
Koester, H. (1989). "The Text of the Synoptic Gospels in the Second Century," in *Gospel Traditions in the Second Century: Origins, Recensions, Text, and Transmission*, edited by W. L. Peterson. Christianity and Judaism in Antiquity, 3. Notre Dame: University of Notre Dame Press, pp. 19–37.
Koester, H. (1990). *Ancient Christian Gospels: Their History and Development*. Philadelphia, PA: Trinity Press International.
Kramer, R. S. (1998). *When Aseneth Met Joseph. A Late Antique Tale of the Biblical Patriarch and His Egyptian Wife, Reconsidered*. New York: Oxford University Press.
Kratz, R. G. (2006). "The Growth of the Old Testament," in *The Oxford Handbook of Biblical Studies*, edited by J. W. Rogerson and J. M. Lieu. Oxford: Oxford University Press, pp. 459–88.
Kraus, T. J. (2007). *Ad Fontes: Original Manuscripts and Their Significance for Studying Early Christianity: Selected Essays*. TENT 3. Leiden: Brill.
Kraus, T. J., and T. Nicklas (2006). "The World of New Testament Manuscripts," in *New Testament Manuscripts: Their Texts and Their World*, edited by T. J. Kraus and T. Nicklas. TENT 2. Leiden: Brill, pp. 1–11.
Kruger, M. J. (2012). *Canon Revisited: Establishing the Origins and Authority of the New Testament Books*. Wheaton, IL: Crossway.
Kruger, M. J. (2013). *The Question of Canon: Challenging the Status Quo in the New Testament Debate*. Downers Grove, IL: InterVarsity Press.
Kruger, M. J. (2014). "Early Christian Attitudes toward the Reproduction of Texts," in *The Early Text of the New Testament*, edited by C. E. Hill and M. J. Kruger. Oxford: Oxford University Press, pp. 63–80.

Kruger, M. J. (2014). "Origen's List of New Testament Books in *Homiliae in Josuam* 7.1: A Fresh Look," in *Mark, Manuscripts, and Monotheism: Essays in Honor of Larry W. Hurtado*, edited by C. Keith and D. T. Roth. LNTS (JSNTS) 528. London: Bloomsbury, pp. 99–117.

Kurek-Chomycz, D. A. (2006). "Is There an 'Anti-Pricscan' Tendency in the Manuscripts? Some Textual Problems with Prisca and Aquila," *JBL* 125(1): 107–28.

Ladd, G. E. (1986). "Pseudepigrapha," in *The International Standard Bible Encyclopedia*, edited by G. Bromiley, gen. Grand Rapids, MI: Eerdmans, pp. 3:1040–3.

Lattke, M. (1991). *Hymnus: Materialien Zu Einer Geschichte Der Antiken Hymnologie*. Freiburg: Novum Testamentum Et Orbis Antiquus; German edition.

Layton, B. (1987). *The Gnostic Scriptures; A New Translation with Annotations and Introductions*. Garden City, NY: Doubleday.

Lazare, B. (2010). *Anti-Semitism: Its History and Causes*. Cosimo Classics. New York: Kessinger Publishing.

Leaney, A. R. C. (1984). *The Jewish and Christian World*. Cambridge: Cambridge University Press.

Leiman, S. Z. (ed.) (1974). *The Canon and Masorah of the Hebrew Bible: An Introductory Reader*. New York: Ktav.

Leiman, S. Z. (ed.) (1976). *The Canonization of Hebrew Scripture: The Talmudic and Midrashic Evidence*. Hamden: Archon Books.

Levine, A.-J. (2017). "Bearing False Witness: Common Errors Made about Early Judaism" in *The Jewish Annotated New Testament*, 2nd ed., edited by A.-J. Levine and M. Z. Brettler. Oxford: Oxford University Press, pp. 118–19, 249–50, 759–63.

Levine, L. I. (2005). *Ancient Synagogue: The First Thousand Years*. 2nd ed. New Haven, CT: Yale University Press, pp. 135–51.

Lewis, J. P. (1991). "Some Aspects of the Problem of Inclusion of the Apocrypha," in *The Apocrypha in Ecumenical Perspective*, edited by S. Meuer. UBS Monograph Series No. 6. New York: United Bible Societies, pp. 161–207.

Lewis, J. P. (2002). "Jamnia Revisited," in *The Canon Debate*, edited by McDonald and Sanders. Peabody, MA: Hendrickson.

Liere, F. van (2012). "The Latin Bible, c. 900 to the Council of Trent, 1546," in *The New Cambridge History of the Bible: From 600–1450*, edited by R. Marsden and E. Ann Matter. Cambridge: Cambridge University Press, pp. 93–109.

Liere, F. van (2014). *An Introduction to the Medieval Bible*. New York: Cambridge University Press, pp. 4–15.

Lieu, J. M. (1994). "'The Parting of the Ways': Theological Construct or Historical Reality?" *JSNT* 56: 101–19.

Lieu, J. M. (2015). *Marcion and the Making of a Heretic: God and Scripture in the Second Century*. Cambridge: Cambridge University Press.

Light, L. (2011). "The Bible and the Individual: The Thirteenth-Century," in *The Practice of the Bible in the Middle Ages: Production, Reception, and Performance in Western Christianity*, edited by S. Boynton and D. J. Reilly. New York: Columbia University Press, pp. 228–46.

Light, L. (2012). "The Thirteenth Century and the Paris Bible," in *The New Cambridge History of the Bible: From 600–1450*, edited by R. Marsden and E. A. Matter. Cambridge: Cambridge University Press, pp. 380–91.

Lightfoot, J. ([1859] 1974). *A Commentary on the New Testament from the Talmud and Hebraica*. First published in 1658 followed by the Oxford University Press, 1st ed. and reprinted by Grand Rapids, MI: Baker Book House. 4 vols.

Lim, T. H. (2009). "'All These He Composed through Prophecy'," in *Prophecy after the Prophets: The Contribution of the Dead Sea Scrolls to the Understanding of Biblical and Extra-Biblical Prophecy*, edited by K. De Troyer and A. Lange with assistance of Lucas L. Schulte. BET 52. Leuven: Peeters, pp. 61–73.

Lim, T. H. (2010). "Defilement of the Hands as a Principle Determining the Holiness of Scriptures," *JTS* 61(2): 1–15.

Lim, T. H. (2013). *The Formation of the Jewish Canon*. AYBRL. New Haven, CT: Yale University Press.

Lim, T. H. (ed.) (2017). *When Texts Are Canonized*. RJS 359. Providence, RI: Brown Judaic Studies, pp. 95–107.

Logan, A. H. B. (1996). *Gnostic Truth and Christian Heresy: A Study in the History of Gnosticism*. Edinburgh: T&T Clark.

Lohse, E. (1976). *The New Testament Environment*. Translated by J. E. Steeley. Nashville, TN: Abingdon.

Lüdemann, G. (1996). *Heretics: The Other Side of Early Christianity*. Translated by J. Bowden. Louisville, KY: Westminster/John Knox Press.

Luijendijk, A. (2002). "Sacred Scriptures as Trash: Biblical Papyri from Oxyrhynchus," *Vigiliae Christianae* 64: 217–54.

Luijendijk, A. (2008)."*Greetings in the Lord:*" *Early Christians and the Oxyrhynchus Papyri*. Harvard Theological Studies 59. Cambridge, MA: Harvard University Press.

Lupieri, E. (2002). *The Mandaeans: The Last Gnostics*. Grand Rapids, MI: Eerdmans.

Maccoby, H. (1988). *Early Rabbinic Writings: Cambridge Commentaries on the Writings of the Jewish and Christian World, 200 BC to AD 200*. Cambridge Commentaries on Writings of the Jewish and Christian World Book 3. Cambridge: Cambridge University Press.

MacMullen, R. (1984). *Christianizing the Roman Empire A.D. 100–400*. New Haven, CT: Yale University Press.

MacMullen, R., and E. N. Lane (eds.) (1992). *Paganism and Christianity 100–425 C.E.: A Sourcebook*. Minneapolis, MN: Fortress Press.

Malherbe, A. J. (1983). *Social Aspects of Early Christianity*. 2nd ed. Philadelphia, PA: Fortress Press.

Mara, M. G. (1992). "Apocrypha," in *Encyclopedia of the Early Church*, edited by A. Di Bernardino. New York: Oxford University Press, pp. 1:56–8.

Marcus, J. (2018). "The Gospel of Peter as a Jewish Christian Document," *NTS* 64(4): 473–94.

Marshall, I. H. in collaboration with Philip H. Towner (1999). *The Pastoral Epistles*. ICC. Edinburgh: T&T Clark.

Martin, R. P. (1982). "Hymns in the NT," in *International Standard Bible Encyclopedia*, gen. edited by G. W. Bromiley. Grand Rapids, MI: Eerdmans, pp. 2:788–90.

Massaux, E. (1986–93). *The Influence of the Gospel of Saint Matthew on Christian Literature before Saint Irenaeus*. Book 3. The Apologists and the Didache. New Gospel Studies 5/3. Leuven: Peeters-Mercer.

McArthur, H. K., and R. M. Johnston (1990). *They also Taught in Parables: Rabbinic Parables from the First Centuries of the Christian Era*. Grand Rapids, MI: Zondervan.

McDonald, Lee Martin (1992). "Anti-Marcionite Gospel Prologues," in *Anchor Bible Dictionary*, edited by D. N. Freedman. Garden City, NY: Doubleday, pp. 1:262–3.

McDonald, L. M. (1993). "Anti-Judaism in the Early Church Fathers," in *Anti-Semitism and Early Christianity: Issues of Polemic and Faith*, edited by C. A. Evans and D. Hagner. Minneapolis: Augsburg Fortress, pp. 215–52.

McDonald, L. M. (1996). "The Theological Integrity of the Biblical Canon in Light of Its Historical Development," *BBR* 4: 1–38.

McDonald, L. M. (2004). "The Gospels in Early Christianity: Their Origin, Use, and Authority," in *Reading the Gospels Today*, edited by S. E. Porter. Grand Rapids, MI: Eerdmans, pp. 150–78.

McDonald, L. M. (2006). *The Biblical Canon: Its Origin, Transmission, and Authority*. Peabody, MA: Hendrickson.

McDonald, L. M. (2011). *The Biblical Canon: Its Origin, Transmission, and Authority*. Revised ed. Grand Rapids, MI: Baker.

McDonald, L. M. (2013). *The Story of Jesus in History and Faith*. Grand Rapids, MI: Baker.

McDonald, L. M. (2013). "Hellenism and the Biblical Canons: Is There a Connection?" in *Christian Origins and Hellenistic Judaism: Social and Literary Contexts for the New Testament*, edited by S. E. Porter and A. W. Pitts. TENT 10. Leiden: Brill, pp. 13–49.

McDonald, L. M. (2014). "The *Odes of Solomon* in Ancient Christianity," in *Sacra Scriptura: How "Non-Canonical" Texts Functioned in Early Judaism and Early Christianity*, edited by J. H. Charlesworth and L. M. McDonald. JCTS, 20. London: Bloomsbury T&T Clark, pp. 108–36.

McDonald, L. M. (2017). *The Formation of the Bible*. Volume 1: *The Old Testament: Its Authority and Canonicity*. London: Bloomsbury T&T Clark.

McDonald, L. M. (2017). *The Formation of the Bible*. Volume 2: *The New Testament: Its Authority and Canonicity*. London: Bloomsbury T&T Clark.

McDonald, L. M. (2019). "The Reception of the Writings and Their Place in the Biblical Canon," in *The Oxford Handbook of the Writings of the Hebrew Bible*, edited by Donn F. Morgan. Oxford: Oxford University Press, pp. 397–413.

McDonald, L. M. (2020). "Forming Christian Scriptures as a Biblical Canon," in *Ancient Jewish and Christian Scriptures: New Developments in Canon Controversy*, edited by J. J. Collins, C. A. Evans, and L. M. McDonald. Louisville, KY: Westminster John Knox Press, pp. 26–44.

McDonald, L. M. (2021a). "A Canonical History of the Old Testament Apocrypha," in *The Oxford Handbook of the Apocrypha*, edited by G. S. Oegema. Oxford: Oxford University Press, pp. 24–51.

McDonald, L. M. (2021). "Fluidity in the Early Formation of the Hebrew Bible," *Hebrew Studies* 61: 73–96.

McDonald, L. M. (2022). "The Emergence of the Biblical Canons in Orthodox Christianity," in *The Oxford Handbook of the Bible in Orthodox Christianity*, edited by E. Pentiuc. Oxford: Oxford University Press.

McGuckin, J. A. (1995). *At the Lighting of the Lamps: Hymns of the Ancient Church*. Oxford: SLG.

McGuckin, J. A. (2008). "Poetry and Hymnography (2): The Greek World," in *The Oxford Handbook on Early Christian Studies*, edited by S. A. Harvey and D. G. Hunter. London: Oxford University Press, pp. 641–56.

Meade, D. G. (1986). *Pseudonymity and Canon: An Investigation into the Relationship and Authority in Jewish and Earliest Christian Tradition*. Grand Rapids, MI: Eerdmans.

Meagher, J. C. (1979). "As the Twig Was Bent," in *Anti-Semitism and the Foundations of Christianity*, edited by A. T. Davies. New York: Paulist, pp. 1–26.

Meeks, W. A. (1983). *The First Urban Christians: The Social World of the Apostle Paul*. New Haven, CT: Yale University Press.

Meeks, W. A., and R. L. Wilken (1978). *Jews and Christians in Antioch in the First Four Centuries of the Common Era*. Missoula, MT: Scholars Press.

Metzger, B. M. (1963). "Explicit References in the Works of Origen to Variant Readings in New Testament Manuscripts," in *Biblical and Patristic Studies in Memory of Robert Pierce Casey*, edited by J. N. Birdsell and R. W. Thomson. Freiberg: Herder, pp. 78–95.

Metzger, B. M. (1968). "The Formulas Introducing Quotations of Scripture in the New Testament and in the Mishnah," in *Historical and Literary Studies: Pagan, Jewish, and Christian*, edited by B. M. Metzger. New Testament Tools and Studies 8. Leiden: Brill, pp. 52–63.

Metzger, B. M. (1972). "Literary Forgeries and Canonical Pseudepigrapha," *JBL* 91: 3–24.

Metzger, B. M. (1979). "St Jerome's Explicit References to Variant Readings in Manuscripts of the New Testament," in *Text and Interpretation. Studies in the New Testament Presented to Matthew Black*, edited by E. Best and R. McLachlan Wilson. Cambridge: Cambridge University Press, pp. 179–90.

Metzger, B. M. (1987). *The Canon of the New Testament: Its Origin, Development, and Significance*. Oxford: Clarendon Press.

Metzger, B. M. (2001). *The Bible in Translation: Ancient and English Versions*. Grand Rapids, MI: Baker.

Metzger, B. M., and B. D. Ehrman (2005). *The Text of the New Testament: Its Transmission, Corruption, and Restoration*. New York: Oxford University Press.

Meyer, B. F. (1986). *The Early Christians: Their World Mission and Self Discovery*. Good News Studies 16. Wilmington, DE: Michael Glazier.

Meyer, M. (ed.) (2007). *The Nag Hammadi Scriptures*. The International Edition San Francisco, CA: HarperSanFrancisco.

Milik, J. T. (1976). *The Books of Enoch: Aramaic Fragments of Qumran Cave 4*. Oxford: Clarendon Press.

Miller, J. (2010). "The Prophetologion: The Old Testament of Byzantine Christianity?" in *The Old Testament in Byzantium*, edited by P. Magdalino and R. S. Nelson. Washington, DC: Dumbarton Oaks Research Library and Collection, pp. 55–76.

Mitchell, M. M. (2006). "The Emergence of the Written Record," in *The Cambridge History of Christianity*, Vol. 1 *Origins to Constantine*, edited by M. Mitchell and F. M Young. Cambridge: Cambridge University Press, pp. 177–94.

Mitton, C. L. (1955). *The Formation of the Pauline Corpus of Letters*. London: Epworth Press.

Moberly, R. W. L. (2017). "Canon and Religious Truth: *An Appraisal of A New New Testament*," in *When Texts Are Canonized*, edited by T. H. Lim. Providence: Brown University Press, pp. 108–35.

Moore, G. F. (1921). "Christian Writers on Judaism," *HTR* 14: 200.

Moore, G. F. (1974). "Definition of the Jewish Canon and the Repudiation of Christian Scriptures," in *The Canon and Masorah of the Hebrew Bible*, edited by S. Z. Leiman. New York: Ktav, pp. 99–125.

Mroczek, E. (2016). *The Literary Imagination in Jewish Antiquity*. New York: Oxford University Press.

Mroczek, E. (2018). "Hidden Scriptures, Then and Now: Rediscovering 'Apocrypha'," *Interpretation* 72(4): 383–95.

Munier, Ch. (1992). "Canonical Collections," in *Encyclopedia of the Early Church*, edited by A. Di Berardino. New York: Oxford University Press, pp. 1:141–3.

Najman, H. (2003). *Seconding Sinai: The Development of Mosaic Discourse in Second Temple Judaism*. JSJSup 77. Leiden: Brill, pp. 1–69.

Najman, H. (2007). "How Should We Contextualize Pseudepigrapha? Imitation and Emulation in 4Ezra," in *The Dead Sea Scrolls and Other Early Jewish Studies in Honour of Florentino Garcia Martinez*, edited by A. Hilhorst, E. Puech, and E. Tigchelaar. Leiden: Brill.

Najman, H., and I. Peirano (2019). "Pseudepigraphy as an Interpretive Construct." In *The Old Testament Pseudepigrapha: Fifty Years of the Pseudepigrapha Section at the SBL*. Early Judaism and Its Literature, edited by Matthias Henze and Liv Ingeborg Lied. Atlanta: Society of Biblical Studies Press, pp. 331–58.

Nardoni, E. (1984). "Origen's Concept of Biblical Inspiration," *Second Century* 4: 9–23.

Neill, S. (1976). *Jesus through Many Eyes*. Philadelphia, PA: Fortress Press.

Nelson, R. S. (1991). "Canons," in *Oxford Dictionary of Byzantium*, editor-in-chief P. Kazhdan. New York: Oxford University Press, pp. 1:374.

Nersessian, V. (2001). *The Bible in the Armenian Tradition*. London: British Library.

Neusner, J. (1984). *Judaism in the Beginning of Christianity*. Philadelphia, PA: Fortress Press.

Neusner, J. (1984b). *Messiah in Context: Israel's History and Destiny in Formative Judaism*. Philadelphia, PA: Fortress Press.

Neusner, J. (1986). *Judaism in the Matrix of Christianity*. Philadelphia, PA: Fortress Press.

Neusner, J. (1987). *Judaism and Christianity in the Age of Constantine*. Chicago: University of Chicago Press.

Neusner, J. (1991). *Jews and Christians: The Myth of a Common Tradition*. Philadelphia, PA: Trinity Press International.

Neusner, J. (1994). *Rabbinic Literature and the New Testament: What We Cannot Show, We Do Not Know*. Valley Forge: Trinity Press International.

Neusner, J. (2002). *The Tosefta: Translated from the Hebrew with a New Introduction*. 2 vols. Peabody, MA: Hendrickson.

Neusner, J., and W. S. Green (1987). *Judaisms and Their Messiahs at the Turn of the Christian Era*. Edited by E. Frerichs. Cambridge: Cambridge University Press.

Neusner, J., and W. S. Green (1989). *Writing with Scripture: The Authority and Uses of the Hebrew Bible in the Torah of Formative Judaism*. Minneapolis, MN: Fortress Press.

Northcott, W. C. (1964). *Hymns in Christian Worship. The Use of Hymns in the Life of the Church*. Ecumenical Studies in Worship 13. Louisville, KY: John Knox, Press, 1964.

Oikonomos, E. (1991). "Deuterocanonicals in the Orthodox Church," in *The Apocrypha in Ecumenical Perspective*, edited by Siegfried Meuer. UBS Monograph 6. New York: United Bible Societies, pp. 17–32.

Osiek, C. (1999). *The Shepherd of Hermas*. Hermeneia. Minneapolis, MN: Fortress Press.

Pagels, E. (1975). *The Gnostic Paul: Gnostic Exegesis of the Pauline Letters*. Philadelphia, PA: Trinity Press International.

Pagels, E. (1979). *The Gnostic Gospels*. New York: Vintage.

Pagels, E. (2014). "Variants and Variance," in *Texts and Traditions: Essays in Honor of J. Keith Elliott*, edited by Peter Doble and Jeffrey Kloha. Leiden: Brill, pp. 25–34.

Paget, J. C. (2010). *Jews, Christians and Jewish Christians in Antiquity*. Tübingen: Mohr Siebeck.

Parker, D. C. (1997). *The Living Text of the Gospels*. Cambridge: Cambridge University Press.

Parkes, J. (1961). *The Conflict of the Church and the Synagogue*. Cleveland: World Publishing.

Patzia, A. G. (2011). *The Making of the New Testament: Origin, Collection, Text & Canon*. 2nd ed. Downers Grove, IL: InterVarsity Press.

Payne, P. B. (2009). *Man and Woman, One in Christ: An Exegetical and Theological Study of Paul's Letters*. Grand Rapids, MI: Zondervan.

Pearson, B. (1986). "Christians and Jews in First-Century Alexandria," in *Christians among Jews and Gentiles*, edited by G. W. E. Nickelsburg and G. W. MacRae. Philadelphia, PA: Fortress Press, pp. 18–36.

Pelikan, J. (2003). *Creedo: Historical and Theological Guide to Creeds and Confessions of Faith in the Christian Tradition*. New Haven, CT: Yale University Press.

Penner, K. M. (2010). "Citation Formulae as Indices to Canonicity in Early Jewish and Early Christian Literature," in *Jewish and Christian Scriptures: The Function of "Canonical" and "Non-Canonical" Religious Texts*, edited by J. H. Charlesworth and L. M. McDonald. Jewish and Christian Texts in Contexts and Related Studies 7. London: T&T Clark, pp. 62–84.

Penner, K. M. (2011). "Dead Sea Scrolls," in *The Oxford Encyclopedia of the Books of the Bible*, editor-in-chief M. D. Coogan. Oxford: Oxford University Press, pp. 1:173–92.

Pentiuc, E. J. (2014a). *The Old Testament in Eastern Orthodox Tradition*. Oxford: Oxford University Press.

Pentiuc, E. J. (2014b). "The Old Testament: Canon," in *The Concise Encyclopedia of Orthodox Christianity*, edited by J. A. McGuckin. Oxford: Wiley/Blackwell, pp. 341–3.

Perelmuter, H. G. (1989). *Siblings: Rabbinic Judaism and Early Christianity at their Beginnings*. New York: Paulist Press.

Perkins, P. (1980). *The Gnostic Dialogue*. New York: Paulist Press.

Perkins, P. (2002). "Gnosticism and the Christian Bible," in *The Canon Debate*, edited by L. M. McDonald and J. A. Sanders. Peabody, MA: Hendrickson, pp. 355–71.

Pfeiffer, R. (1998). *History of Classical Scholarship: From the Beginning to the End of the Hellenistic Age*. Oxford: Clarendon Press.

Piovanelli, P. (2013). "Scriptural Trajectories through Early Christianity, Late Antiquity, and Beyond," in *Forbidden Texts on the Western Frontier*, edited by T. Burke. The Christian Apocrypha in North American Perspectives. Eugene, OR: Cascade, pp. 95–110.

Poliakov, L. (1962). *The History of Anti-Semitism*. Translated by R. Howard. New York: Vanguard.

Porter, S. E. (1995). "Pauline Authorship and the Pastoral Epistles: Implications for Canon," *BBR* 5: 105–23.

Porter, S. E. (1996). "Pauline Authorship and the Pastoral Epistles: A Response to R. W. Wall's Response," *BBR* 6: 136.

Porter, S. E. (2007). "The Ending of John's Gospel," in *From Biblical Faith to Biblical Criticism: Essays in Honor of Lee Martin McDonald*, edited by C. A. Evans and W. Brackney. Macon, GA: Mercer University Press, pp. 55–73.

Porter, S. E. (2013). *How We Got the New Testament: Text, Transmission, Translation*. ASBT. Grand Rapids, MI: Baker.

Porter, S. E. (2015). *How We Got the New Testament: Text, Transmission, Translation*. ASBT. Series editors Craig A. Evans and Lee Martin McDonald. Grand Rapids, MI: Baker.

Porter, S. E., and A. W. Pitt (2008). "Paul's Bible, His Education and His Access to the Scriptures of Israel," *JGRChJ* 5: 9–41.

Porter, S. E., and A. W. Pitts (2015). *Fundamentals of New Testament Textual Criticism*. Grand Rapids, MI: Eerdmans.

Quasten, J. ([1950] 1975). *Patrology, Vol. II, The Ante-Nicene Literature After Irenaeus*. Utrecht: Spectrum, pp. 2:273–82.

Rajak, T. (2009). *Translation and Survival: The Greek Bible of the Ancient Jewish Diaspora*. Oxford: Oxford University Press.

Reed, A. Y. (2008). "Pseudepigraphy, Authorship, and the Reception of 'The Bible' in Late Antiquity," in *The Reception of and Interpretation of the Bible in Late Antiquity*, edited by L. DiTommaso and L. Turcescu. Leiden: Brill, pp. 467–89.

Reed, A. Y. (2009). "The Modern Invention of 'Old Testament Pseudepigrapha'," *Journal of Theological Studies*, New Series, 60(2) (October): 403–36.

Reed, A. Y. (2015). "The Afterlives of New Testament Apocrypha," *JBL* 133(2): 401–25.

Reicke, B. (1968). *The New Testament Era: The World of the Bible from 500 B.C. to A.D. 100*. Translated by D. E. Green. Philadelphia, PA: Fortress Press.

Reuss, E. W. (1891). *History of the Canon of the Holy Scriptures in the Christian Church*. Translated by D. Hunter. Edinburgh: Hunter.

Richards, E. R. (2004). *Paul and First-Century Letter Writing: Secretaries, Composition and Collection*. Downers Grove, IL: InterVarsity Press.

Richards, E. R. (2013). "Reading, Writing, and Manuscripts," in *The World of the New Testament: Cultural, Social, and Contexts*, edited by J. B. Green and L. M. McDonald. Grand Rapids, MI: Baker, pp. 345–66.

Richardson, C. C. (1970). *Early Christian Fathers*. New York: Macmillan.

Riesner, R. (1988). *Jesus als Lehrer: Ein Üntersuchung zum Ursprung der Evangelien-Überlieferung*. 3rd ed. WUNT 2.7. Tübingen: Mohr Siebeck.

Rist, M. (1972). "Pseudepigraphy and the Early Christians," in *Studies in New Testament and Early Christian Literature: Essays in Honor of Allen Wikgren*, edited by D. A. Aune. SNT 33. Leiden: Brill, pp. 75–91.

Roberts, M. J. (2008). "Poetry and Hymnography (1) Latin Poetry," in *The Oxford Handbook on Early Christian Studies*, edited by S. A. Harvey and D. G. Hunter. London: Oxford University Press, pp. 628–40.

Robinson, J. M. (1971). "Introduction," in *Trajectories through Early Christianity*, edited by J. M. Robinson and H. Koester. Philadelphia, PA: Fortress Press, pp. 1–19.

Robinson, J. M. (ed.) (1987, 1988, 1990). *The Nag Hammadi Library in English*. 3rd ed. San Francisco, CA: Harper & Row.

Rokeah, D. (1989). "Behind the Appearances," *Explorations* 3: 2–3.

Romodanovskaya, V. A. (2005). "Gennady's Bible," in *Orthodox Encyclopedia* (in Russian). Moscow: Russian Orthodox Encyclopedia, pp. 10:584–8.

Rompay, L. Van (2020). "1.1.3 The Syriac Canon," in *Textual History of the Bible: The Deuterocanonical Scriptures*, Vol. 2A, edited by A. Lange, gen. ed. F. Feder and M. Henze. Leiden: Brill, pp. 136–65.

Rothschild, C. K. (2017). *New Essays on the Apostolic Fathers*. WUNT 375. Tübingen: Mohr Siebeck.

Rothschild, C. K. (2018). "The Muratorian Fragment as Roman Fake," *NovT* 60: 55–82.

Rothschild, C. K. (2022). *The Muratorian Fragment*. WUNT. Tübingen: Mohr Siebeck.

Rouwhorst, G. (2012). "The Bible in Liturgy," in *The New Cambridge History of The Bible from the Beginnings to 600*, edited by James Carleton Paget and Joachim Schaper. Cambridge: Cambridge University Press, pp. 822–42.

Rudolph, K. (1983). *Gnosis: The Nature and History of Gnosticism*. San Francisco, CA: Harper & Row.

Ruether, R. (1974). *Faith and Fratricide: The Theological Roots of Anti-Semitism*. Minneapolis, MN: Seabury.

Salveson, A. (2006). "The Growth of the Apocrypha," in *The Oxford Handbook of Biblical Studies*, edited by J. W. Rogerson and Judith M. Lieu. Oxford: Oxford University Press, pp. 489–517.

Sanders, E. P. (ed.) (1980). *Jewish and Christian Self-Definition*. I. *The Shaping of Christianity in the Second and Third Centuries*. London: SCM.

Sanders, James A. (1991). "Stability and Fluidity in Text and Canon," in *Traditions of the Text: Studies Offered to Dominique Barthélemy in Celebration of His 70th Birthday*, edited by G. Norton and S. Pisano. Göttingen: Vandenhoech & Ruprecht, pp. 203–17.

Sanders, J. A. (1995). "Scripture as Canon for Post-Modern Times," *Biblical Theology Bulletin* 25: 56–63.
Sanders, J. A. (1997). "Non-Masoretic Psalms," in *Pseudepigraphic and Non-Masoretic Psalms and Prayers*, edited by J. H. Charlesworth with H. Rietz. PTSDSSP 4A. Tübingen: Mohr Siebeck; Louisville, KY: Westminster John Knox.
Sanders, J. A. (1999). "Intertexuality and Canon." in *On the Way to Nineveh: Studies in Honor of George M. Landes*, edited by S. Cook and S. Winter. Atlanta, GA: Scholars Press, pp. 316–33.
Scanlin, H. P. (1996). "The Old Testament Canon in the Orthodox Churches," in *New Perspectives on Historical Theology: Essays in Memory of John Meyendorf*, edited by B. Nassif. Grand Rapids, MI: Eerdmans, pp. 300–12.
Schaff, P. (1980). *History of the Christian Church*, Vol. 2: *Ante-Nicene Christianity A.D. 100–325*. Grand Rapids, MI: Eerdmans, reprinted from Charles Scribner's Sons, 1910.
Schaff, P. ([1983] 1998). *The Creeds of Christendom with a History and Critical Notes*, 6th ed. Revised by D. S. Schaff. Grand Rapids, MI: Baker reprint from Harper & Row, 1931. 3 vols.
Schlatter, A. (1955). *The Church in the New Testament Period*. Translated by P. P. Levertoff. London: SPCK.
Schmidt, D. D. (2002). "The Greek New Testament as a Codex," in *The Canon Debate*, edited by L. M. McDonald and James A. Sanders. Peabody, MA: Hendrickson, pp. 469–84.
Schminck, A. (1991). "Canon Law," in *Oxford Dictionary of Byzantium*, editor-in-chief P. Kazhdan. New York: Oxford University Press, pp. 1:372–4.
Schnabel, E. J. (2004). "Textual Criticism: Recent Developments," in *The Face of New Testament Studies: A Survey of Recent Research*, edited by S. McKnight and G. R. Osborne. Grand Rapids, MI: Baker, pp. 59–75.
Schnabel, E. J. (2009). "Pharisees," in *New Interpreter's Dictionary of the Bible*. Katherine Sakenfeld, general editor. Nashville, TN: Abingdon, pp. 4:485–96.
Schnackenburg, R. (1992). *The Johannine Epistles: A Commentary*. New York: Crossroad, pp. 44–6.
Schneemelcher, W. (ed.) (1991–2). *New Testament Apocrypha*. 2 vols. Revised ed. Louisville, KY: Westminster John Knox Press.
Schneemelcher, W. (ed.) (1992). "3. Acts of Paul," in *New Testament Apocrypha, Vol. Two: Writings Relating to the Apostles; Apocalypses and Related Subjects*. Revised ed. Cambridge: James Clarke, pp. 2:213–70.
Schrenk, G. (1964–76). "γραφη, κτλ," in *Theological Dictionary of the New Testament*, edited by G. Kittel and G. Friedrich and translated by G. W. Bromiley. 10 vols. Grand Rapids, MI: Eerdmans, pp. 1:742–73.
Schröter, J. (2018). "The Contribution of Non-Canonical Gospels to the Memory of Jesus: The Gospel of Thomas and the Gospel of Peter as Test Cases," *NTS* 64(4): 435–54.
Schürer, E./Revised by G. Vermes, F. Millar, and M. Goodman (1987). *The History of the Jewish People in the Age of Jesus Christ, 175 BC–A.D. 135*. Edinburgh: T&T Clark.
Scouteris, C., and C. Belezos (2015). "The Bible in the Orthodox Church from the Seventeenth to the Present Day," in *The New Cambridge History of the Bible: From 1750 to the Present*, edited by J. Riches. New York: Cambridge University Press, pp. 4:523–36.
Segal, A. (1953). *Sefer Ben-Sirah ha-Shalem*. Jerusalem: Bialik.
Segal, A. F. (1986). *Rebecca's Children: Judaism and Christianity in the Roman World*. Cambridge, MA: Harvard University Press.
Setzer, C. (1994). *Jewish Responses to Early Christians: History and Polemics: 30–150 C.E.* Minneapolis, MN: Fortress Press.

Siker, J. S. (1991). *Disinheriting the Jews: Abraham in Early Christian Controversy*. Louisville, KY: Westminster/John Knox.

Simon, M. (1986). *Verus Israel*. Translated by H. McKeating. New York: Oxford University Press.

Somov, A. (2021). "The Martyrdom of Daniel and the Three Youths," *JSP* 30(4): 198–227.

Souter, A. (1954). *The Text and Canon of the New Testament*. Studies in Theology. Revised by C. S. C Williams. London: Duckworth.

Stambaugh, J. E., and D. L. Balch (1986). *The New Testament in Its Social Environment*. LEC. Philadelphia, PA: Westminster.

Stendebach, F. J. (1991). "The Old Testament Canon in the Roman Catholic Church." in *The Apocrypha in Ecumenical Perspective: The Place of the Late Writings of the Old Testament among the Biblical Writings and Their Significance in the Eastern and Western Church Traditions*, edited by S. Meurer. Translated by P. Ellingworth. United Bible Societies. Monograph Series 6. New York: United Bible Societies, pp. 33–45.

Stevenson, J. A. (1957). *A New Eusebius: Documents Illustrative of the History of the Church to A.D. 337*. London: SPCK.

Stone, M. E. (ed.) (1984). *Jewish Writings of the Second Temple Period*. CRINT 2/2. Philadelphia, PA: Fortress Press.

Stroker, W. D. (1989). *Extracanonical Sayings of Jesus*. SBLRBS. Atlanta, GA: Scholars Press.

Stubbs, David L. (2020). *Table and Temple: The Christian Eucharist and Its Jewish Roots*. Grand Rapids, MI: Eerdmans.

Stuckenbruck, L. (2010). "Apocrypha and Pseudepigrapha," in *The Eerdmans Dictionary of Early Judaism*, edited by J. J. Collins and D. C. Harlow. Grand Rapids, MI: Eerdmans, pp. 143–62.

Stuckenbruck, L. (2013). "The Book of Enoch: Its Reception in Second Temple Jewish and Christian Tradition," *Early Christianity* 4: 7–40.

Stuhlmacher, P. (1991). "The Significance of the Old Testament Apocrypha and Pseudepigrapha for the Understanding of Jesus and Christology," in *The Apocrypha in Ecumenical Perspective*, edited by S. Meuer. UBS Monograph Series No. 6. New York: United Bible Societies, pp. 1–15.

Sundberg, A. C. Jr. (1964). *The Old Testament of the Early Church*. Cambridge, MA: Harvard University Press.

Sundberg, A. C. Jr. (1975). "The Bible Canon and the Christian Doctrine of Inspiration," *Interpretation* 29: 352–71.

Sundberg, A. C. Jr. (2002). "The Septuagint: The Bible of Hellenistic Judaism," in *The Canon Debate*, edited by L. M. McDonald and J. A. Sanders. Peabody, MA: Hendrickson, pp. 68–90.

Swanson, R. (ed.) (2003). *New Testament Greek Manuscripts: Variant Readings Arranged in Horizontal Lines Against Codex Vaticanus. 1 Corinthians*. Wheaton, IL: Tyndale House Publishers.

Theron, D. (1980). *Evidence of Tradition*. Grand Rapids, MI: Baker Book House.

Tov, E. (2002). "The Status of the Masoretic Text in Modern Text Editions of the Hebrew Bible," in *The Canon Debate*, edited by L. M. McDonald and J. A. Sanders. Peabody, MA: Hendrickson. Second edition by Grand Rapids, MI: Baker, 2019, pp. 234–51.

Tuckett, C. (2003). "Nomina Sacra: Yes and No?" in *The Biblical Canons*, edited by J.-M. Auwers and H. J. de Jonge. Bibliotheca ephemeridum theologicarum lovaniensium 163. Leuven: Louvain University Press, pp. 431–58.

Tuckett, C. (2015). "Introduction: What Is Christian Apocrypha," in *Oxford Handbook of Early Christian Apocrypha*, edited by A. Gregory and C. Tuckett. Oxford: Oxford University Press, pp. 2–12.

VanderKam, J. C. (1996). "1 Enoch, Enoch Motifs, and Enoch in Early Christian Literature," in *The Jewish Apocalyptic Heritage in Early Christianity*, edited by J. C. VanderKam and W. Adler. CRINT. Minneapolis, MN: Fortress Press, pp. 33–101.

VanderKam, J. C. (2000). *From Revelation to Canon: Studies in the Hebrew Bible and Second Temple Literature*. Journal for the Study of Judaism Supplement 62. Leiden: Brill.

VanderKam, J. C. (2002). "Questions of Canon Viewed through the Dead Sea Scrolls," in *The Canon Debate*, edited by L. M. McDonald and J. A. Sanders. Peabody, MA: Hendrickson, pp. 91–109.

Van Voorst, R. E. (2000). *Jesus Outside the New Testament: An Introduction to the Ancient Evidence*. Grand Rapids, MI: Eerdmans.

Vassiliadis, P. (2004). "Canon and Authority of Scripture: An Orthodox Hermeneutical Perspective," in *Das Alte Testament als christlichen Bibel in orthodoxer und westlicher Sicht*, edited by I. Z. Dimitrov, J. D. G. Dunn, Ulrich Luz, and K.-W. Niebuhr. Tübingen: Mohr Siebeck, pp. 259–76.

Verheyden, J. (2003). "The Canon Muratori: A Matter of Dispute," in *The Biblical Canons*, edited by J.-M. Auwers and H. J. de Jonge. Bibliotheca ephemeridum theologicarum lovaniensium 163. Leuven: Louvain University Press, pp. 487–556.

Verheyden, J. (2012). "The New Testament Canon," in *The New Cambridge History of the Bible, Vol. 1: From the Beginnings*, edited by J. C. Paget and J. Schaper. Cambridge: Cambridge University Press, pp. 1:389–411.

Voicu, S. J. (2010). *Apocrypha. Ancient Christian Commentary on Scripture, Old Testament XV*. Edited by T. C. Oden. Downers Grove, IL: InterVarsity Press.

Wahlde, U. C. (2006). "Archaeology and John's Gospel," in *Jesus and Archaeology*, edited by J. H. Charlesworth. Grand Rapids, MI: Eerdmans, pp. 523–86.

Wall, R. W. (1995). "Pauline Authorship and the Pastoral Epistles: A Response to S. E. Porter," *BBR* 5: 125–8.

Walsh, M. (1986). *The Triumph of the Meek: Why Early Christianity Succeeded*. San Francisco, CA: Harper & Row.

Wegner, P. D. (1999). *The Journey from Texts to Translations: The Origin and Development of the Bible*. Grand Rapids, MI: Baker Academic.

Weitzman, M. P. (1999). *The Syriac Version of the Old Testament: An Introduction*. Cambridge: Cambridge University Press.

Wellesz, E. (1949). *A History of Byzantine Music and Hymnology*. Oxford: Oxford University Press.

Wilde, R. (1949). *The Treatment of the Jews in the Greek Christian Writers of the First Three Centuries*. Washington, DC: Catholic University of America Press.

Wilken, R. L. (1971). *Judaism and the Early Christian Mind*. New Haven, CT: Yale University Press.

Wilken, R. L. (1984). *The Christians as the Romans Saw Them*. New Haven, CT: Yale University Press.

Williams, A. L. (1935). *Adversus Judaeos*. Cambridge: Cambridge University Press.

Williams, P. J. (2013). "The Syriac Versions of the Bible," in *The New Cambridge History of the Bible, Vol. 1: From the Beginnings*, edited by J. C. Paget and J. Schaper. Cambridge: Cambridge University Press, pp. 1:527–35.

Williamson, C. M., and R. J. Allen (1989). *Interpreting Difficult Texts: Anti-Judaism and Christian Preaching*. London: SCM Press.

Wilson, S. G. (1995). *Related Strangers: Jews and Christians, 70–170 C.E.* Minneapolis, MN: Fortress Press.

Wink, W. (1993). *Cracking the Gnostic Code: The Powers in Gnosticism.* SBL Monographs Series 46. Atlanta, GA: Scholars Press.

Wisda, L. (2019). "Marcion and New Testament Canon," *Jurnal Theologia Aletheia* 21(17), September: 23–39.

Wright, N. T. (1991). "How Can the Bible Be Authoritative?" *Vox Evangelica* 21: 14.

Yamauchi, E. M. (1973). *Pre-Christian Gnosticism: A Survey of the Proposed Evidences.* London: Tyndale.

Yarbro-Collins, A. (1986). "Vilification and Self-Definition in the Book of Revelation," in *Christians among Jews and Gentiles: Essays in Honor of Krister Stendahl on His 65th Birthday*, edited by G. W. E. Nickelsburg and G. W. MacRae. Philadelphia, PA: Fortress Press.

Zahn, T. (1893). *Forschungen zur Geschichte des neutestamentlichen Kanons und der altkirchlichen Literatur.* 10 vols. Leipzig: A Deichert, 1881–1929.

INDEX OF BIBLICAL AND OTHER ANCIENT REFERENCES

Hebrew Bible/Old Testament

Genesis
1:1   80
1:27   79
2:24   79
4:1–8   79
4:7   80
12:1–3   14
12:10, 46   80
14:21   80
16:4, 15   80
17:10–12   80
21:17   80
21:19   80
22:27   80
26:19   80
28:12   80
28:30   80
33:11   80
34:6   80
40:55   80
48:22   80

Exodus
3:6   79
7:1   80
15:1–18   113
20:7   79
20:12–16   79, 82
20:13   79
20:14   79
21:12   79
21:17   79
21:24   79
23:20   79
24:6–11   13
24:8   79
24:18   175
29:37   79
30:29   79
31:18   118

Leviticus
12:14   20
14:2–32   79
17:10–14   80
19:2   12
19:12   79
19:18   79
20:10   80
23:34   80
23:36   80
23:40   80
24:9   79
24:16   80
24:17   79
24:20   79
Rabbah 23   20

Numbers
5:12   80
9:12   80
12:2   80
12:8   80
14:23   80
16:5   82
16:28   80
21:8   80
27:21   80
28:9–10   70, 79

Deuteronomy
1:1   176
1:16   80
1:35   80
2:14   80
4:2   137, 141
4:12   80
5:16–20   79, 82
5:17   79
5:18   79
6:4, 5–8   100
6:4–5   79
6:4–9   103
6:13   79

6:16	79	2 Chronicles	
7:1–6	26	5:13	113
8:3	79	24:20–22	79
11:29	80	34:14	176
12:5	80	35:25	113
13:2	79	Ezra	
17:7	80	2:41	113
18:15	80		
19:15	79, 80	Nehemiah	
21:23	80	5–7	154
22:22–24	80	7:1	113
23:22	79	12:27–47	113
24:1	79	12:39	80
24:16	80		
27:12	80	Esther	
27:26	80	*m. Meg.* 3.6	20, 122
30:4	79	*m. Megillah* 4:1	20
30:6	80	*t. Megillah* 2:1a	20
32:43	67		
		Job	
Joshua		24:13–17	80
7:19	80	31:8	80
		37:5	80
Judges			
5	113	Psalms	
		2:2	80
Ruth.		2:7	67, 80
b. Megillah 7a	20	5:3	82
		6:9	79
1 Samuel		7:1	82
21:2–7	79	7:6	82
		8	113
2 Samuel		8:3	79
7:12	80	15:2	80
13:25	80	17:21	82
		22	113
1 Kings		22:1	70
10:4–5	79	22:2	79
10:13	79	22:19	80
17:1, 8–16	79	22:23	80
		24:4	79
2 Kings		25:5	80
5	79	29	113
5:7	80	30	113
10:16	80	31:6	79
14:25	80	31:10	80
19:15	80	32:2	80
19:19	80	33	113
22:8–13	176	33:6	80
		35:19	80
1 Chronicles		35:23	80
15:16–28	113	37:11	79

40:6–8	16	11:5	80
40:11	80	48a	20
41:10	80	100a	20
45	113	Hist. 3.25.4–7	189
48:3	79	Rabbah 1:3; 11:9	20
50:14	79		
51:7	80	Song of Songs	
63:2	80	m. Eduyyot 5:3	20
66:18	80	m. Yadayim 3:5	20
68	113	t. Sanhedrin 12:10	20
69:4–9	70	t. Yadayim 2:14	20
69:5	80	b. Sanhedrin 101a	20
69:10	80	b. Megillah 7a	20
75	113		
78:24	80	Isaiah	
78:71	80	2:3	80
80	113	4:33–34	173
80:2	80	5:1–2	79
82:6	77, 80	6:1	80
85:11	80	6:9–10 LXX	173
89:4	80	6:9–10	27, 79
89:27	80	6:10	80
92:16	80	8:14–15	79
95:7	80	8:23	80
109	113	8:6	80
110:1	79	[9:1]	80
118:22–23	79	9:2	80
118:26	79	11:2	80
154 (11QPs a XVIII, 18.3–6)	75	12:3	80
		13:10	79
104	113	14:13, 15	79
107:30	80	23	79
111	113	24–27	176, 181, 187
113	113	26:17	80
118:20	80	28:11–12	77
119:142, 160	80	29:13	79
122:1ff.	80	32:15	79
132:16	80	34:4	79
145:19	80	35:4	80
		35:5–6	79
Proverbs		37:20	80
1:28	80	40:3	80
3:6	12	40:9	80
8:22	80	42:8	81
15:8	80	43:10	81
15:29	80	43:13	81
18:4	80	43:19	81
30:4	80	45:19	81
		46:10	81
Ecclesiastes		52:13	81
2.1	178	53:4–9	67
3:5	20	53:7	81

53:10–12	79	Obadiah	
53:12	79	1:12–14	81
54:13	81		
55:1	81	Jonah	
56:7	79	2:1	79
57:4	81	3:5–9	79
58:6	79		
60:17 (42.4–5)	96	Micah	
61:1–2	79	5:1	81
64:3	82	6:15	81
66:1	79	7:6	16, 79
Jeremiah		Zephaniah	
1:5	81	3:13	81
6:16	79	3:14	81
7:11	79	3:15	81
31:31–34	13		
		Haggai	
Ezekiel		2:9	81
15:1–8	81		
26–28	79	Zechariah	
34:11–16	81	1:5	81
34:23	81	9:9	79, 81
36:25–27	81	12:10	81
37:24	81	13:7	79, 81
37:27	81	14:8	81
47:1–12	81		
		Malachi	
Daniel		1:6	81
1:2	81	3:1	79, 90
5:5–9	118	3:23–24	79, 81
7:13	79	12:12	79
8:18–26	173		
9:27	16, 79	**Apocrypha or Deuterocanonical Books**	
11:31	79		
12:2	10	4 Ezra	
12:2–9	173	1:37	82
12:4	170	4:8	82
12:11	79	12–14	170, 173
		14:19–47	185
Hosea			
4:18	81	Tobit	
6:2	81	4:10	193
6:6	79	4:6	82
10:8	79	6:7–11	193
11:1	67	12:15	72
		12:9	193
Joel		14:5	72
2:28–32	10	14:10–11	193
4:13	79		
		Judith	
		29:10–11	73

INDEX OF BIBLICAL AND OTHER ANCIENT REFERENCES

Wisdom of Solomon	
2:13	72
2:16	82
2:18–20	72
2:23–24	82
2:24	82
3:7	72
3:9	82
5:4	82
5:22	72
6:18	73, 82
7:25	16, 191
8:8	82
9:1	82
14:22–31	82
16:26	73

Sirach	
3:30	193
4:1	82
9:8	72
10:14	72
11:19	72
16:21	82
17:26	82
24:19–22	74–75
24:21	82
24:40, 43	82
49:8	20
51:23, 26	73, 75
51:26–27	73

Baruch	
3:29	82
6	173
2 Baruch 18:9	82
3:19	82
5:35	82
39:7	82

1 Maccabees	
4:46	23
4:59	82
9:27	23
9:39	82
10:7	82
14:41	23

2 Maccabees	
2:13–15	78
3:26	72

12:39–42	193
15:36	20

New Testament

Matthew	
1:18–21	75 n.2
2:1	79
2:15	67
3:1–6	
3:16–17	49
3:3	90
3.39.14–6	86
4:10	79
4:1–11	84
4:4	73, 79
4:7	79
5:17	55, 77
5:17–20	9, 20
5:18	12
5:21	79
5:27	79
5:28	72
5:31	79
5:33	79
5:34–35	79
5:35	79
5:38	79
5:38–48	54
5:43	79
5:48	79
5:5	79
5:8	79
5–7	129
6:20	73
6:26	73
6:29	79
6:5	50
6:9–13	109
6:9–13	123
7:12	77
7:15	97, 105
7:23	79
8:4	79
9:13	79
10:10	86
10:15	79
10:35–36	16, 79
11:5	79
11:10	79
11:21–22	79
11:23	79

11:23–24	79	23:39	79
11:25–28	75	23:8	55
11:28	73	24:11, 24	97
11:28–30	75	24:15	8, 16, 79
11:29	73, 79	24:24	79
12:11	79	24:29	79
12:3–4	79	24:30	79
12:39	79	24:31	79
12:4	79	24:37–39	79
12:41	79	24:39	79
12:42	79	25:31	74
12:5	70, 79	25:34–46	67
13:1–17	173	26:17–30	14
13:14–15	79	26:24	74
13:39	73	26:28	13, 79
15.3–4, LCL	123	26:31	79
15:4	79	26:36–46	134
15:8–9	79	26:64	74
16.16	11, 49, 100	27:43	72
16:4	79	27:46	79
17:5	49	28:18	87
18:10	72	28:18–20	100, 107
18:15–20	96	28:19–20	67, 69, 86
18:16	79		
18:22	79	Mark	
19:12	55	1:1	143–4
19:18	79	1:1b	179
19:18–19	79	1:2	79
19:28	74	1:11	49
19:4	79	1:15	72
19:5	79	1:4–8, 14–15	67
19:8	79	1:44	79
20:28	79	2:1–3:6	24
21:1–11	79	2:13–3	9
21:12–17	14	2:23–3:6	9
21:13	79	2:25–26	79
21:16	79	3:5–9	79
21:33	79	3:21	90
21:42	79	3:22	32
21:42–43	26	3:27	73
21:44	79	3.39.14–6	86
22:14	110	4:10–12	173
22:32	79	4:12	79
22:37	79	4:29	79
22:37–40	12	4:38	90
22:39	79	6	9
22:44	79	7:10	79
23:16	27	7:1–13	9
23:17, 19	79	7:6–7	79
23:29–36	27	8:17–21	90
23:30	79	8:24	90
23:35	79	8:31	79

8:34–35	69	4:16–21	122, 123
9:7	49	4:17	77
9:12–13	79	4:18–19	79
9:45	102	4:25–26	79
10:5	79	4:27	79
10:6	79	4:4	79
10:7–8	79	4:8	79
10:19	79, 82	5:14	79
10:45	79, 100, 107	6:24	74
11:1–10	79	6:3–4	79
11:14	79	6:36	79
11:15–19	14	6:4	79
11:17	79	7:22	79
12:1	79	7:27	79
12:10–11	79	9:35	49
12:25	73	10:7	86
12:26	79	10:12	79
12:29–31	79, 100, 107	10:13–14	79
12:31	79	10:15	79
12:36	79	10:23–24	173
12:37–40	27	10:27	79
13:14	79	11:31	79
13:24–25	79	11:32	79
13:26	79	11:37–52	9
14:1–2, 53–65	9	11:51	79
14:12–25	14	12:19–20	72, 74
14:23–24	13	12:27	79
14:24	79	12:53	79
14:27	79	13:1–3	67
14:32–42	134	13:27	79
14:62	79	13:35	79
15:34	70, 79	15:11–32	138
16:8	134	16:10–12	109
16:9–12	90	16:26	74
16:9–20	51, 129, 142, 179, 181	17:11–12	79
		17:14	79
Luke		17:20–21	37
1:5	75 n.2	17:26–27	79
1:1–2	90, 93	18:20	79
1:1–3	88	19:29–40	79
1:2	99	19:44	72
1:19	72	19:45–48	14
1:46–55	113	19:46	79
1:52	72	20:17	79
2:41–52	14	20:18	79
3:21–22	49	20:37	79
3:3–14		20:42–43	79
3:4	90	20:9	79
4:1–12	84	21:24	72
4:12	79	21:25	72, 79
4:16–19	5–6	21:27	79
4:16–20	14	21:28	74

22:20	13	3:8	82
22:37	79	4:10	80, 81
22:39–46	134	4:10, 7:38	81
22:43–44	134	4:11	80
22:69	79	4:14	81
22:7–23	14	4:20	80
23:46	79	4:22	80
24:4	72	4:36	80
24:27	76	4:37	80, 81
24:44	9, 76, 78	4:48	82
24:49	79	4:5	80
		4:9	82
John		5:10	81
1:1	80	5:10–18	27
1:11–12	37	5:18	82
1:12	37	5:2	80
1:1–3, 12–14	100	5:21	80, 81
1:1–3, 12–14, 49	107	5:22	82
1:14	81, 82	5:25–29	37
1:17	80	5:30	80
1:2	80	5:35	80
1:4	75 n.2	5:37	80
1:9	82	5:39	9
1:21	80, 81	5:44	80
1:23	80	5:46	80
1:2–4	14	5:5	80
1:29	81	6:21	80
1:3	80, 82, 100, 107	6:31	80
1:32	80	6:32	80
1:41	80	6:35	82
1:45	77	6:41–59	27
1:46	80	6:45	81
1:47	80, 81	6:49	80
1:49	80, 81, 100	6:53	80
1:51	80	6:68–69	100, 107
2:11	70, 80	7:1, 10–13	27
2:13	81	7:17	80
2:13–25	14	7:18	80
2:17	80	7:2	80
2:5	80	7:22	80
3:12	82	7:34	80
3:13	80, 82	7:37	80, 81
3:13b	51, 142, 179, 181, 183	7:38	80, 81, 82
3:14	80	7:42	80, 81,82
3:20	80	7:49	80
3:21	82	7:51	80
3:22–24	12	7:52	80
3:27	82	7:53–8:11	51, 134, 142, 179, 181
3:29	82	8:12	81
3:3	37	8:21	80
3:35	81	8:28, 58	81
3:5	81	8:3	80

8:32	81	15:19	55
8:34	80	15:25	80, 82
8:40	80	15:3	82
8:44	82	15:6	81
8:48–59	27	15:9–10	82
8:49	81	16:13	80
8:5	80	16:21	80
8:52	81	16:22	81
8:53	82	16:32	81
8:58	81	17:12	80, 81
8:7	80	17:17	80
9:16	82	17:21	81
9:24	80	17:3	82
9:29	80	18:14–16	82
9:31	80	18:20	81
9:34	80	18:22	80
9:4	81	19:24	80
9:7	80	19:28	80
10:3	80	19:31	80
10:4	80	19:36	80
10:9	80	19:37	81
10:10	37	20:17	80
10:11	81	20:22	82
10:16	81	20:28	80, 82, 100, 107
10:20	82	20:30	84, 91, 92
10:33	80	20:31	37
10:34	77, 80	21	179
10:36	81	21:15–17	130
11:19	81	21:16	80
11:50	81	21:24	130
11:51	80	24:22	80
11:54	80	58:11	81
12:13	80, 82	60:1, 3	81
12:15	80–81	66:14	81
12:26	82		
12:27	80	Acts	
12:29	80	1:12–26	181, 195
12:34	80, 81	1:36	67
12:38	81	1:6–7	15
12:40	80	1:9–11	45
12:41	80	2:16–33	10
13:16	81	2:22–36	100, 107
13:18	80	2:29–36, 42	112
13:19	81	2:37–38	12
13:34	55	2:38	113
14:1	80	2:42	x, 68, 195
14:15	73, 82	2:44–25	48
14:27	81	3:1–11	14
14:28	45	4:12	8
15:1	82	4:1–6	9
15:11	82	4:32–37	48
15:15	80	5:17–42	9

6:1–7	96	21:17–27	14
6:3–5	96	21:26–27	14
6:42	113	24:14	35
8	x	24:5, 14	7
8:12, 36–38	12	26:28	35
8:28–35	67	28:17–28	14
8:36–37	100, 107	28:17–31	34
8:9–24	53, 57	28:22	7, 35
9:18	12	28:23	77
10:9–29	9	28:25–29	27
10:9–48	15		
10:34–48	12, 14	Romans	
10:48	113	1	107
11:1–18	8, 14, 15	1:3–4	67, 68, 100, 107
11:19–26	14, 19	1:7	96
11:19–30	15	1:16–17	10, 14
11:2–12	9	1:24–32	82
11:21–26	15	2:25–29	8
11:2–3	47	3:10–19	77
11:26	35	3:21	77
11:30	96	4:1–5	15
13:1–3	15, 19, 96	4:1–15	10
13:14	14	4:1–18	26
13:14–45	19	4:25	100, 107
13:15	77, 122, 123	4:5	54
13:27	77	5:1–11, 18–21	15
14:1	14	5:12–21	82, 83
15	9, 159	6:17	99
15:1–11	8	6:3–4	12
15:1–21	15	7:6	15
15:1–35	14	7:7	83
15:1–5	47	7:7–12	15
15:1–6, 22–23	96	8:11	9
15:6–30	96	10:11–14	10
16:13	14	10:9	ix–x, 9, 19, 19, 67, 68, 86, 93, 95, 100, 103
16:16–40	38		
16:3, 13	14, 19	10:9–10	9, 103
16:31	100, 107	11:11, 15, 23–24	27
16:4	99	11:1–23	10
17:1, 10, 17	14	11:13–24	8
17:1–2	19	11:17–24	25
17:24	14	11:17–30	27
18:14, 18	19	11:25–27	26
18:18	14	11:25–32	25, 85
18:18b	14	11:25–36	10
18:4	14	11:28–29	26
19:5	113	16:1–2	136
19:8	14	16:1–3	96
20:25	92	16:14	161
20:35	109	16:25–27	179, 181
20:6, 16	14	16:7	134, 181
21:17–26	9	16: 18–23	9

INDEX OF BIBLICAL AND OTHER ANCIENT REFERENCES

1 Corinthians		1:6–8	44
1:2	96	2:11–14	8, 9, 14, 15, 47
1:14–16	12	3:19–21	15
1:23	29	3:5–18	26
2:8	27	3:6–9, 13–14	10, 26
2:9	82	3:6–10, 21–29	15
5:1–6	96	3:6–14	8, 14
5:9–13	96	3:8–14, 21–29	47
6:1–6	96	3–4	27, 54
6:1–7	96	4:5:2–15	47
7:10, 12, 17, 25	87, 92, 98	5:11–12	47
7:10–11:23–25	89	6:12–15	47
8:6	14, 100, 107, 108	6:15–16	10, 85
8–11	98	6:18	26
9:1	195		
9:1–2	181	Ephesians	
9:19–20	14	1:3–14	100, 107
9:20–21	15	2.2	95
11:2	99, 100, 107	4.1	95
11:2, 6, 23	98	5:18–21	113
11:23–25	92	5:21 and 22	143
11:23–26	x	7:2	101, 108
11:23–29	100	18:2	101, 108
11:5	134	19:1	101, 108
12:28	181		
12:3	100, 107	Philippians	
12:31	103	1:1	96
14:21	77	2:3	92
14:33b–36	179	2:6–11	x, 10, 19, 92, 93, 100, 107, 109, 110, 113
14:34–35	134, 142		
14:37	92, 109	2:9–11	67
15:1–11	98	2:10–11	25
15:2–3	99	3:1–5	14
15:3–11	9, 68	3:1b	51
15:3–8	92, 95, 100, 103, 107, 181		
		Colossians	
15:11	95	1:12–20	100, 107
15:12–19	46	1:15–16	14, 100, 107
44.4–6	96	2:8–16, 20–23	46
		2:8, 20–23	46
2 Corinthians		2:9–15	100, 107
1:1	96	2:20–23	44
3:15	122	3:16	113
5:1–5	83	4:16	55, 123, 127
8:1–9:13	51		
11:3	83	1 Thessalonians	
11:14	83	2:14–16	27, 34
12:2	83	4:14–18	45
		4:15	87, 92
Galatians		5:5–7	58
1:1	195		
1:2	96, 127		

2 Thessalonians		4:5	82
2:1–3	46, 181	5:7–11	68
2:2	37	Vita 29:2	82
2:15	98, 100, 107		
2:2–3; 3:17	191	1 Peter	
3:6	98, 100, 107	1:1–3	68, 96
		3:12	150
1 Timothy		3:18	100, 107
1:15	184	3:19	102
2	44	4:16	35
2:4	83	5:1–5	96
2:5–6	107		
2:6	100, 107	2 Peter	
2:8–15	134	1:18	191
2:12	135	1:2	150
3:1–13	96	2–3	152
3:16	100, 107	2:1–3	191
4:1–5	44	2:4	82
5:18	86	2:9	150
6:20	44	2:20	150
14	100	2:21	99
		3:1	175
2 Timothy		3:1–4	45
1:15	184	3:3–7	36, 44
1:15–18	180	3:6	82
2:2, 14	96		
2:8	100, 107	1 John	
2:19	82	4:1–3	46
3:1–9	44	4:2–3	44, 46, 59, 100, 104, 107, 108
3:16–17	36, 157		
4:5–21	180	5:7–8	51, 130, 132, 142, 179, 181, 183
4:6–8	180		
4:6–18	184	5:11–13	37
4:13	119	5:12	37
4:13	120, 122, 148		
4:14–22	180	2 John	
Titus		7–11	97
1:5–16	181		
		3 John	
Hebrews		5–10	97
1:2–3	191		
1:3	16, 82	Jude	
1:5–6	67	14	84, 191
1:6	82	5–8	44
10:5–7	16		
10:32	38	Revelation	
13:20–21	68	1:3	36
Vita 13–14	82	1:9	187
		2–3	120
James		2:6, 14, 20, 24	44
1:1	68, 96	2:9–10	38
1:17	82	2:14–15, 20–24	46

3:9–10	38	*4 Maccabees*	
3:10–11	36	17:20	82
4:8, 11	113	44:19	82
4:11	107	50:25–26	82
5:1–5	119, 170	*Acts of Paul and Thecla*	180
5:1–8:5	118		
5:2	118	*Ag. Haer*	
5:9–10, 12–13	113	3.3.3, ANF	99
6:1–8:1	119	3.4.1 ANF	99
10:4–11	170	*Against the Jews (Jewish synagogues)*	
13:18	140	2	26
22:2	83	4	26
22:12	36	Ambrose, Ep. 42.5	106-7
22:18–19	119, 137		
22:20	36	*Apoc. Mos.*	
		17:1	83
Other Ancient Sources		19:3	83
		24:1–26:4	83
1 Clement		36:3	83
13.1–4, LCL	87	37:5	83
13:1	109		
44.1–4	105	*Apol.*	
46.7–8, LCL	87	5.3–4	38
45.2–3	21		
		Ascen. Isa.	
1 Enoch		11:34	82
1:9	82, 191		
8.1	178	*Athanasius*	
10.4	82	Festal Letter 19.3–4	27
15.6–7	73	Athenagoras, Plea 3	38, 46
16.1	73		
19.1	178	*Augustine*	
19.3	178	*Contra Faustus*	
83.3–5	82	19:13	26
99.6–7	178		
21.1	178	*Hippolytus*	11, 33, 44, 46, 104–105
22.9–10	73–74		
38.2	74	*In Gen.* 49.86	33
51.2	74	*Against the Heresy of Noetus*	109
6.6	178		
62.2–3	74	*Ref* . 7.34.12; 7.35.1–2; 9.13.2–3; 9.15.2; 9.17.2	49
69.27	74, 82		
94.8	74	*Ref. Prol* . 7.7–9; 7.33.1–2	49
97.8–10	74		
chs. 37–71	75	*On Christian Teaching* 2.8.12.24–13.29	166
2 Clement			
8:5	109		
3 Corinthians	119, 152–153, 158, 174, 180, 192	*b. Baba Bathra*	
		14b 16,	76, 77

b. Ber.		7:1–4	x
63a, 18	12	9:1–5	x
b. Gitt.		5.14.23	29
57a, MS. M	33	Didascalia	159
60b	19	*Elenchus*	
		8.19.1	62
b. Hagigah			
13a	20	*Enoch*	
		71:5–17	75
b. Menahot		*Ep. Barnabas*	103, 110, 125, 127,
45a	20		165, 167, 180,
			189, 196
b. Shabbat		2–3, 4.6–8, 6.6–8	28
13b	20	4:14	110
30b	20	*Diogn.* 3–4	28
b. Temura		*Ep. Diog* (Aurelius, Marcus)	
14b	19	11.1, LCL	98
Birkath ha-Minim	25, 31–32	*Epigr.* 1.2	148
byblos	118		
Cerinthians	11, 29	*Epiphanius*	
Chron	79	*Haer* 72.3	104, 109
24:20–22	79		
4:24	79	*Pan*	
6–7	79	11.9–11	51
19	79	28.1.3	11
Cicero (14.190)	148	2.3	11
Claudius 25.4)	38	4.1–2	11
Clement 44.1–2	96	29.9.1	32
Clement of Alexandria	161		
		Eusebius	
Strom.		*Hist. eccl.*	164
1.1.13	178	1.1.2 [LCL]	30
2.1	161	1.13	126
2.9	161	2.17.2 [LCL]	28
2.12	161	2.20.2	104, 109
4.9	161	2.6.3–7	30
6.2, 8.1	25	3.18.4	38
6.15	161	3.20	31
6.12, 8.3	21	3.25	183, 184
Decretum Gelasianum	162	3.25.1	91, 185
		3.27.1–2	48
Didache		3.27.3–6, LCL trans	48
1–6	29	3.27.4	48
8.2	50, 109	3.37.1–6	47–48
8–10	123	3.39.16	157
11.1–10	62	3.39.4, 14–16	37, 86, 90, 93
11–13	37, 97	3.5–6	30
16	123	3.7.1 [LCL]	30
		4.26.13–14	22, 78
apost.		4.26.9	38
1.6.7–11	26	4.29.1–2, LCL	53

5.14–19	61	*Magn.*	
5.16.3–4, LCL	64	6.1–2	95
5.20.2, LCL	140	7.1–2	95
5.22	30, 31	13.2	95
6.12.3–6	182	8–10	
6.17	11, 49		
6.24–25	178	*Phld.*	
6.25	193	5–6	28
6.25.1–14	164	2.1–2	95
6.25.13	179, 183	7.1–2	95
6.25.3–6	164		
7.13	31	*Smyrn.*	
7.25	183	2.	59
8.2.1	38	8.	96
8.5–6	38		
11.9	154	*Trall.*	
		2.1	95
Prin.		3.1	95
2.1.5	193	9	107
4.4.8	178	9.1–2	100, 104, 108
Gospel of Philip	58, 59	10.1	59
83.18–30		13.2	95
Hippolytus		*In ev. Ioann*	
Ref.		32.16	101
7.7–9	11		
7:33.1–2	11	*Irenaeus*	
7.34.12	11	*adv. Haer.*	
7.35.1–2	11	1.1.1	178
9.13.2–3	11	1.10.1	102, 108
9.15.2	11	1.10.1, ANF	111
9.17.2	11	1.26.1–2	11, 49, 56
10.28–30	101	1.27.1	53
		1.28.1, ANF	58
Ref. of All Heresies		1.31.1	84
8.12	63	1.110.1–3	26
7.22–26	61	2.20.2	161
		3.2.1	60
Homer		3.3.1	59
14.184	148	3.3.3	105
		3.3.4	11, 44
Ignatius		3.4.1	105
Eph.		3.4.2	102, 108
1:3–14	100, 107	3.11.1–9	80
2.2	95	3.11.7	48
4.1	95	3.21.1	11, 44, 49
5:18–21	113	3.21.2	21
5:21 and 22	143	3.33.1	26
7.1–2	59	4.21.3	33
7:2	101, 108	3.33.4	11, 49
18:2	101, 108	4.4.1–2	30
19:1	101, 108	4.9.1	26

4.13.4	30	*Jos. Asen.*	
4.15.1	26	1.1	75 n.2
4.17.3	26	1.48	75 n.2
4.16.2	26	10.11	75 n.2
4.20.2	161	10.2	75 n.2
30	49	15.18	75 n.2
		10.4	75 n.2
Mand		20.22	75 n.2
1.1	161	11.12	75 n.2
		2.52	75 n.2
Jerome	4, 17, 18, 20, 32, 140, 141, 154, 155, 158, 166, 179, 195	11.4	75 n.2
		5.43–48	75 n.2
		12.15	75 n.2
Ep. 112.13	32	6.23	75 n.2
		12.2	75 n.2
Esaiam		1.10	75 n.2
8.11–15	11, 49	12.2	75 n.2
9.1; 11.1–3	11, 49	1.27	75 n.2
29.17–21	11, 49	12.5	75 n.2
31.6–9	11, 49	3.5	75 n.2
In Dan 1.29.21	33	14.2	75 n.2
Latin translation of Stridon and Bethlehem	17	1.17	75 n.2
		19.11	75 n.2
	166	20.28	75 n.2
		21.1	75 n.2
Joseph		5.13	75 n.2
b. Sanh.		21.21	75 n.2
43a	33	6.3	75 n.2
100a	20	22.3	75 n.2
101a	20	29.5	75 n.2
106a	32, 33	6.19–21	75 n.2
107b	32	4.10	75 n.2
		10.21	75 n.2
Sota		4.7	75 n.2
47a	32	7.44	75 n.2
		6.6	75 n.2
Josephus		7.1	75 n.2
Against Apion	33	11.7	75 n.2
1.37–43	20, 76, 77, 78	7.4	75 n.2
2.289–92	122	28	75 n.2
		8.9	75 n.2
Ant.		13.23	75 n.2
11.184–296	20	*Jubilees*	16, 159, 175, 179, 194
13.12–15	9		
13.171–173, 288–298	10	5.3	73
17.41–44	10	5.9–11	73
18.11–15	10	*Judas*	83
18.171–72	9	1 *Apol.* 31.1–5	21, 104, 108
Life 10–12	9		
		Dial. 1	
War		8.1	21
1.107–114	10	19:5–6	26
2.162–166	10		

INDEX OF BIBLICAL AND OTHER ANCIENT REFERENCES

22:11	26	6.25	178
46:5	26		
89–98	104	*Contra Celsum*	
89–98	108	1.23	52
100.1	109	1.38 LCL	43
117	30	1.6, 68	43
123, 135	26	1.9 LCL	43
		2.1	48
Dial. with Trypho		2.13	31
10:3	26	2.18	31
19:3–4	26	2.4.1–2	31
Trypho	11, 12 26	2.9.1	31
16	33	26, 28, 34, 39, 41	31
17	33	5.52–55	178
32	33	5.61	48
34	33	5.65	48
110	26	7.20	30
117	33	16.355.5–6	170
131	33	16.329.26–28	170
133	33	*Epist ad Titum* 3.11	48
136	33	*Epist ad Rom* 3.11	48
137	33	GCS , 7.510.14	25
Livy 14.190	148	*Genes. Hom.* 13.3	33
Lucian, On the	42	*Hom in Gen* 3.5	48
Death of Peregrinus		*Hom in Jer* 10.8.2 32,	48
11–14 LCL		14.13 30, 19.12	
		Hom on Josuam 7.1	164
Mart. Pol.		*Hom in Luk* 17	48
12.2	33	*In Lib. Jud. Hom.* 8.2	25
12–13	24	*Matt. Comm. Ser* 79	48
13.1	33	*On Prin.* 1.3.3; 4.1.11	161
17.2	33	Ovid (14.192)	148
17–18	24	*Pastorals*	4, 51 n.3, 120, 172,
18.1	33		180, 196
Minusius Felix,	38	*Philo*	10, 12, 18, 33
Octavius 9		in Alexandria	28
Nat. (Romans)	148		
13.74–82		*De Vita Contemplativa*	
Nero 16.2	38	3.25–26, 28, 33, 76,	33
		78 On the Embassy	
Ode (Odes of Solomon)		to Gaius	
33.5–11	114	*Spec. Laws* 2.60–62	122
27.1–3	114		
42.1–2	114	*Ep. Pliny*	
8.5–6	114	10.96.1	38
41.12	114	10.96–97	38
42.11–13	114	10.97, LCL	41
41.11–16	114	53.8	20
		Pliny the Younger,	114
Origen		Letter 10.96.7	
Comm. John		*Polycarp Phil.* 2	100, 107
5	164	*Praescr.* 38.7, ANF	53

Haer. 42	60	*Cult. fem.*	
On Prescription	109	1.3	178
Against Heretics		2.10	178
19, ANF		*De Praesc*. 32.3–5	49
Shemonah Esrey	31		
Shepherd of Hermas		*De mensuris et ponderibus*	
31:2-7,	103, 125, 150, 159,	4–5	165
	160, 161, 165, 166–	22–23	165
	167, 180, 196	PG 43:244	193
		De orat.	160
Silvanus		*De Pudicitia* 160*Idol*. 4.2–3 178	
5:12	187		
Socrates Scholasticus		*Marc.*	
Ecclesiastical History 3.20	30	1.19	53
Hist. eccl. 7.13; 3.20; 5.22	31	3.473–475	51
		4.2, ANF	54
Suetonius, *Dom.*		5.16–18	54
12.2	38	5.18.1, ANF	54
23.1–2	38	primordial law	26
		secondary laws	26
t. Sanh.		*Torah*	12, 20, 22,
10.11	33		29, 70, 76
t. Shabbat		*Tosefta*	
13:5 A–F	23	*Abod. Zar.*	
		16b	8
Tacitus		405	23
Ann 15.44	38		
Ann. 15.44.2–8	39	Virgil	
Tatian, *Diatessaron*	158	14.186	148
Tertullian	11, 24, 28, 32,		
	44, 46, 60, 64,	*Vita* (*Life of Adam and Eve*)	
	96, 160	44:1–5	83
Ad Nat. 1.7.8–9	38	9:1	83
		29:2	83
Adv. Jud.			
4.6.4–5	27	*Wisdom and Sirach*	
4.8.1 ANF	32	*Panarion*	
		76.22.5	165
Ag. Marc.		8.6.1–4	165
2.18	26		
2.19	28	*y. Sanh*	
3.1	109	7.16	33
3.23	28	67a	33
4.11	26		
5.4	28		

SUBJECT AND AUTHOR INDEX

Note: Endnotes are indicated by the page number followed by "n" and the endnote number e.g., 20 n.1 refers to endnote 1 on page 20.

Abraham 14, 26, 142, 188
  patriarchal age of 27
act of writing 118–122
Adler, W. 173, 178
Against Heresies (Irenaeus) 57, 84, 105, 140
Agrapha 69
Aland, Barbara 131, 136
Aland, Kurt 131, 136, 180
Alcuin Bible 128
Alexandrinus 16, 18, 78
  baptismal affirmations 101
"allepigraphy" 172
Allert, Craig D. 157
"allonymity" 172
Alogi 62
Ambrose 28, 31, 107
Ambrosiaster (*ad Gal. Prol.*) 11
Amphilocius of Iconium (*c.*380) 21, 165
ancient artifacts 147
Anderson, P. N. 80
ante-Nicene 21
anti-Jewish 28
  from Christianity 27–8
  sentiment 27, 52
  statements 34
Antioch 14, 15, 19, 25
anti-Semitism 27–8
Antony, David 49
Aphraat 28
apocalyptic eschatology 13, 190
apocrypha
  books 4, 5, 18, 15, 17, 22, 70
  in early Christianity 169
"Apocryphal New Testament" 180
Apostles' Creed 98, 100, 101, 102, 104, 107
Apostolic Canons 85 165
Aquila 17
Aramaic texts 15, 16, 17
Athanasius 21, 26–7

Festal letters 125, 178
Thirty-Ninth Festal Letter 176
Athanasius of Alexandria 164–5
Athenagoras 46
Augustine 17, 26, 32
Aune, D. E. 174
Aurelius, Marcus 98

Babylon 9
  Talmud 16, 32
Bakke, O. M. 98
baptisms 2, 12
  affirmations x, 196
Bar Kochba(Kochbah) 15
  Jewish 9
  rebellion 23, 25, 52
Barber, M. P. 26, 27
Bar-Ilan, M. 118
Barton J. 49, 51, 52, 54
Bauckham, R. 176
Bauer, W. 46, 108
Baur, F. C. 171
Beckwith, Roger 70–1, 75
BeDuhn, J. D. 52
Benko, S. 38
Beza, Theodore 142
"Bible" x, 1, 4, 195
biblical canon 2, 4, 5, 21
Bichel, M. A. 116
bishop of Milan 28
"bishops and deacons" 96
"blood of the covenant" 13
Boccaccini, Gabriele 25, 75
Bohak, Gideon 75
Bokedal, Tomas 149
Bonaventure Elzevir 142
Borges, Jorge Luis 135
Brakke, D. 176, 178
Brock, S. 116
Brown, M. P. 11

Bryennios 164
Burke, T. 180, 187

Caesarea Maritima 14, 15, 19
Cairo Geniza 7, 16
Callan, T. 29
Campenhausen, Hans von 47, 50, 62–3, 89–90, 95, 98
Candlish, J. S. 171
"canon of faith" 111
"canon" 2
canonical pseudonymous literature 187–190
canonical texts 71
capital lettered manuscripts 132
Cassey, R. 55
Cassiodorus' pandect 128
"Cataphrygians" 61
Catholic Christians 8, 16
Catholic Epistles 36
Catholics 159
Celsus (fl.c. 178–180) 42–3
Chadwick, H. xi, 19, 24
Charles, R. H. 170
Charlesworth, James 69, 75, 80, 116, 174, 175, 176, 187
Christ, Jesus 9, 13, 24
  crucifixion of 27
  identity, teachings, and mission 20
  and Paul 26
  psalms 76
Christian 32, 35
  "beliefs" 8, 19
  baptism 12, 13, 14
  biblical manuscripts 22
  challenges of early followers 35–7
  Judaism and 7
  production and use of pseudepigraphal writings 179–187
  Protestant 8
  proto-orthodoxy 89
  scriptures 4, 15, 17, 86, 100
  writings, against Jews 5, 28
Christianity 2, 35
  second-century 44, 56, 96, 111
  third-century 111
Chronicles 21
Chrysostom, John 10, 27, 28
  Against the Jews 28
  An Answer to the Jews 28
  Homily 8 28
  PG 28
Church, F. F. 116

Church's scriptures
  canon lists 163
  local council decisions and 159–163
  NT Canon Lists from East 164–5
  NT Canon Lists from the West 165–6
  OT Canon Lists from East 164–5
  OT Canon Lists from the West 165–6
  translations of 152–9
Cicero 148
Clabeaux, J. J. 53
Clarke, K. D. 171, 175, 181, 191
Claudius Nero (c. 37–68) 38
Clement of Alexandria 7, 21, 161
Clement of Rome 21, 87
Clementine Homilies and Recognitions 29
Codex Alexandrinus 51 n.3, 127–8, 161
Codex Ambrosianus 128
Codex Amiatinus 128
Codex Claromontanus 128, 161, 165
Codex Dublinensis 154
Codex Fuldensis 154
Codex Sangermanensis 128
Codex Sinaiticus (Aleph or א a, c. 375–380) 51 n.3, 125, 127, 137, 156, 161, 180
Codex Vaticanus (c. 350–375) 51, 125, 127, 134
Codex Venetus 128
Codices 18, 21
Cohen, S. J. D. 11, 28, 31
Collins, John J. 5, 117, 171, 175
Collins, Raymond 50, 62
Constantine 11, 30
core creeds 69, 95
Cornelius Tacitus (c. AD 55–120) 38–9
Council of Laodicea 161–2, 196
Council of Nicea 106, 163, 196
Council of Rome 162
Council of Trent 18, 158, 159, 163
Councils of Hippo and Carthage 162–3, 166
Crawford, Sidnie White 176
creeds
  addressing "Heresies" 104–5
  affirmations x, 108, 110
  early and later 100
  expansion of 105–9
  NT Creeds 100–4
cursivus manuscripts 122
Cyprian 46
Cyril of Alexandria 28, 31
Cyril of Jerusalem 164

Dahl, N. A. 53, 55
Damascus Document 16

Daniel and Esther 162, 163, 173, 176, 178, 194
Daniel and Revelation 13
Daniel as prophet 8
Daube, D. 12
Davila, J. R. 176
Dead Sea Scrolls (DSS) 3, 10, 16, 18, 21, 69, 119, 176
Decius (250–251) 37–8, 41
Delling 116
Demiurge 51 n.4
deSilva, David A. 5, 183, 194
"deuterocanonical" scriptures 8, 16, 17, 18, 173
Dibelius, Martin 70
Diocletian (303–305) 37–8
Dionysius 183
Docetism 11
  controversy 46, 110
  views of Jesus 44
Domitian (*c.* 51–96) 38
Donelson, L. R. 171, 179, 188
Dungan, David 103
Dunn, J. D. G. 11, 24, 21, 35, 68, 88, 180

"Early Christian Apocrypha" 180
early Christianity
  gatherings 113
  sacred tradition in 98
early church's first scriptures 15
early core traditions 112–16
early Jewish-Christian beliefs
  and other Jewish-Christian sects 11
Ebionites 11, 29, 47–9
  views of Jesus 44
"eclectic" texts 138
Edgecombe, Kevin P. 79 n.2
Edrei, Arye 16, 76, 77
Egypt 5
Ehrman, B. D. 48, 103, 130, 132, 133, 142, 155, 171, 172, 188
Eighteen Benedictions 31
Eldad 23
Elias 171
Elkasaites 11, 29
Elliot, J. K. 158, 173, 175, 180
Ellis, E. E. 75
"embryonic Christianity" 35
Ephraem 28
Epiphanius 11, 49, 50, 104, 165
Epiphanius of Salamis 50, 165
episcopate 44, 45, 95–8
Epp, Eldon 125, 126, 129

Erasmus, Desiderius 133–4
Essenes 24, 32
Eucharist 13, 191
  affirmations x, 196
  communion affirmations 85
Evangelists 70
Evans, Craig A. 5, 15, 69, 117, 132, 171, 180, 181

"false prophecy" 63
Ferguson, E. 9, 12, 13, 43, 101, 116
fifth-century codex manuscripts 16
first-century
  Christianity 96, 99
  Judaism 26
Flint, P. W. 171, 173, 181
Flusser, D. 29, 32
Foucault, M. 169
Frend, W. H. C. 56, 61
Frey, Jörg 173, 180
Fricke, K. D. 193

Gager, J. 34
Gaius Suetonius Tranquillas (*c.* 69–140) 38
Galilee region 68
Gallagher, E. L. 16, 164, 189
Gamaliel 9
Gamble, H. Y. 37, 120
Geniza, Cairo 7
Gentile Christians 17, 24, 47, 196
Gerhardson, B. 92
Gnostic Christians 11, 14, 47, 56–61, 110
  writings 83
Gnosticism 56–61
  views of Jesus 44
Goppelt, L. 65
Gospels God 2, 4, 9, 13, 14
Grant, R. M. 53, 59, 193
Greco-Roman Empire
  Jews in 36
Greek 17
  Scriptures (LXX) 16, 18, 19
The Greek New Testament 142
Greek text 142–3
Green, W. S. 20
Greenblatt, Stephen 135
Gregory of Nazianzus 165
Gupta, Nijay 184
Guthrie, Donald 171, 181

Haggmark, S. 50
Hagiographa 23, 76, 78

Hahneman, G. M. 55, 56
Halakah 11
Harnack, Adolf von 47, 52, 60
Harrington, Daniel J. 82
Hebrew alphabet 177
Hebrew Bible (HB) 70, 119, 152, 173
  Scriptures 2, 4, 7, 8, 15, 17, 18, 19, 25, 29, 59, 67, 99
Heemstra, Marius 31–2
Hegesippus 44
Hellenistic model 100
Hellenistic philosophy 57
Helmut Koester 46, 139
Hendel, R. 135, 136
Hengel, Martin 17
heresy in early Christianity 44, 64–5
"heretical" 11
Hilary of Poitiers 165
Hill, C. E. 189
Hillel 9, 12, 77
Hofius, O. 69
Holmes, Michael 105, 137, 140, 142
"Holy Bible" 4, 164, 166, 195
Holy Spirit 10, 27, 48, 61, 100, 101, 106–7, 133, 181
"Holy Tetrad" 91, 185
Homer 135, 148
Houghton, A. G. 158
Hovhanessian, V. S. 154, 158
Hultgren, A. J. 50
Hurtado, L. W. 5, 88, 120, 122, 126–7, 149
Hurtado, Larry 139
Hutson, C. R. 184
hymns x, 2, 95, 112–16, 196

Iamblichus 171, 172
Ignatius of Antioch 25, 28, 97, 120
Iranian Zoroastrian theology 57
Israel 9, 10, 23, 24, 27, 85

Jamnia (Javneh) 9, 25
Jenson, R. W. 99
Jeremias, J. 69
Jerusalem 14, 25, 29–30, 52, 56, 68, 72, 76, 149, 159, 190, 194
Jesus of Nazareth 24, 59, 67, 93
Jewish 2, 25
  apocalypticism 58
  challenges for 35–6
  Christianity and Late Second Temple Judaism 7
  Christians 14, 17, 24, 27
  gatherings 113
  production and use of pseudepigraphal writings 175–9
  Sabbaths 15
  scriptures 24, 194
  synagogues 10
  writings 5
Johannine Comma 133
Johnson, L. T. 36
Jonas, H. 59
Judaism
  and early Christianity 7
  separation of Christians from 24

Kelley 101
King James Version (KJV) 189
King, Karen 52, 59, 60
Klassen, W. 28
Klugkist, A. C. 48, 150
Koester, Helmut 46, 108, 135
Kramer, R. S. 75
Kurek-Chomycz, D. A. 134

Landau, B. 180, 187
Laodiceans 50 n.2, 154, 158, 165
Last Supper 13, 14
Late Second Temple Judaism 35, 47, 69, 86, 123, 127, 92 n.3
  and early Christianity 13
Latin translations 17–18, 142, 158
  of LXX manuscripts 152, 153
Latin Vulgate 141, 155, 163
Lattke, M. 116
"Law and the Prophets" 55, 76, 77, 78, 190
Law of Moses (Pentateuch) 7, 8, 17, 26, 35, 45, 47, 76, 84, 88
Layton, B. 51 n.4, 57, 59
Lazare, B. 29
lectionaries 117, 122–4, 196
Leiman, S. Z. 23, 77
Levine, A.-J. 10, 15
Levine, L. 123
Lewis, J. P. 20, 194
Liere, F. van 153
Lieu, J. M. 25, 49
Lim, T. H. 19, 102
literary artifacts 121, 147
"literate amateurs" 131, 148
Logan, A. H. B. 59
Lord's Supper 13
Lucian of Samosata (*c.* AD 120–80) 41–2, 97, 124

SUBJECT AND AUTHOR INDEX 245

Luijendijk, AnneMarie 151
Lupieri, E. 57
Luther, Martin 116, 175, 193

Maccoby, H. 31
Magdalene, Mary *vs.* Mary 32
Magus, Simon 53, 56, 57
manuscripts 117
  and Christian scripture 124–7
  majuscule/uncial 117, 121, 127–8, 132
Marcionism
  views of Jesus 44
Marcionites 11, 14, 47, 49–56, 110
Marcus Aurelius (c. 161–180 CE) 98
Marshall, I. H. 172
Martyr, Justin 26, 115
McDonald, L. M. 10, 16, 21, 22, 34, 41, 64–5, 76, 77, 91, 100, 117, 126, 159, 164, 167, 171, 188, 189, 193, 194
McGuckin, J. A. 116
Meade, J. 16, 164, 180, 189
Meagher, J. C. 31
Mediterranean world 7
Meeks, W. A. 36
Melito in Sardis 21, 22, 27, 78, 164
Mendels, D. 16, 76, 77
Metzger, B. M. 47, 86, 87, 131, 132, 133, 141, 153, 155, 158, 159, 169, 171, 173, 174, 175, 181, 187, 189, 194
Meyer, M. 57
midrash 20 n.2, 22, 69, 92 n.3
Mill, John 137
Miller, J. 123
"Minor" 196
minuscule manuscripts 122, 132, 142
minuscule/lowercase manuscripts 133
Mishnah (*m. Megilla*) 10 n.1, 11, 12, 19, 21, 22, 76, 77, 78, 89
Mitton, C. L. 171
Moffatt, James 174
Mommsen/Cheltenham List 165
Montanists 11, 23, 37, 47, 61–4, 96, 160, 165
  views of Jesus 44
Moore, George Foote 23, 30–1
Mosaic Law 26
"Moses and the Prophets" 77
Moule, C. F. D. 16
Mroczek, E. 175
Mt Athos manuscript 124
Mulry, T. J. 116
Muratorian Fragment (MF) 160, 161, 165, 176, 189, 192

Najman, H. 170, 172, 179, 189
Nazarene 11, 25, 32, 49
Nazoreans 29, 32
Neill, Stephen 29
Neusner, Jacob 9, 10, 11, 20
The New New Testament (Taussig, Hal) 103
"the new Socrates." 41
New Testament (NT) 1, 7, 22, 35, 54, 62, 85, 95, 103, 130, 119, 138, 169
  scriptures 67
  writings 147
"New Testament Apocrypha" 180
Nicene Creed 21, 98, 100, 101, 104, 106–7, 108
  affirmations 105
Noetus 104
Nomina Sacra (sacred names)
  Christian use of 148–152
"non-canonical scripture" 16
noncanonical texts 70, 71, 82
"non-Masoretic" texts 18
Novum Testamentum Graece 78, 121, 142

"Oedipodean intercourse" 38
Oikonomos, E. 193
Old Roman Creed 100, 101, 104, 106, 108
Old Testament (OT) xi, 1, 3, 7, 22, 65, 102, 121, 162, 169, 177
  scriptures 67
  texts 148
Olympiodorus 171
"Oral Torah" 19, 22
"original manuscripts" 129, 143
Orthodox Christianity 57, 104, 194
Osiek, C. 160
Oxyrhynchus 126, 129

Palestine 3, 7, 9, 19, 23, 36, 41, 71, 76, 84, 89, 127, 154, 175
  Christian Gospels in 23
Palestinian Talmud 10 n.1, 32
Panayotov, A. 176
Papias 37, 55, 86, 90, 93, 147, 157
papyrus manuscripts 91, 118, 133, 143
Paris Bibles 128, 195
Parker, D. C. 137
Pastoral Epistles 96, 121, 125, 171, 172, 180, 181, 184
Payne, Philip B. 135
Payne-Smith, R. 178
Peirano, Irene 170, 172, 176, 179, 189
Pelikan, Jaroslav 103

Penner, K. M. 86
Pentecost parallels 13
Perelmuter, H. G. 36
Perkins, P. 52, 59, 60
Pesher 92 n.3, 179
Pharisaic
  Judaism 9, 33
  rabbis 9
Pharisees 9, 10, 19, 24, 25, 70
Pilate, Pontius 39, 100, 104, 108, 196
Plato 19, 51 n.4, 171
Platonism 57
Pliny the Younger (c. 61–114) 39–40, 114
"Pocoke" 178, 196
Poliakov, L. 27, 36
Pope Damasus 141, 162
Pope/Bishop of Rome Innocent I 166
Porter, S. E. 122, 130, 181, 191
preaching x, 10, 14, 60, 69, 92, 98, 113–14, 166, 185
"priest" 41 n.1, 61
Priscilla 61, 134
"Prophetologion" 124
"prophets" 20, 21, 25–6, 32, 46, 61, 70, 72, 75–6, 78, 84, 90, 96, 99, 107, 110, 115, 119, 122, 123, 158, 161, 163, 177, 190
Protestants 18, 45, 71, 159, 175, 193
  Bibles 175, 193, 194
  Christians 8, 18
  ecumenical Bibles 176
  OT 71
Protocanonicos 158
proto-orthodox 45, 46, 48, 103–4, 111
  Christians 11, 37, 44, 48, 57, 61, 89, 103–4, 105, 111, 141, 158
pseudepigraphal writings
  books 4, 5, 17, 18
  canonical pseudonymous literature 187–190
  Christian production and use of 179–187
  importance of 190
  in early Christianity 169
  Jewish production and use of 175–9
  origin and meaning of 170–5
  texts 70
pseudonymous writings 110, 168–170, 181–2, 188
  Acts 186
  Apocalypses 186 n.2, 186–7
  Christian 57
  Epistles 186
  Gospels 185–6
  importance of 190

Ptolemy 51 n.4, 59, 87, 88
Pythagoras 171, 172

Q Community hypothesis 95
"quadripartite" divisions of Law 16, 18, 77
Qumran 3, 12, 21, 23, 69, 75, 92 n.3, 119, 135, 175, 176

rabbinic Judaism 8, 10, 22, 26, 76, 156
Rahlfs 124, 194
Rajak, T. 16, 17
"received text" (*Textus Receptus*) 142, 143
Reed, A. Y. 171, 178
"reformed documentary" type of writing 120
regula fidei ("rule of faith") 109–10
  and Christian scripture 110–12
Reinink, G. L. 48, 158
"rewritten Scriptures" 175
Richards, E. R. 122
Riesner, R. 92
Rist, M. 171, 173, 175, 180, 191
Roberts, M. J. 116
Robinson, J. M. 57
Rokeah, D. 33
Roman Catholics 45
Roman Creed 102
Roman persecutions
  of Christians 37–43
  and philosophical disputes 37
Rome 9, 15, 21
Rothschild, C.K. 161
Rouwhorst, Gerard 122, 123
Rudolph, K. 59
Ruether, R. 27, 30
Rufinus of Aquileia 166
"rule of faith" (*regula fidei*) 109

Sabbath 8, 9, 11, 13, 19, 24, 26, 35, 45, 47, 48, 122
sacred traditions 67, 86, 95, 98, 102, 105, 112, 116, 167, 185, 192
Sadducees 9, 24, 177
Sanders, James 14, 18, 29, 126
Saturninus 5 2, 57
Scanlin, H.P. 124, 188
Schaff, P. 98, 101
Schmidt, Daryl 124, 125
Schnabel, E.J. 9, 132, 137
Schnackenburg, R. 133
Schneemelcher, W. 63, 64, 180
Scriptoria 131
"scripture" 2, 46, 195

Sea of Galilee 8
Second Temple Judaism 4, 7, 10, 12, 13, 14, 86, 96, 123, 171, 176, 179, 191
    and early Christianity 9–11, 13
Segal, A. F. 29, 30–1, 32, 34
Sepphoris (Zippori) 8
Seventh Ecumenical Council 163
Shimon Kosiba 25
Siker, J. S. 26
Silvan 171
Simon Bar Kochba *see* Bar Kochba
Simon, Marcel 9, 27, 28, 31
Sinaiticus 16, 18, 21
songs 112–16
Sozomen (*c.* 425–430) 30
spiritual songs x, 5, 14, 112, 113, 116
Stendebach, F. J. 194
Stevenson, J. A. 39
Stichometry of Nicephorus 117, 191–2
Stroker, W. D. 69
Stubbs, David L. 13
Stuckenbruck, L. 171, 173, 183, 192
Stuhlmacher, Peter 75, 82, 85
Susanna 153, 164, 180, 192
Swanson, R. 168
Symmachians 11, 49
"Syndogmaticon" 103
Synod of Laodicea 165
Synoptic Gospels 37, 70, 79, 80, 81, 95, 102, 134
Syriac Peshitta ("common") translation 130, 153, 156, 158

Talmudim 19, 20 n.2, 22, 77, 89
Talmuds 10 n.1, 11, 12, 32
Tanakh Scriptures 2, 7, 16, 23
Tarfon, R. 23
Tatian 21, 55, 58, 152, 154, 158
teaching, of Jesus x, 9
Temple in Jerusalem 25, 30
Ten Commandments 26
textual variants
    ancient acknowledgment of 140–2
    and their importance 128

Theodosius 28, 31
"theological anti-Judaism" 27
Theron, D. 52, 53, 56
third-century
    Christianity 111
    churches 99
Toldoth Yeshu 32
Trajan (Roman emperor, *c.* 98–117) 40–1
translations of Church's scriptures 152–9
    Armenian Versions 154
    Coptic Versions 154
    dialects 154
    Ethiopic Version 154
    Georgian Version 154
    Gothic Versions 154
    Harclean Version 153
    Latin Versions 153–4
    Latin Vulgate version 154
    Palestinian Syriac version 153
    Philoxenian version 153
    Syrian Versions 152–3
Traube, Ludwig 149
"tripartite" divisions of Law 18, 20
"true spiritual Israel" 25–6
Trullan Synod 163
Tuckett, C. M. 149, 171, 173
Turner, E. G. 120
Twain, Mark 176

Valentinus 57, 58, 165
Van Voorst, R. E. 11
VanderKam, James 71, 75
Verheyden, J. 158

Wahlde, U. C. 80
Wegner, P. D. 122
Weitzman, M. P. 153
Wellesz, E. 116
Wilde, R. 28
Wilken, R. L. 28, 38
Williams, A. L. 27, 158
Wink, W. 52, 58

Zealots 24

www.ingramcontent.com/pod-product-compliance
Lightning Source LLC
Chambersburg PA
CBHW080936300426
44115CB00017B/2834